MAKING WOMEN COUNT

For Katriona and Alex

Making Women Count

Integrating Gender into Law and Policy-Making

Edited by

FIONA BEVERIDGE
Feminist Legal Research Unit
The University of Liverpool

SUE NOTT
Feminist Legal Research Unit
The University of Liverpool

KYLIE STEPHEN
Feminist Legal Research Unit
The University of Liverpool and
The Women's Unit, Cabinet Office

ASHGATE

DARTMOUTH

Published by
Dartmouth Publishing Company
Ashgate Publishing Limited
Gower House
Croft Road
Aldershot
Hants GU11 3HR
England

Ashgate Publishing Company
Suite 420
101 Cherry Street
Burlington, VT 05401-4405
USA

Ashgate website: http://www.ashgate.com

British Library Cataloguing in Publication Data
Beveridge, Fiona
Making women count : integrating gender into law and policy-making
1. Feminist jurisprudence 2. Women - Legal status, laws, etc.
3. Law and society
I. Title II. Nott, Sue III. Stephen, Kylie
340'.082

Library of Congress Control Number: 00-135331

ISBN 0 7546 2014 X

Reprinted 2003

Printed in Great Britain by Biddles Limited,
Guildford and King's Lynn.

Contents

Biographical Notes on Contributors

Fátima Arranz is a Professor in the Department of Sociology IV (Methodology in Social Research) in the Faculty of Political Sciences and Sociology at the Complutense University of Madrid. In addition to teaching research methods in Social Sciences, she also teaches Feminist Epistemology and Methodology in the Doctoral Programme 'Gender in the Social Sciences'.

Fiona Beveridge is a lecturer in Law at the University of Liverpool where she teaches European Union Law, Public International Law and International Economic Law, and is a member of the Feminist Legal Research Unit. Her research interests include international economic law, taxation in international law and in EC law, EU social law and policy and the impact of the European Union on women. She has published on foreign investment, including the impact of privatisation on foreign investment, taxation in the EC, women in the EC and gender-auditing.

João Casqueira Cardoso graduated both in Law and Political Science at the University of Paris X in 1990. He was an ERASMUS student at Reading University, where he completed an M.A. in International Studies in 1992. In 1997, he obtained a doctoral degree in Law from both the European University Institute of Florence and the University of Paris X. In 1997 he was appointed Auxiliary Professor of International Law at the University Fernando Pessoa in Oporto, where he is currently co-ordinating scientific research on 'Culture and Political Science'. He has published several articles on labour law, positive action and sexual harassment, mainly in French and Portuguese but also in Italian and English.

Mary Donnelly is a lecturer in Law at the Faculty of Law, University College Cork, lecturing in a wide range of subjects including Equality and the Law, Medical Law and Banking Law. She also teaches on the M.A. in Womens' Studies at University College Cork and contributes to the Gender and the Law module for the M.A. in Equality Studies at University College Dublin. She has published in the areas of gender, medical law and banking law. She is especially interested in the development of feminist perspectives on medical ethics.

Minna Gillberg is a research fellow at the Sociology of Law Institute, Lund University and a reader in Environmental Science at Malm University. She has worked on research projects commissioned by the Nordic Council of Ministers and by the Swedish and Danish Governments. These projects have focused on the development of alternative implementation strategies for environmental agreements and on the democracy/equality dimension of sustainable development (mainstreaming as part of eco-streaming). Dr. Gillberg has also carried out research for the Swedish Government on market based mechanisms (self-regulation) and their application to environmental issues and equal opportunities, and the possibilities of integrating the equality dimension with existing environmental standards such as ISO 14000 and EMAS (equality labelling).

Siobhán Mullally is a lecturer in Human Rights and Public International Law at the Faculty of Law, University College Cork. She was previously a lecturer in Law at the Law School, University of Hull, UK (1990-95) and was a visiting lecturer at the Faculty of Law, University of Peshawar, Pakistan, from 1992-93 and also from January-April 1995. She is currently working on a Ph.D. at the European University Institute, Florence on the subject of feminist theory and human rights and is widely published in the field of women and human rights.

Sue Nott LLB, BCL is a senior lecturer in the School of Law, University of Liverpool and a member of the Feminist Legal Research Unit. She lectures on Law and the Sexes and her main research interest is law and gender. She is the co-author of a book on working women and another on women and wealth. In addition, she has published articles on women and the EC, mainstreaming and the law as an instrument for combating poverty.

Beatriz Quintanilla (Ph.D. in Political Science) is a Professor of Labour Law in the Department of Labour Law and Social Security in the Faculty of Political Sciences and Sociology at the Complutense University of Madrid. Dr. Quintanilla teaches courses on Labour Law, Social Legislation in the European Union, Industrial Relations, and Social Security. Her main areas of research are non-discrimination principles between men and women in the labour place and labour conditions, atypical employment, part-time employment and affirmative action policies.

Olivia Smith BCL, LLM (NUI) was the researcher on the *Predicting the Impact of Policy* project at the Faculty of Law, University College Cork where she also tutored and contributed to the LLM module on Equality Law. She is currently a lecturer in Equity and Labour Law at University College Cork. Her research interests lie in the field of anti-discrimination law with particular reference to disability discrimination.

Kylie Stephen was, between February 1998 and August 1999, the researcher on the Predicting the Impact of Policy project for the Feminist Legal Research Unit, University of Liverpool. She holds a political science degree and gained a doctorate in feminist theory and political science from the University of Queensland (Australia). Her doctoral dissertation was entitled 'Proprietal Subjectivity: Women's Subjectivity and Citizenship'. Her research interests are in the fields of feminist theory, theories of citizenship, reproductive technologies and gender mainstreaming. She has worked as a tutor and senior research assistant at the University of Queensland and as a part-time lecturer at the University of Kent at Canterbury, England. Since August 1999 she has worked in The Women's Unit of the UK government on a project to develop the government's mainstreaming agenda. The views in this book, however, are entirely personal and do not represent the opinions of the Women's Unit.

Mieke Verloo is a lecturer in Political Science and Women's Studies at the School of Public Affairs, University of Nijmegen, the Netherlands. She developed the EER, the Dutch Emancipation Impact Assessment instrument (with Conny Roggeband) in 1994. She was the chairwoman of the Group of Specialists on Gender Mainstreaming at the Council of Europe. She was a member of the reference group for the evaluation study on women and development. Currently she is working on a second project on gender mainstreaming in Human Resource Management for the Ministry of the Flemish Community in Belgium (with Yvonne Benschop).

Cristina Velázquez is a sociologist with a Masters degree in Social Sciences from the University of California, Irvine (1995). She is currently affiliated to the Department of Political Science I (Faculty of Political Sciences and Sociology) Complutense University of Madrid as an Assistant Professor. There she teaches Political Behaviour and is also working on the final stages of her Political Sciences doctoral dissertation — a comparative study of the influence of liberal ideology on the political participation of the lower classes in the United States.

Acknowledgements

Making Women Count is based on findings from the research project *Predicting the Impact of Policy* which was funded by the EC Commission Targeted Socio-Economic Research Funds (Contract ERB-SOE2-CT97-3040) and co-ordinated by Fiona Beveridge and Sue Nott of the *Feminist Legal Research Unit*, University of Liverpool. Many individuals gave their time and support to the project and we would like to record our thanks to them all. We would like to thank in particular our co-editor and the UK researcher on the project, Dr. Kylie Stephen, for her efficiency and patience in the face of many provocations. Our research partners and fellow contributors to *Making Women Count* also deserve special mention for their hard-work and enthusiasm.

Some of the ideas discussed in this book first saw light of day at the Colloquium *Predicting the Impact of Policy* in Manchester in May, 1999. We would like to thank all those who participated and provided constructive criticism of our findings and ideas. In particular we would like to thank the speakers, Fiona Reynolds of the Women's Unit, Anna Havnoer of the European Commission, Christopher McCrudden of Lincoln College, Oxford, Mieke Verloo of the University of Nijmegen, Fiona Mackay of the Unit for the Study of Government in Scotland, University of Edinburgh and Professor Teresa Rees of the EOC and the University of Bristol.

We would like to thank Fadila Boughanémi of the European Commission and our colleagues at the University of Liverpool, particularly Steve Cooper, Anne Porter, Marie Ball, Hadassah Max, Anne Morris and Brian Thompson for their respective contributions, whether in ensuring the smooth-running of the project, commenting on work in progress or grappling with much-altered typescripts. Finally we would like to thank Liverpool Classical Monthly for typesetting.

Fiona Beveridge
Sue Nott

1 Setting the Scene: The Why, What and How of Promoting Equality between the Sexes

FIONA BEVERIDGE, SUE NOTT AND KYLIE STEPHEN

Introduction

It is a truth universally acknowledged that inequalities between the sexes still persist despite the effort and resources that have been invested in promoting equality during the course of this century. Whilst it is undeniable that there have been gains, and quite considerable gains at that, low wages, occupational segregation, high unemployment rates, difficulties in combining work and family life, exclusion from the decision-making process, domestic violence and poverty are still remarkably common experiences for women in Europe.[1] These situations persist despite the range of measures — anti-discrimination legislation, equality agencies and rights strategies to name but a few — which European states employ in attempting to eradicate inequalities between the sexes. The European Union (EU) has also actively promoted equal opportunities for women for several decades and its efforts would be expected to reinforce national programmes. Whilst the presence of this supra-national body has clearly had an advantageous effect in some national contexts, the impact of the EU's actions has been uneven and has largely left untouched deeply-rooted prejudice.

The act of acknowledging the qualified success of the campaign to promote equal opportunities between the sexes does not, however, shed any light on the reasons why this should be so. Analyses have frequently been undertaken of individual state[2] and EU practice in respect of sex equality,[3] offering detailed and highly informative accounts of the strengths and failings of specific laws and policies. Less commonly encountered is an evaluation of equal opportunities strategies *per se* as currently employed in Europe and

1. See, for example, the statistics complied by national equality agencies such as the Equal Opportunities Commission (*Facts about Women and Men in Great Britain*), Statistics Sweden (*Women and Men in Sweden*) and by Eurostat on behalf of the European Union.
2. See further the chapters on state practice in this volume for a critique of national equality laws.
3. See, for example, Ellis, E. (1998), *EC Sex Equality Law*, Second Edition, Oxford: Clarendon Press; Hervey, T. and O'Keeffe, D. (1996), *Sex Equality Law in the European Union*, Chichester: Wiley; Hoskyns, C. (1996), *Integrating Gender*, London: Verso.

what causes them to succeed or fail. *Making Women Count* offers such an analysis. It considers the equality strategies employed in six European states with a view to identifying what strategies work best and in which circumstances. It examines whether success or failure depends on the nature of a procedure or the legal and political context in which it operates. The states featured in *Making Women Count* are Ireland, the Netherlands, Portugal, Spain, Sweden and the United Kingdom. This list does not claim to be exhaustive rather it is representative of certain political and social trends in Europe. In the first place all the states in question are members of the EU. This is deliberate since one of the issues which *Making Women Count* aims to inquire into is the degree of influence exerted by EU equal opportunities measures on national practice. It is commonly assumed that one of the consequences of EU membership is a convergence of Member States' practice. There is, however, little research on whether or not this is so. Choosing these particular states, some of which are recent entrants to the EU whilst others are long-standing members, allows this proposition to be scrutinised. Secondly, the states chosen present a range of political backgrounds. Some countries, such as the Netherlands and Sweden, have a long tradition of stable democratic government. In contrast, Portugal and Spain have emerged comparatively recently[4] from a period of political repression. The states selected are, rightly or wrongly, also perceived in the world at large as displaying varying degrees of commitment to the promotion of equal opportunities between the sexes. On the one hand, Sweden is regarded as having an exemplary record on this subject. On the other hand, the United Kingdom has, until very recently, been seen as fiercely opposed to equal opportunities initiatives and as regularly defaulting on its Community obligations in this respect. As for Spain and Portugal, they are normally categorised as very traditional in their approach to the 'appropriate' roles of men and women.

Five of the states included, Ireland, Portugal, Spain, Sweden and the UK were subjected to scrutiny as part of an international research project, *Predicting the Impact of Policy*, funded by the European Commission.[5] This project had as its subject matter the continued significance of gender as a factor in social exclusion in the EU. In its early stages the project compared formal laws directed at eliminating gender-based discrimination and promoting equal opportunities in the participating states and analysed how those states

---

4. In 1974 and 1978 respectively.
5. *Predicting the Impact of Policy: Gender-auditing as a Means of Assessing the Probable Impact of Policy Initiatives on Women* was funded by the European Commission through the Targeted Socio-Economic Research (TESR) programme. The project was co-ordinated by Liverpool University's Feminist Legal Research Unit and further details of the project can be obtained by visiting the Unit's Web site: http://www.liv.ac.uk/~scooper/flru.html The Netherlands was added to the studies in *Making Women Count* for comparative purposes.

had employed their policy-making processes and institutions towards achieving greater substantive equality for women. The overall aim of the research was to suggest how equality concerns could best be integrated into the process of planning, implementing, monitoring and evaluating all policies, measures and activities at Community, national, regional and local level. The data assembled at the start of the project regarding existing state practice provided the inspiration for this book. It demonstrated a notional uniformity in the strategies each state employed to promote equality between the sexes. But beneath this uniformity there was clearly diversity in the participating states' institutional, legal and political landscapes. Areas which had been the subject of extensive attention from law and policy-makers in one country had not been problematised in another. A strategy that worked moderately well in one state, might produce disappointing results in another. This inevitably led to the question — why? An immediate response is to attribute this disparity in results to specific domestic circumstances, arguing that the particular forms which gender discrimination takes, and hence the solutions required, are sufficiently culturally specific to defy common solutions. If that were so it would mean that in some states with 'adverse' domestic situations (whatever that might mean) it would be impossible to promote equality between the sexes utilising certain strategies. This, however, does not seem an adequate explanation of the differences which exist. An alternative explanation is that some equality strategies simply do not work. This is equally unsatisfactory since strategies which sometimes fail in one state patently do work in others. A further explanation is that equality strategies cannot be assessed, and 'best practice' identified, in isolation from the context in which they operate. In other words a crucial element in the success of equality strategies may be their appropriateness to the context in which they are to function.

Making Women Count devotes its opening chapters to reviewing the practices of six individual states. These chapters give the reader an overview of the law and policy-making framework in that particular state. The role of the state's equality laws and its procedures for promoting equal opportunities are then analysed against this background. In writing these accounts a balance has been struck between the need to produce chapters which are broadly similar in orientation and content and the need to allow different national perspectives to shine through. The desire is to allow the authors of these chapters to 'tell it as they saw it' with due emphasis on aspects which were regarded as particularly significant from the contributors' own points of view. These chapters seek also to recognise the gap between law in books and law in action which has long been recognised and which provided an important reference point for these analyses of national practice. Finally it is intended that these chapters will present the reader with a critical account of national equality measures as well as a national perspective on the effect of EU gender initiatives.

The final four chapters of *Making Women Count* consider what conclusions can be drawn from the similarities and differences in individual state practice. National perspective is undoubtedly extremely important. Equally important, however, is the light it sheds on the general perspective. *Making Women Count* will consider by turn equality laws, equality agencies and alternative equality strategies, such as mainstreaming. The intention is to offer a critical insight into the ways in which different equality strategies have been deployed and have operated in the states under consideration, and to consider what factors are essential for success if each of these strategies is to play a part in promoting equal opportunities.

Before any discussion can take place, however, three preliminary issues need to be clarified. Thought has to be given to *why* states feel obliged to promote equality between the sexes, *what* they understand that duty to include and *how* they choose to go about this task. Equality between the sexes is in some respects a modern day mantra. Like motherhood and apple pie everyone is in favour of it. Why states are in favour of it and to what ends is another matter. But the issue is worthy of further examination, since the reason why a state feels obliged to pursue equality may dictate the notion of equality it chooses to pursue. 'Equality' can mean different things to different bodies or individuals in different contexts. It is unwise to assume that when a reference is made to 'equality' in the Portuguese Constitution, the concept is the same as that employed by feminists in the United Kingdom. Part of this chapter will therefore be devoted to an analysis of the term 'equality' so that its range of meanings can be appreciated. The significance of the term 'equality' often depends on its source — international convention or feminist theory — and the impetus behind a state's decision to promote equality between the sexes. A country that traces its equal opportunities measures back to the European Union may develop a very different notion of equality from a state which has acted on feminist pressure. It is also important to explore the strengths and weaknesses of the mechanisms that can be used to put the concept of equality into practice. One of the most popular ways of attempting to secure equality between the sexes is by employing legislation. Laws may provide that everyone is to be treated equally and/or may make sex discrimination unlawful. A state's constitution, which is a higher or more fundamental form of law, may also make provision for all groups in society to receive equal treatment. In addition, there are extra-legal ways of securing equality such as the setting of targets in order to increase the numbers of women in particular professions or in government. Each of these mechanisms has specific advantages and disadvantages which need to be taken into account when deciding how precisely to go about promoting equality.

The sources of the equality imperative

Equality between the sexes is accepted as a given value in present day developed countries. To acknowledge that equality between the sexes is totemic is not, of course, to claim that it is a value which is comprehensively observed. Exploring the pressures at work behind this level of acceptance is, however, helpful since, depending on the source, notions of equality can and do vary. It is possible to identify three major actors at work urging states to promote equality. These are the feminist movement, the European Union and international organisations, most particularly the United Nations. Each of these will be considered in turn to determine the extent of the influence they may have exerted in persuading the states featured in this book to promote equality between the sexes.

Each of the states dealt with in *Making Women Count* has a national feminist or women's movement.[6] Feminism and women's movements are important for a variety of reasons. In the first place, feminist academics and activists are often a source of criticism of current laws, policies and institutions as well as suggestions for how best to promote equality. Secondly the feminist movement is frequently politically active campaigning for changes such as better treatment for rape victims or laws to make sexual harassment illegal. Thirdly the notion of equality promoted by the feminist movement is sometimes very radical, calling not for changes to the law but for changes to the way in which society is organised. Indeed some feminists regard the law and state institutions as organised around male values and hence as unreliable avenues for delivering substantive change.[7] However it should also be recognised that feminism and feminists are rarely a united movement. There is normally a great deal of friction within the movement and dissent over the

6. The degree of activism associated with that feminist movement varied.
7 See, for example, the work of the American feminist Catherine MacKinnon. MacKinnon, C. (1989), *Toward a Feminist Theory of the State*, Cambridge, Mass: Harvard University Press.

concept of equality to be pursued. Moreover many feminist perspectives are highly situational, being closely related to a particular local issue, dispute or area. Thus feminist movements tend to propound a range of views about 'equality' and disadvantage, rather than a single uncontested concept.[8]

Whilst feminism often provides the impetus for change, its influence on the form which such changes take is much harder to calculate. This is because in order to exercise the greatest degree of influence feminists must be able to feed into the political decision-making process. This can occur if channels of communication are opened up between government, equality agencies and feminists. In some of the countries featured in this book this had not occurred. For example in Spain it was said

> ... the public policies on women's issues, developed at the national as well as regional and local level, have practically excluded the feminist movement.[9]

In Great Britain, the Equal Opportunities Commission, the main equality agency, has been criticised in the past for not establishing links with feminist grass roots groups.[10] In other countries, however, such as Sweden, the women's movement has succeeded, not only in opening channels of communication, but in bringing pressure to bear on the established political parties. In the 1994 General Election campaign

> . . . a 'task force' coalition of feminists from different spheres, managed to exert great pressure on the political parties by threatening to form a women's political party. The result was that the Social Democratic Party decided that every other candidate on their election lists should be a woman. It also led to several measures being taken and implemented in favour of equality, both within the work process of Parliament and through legislation.[11]

Beside the pressures that feminists can bring to bear on governments to secure changes to policies or the law, they may also draw attention, as happened in Sweden, to women's low levels of participation in public life. There is evidence that the presence of women in government, even those who would reject any attempt to label them as 'feminists', can have an effect on a government's

8. For a discussion on the meaning of equality, its definition in terms of sameness to men or difference from men and the consequences see Majury, D. (1991), 'Strategizing in Equality', in Fineman, M. A. and Thomadsen, N. S. (eds), *At the Boundaries of Law*, London: Routledge. See also Chapter 10, this volume.
9. See further Chapter Five, this volume at p. 129.
10. Lovenduski, J. (1995) 'An Emerging Advocate — The Equal Opportunities Commission in Great Britain', in Stetson, D. M. and Mazur, A. G. (eds), *Comparative State Feminism*, USA: Sage, p. 123.
11. See further Chapter Six, this volume at pp. 134-5.

agenda and its policies.[12] The notion that it was possible for politicians and public servants who were male, middle-class and white to represent the views of women, ethnic minorities or unskilled workers has lost credibility. Instead positive efforts are being made in countries such as Ireland[13] to make government more representative. It is becoming more commonplace to find politicians holding key positions who are overtly feminist in their sympathies, though radical feminists frequently challenge the feminist credentials or commitment of such politicians, arguing that they cannot make real gains by working inside inherently male state apparatus.[14] Moreover whilst it is important to make government more representative, this will achieve little if women remain excluded from the real focus of power in a state. A national legislature where women make up half of its membership is commendable, but this gain loses some of its significance if that legislature is rubber-stamping decisions taken by a coalition of business, trade union and government representatives where women are not represented.[15]

As well as reacting to the pressures of the women's movement, each of the states featured in *Making Women Count* is a member of the European Union (EU). For a variety of reasons it would appear, at least in principle, that the EU is capable of exercising a considerable influence on how Member States pursue gender equality. The truth of this assumption and the degree of influence the EU actually exerts on Member States is one of the themes of *Making Women Count*. At this stage, therefore, it is sufficient to outline the reasons why the EU has the potential to influence the behaviour of Member States. In the first place the EU is a source of legally binding measures such as the Equal Treatment Directive[16] which Member States are under a duty to implement and which, should they neglect that duty, is capable of having direct effect.[17] Moreover the totemic status of equality may make it difficult politically for states to resist legislative initiatives at EU level. Secondly the EU has a range of procedures available to ensure that Member States honour their obligations. These include litigation in the European

12. Norris, P. (1996), 'Women Politicians: Transforming Westminster?', *Parliamentary Affairs*, 49(1): 89-102.
13. See further Chapter Two, this volume.
14. MacKinnon, op cit, n. 7.
15. On this point see Stetson and Mazur, op cit, n. 10, p. 7-8.
16. Equal Treatment Directive 76/207/EEC, OJ 1976 L39/76.
17. Direct effect meaning the ability of an individual to rely on a Directive even though it had not been implemented by the particular Member State. See Case 152/84 *Marshall v Southampton and South West Hampshire Area Health Authority* [1986] ECR 723 where the European Court of Justice limited that direct effect to actions involving the state (vertical direct effect) rather than private individuals (horizontal direct effect).

Court of Justice to determine whether a Member State's law is in accordance with Community law.[18] Thirdly the EU can use its financial muscle to promote equality between the sexes. For example, the Community has over the years utilised its structural funds, such as the European Social Fund and the European Regional Development Fund, to fund initiatives of particular significance for women. The New Opportunities for Women (NOW) programme allocated funds to Member States for the promotion of employment opportunities for women.[19] More recently the Regulations governing the administration of the structural funds have been 'mainstreamed' in order to ensure that gender and equal opportunities are major factors in the management and allocation of these funds.[20]

As well as the EU, other international organisations, such as the United Nations, have encouraged the conclusion of international agreements relating to equality between the sexes.[21] These efforts seem to have produced results at least to the extent that each of the states featured in *Making Women Count* is a signatory to a range of international agreements with a bearing on equality between the sexes. Portugal, for example, is a party to the Convention on the Elimination of All Forms of Discrimination Against Women (CEDAW)[22] as well as International Labour Organisation (ILO) Conventions on Underground Women's Work,[23] Equal Pay,[24] the Protection of Motherhood,[25] Discrimination in Employment and Occupation,[26] and Workers with Family Responsibilities.[27] It is, however,

---

18. This can include action taken by the European Commission against a Member State which it believes is in breach of its obligations under EU law (*Commission of the European Communities v United Kingdom* Case 61/81[1982] ECR 2601) or a reference to the European Court of Justice by a national court. The courts in the United Kingdom frequently make such references. The *Marshall* case (see n. 17) was one such reference by the United Kingdom courts.
19. For details of the NOW programme see Rees, T. (1998), *Mainstreaming Equality in the European Union*, London: Routledge.
20. For the text of these Regulations see http://www.inforegio.org/wbdoc/docoffic/sf20002006/regul_en.htm.
21. For a compilation of international agreements with a bearing on the human rights of women, including those dealing with the elimination of gender discrimination, see Alfredsson, G. and Tomasevski, K. (1995), *A Thematic Guide to Documents on the Human Rights of Women*, The Hague: Martinus Nijhoff Publishers.
22. Adopted by the General Assembly of the United Nations by resolution 34/180 of 18 December 1979.
23. International Labour Organisation, Convention no 45. For the text of this Convention and any others mentioned see ILO. (1982) *International Labour Conventions and Recommendations, 1919-1981*, Geneva: International Labour Office.
24. Ibid, Convention no 100.
25. Ibid, Convention no 103.
26. Ibid, Convention no 111.
27. Ibid, Convention no 156.

difficult to determine what concrete effects such international agreements have. At first sight they would seem likely to have less impact on state practice as compared with EU law perhaps because they tend to be cast in fairly general terms and perhaps also because the mechanisms for their implementation are far weaker. Some states possess monist legal systems which means that international agreements are automatically regarded as part of the national legal order without the need for implementation.[28] In principle this means that women can use such international legal instruments to challenge national laws. In practice, however, there is little evidence of this happening. By way of contrast, other states, such as the United Kingdom, possess dualist legal systems which means that in order for an international agreement to be integrated into national law the state had to agree legislation to this effect. Until such legislation is in place, women derive little, if any, direct benefit from such international agreements.

Despite this problem, some international agreements can have an impact on state practice because they oblige states to report periodically on their progress in achieving the goals set out in the agreement. The Convention on the Elimination of all Forms of Discrimination against Women (CEDAW) requires signatories to report periodically and explain any lack of progress to a special UN committee.[29] The Beijing Platform for Action[30] also appears to have produced a sustained effect on states which is once again attributable to the existence of follow-up measures designed to assess progress on implementing the Platform for Action. Using some form of reporting mechanism would therefore seem a useful device for ensuring state compliance. Its downside is the tendency for some states to exaggerate what they have achieved.[31] Moreover in some instances such reports were not readily available to the public at large.

Given the number of such international agreements with a bearing on equality it is not possible here to analyse each one in detail. The influence of such agreements can be seen in the chapters on state practice. It is, however, worth stressing that the ability of the EU and the UN to secure change depends not only on the willingness of states to act on their pronouncements but also on the concept of equality those organisations employ. The EU, for

28 For an example of a monist state see further Chapter Three, this volume at p. 53.

29. Article 18, CEDAW requires states parties to submit an initial report on the legislative, administrative or other measures they have adopted to give effect to CEDAW. Thereafter they have to submit a report every four years detailing their progress.

30 The Beijing Declaration and Platform for Action, Fourth World Conference on Women, Beijing, China, 4-15 September 1995.

31. See further Chapter Two, this volume at pp. 45-7.

example, has in the past used a notion of equality based primarily on equal treatment.[32] International agreements such as CEDAW employ in the main an equal rights concept of equality.[33] As subsequent chapters will demonstrate more recently the EU and the UN have recognised the limitations of equality defined as equal treatment or equal rights and have attempted to use alternative strategies to promote equality such as mainstreaming. In order to illustrate how significant the definition of equality can be the following section will explore the range of meanings that can be attached to this deceptively straightforward term.

What does equality mean?

The term 'equality' in the context of equality between the sexes carries a variety of meanings. Historically the notion of equality for women meant securing equal rights under the law for women. This was because until the twentieth century women did not often possess the same civil and political rights as men, such as the right to vote. Their position under the law was in almost every respect a subordinate one to that of men.[34] Countless explanations are given as to why women were regarded as men's inferiors. Even in the nineteenth century writers such as John Stuart Mill asserted that there was no logic to this situation.

> . . . the adoption of this system of inequality never was the result of deliberation, or forethought, or any social ideas, or any notion whatever of what conduced to the benefit of humanity or the good order of society. It arose simply from the fact that from the very earliest twilight of human society, every woman (owing to the value attached to her by men, combined with her inferiority in muscular strength) was found in a state of bondage to some man.[35]

---

32. For example in the Equal Treatment Directive 76/207/EEC, OJ L39/76. It is, however, worth remarking that the European Court of Justice interpreted the concept of equal treatment in a more constructive fashion than some national courts, such as those in the United Kingdom. This was particularly true in relation to pregnancy discrimination. See further Chapter Eight, this volume.
33. The problem with using a rights based approach to the promotion of equality is discussed in McColgan, A. (2000), *Women under the law: the false promise of human rights*, Harlow: Longman.
34. For example it was common for the law to provide that on marriage a woman would lose the right to dispose of her property or income as she wished. Instead that power would pass to her husband. This was the case in Sweden where married women did not gain that right until 1874.
35. Mill, J. S. (1869), 'The subjection of women' published in 1970 in Mill, J. S. and Mill, H. T. (eds), *Essays on Sex Equality*, Chicago: University of Chicago Press, pp. 129-130.

In Mill's opinion, the law simply reflected the 'accepted' view of women as men's inferiors and denied them the rights that men enjoyed. This relegation of women for whatever reason to the 'other', to the less valued sex, is at the heart of inequality. In the nineteenth century it was common to see the view expressed that women were men's inferiors, whose mental capacities were far outstripped by those of men. In one notorious case in the United Kingdom[36] a group of women took legal action in order to be allowed to attend medical school and graduate from university but were unsuccessful. One of the reasons for this was the perception that they were not equipped to benefit from a university education.

> It is a belief, widely entertained, that there is a great difference in the mental constitution of the two sexes, just as there is in their physical conformation. The powers and susceptibilities of women are as noble as those of men; but they are thought to be different, and, in particular, it is considered that they have not the same power of intense labour as men are endowed with. If this be so, it must form a serious objection to uniting them under the same course of academical study. I confess that, to some extent, I share in this view, and should regret to see our young females subjected to the severe and incessant work which my own observation and experience have taught me to consider as indispensable to any high attainment in learning.[37]

Ridiculous though these sentiments now appear, it is important to stress, when exploring the notion of equality, that, whilst some prejudices may have disappeared, many still remain, either overtly or covertly, insinuating society and its institutions. As Simone de Beauvoir so accurately points out, one is not born, but rather one becomes a woman.[38] In other words society still takes the differences between the sexes, such as biological differences, and constructs from them its own version of what women can and cannot do, how they should or should not behave and what the relationship of one sex is to the other. Whatever progress has been made, many women still regard themselves as the 'other' in a society which takes the male standard as its norm.

Rather than addressing the underlying causes of inequality early campaigners focused on obtaining equal rights for women. They sought formal legal equality with men and whilst, as Carol Smart has pointed out, 'it is unlikely

36. *Jex-Blake v Senatus of Edinburgh University* (1873) 11M 784.
37. Ibid, p. 833.
38. de Beauvoir, S. (1949), *The Second Sex*, translated and edited by Parshley, H. M. (1972) London: Penguin.

that we would willingly give up any of the legal reforms they achieved',[39] this notion of equality proved very restricted in what it could achieve. It removed overt discrimination but did nothing to tackle the whole wealth of beliefs and preconceptions surrounding women. These early movements demanding equal rights for women, however, have had a considerable influence on subsequent campaigns for equality. They have given a spurious importance to the notion of individual rights and an inflated view of what those rights can achieve. Individual rights secure change only when it is possible to enforce or act upon them. For example, the right to abortion means nothing if there are insufficient doctors and hospital places to make that right a reality to those women who wish to terminate a pregnancy. The language of individual rights tends to be open-textured and often requires interpretation. This gives those officials or judges who are charged with this task the opportunity to restrict who can benefit from them. Finally it is not uncommon for one set of rights to conflict with another.[40] Elsewhere in this book the example is given of the rights of the disabled to have their needs accommodated being trumped by the right of the individual (in this case employers who would be forced to make changes to their businesses) to earn a living.[41]

As women soon discovered, being the recipients of rights is not an immediate solution to centuries of prejudice. If it is part of a society's culture that women do not work or only engage in certain types of employment or are financially dependent on their husbands, this does not change overnight simply because women are given the right to enter the medical profession or dispose of their own property as they think fit. Women continued to be the target of discrimination and it remained common, for example, to pay women less since they were not 'bread winners': that is, it was assumed that they did not have the responsibility of supporting a family.

In some countries not only did women obtain individual civil and political rights but the constitution granted everyone, irrespective of their sex, race or religion, equality under the law or in other ways guaranteed equality. Important as such provisions are either as a statement of intent or for their educative value, their practical effect can and does vary. This will, however, become apparent in the chapters reviewing national practice. What is significant from the point of view of exploring the meaning of equality is that 'equality before the law' signifies a shift in emphasis when compared with equality in the sense of equal rights. Equality before the law indicates

---

39. Smart, C. (1989), *Feminism and the Power of Law*, London: Routledge, pp 138-139
40. For a critique of rights as a means of promoting equality see McColgan, op cit, n. 33
41. See Chapter Two, this volume p. 35.

that everyone is entitled to equal treatment and should not be the target of discrimination because of their sex, race or religion. This corresponds with the pressure exerted by women's organisations to obtain legislation condemning sex discrimination which is also based on the concept of equality as equal treatment.

Equality as equal treatment often manifests itself in legislative provisions which outlaw sex discrimination. This demands that women are treated no less favourably than men (direct discrimination). Alternatively the definition of discrimination may be extended by outlawing indirect as well as direct discrimination. Indirect discrimination occurs when an apparently 'neutral' requirement, such as an age limit, is applied to both men and women. If, however, a comparison is made between the number of men and the number of women who can comply with that requirement it will emerge that substantially fewer women can comply. In those circumstances indirect discrimination will have occurred unless the requirement in question can be justified on some basis other than sex. Indirect discrimination acknowledges that discrimination is more subtle than a simple refusal to employ or promote women. It can and does tackle covert inequality but only within narrow limits. If an employer can justify a requirement, such as the need for potential employees to possess certain educational requirements, the fact that very few women have these qualifications is irrelevant. The concept of indirect discrimination is not capable of tackling deep-rooted gender differences that cause men and women to pursue different paths in life. At most it can tackle some of the obvious manifestations of this phenomenon. Moreover it can do this only if states use the concept, which not all states do, and employ it in as productive a manner as the concept allows, which is often far from the case.[42]

The problem with defining equality as equal treatment is that women have to adhere to male standards to succeed and many find it difficult or impossible to do so. In addition the notion of equal treatment is regarded as an inappropriate standard to be applied to certain aspects of human behaviour. This is particularly true of the so-called private sphere of the family. Within the family, relationships, so it was thought, should be organised on a basis of love, mutual respect and sharing, as opposed to law. The law was simply to be concerned with regulating the initiation and dissolution of family relationships. The state, whilst it might offer 'incentives' such as tax concessions to encourage the formation of family relationships such as

42 For an analysis of how (and in the case of indirect discrimination whether) the concepts of direct and indirect discrimination are employed by individual states see the chapters detailing state practice. See also Chapter Eight, this volume. For a more general analysis of direct and indirect discrimination see Bacchi, C. L. (1999), *Women, Policy and Politics*, London. Sage, pp. 93-98.

marriage, scarcely ever intervened in those relationships once they were formed and might not even recognise the desire of one (or both) of the partners to dissolve the union. The reluctance of the state to regulate the private sphere of the family has been eroded by the exposure of such phenomena as domestic violence and child abuse. As long, however, as the equality as equal treatment standard is confined largely to the workplace and the marketplace, the inequalities still practiced in the private sphere of the family will adversely affect its ability to eliminate inequalities between the sexes.

> [T]he weakness of the equal treatment approach lies in a lack of analysis of the relationship between public and private spheres. In effect, public life is ring-fenced as if it were unaffected by inequalities in the arena of private life. . . . Granting equal access to men and women will only benefit certain women: those whose cultural capital, experiences, family circumstances and share of domestic responsibilities are similar to those of men as a group.[43]

Equality as equal treatment is clearly unequal to the task of dealing with the disadvantages, both biological and cultural, which some women experience and most men do not.

> For a long time — and it is often still the case — gender equality in Europe was defined as giving girls and boys, women and men, *de jure* equal rights, equal opportunities, equal conditions and equal treatment in all fields of life and in all spheres of society. Nowadays, it is recognised that equality *de jure* does not automatically lead to equality *de facto*. It is important to understand that men's and women's living conditions are very different — to some degree because of the childbearing function of women. The main point is not the mere existence of such differences, but the fact that these differences should not have a negative impact on the living conditions of both women and men, should not discriminate against them and should contribute to an equal sharing of power in economy, society and policy-making processes. Gender equality is not synonymous with sameness, with establishing men, their life style and conditions as the norm.[44]

---

43 Rees, op cit, n. 19, p. 29.

44. Council of Europe (1998), *Gender Mainstreaming: Conceptual Framework, Methodology and Presentation of Good Practices, Final report of the Group of Specialists on Mainstreaming* (EG-S-MS (98) 2), Strasbourg: Council of Europe, p. 4.

If equality means devising some way of accommodating or even celebrating difference rather than penalising it, then the question must be — how? Feminist theory has found it very difficult to give a satisfactory answer to this question for a number of reasons. In the first place the obvious response to any differences which cause individuals to suffer is to compensate them in some positive way for this negative impact. The problem with achieving equality by means of special treatment or affirmative action is that it is in direct conflict with the notion of equality as equal treatment. This, as will be seen later, can cause grave problems if it is necessary to reconcile both notions within a single legal system.[45] Secondly this approach to securing equality between the sexes is often not seen as a way of redressing past inequalities or addressing the social or cultural stereotypes associated with women. Instead it is viewed, even by some women, as a way of privileging them and penalising men. States may often have to be circumspect in their use of such a strategy, resorting to conciliatory language — targets rather than quotas — and often leaving the decision whether or not to use positive or affirmative action to the discretion of individual employers or organisations. Attempts to move beyond the formal equality of equal treatment to a more radical but substantive notion of equality acknowledge that in order to attain equality women may require *more* than equal treatment, but if such strategies involve taking 'benefits', in the shape of employment, promotion, or public office, away from men they are likely to meet with objections.

Recent efforts to discover a way to move the equality debate beyond formal equality have put forward an alternative strategy to achieve substantive equality commonly referred to as mainstreaming.[46] Mainstreaming requires that the impact that laws or policies will have on gender equality be evaluated prior to their implementation. The strategy is not seen as singling out women for special treatment since it applies equally to men. Mainstreaming is regarded as having considerable potential to transform the current situation of women since it inquires what positive or negative effects will this policy have on gender equality. The problem is, however, that expressing the desire to promote substantive equality by resorting to mainstreaming or affirmative

45. This proved to be the case in the United Kingdom where an attempt by a political party to increase the numbers of women elected to Parliament by creating all women short lists for winnable Parliamentary seats was held to constitute sex discrimination. *Jepson and Dyas-Elliott v The Labour Party* [1996] IRLR 116.

46. For a definition and general discussion of mainstreaming see Council of Europe, op cit, n. 44, Commission of the European Communities (1996), *Communication on Incorporating Equal Opportunities for Men and Women into all Community Policies and Activities*, COM (96)67, 21/02/96.

action leaves unanswered what exactly substantive equality stands for. The notion of equal treatment is a comparatively simple one but substantive equality is often presented as a desirable goal without any detailed articulation of what it represents. If substantive equality were achieved, in what ways would society be transformed? Would there be equal numbers of women and men in company boardrooms, in national legislatures and in the professions? Would the task of childcare be split equitably between a child's parents? Would wealth be equally distributed between the sexes so that the process of the feminisation of poverty would be reversed?

The quest for equality is further complicated by the work of those feminist commentators who have revealed that the neutrality of laws and legal reasoning is illusory.[47] Maleness and male values are said to permeate the very core of a state's values and institutional landscape. If this is so then there must be doubts over the ability of such a system to deliver substantive equality. Laws which are meant to secure real progress in securing equality between the sexes could be undermined by a hostile interpretation on the part of a [male] judiciary. Even if as many women hold judicial office as men, there is no guarantee that the training in legal reasoning that these women have will not blind them to the 'maleness' of that reasoning.

Furthermore, post-modern feminism has directed its attention to the use of terms such as 'men' and 'women'. To ask questions such as 'does this policy have a negative impact on women?' is to run the risk of essentialism; that is, regarding the category of 'women' as a group of individuals with exactly the same needs and aspirations.[48] This is patently not the case. The needs of black women or poor women may be very different from those of white, middle class professional women. Yet those involved in the search for more effective equality strategies have to be aware of the fact that the 'woman of legal discourse' or the woman who is the focus of the policy-makers' concern is such an attempt to essentialise women.[49] As a consequence only those women whose behaviour most closely corresponds to the law or policy-makers' image of 'women' may be able to benefit from any attempts to improve equality strategies.

Viewed from this perspective, it could appear that the barriers which exist to promoting equality between the sexes are so formidable that there is no point in embarking on this task. The chapters which follow, however, will demonstrate that, whilst the task is not an easy one, there is every reason to persevere. An awareness of the dangers of essentialism is not a reason for

---

47. MacKinnon, op cit, n. 7.
48. Brooks, D. (1994) 'A commentary on the essence of anti-essentialism in feminist legal theory', 2 *Feminist Legal Studies* 115.
49. Smart, C. (1992), 'The woman of legal discourse', 1 *Social and Legal Studies* 29

abandoning the quest for equality, but an indication that the different causes of inequality — sex, race, age or disability for example — cannot be compartmentalised and treated as if there were no links between them. The same is true of the alleged maleness of the state. To be forewarned is to be forearmed, it is not a reason to admit defeat. Finally the search for the paradigm that is equality must also be put into perspective. Anyone involved in the pursuit of equality has to be aware of the shades of meaning attached to this term.[50] Rather than forcing them to take sides, this should alert them to the fact that arguments over the 'correct' meaning of equality can divert attention away from what in any given situation is the best method of promoting equality between the sexes.

The mechanics of promoting equality

Apart from determining which notion, or indeed notions, of equality it wishes to pursue, a state also has to select the appropriate mechanism for implementing this policy goal. There are a range of options available but the ones which will be encountered most frequently in *Making Women Count* are guarantees in a state's constitution of equal treatment or equality under the law, hard and soft law measures as well as extra-legal initiatives such as setting targets for the number of women holding public office. Each of these mechanisms has its particular strengths and weaknesses *as a mechanism* irrespective of the content of any equality policy which it is used to promote. If, for example, a state includes in its constitution a guarantee of 'equal treatment for men and women', it is possible not only to criticise the wording of that guarantee and the wisdom of using a rights strategy to promote equality but also to analyse the practical difficulties of employing a constitutional guarantee. Clearly, these issues are interrelated but equally clearly when a state decides to promote equality by pursuing a particular strategy or policy it must consider what is the best vehicle for doing this. As the chapters devoted to state practice will show, no state relies on a single mechanism in order to promote equality, preferring instead to use a combination of approaches. This will often be influenced by a state's political, institutional or cultural landscape. The European Union can also exert an influence on the choice of mechanism by insisting that Member States put legally binding measures in place in order to implement their Community obligations.

---

50. Majury, op cit, n. 8.

In the chapters that follow, therefore, it is important to be alive to the fact that some of the criticisms leveled at the states featured in *Making Women Count* may be as a consequence of the mechanisms they have chosen to implement their state policy. Where a state has decided to insert a guarantee of equality in its constitution, its practical impact may depend on whether individuals can enforce such a guarantee as well as the nature of the body entrusted with the task of determining whether this guarantee has been breached. In the Netherlands no way exists of enforcing the rights, including the right to equality, in the constitution. In Ireland and Spain, however, the courts are given the task of interpreting the constitution and ensuring its terms are observed. Arranz, Quintanilla and Velázquez are very positive in their comments regarding the Spanish Constitutional Court and how it has chosen to interpret the constitutional guarantees of equality.[51] In contrast, Donnelly, Mullally and Smith are much more critical of the approach taken by the Irish Supreme Court.[52]

There can also be difficulties if a state decides to use hard law — that is primary or secondary legislation — to give effect to its equality policy. In some respects the issues are the same as those associated with constitutional guarantees — that is how the rights and duties set out in the legislation are to be enforced. In Ireland and the United Kingdom an individual has to take legal action in order to enforce the rights given to her in legislation. This can be a costly and discouraging process since, initially at least, the burden falls on the individual to prove that she has been treated unlawfully by being made the target of sex discrimination. In other countries, such as Sweden, a dedicated official, the Equality Ombudsman, is entrusted with the task of enforcing the legislation rather than requiring the injured party to take action.

Apart from the issue of how hard law initiatives are to be enforced, there is also the question of how sympathetically the individuals or bodies entrusted with this task will go about it. There is a possibility that if enforcement is the responsibility of a specific individual or organisation, such as an Equality Commission or Ombudsman, the task of interpretation may be performed more constructively and efficiently than if it is assigned to some more generalist body such as the courts. A body which constantly deals with allegations of sex discrimination and has prime responsibility for interpreting the legislative framework which is meant to secure equality is likely to measure its own progress in terms of the successful implementation of that legislation. By way of contrast, those institutions which deal with allegations

51. See Chapter Five, this volume at pp. 113-116
52. See Chapter Two, this volume at p. 33.

of sex discrimination on an occasional basis, where these cases represent only a fraction of their complete caseload, may fail to appreciate the purpose behind the legislation.[53] The membership of decision-making bodies can also have a bearing on how sympathetically equality legislation is applied and interpreted. For example a court accustomed to dealing only with individual rights might regard equality legislation in a very different manner from a tripartite tribunal accustomed to dealing with industrial relations and with balancing trade union and employee concerns.

As well as hard law measures, some states make use of so-called soft law initiatives. The term 'soft law' is frequently employed in the context of international and Community law in order to refer to initiatives which, whilst they are not legally binding (hard law), may have some indirect legal impact.[54] The European Union's Recommendation on the Protection of the Dignity of Men and Women at Work and its associated Code of Practice on sexual harassment[55] are good examples of soft law. In the opinion of the European Court of Justice[56] a Member State, and in particular its national courts, would be obliged to take this measure into account when deciding relevant disputes. This would be especially true if the measure had been acted on by the state in question or was designed to supplement a binding Community initiative such as a Directive.

The states featured in *Making Women Count* are, therefore, exposed to soft law equality measures either as a consequence of their membership of the European Union or as a result of national efforts. States can of course decide that they wish to act on an EU recommendation and use primary legislation to do so. This is not a frequent occurrence since soft law is perceived as possessing qualities which mean that, in certain contexts, it is a more useful mechanism to promote equality than hard law. The particular advantages of soft law are said to be that it can be adopted speedily and used to encourage or reinforce positive behaviour patterns among its target group. Its major drawback is seen as being the fact that compliance with a soft law measure is largely voluntary rather than obligatory.

53 The Equal Opportunities Commission recommends that discrimination cases should be heard by specialist tribunals. Equal Opportunities Commission (1998) *Equality in the 21st Century: A New Approach*, Manchester: Equal Opportunities Commission, para 96.

54. Beveridge, F. and Nott, S. M. (1998), 'A Hard Look at Soft Law', in Craig, P. and Harlow, C. (eds), *Lawmaking in the European Union*, London: Kluwer Law International.

55. Commission Recommendation on the protection of the dignity of men and women at work, 91/131/EEC, OJ L49/1, 1991.

56. *Grimaldi v Fonds des Maladies Professionelles* Case 322/88 [1989] ECR 4407.

Soft law may emanate from government but state equality agencies are often a source of such guidance. Governments frequently impose a duty on state equality agencies to promote equality and this may include the drawing up and dissemination of advice on best practice in the form of Codes of Practice or guidelines. Soft law, in the shape of such measures as Codes of Practice, is essentially used to encourage certain behaviour which is seen as helpful in promoting equality. In the case of sexual harassment, for example, some of the states featured in *Making Women Count* have adopted hard law measures to provide those women who are the victims of such behaviour with specific redress.[57] It is, however, far better if the sort of behaviour which constitutes sexual harassment either does not occur in the first place or is dealt with immediately before it gets out of hand. Soft law measures can be used to provide employers or other organisations with guidance on how to tackle such behaviour. Advice can be offered on what constitutes sexual harassment, what complaints machinery can be put in place to deal with allegations of such conduct and how to train employees to refrain from behaving in this manner. Whilst employers are not obliged to take heed of such advice, the knowledge that by following it they could avoid the disruption, unhappiness and litigation that sexual harassment can bring, may be a powerful incentive to comply.

Apart from the decision on the part of government, and those agencies which form part of government, to offer advice to others on promoting equality, there are also occasions when a government will use its domination of the policy-making process to achieve equality between the sexes. A government may announce its adoption of the strategy of mainstreaming, that is its commitment to evaluate all future, or indeed existing, policies for their gender impact. It may set targets for the numbers of women to be employed in the public service. It may decide that certain government grants are to be awarded only to those organisations with a proven record on promoting equality between the sexes. Why governments choose to make such extra-legal commitments depends, as subsequent chapters will show, on a variety of factors. These include international pressure, internal political pressures and the degree of responsibility a particular government feels for promoting equality. Indeed a government which, for whatever reasons, is willing to adjust its own behaviour may often be persuaded to impose such obligations on regional governments or provide an example which regional or local government is willing to follow.

57. For example, Sweden. Equal Opportunities Act 1991 as amended by SFS 1998:208.

The difficulty with relying on extra-legal mechanisms is that such positive policies may disappear when the government in question loses power or is faced with some more pressing crisis. Moreover it is sometimes the case that governments which commit themselves to strategies such as mainstreaming do so in name only. There may be little practical evidence that they are willing to devote the resources to ensuring that such strategies work in practice.

Conclusion

The major purpose of this chapter has been to set the scene for the analyses of national practice and of equality strategies which follow by introducing what will be recurring themes throughout *Making Women Count*. Equality is not only a national concern but also represents a preoccupation of supranational bodies such as the European Union. As a consequence of such pressures states are faced by a conflicting array of definitions of what equality means and an equally confusing range of strategies for promoting equality. These are then filtered through a state's own particular institutional and political landscape. What is lacking, and what *Making Women Count* aims to provide, is clear guidance on what the objectives of particular strategies are and how best to go about achieving these objectives.

2 Making Women Count in Ireland

MARY DONNELLY, SIOBHÁN MULLALLY AND OLIVIA SMITH

Recent years have witnessed significant changes in the policy-making processes in Ireland. The partnership approach to policy-making has been expanded to include the Community and Voluntary sector, giving groups such as the National Women's Council of Ireland (NWCI) a direct input into the policy process. This expansion of the partnership process has coincided with an increased emphasis on inequality and social exclusion. The national agreement, *Partnership 2000, for Inclusion, Employment and Competitiveness*,[1] negotiated between the Government and the Social Partners in 1996 sets out a detailed programme designed to tackle the many and varied mechanisms of social exclusion in Irish society. The agreement identifies three principal equality strategies: constitutional reform, the introduction of employment equality and equal status legislation and improved administrative procedures to 'equality proof' law and policy proposals. A number of steps have already been taken. In 1998, the Employment Equality Act was signed into law. The Act extends the scope of equality protection beyond gender to include such categories as age, race and disability. It also includes, for the first time, a statutory prohibition of sexual harassment. The Equal Status Bill, 1999, if enacted into law, will extend equality protection beyond the sphere of employment, to include areas such as education and the provision of goods and services. The Constitution Review Group, established by the Government in 1995, has made a number of recommendations for constitutional reform, including a recommendation that Article 41.2.2°'s reference to women's 'duties in the home' be deleted. As yet, however, no action has been taken to implement this recommendation. As part of a mainstreaming approach to gender equality a range of administrative procedures have been introduced to 'proof' policies for their impact on women.[2] The need for gender mainstreaming is now increasingly accepted within the political system. No

1 (1996), Dublin: Government Stationery Office.

2 See Department of the Taoiseach. (1998), *Cabinet Handbook*, Dublin: Government Stationery Office, p 19; Department of Justice, Equality and Law Reform. (1999), *Discussion Document on Gender Proofing*, Dublin; Mullally, S. (1999), *Guidelines for Gender Proofing within the Context of the Structural Funds*, Dublin: Department of Justice, Equality and Law Reform. See also Department of Social, Community and Family Affairs. (1998), *Guidelines on Poverty Proofing within the context of the National Anti-Poverty Strategy* (see infra p. 46).

longer is the pursuit of equality to be seen as the preserve of specialised Government units or projects. Bringing equality 'out of the margins', it is recognised, requires a process of integrating equality into the mainstream of policy work and service delivery.

These changes in the legislative and policy framework on equality have coincided with an unprecedented economic boom in Ireland. Women are entering the labour force in increasing numbers. Rates of female participation in the labour force have risen from 30.9 per cent in 1986 to approximately 44 per cent in 1999.[3] Women and men, however, are not benefiting equally from the Tiger economy. Women remain concentrated in low and semi-skilled service occupations and significant disparities continue to exist between average male and female earnings.[4] Women's maternal status continues to be a primary determinant in labour force participation, highlighting, yet again, the failure to assist workers in combining paid employment with family responsibilities.[5] A recent report on women and poverty in Ireland notes that gender continues to be a significant factor in poverty and social exclusion.[6] This exclusion is particularly evident in women's under-representation within policy-making processes. Despite an increasing awareness of the need to mainstream gender equality, this has not yet translated into systematic changes in the way in which such processes operate.

The Political and Legal Landscape in Ireland

Irish law is comprised of European Community law, the 1937 Constitution *Bunreacht na hÉireann*, legislation passed by or under the authority of the *Oireachtas*[7] and the common law. The supremacy of Community law was ensured by a constitutional amendment providing that any legislative or administrative acts of the Community institutions would be free from

3. Pollak, A. (1999), 'Number of Families Where Both Parents Work Doubles', *Irish Times*, 2 June.
4. See Ruane, F. and Sutherland, J. (1999), *Women in the Labour Force*, Dublin: Employment Equality Agency. The Report notes that 70 per cent of people with a scientific or technological qualification in 1996 were male. In 1997, the average weekly earnings of women were 64.37 per cent of men's average weekly earnings. This disparity is a result of women on average working a shorter number of hours than men.
5. Ibid.
6. See Nolan, B. and Watson, D. (1999), *Women and Poverty in Ireland*, Dublin: Combat Poverty Agency. The Report notes the particular risks of poverty faced by female headed households.
7. Also included is legislation passed by the English Parliament, prior to 1922, that remained in force post independence. Whether or not legislation remains in force depends on its compatibility with constitutional requirements.

constitutional scrutiny.[8] Subsequent amendments to the Constitution have provided for the ratification of the Single European Act and the Maastricht and Amsterdam Treaties. However, despite the apparent acceptance of Community law supremacy, there have been some hints that the national courts may be reluctant to yield total supremacy in the area of fundamental rights. This reluctance has been most evident in debates on the question of abortion.[9]

The development of a strong 'rights culture' has been an important feature of Irish constitutional jurisprudence. The fundamental rights provisions of the Constitution are set out in Articles 40-44 and include rights to: equality before the law, personal liberty, freedom of expression and assembly, freedom of association, family and education rights, property rights and freedom of religion. By contemporary standards, the list of rights expressly protected is incomplete. This has been remedied somewhat by the recognition of a large body of 'unenumerated' personal rights under Article 40.3.1°,[10] including the right to bodily integrity[11] and the equal right of men and women to an adequate means of livelihood.[12]

Ireland is a party to a number of international human rights treaties including the 1979 UN Convention on the Elimination of All Forms of Discrimination Against Women (CEDAW) and the European Convention on Human Rights (ECHR).[13] Neither of these treaties is incorporated into domestic law.[14] The Constitution Review Group considered the question of incorporation of the ECHR. It concluded against it, however, on the ground that it would not lead to any significant improvement in the protection of

8. See Article 29. 4. 3°-6°. The incorporation of Community law into the law of Ireland was completed by the European Communities Act, 1972.
9. See generally, Kingston, J., Whelan, A., and Bacik, I. (1997), *Abortion and the Law*, Dublin: Roundhall Sweet and Maxwell.
10. Article 40. 3. provides that:
    The State guarantees in its laws to respect, and, as far as practicable, by its laws to defend and vindicate the personal rights of the citizen.
    The State shall, in particular, by its laws protect as best it may from unjust attack and, in the case of injustice done, vindicate the life, person, good name, and property rights of every citizen.
11. *Ryan v Attorney General* [1965] IR 294.
12 *Murtagh Properties v Cleary* [1972] IR 330.
13. Ireland has acceded to the 1979 UN Convention on the Elimination of All Forms of Discrimination Against Women; the 1966 UN International Covenant on Civil and Political Rights and both Protocols to the Covenant; the 1966 UN International Covenant on Economic, Social and Cultural Rights and the 1989 UN Convention on the Rights of the Child. It remains the only EU Member State that has not yet ratified the 1966 UN Convention on the Elimination of All Forms of Racial Discrimination.
14. Because of the dualist nature of the Irish legal system, they are not, therefore, directly enforceable in domestic courts (Article 29. 6 of the Constitution).

fundamental rights. Instead, it recommended an amended list of fundamental rights drawing on the ECHR, the UN International Covenant on Civil and Political Rights and those 'unenumerated rights' already identified by the judiciary.[15] In the *Good Friday Agreement*, concluded between the British and Irish governments on 10 April 1998, the Irish Government committed itself to improving human rights protection in Ireland. Given developments within Northern Ireland and the Irish Government's commitment to ensure 'at least an equivalent level of protection of human rights' in the Republic, it is likely that the question of incorporation will be returned to again in the near future.

The Political Structures

The Constitution, *Bunreacht na hÉireann*, provides for three main branches of government, the executive, the legislature and the judiciary. The executive function is carried out by the Government. Both the Government and the *Taoiseach* (Prime Minister) are elected by the *Dáil*. The Cabinet, including the *Tánaiste* (deputy Prime Minister), is appointed by the *Taoiseach*. The legislature or law-making body is the *Oireachtas* (the Parliament). It consists of two houses, an upper house, the *Seanad*, and a lower house, the *Dáil*. The *Dáil* (consisting of 166 members) is directly elected by means of a secret ballot using the single transferable vote system of proportional representation (PR-STV). Although referred to as the 'lower house', the *Dáil* is the primary law-making body. Although legislation may be initiated by any member of either House of the *Oireachtas*, most legislation is initiated in the *Dáil* by the Government Minister with responsibility for the subject area in question.

The *Seanad* is primarily a deliberative body, with limited powers of initiation and review of legislation. It is composed of sixty members. Eleven are nominated by the *Taoiseach* (Prime Minister), six are elected by the graduates of two universities (the National University of Ireland and the University of Dublin) and the remaining forty-three are elected from five panels representing various social sectors. The electorate consists of *Dáil* members, members of the outgoing *Seanad* and all county councils and county borough council members. Although originally established to ensure representation for groups that were under-represented in the *Dáil,* the *Seanad* has now largely lost this function. Increasingly, its membership reflects the political complexion of the *Dáil.*

The judicial system in Ireland is divided into four distinct levels: the District Court, the Circuit Court, the High Court and the Supreme Court.The District and Circuit Courts are courts of local and limited jurisdiction. The

---

15. (1996), *Report of the Constitution Review Group*, Dublin: Government Stationery Office, pp. 216-19.

High Court is invested with full original jurisdiction in both civil and criminal matters. The Supreme Court is the court of final appeal. Both the High Court and the Supreme Court have power to review the constitutionality of legislation. Under Article 26 of the Constitution, the Supreme Court also has power, following a Presidential referral, to review the constitutionality of any legislative proposal. As of April 1999, the gender breakdown of the judiciary was as follows:

	Total Number of Judges	Number of Women	Number of Men	% Female
Supreme Court	8	1	7	12.5%
High Court	24	4	20	16.6%
Circuit Court	25	5	20	20%
District Court	51	9	42	17.6%

The 1937 Constitution also provides for the establishment of the office of President. Although the President is often colloquially referred to as 'Head of State' in fact the constitutional role accorded to the President is primarily a ceremonial one. Additional powers conferred by legislation are relatively insignificant and primarily formal in nature.[16] Ironically, it is within the confines of this largely ceremonial role that women have made the most significant impact. The last two Presidents have both been women. In the last Presidential election, four of the five Presidential candidates were women. Women's successes within the political process, however, have largely remained confined to this ceremonial office. Women remain under-represented within both houses of the *Oireachtas*, accounting for just over 12 per cent of *Dáil* members and 18 per cent of *Seanad* members.[17] In the current centre-right Government, women account for only three Cabinet Ministers (including the *Tánaiste*) and two Ministers of State. In *Oireachtas* (Parliamentary) Committees, women's representation tends to be concentrated in areas relating to health, children and equality. Women remain under-represented also at the level of local government, constituting approximately 16 per cent of the elected members. In elections to the European Parliament, women have fared slightly better, gaining one third of the parliamentary seats in the 1999 elections.

The under-representation of women in political processes has been attributed, in part, to the historically low rates of female participation in the labour force and, in part, to the electoral system — PR-STV — combined with

16. See generally Hogan, G. and Whyte, G. (1994), *Kelly, J.M., The Irish Constitution*, Third Edition, London: Sweet and Maxwell, pp. 79-98.
17. See http://www.irlgov.ie/oireachtas/com28th/comindex.html

relatively small constituencies. Political candidates tend to be nominated on the basis of their local electability rather than the need for a social mix of candidates. Strategies to remedy this gender imbalance have never seriously been addressed by mainstream political parties. The smaller political parties, both left and right, continue to select and elect women in greater proportions than the more established centre-right parties. Neither of the main political parties, *Fianna Fáil* or *Fine Gael*, favour the use of minimum party quotas for women, preferring instead less quantitative positive action strategies.[18] Some consideration has been given to reforming the system of election to the *Seanad*. Suggestions have included extending the current panel system, to include each of the four pillars of the Social Partnership[19] and electing women and men in equal numbers from two sub-panels, divided on the basis of sex.[20] As yet, however, no action has been taken to implement these recommendations. Where positive action strategies have been adopted, they have met with some success. The adoption of a minimum quota for women in Government appointments to State Boards, for example, has increased women's representation in direct appointments from 17 per cent in 1992 to 35 per cent in 1997.[21] A limited form of positive action was provided for in the 1997 Electoral Act. Political parties are now required to provide a yearly statement setting out the budget allocated by the party to promoting the participation of women and young persons in political activity. Although this has led to an increased awareness of gender issues in political participation, it has not yet translated into concrete improvements for women.[22]

One of the most significant developments within the policy process in Ireland has been the development of social partnership. The first partnership institution, the National Economic and Social Council (NESC) was established in 1973 as an advisory body on issues relating to economic development and

18. See Government of Ireland. (1999), *Third Progress Report on the Implementation of the Recommendations of the Second Commission on the Status of Women*, Dublin: Government Stationery Office, p. 115.
19. See generally, Lynch, K. (1996), 'Submission to the Constitution Review Group. Appendix 6' in *Report of the Constitution Review Group*, supra n. 15.
20. The Second Commission on the Status of Women recommended that all political parties in the *Oireachtas* should nominate women and men in equal numbers for the panel seats. Second Commission on the Status of Women. (1993), *Report to Government*, Dublin: Government Stationery Office, p. 222. This recommendation has not met with a positive response from political parties. However, the All Party Oireachtas Committee on the Constitution has recommended that women and men be elected in equal numbers from two sub-panels. In addition the Committee has recommended that the *Taoiseach* maintain a gender balance in his / her appointments. See Government of Ireland, op cit, n. 18, p. 117.
21. A target of 40 per cent was adopted by Government following a recommendation of the Second Commission on the Status of Women, op cit, n. 20 p. 223. See NWCI. (1997), *Who Makes the Decisions?*, Dublin: NWCI.
22. Government of Ireland, op cit, n. 18 pp. 114-17.

social justice. Its membership was drawn from the traditional social partners, business, trade union and farming groups. The 1990s have witnessed an expansion of the 'partnership' process, reflected both in the range of economic and social policies considered and the range of partners included in the process. Initially, the expansion of social partnership had involved an increased emphasis on policy issues relating to unemployment, poverty and social exclusion. Subsequently, the issue of inclusion in the process itself became a focus for discussion.

Before 1993, the conferral of partnership status was confined to the traditional economic players. In 1993, a second partnership institution was established, the National Economic and Social Forum (NESF). The Forum included representatives from the Community and Voluntary sector. The Forum is responsible for developing economic and social initiatives with a focus on unemployment and contributing to the formation of a national consensus on social and economic policies. It has 45 members drawn from three different strands: elected representatives from all the main political parties (Strand 1); Social Partners — IBEC (Irish Business Employers Confederation), Farmers and Trade Unions (Strand 2); and Community and Voluntary Sector (Women, Disadvantaged, Unemployed, Youth, Elderly, Environment and People with a Disability) (Strand 3). The Partnership 2000 agreement assigns the NESF a role in monitoring the implementation of the agreement's equality provisions.

The status and composition of both the NESF and the NESC is presently under review. Proposals to broaden the membership of the NESC — to include the Community and Voluntary sector — and to place both the NESC and the NESF on a statutory footing are being considered.[23]

The expansion of social partnership has given women and other disadvantaged groups greater input into the policy process. The current national agreement, Partnership 2000, was negotiated both by the traditional Social Partners and the Community and Voluntary sector. This more inclusive approach to policy making is reflected in the agreement's extended focus on poverty and social exclusion. However, despite the move towards a more participatory approach to policy-making, the Government of the day retains a virtual monopoly in proposing policy and legislation.

The Law and Policy-Making Process

The procedures to be followed in designing policy are set out in the Cabinet Handbook.[24] Policy proposals, not falling within the ambit of existing

23. See Goverment Legislation Programme, http://www.irlgov.ie/taoiseach/legislation/default.html
24. Department of the Taoiseach, op cit, n. 2.

Government policy, must first be submitted to Government for approval, in the form of a Memorandum for Government. Memoranda set out general strategy and policy and are prepared by the relevant Government Department, following consultation with other concerned Departments. All Memoranda for Government are required to state the implications of a proposal for women and in the case of 'significant' policy proposals, the implications for persons in poverty or at risk of falling into poverty. Once approved, a policy proposal may become the subject of legislative action. Cabinet Procedure Instructions for legislative drafting require government approval of a 'General Scheme'. Once that scheme is approved, consultation with outside bodies may take place, 'if necessary'. Draft legislation is not at any point disclosed to third parties, however, and does not enter the public domain until introduced in the *Oireachtas*. Legislation is initially introduced in the form of a Bill.[25] A Bill passes through five stages in the initiating House. Upon successful passage, the Bill is then sent to the other House for approval. Following its successful passage through both Houses of the *Oireachtas*, the President signs the Bill into law. If the President has any doubt as to the Bill's constitutionality, she may refer it to the Supreme Court (it is this power of referral that has earned the President the title of 'Guardian of the Constitution').

The selection of measures to be included in the law and policy-making agenda is primarily a matter for the Government. In recent years, however, dissatisfaction with a highly centralised approach to government has grown. The development of the partnership process from the mid 1980s onwards heralded an era of negotiated social and economic governance.[26] The first national agreement, *Programme for National Recovery, 1987-1990*,[27] was negotiated between Government and the traditional Social Partners against a background of a severe economic and social crisis. This more participatory approach to government had little impact on women, however. Women remained marginalised both within Government and within the Social Partners.[28] With the establishment of the NESF, women's representation within partnership negotiations improved.[29]

The expansion of the partnership process can be seen in the growing number of Task Forces and *ad hoc* Working Groups participating in the policy process. It would now be 'unthinkable' to establish a task force or policy committee without social partner representation.[30] Of the groups presently

25. See generally Chubb, B. (3rd1992), *The Government and Politics of Ireland*, London: Longman.
26. O'Donnell, R. and Thomas, D. (1998), 'Partnership and Policy-Making' in Healy, S. and Reynolds, B. (eds), *Social Policy in Ireland*, Dublin: Oak Tree Press.
27. Government of Ireland. (1987), Dublin: Government Stationery Office.
28. See Second Commission on the Status of Women, op cit, n. 20, pp. 214-15. The Commission recommended as a 'temporary special measure' that reserved seats for women be established in executive decision-making forums. The recommendation has been taken up by the Irish Confederation of Trade Unionists (ICTU). However, it is considered 'impractical' by IBEC. See Government of Ireland, op cit, n. 18, p. 113.
29. At present, women account for 51 per cent of the Forum's members.
30. O'Donnell, R. and Thomas, D, op cit, n. 26, p. 126.

existing, those of particular interest to women include: the Expert Working Group on Childcare; the Working Group on Gender Proofing, the Commission on the Family and the National Steering Committee on Violence Against Women. The Reports produced by such bodies widen the range of inputs into the policy process, as does the consultative process surrounding the preparation by Government of Green and White policy papers.[31] No particular format is followed in preparing these position papers. In recent years, however, it has become the norm to make this stage of the policy-making process more consultative.

Despite the fact that consultative and partnership processes have broadened the range of inputs into the policy process, it remains at the discretion of the Government to decide whether or not to follow through on the measures proposed. The partnership process has made some inroads into that monopoly.[32] However, concern has been expressed that a two tier system has developed within the partnership process itself. The Community and Voluntary sector continues to be excluded from the NESC. A wide range of public policies are determined at the NESC in negotiations with the traditional Social Partners, leaving the NESF with only an 'invitation to comment'.[33] This hieraracby is a highly gendered one. As women continue to be under-represented amongst the traditional social partners, failing to include the Community and Voluntary sector reinforces the marginalisation of women within the policy process.

A lack of transparency in Government decision-making has also limited the possibilities for a more participatory approach to governance. Recent years, have witnessed some changes in the 'openness' and 'transparency' of government, however.[34] Following the launch of a programme of public service reform in 1994 — the Strategic Management Initiative — freedom of information has become increasingly linked with accountability and

31. See generally: Report of Partnership 2000 Expert Working Group on Childcare. (1999), *National Childcare Strategy*, Dublin: Government Stationery Office; Commission on the Family. (1998), *Strengthening Families for Life*, Final Report to the Minister for Social, Community and Family Affairs, Dublin: Government Stationery Office; Office of the Tánaiste. (1997), *Report of the Task Force on Violence against Women*, Dublin: Government Stationery Office. Government Ministers have the authority to order the preparation of Green and White Papers on a particular issue. A Green Paper provides a framework for discussion and aims to stimulate further debate on a particular policy area. A White Paper sets out agreed government policy and provides a framework for future government action.
32. A recurring concern with the partnership process is that it has sometimes amounted to little more than participation without power. See Employment Equality Agency. (Summer 1999), 'Interview with Niall Crowley', *Equality News*, 18, pp. 14-15.
33. NESF. (1997), *A Framework for Partnership: Enriching Strategic Consensus through Participation*, Dublin: Government Stationery Office, pp. 20-1.
34. See the Official Secrets Act 1963.

efficiency in public service.[35] The Second Programme for Government issued in 1994, by the then centre-left Coalition Government, had promised legislative reform to ensure greater transparency and openness in policy-making.[36] This led, in 1997, to the enactment of the Freedom of Information (FOI) Act and to constitutional changes in the rules governing cabinet confidentiality.

Freedom of Information

The FOI Act came into effect on 21 April 1998, establishing three new statutory rights:[37]

- to access information held by public bodies;
- to have official information relating to oneself amended where it is incomplete, incorrect or misleading;
- to obtain reasons for decisions affecting oneself.

Under the Act, all public bodies have been required to publish the rules, procedures, practices and guidelines used for decision-making. Providing access to official information as a matter of right marks a significant departure from the traditional approach to disclosure of official information. However, some concern has been expressed at the limited scope of the legislation. At present the Act applies to five distinct categories of public bodies: central government departments, State Boards and offices, local authorities, health boards and State or State controlled bodies, organisations or groups. Provision is made for the Minister for Finance to bring statutory bodies and bodies funded by the State within the scope of the Act by an additional regulation. Whether or not this step is taken will depend on the political commitment to promoting transparency and openness at all levels of policy-making. Rights of access to information are also limited. Some records are excluded entirely from the application of the Act, while others may be exempted subject to the satisfaction of specified tests, including, *inter alia*, public interest and injury tests. The Act does not apply to records concerning undertakings of a legislative or judicial nature, and neither does it apply to the workings of certain offices.[38]

---

35. Government of Ireland. (1996), *Delivering Better Government: A programme of change for the Civil Service. Second Report of the Co-ordinating Group of Secretaries*, Dublin: Government Stationery Office.
36. Government of Ireland. (1994), *A Government of Renewal: A Policy Agreement between Fine Gael, the Labour Party and Democratic Left*, Dublin: Government Stationery Office.
37. See generally, McDonagh, M. (1998), *Freedom of Information Law in Ireland*, Dublin: Roundhall Sweet and Maxwell.
38. It does not apply to courts, tribunals, the Attorney General, the Director of Public Prosecutions, the Comptroller and Auditor General, the Ombudsman, the President and the *Oireachtas* in relation to the private papers of members. S. 46 (1).

Access to information is further restricted by constitutional requirements concerning Cabinet confidentiality. Government records (for example Memoranda for Government and other records relating to proceedings or decisions of the Government) are withheld from access for five years. After this time, they may, subject to other exemptions, be accessible to outside bodies.[39] Information concerning actual discussions (as distinct from decisions) at Government meetings is exempt from disclosure under the Act. This is in line with constitutional requirements, which provide that discussions at Cabinet level are to remain strictly confidential unless the High Court determines that the public interest justifies disclosure.[40] It is too early to know whether the numerous exceptions in the Act will prevent it from operating as an effective means of access to information. Much will turn on the interpretation and application of the 'public interest' requirements. It remains to be seen whom the 'balancing of interests' will favour. For the moment, the secrecy surrounding Memoranda for Government continues to limit the potential for an open and transparent approach to gender mainstreaming.

Equality Legislation in Ireland

From a doctrinal perspective, equality is protected in Ireland through a combination of legislation and a constitutional guarantee. Neither method of equality protection has proved to be entirely satisfactory. Article 40.1 of the Constitution of Ireland provides a constitutional guarantee of equality:

> All citizens shall, as human persons, be held equal before the law. This shall not be held to mean that the State shall not in its enactments have due regard to differences of capacity, physical and moral, and of social function.

Unfortunately, the Supreme Court has tended to rely on the second, limiting clause in Article 40.1 in its interpretation of the constitutional guarantee of equality.[41] As a result, the guarantee has been of very limited effectiveness. The reference to differences of social function has been particularly problematic for women. It has been used by the courts to uphold legislation based on questionable stereotypes.[42] This is compounded by the inclusion of

39. S. 19.
40. Article 28. 4. 3° of the Constitution. The High Court can only take such a decision following an application from a Tribunal established by Government to inquire into matters of 'public importance'. This provision was inserted into the Constitution, following a referendum in 1997. Prior to 1997, the doctrine of 'collective responsibility' of Government had been held to require an absolute prohibition on the disclosure of Cabinet discussions. *Attorney General v Hamilton* [1993] 2 IR 250.
41. See *de Búrca v Attorney General* [1976] IR 38.
42. See *Dennehy v Minister for Social Welfare* Unreported High Court 26 July 1984.

Article 41.2.2° in the Constitution. This Article provides that the State shall endeavour to ensure that mothers shall not be obliged by economic necessity to engage in labour to the neglect of their duties in the home. In its recent report, the Constitution Review Group has recommended the replacement of both the equality guarantee and Article 41.2.2°.[43]

Equality legislation in Ireland is currently in a state of flux. At the time of writing, the main pieces of legislation governing equality between women and men in employment are:

- The Anti-Discrimination (Pay) Act, 1974 (implementing Directive 75/117/EEC)
- The Employment Equality Act, 1977 (implementing Directive 76/207/EEC)
- Unfair Dismissals Acts, 1977-1995
- Social Welfare (No.2) Act, 1985 (implementing Directive 79/7/EEC)
- Pensions Act, 1990, Part VII (implementing Directive 86/378/EEC)
- The Worker Protection (Regular Part-Employees) Act, 1991
- Maternity Protection Act, 1994.

Much of this legislation had its origins in European law and the main pieces of Irish legislation are implementations of the EC Equality Directives.

However, the legislative structure will change considerably when the Employment Equality Act, 1998 (hereafter the 1998 Act) commences[44] and when (and if) the Equal Status Bill, 1999 becomes law. This legislation repeals the Anti-Discrimination (Pay) Act, 1974 (hereafter the 1974 Act) and the Employment Equality Act, 1977 (hereafter the 1977 Act) which will only be referred to in the following section for comparative purposes.

The Anti-Discrimination (Pay) Act, 1974 and the Employment Equality Act, 1977

The Anti-Discrimination (Pay) Act, 1974 and the Employment Equality Act, 1977 are construed together as one Act.[45] No mention is made of indirect discrimination in the 1974 Act. This omission was remedied by the 1977 Act. The decision of the Supreme Court in *Nathan v Bailey Gibson*[46] confirmed that indirect discrimination is prohibited by section 3 of the 1977 Act (rather

43. Constitutional Review Group. (1996), *Report of the Constitutional Review Group*, Dublin: Government Stationery Office, pp. 220-42, 333-37.
44. It was signed into law on 18 June 1998 and is expected to commence in September 1999.
45 S. 56 (2) of the 1977 Act.
46. Unreported Supreme Court 29 February 1996.

than by section 2 (c) of the Act which had, up to this time, been considered to be the relevant section). The judgment delivered by the Supreme Court substantially changed the legal framework governing indirect discrimination. To establish a complaint of indirect discrimination, a complainant must show:

> . . . that the practice complained of bears significantly more heavily on members of the complainant's sex than on members of the other sex. At that stage the complainant has established a prima facie case of discrimination and the onus of proof shifts to the employer to show that the practice complained of is based on objectively verifiable factors which have no relation to the plaintiff's sex.[47]

Both the 1974 Act and the 1977 Act were considered to be limited in effectiveness. The adherence to a 'comparator' method limited the usefulness of the legislation for those women who had not had the opportunity to be 'similarly situated' to men in the workplace. In addition, both the 1974 Act and the 1977 Act are primarily instruments giving remedies to individuals in cases of individual grievances.

The limitations of the existing legislation led to a move to introduce the Employment Equality Act, 1998.

The Employment Equality Act 1998

When the Employment Equality Bill, 1996 was first presented to the President for signature, the President referred the Bill to the Supreme Court for consideration of its constitutionality.[48] The Supreme Court identified three areas in which provisions in the Bill failed to comply with constitutional requirements.[49] The Equal Status Bill, 1996 (which had dealt with equality in areas other than employment) had a similar fate. In this instance, the Supreme Court[50] noted that the two Bills were 'inextricably linked' and that the Equal Status Bill was therefore also unconstitutional.

---

47. Ibid. at p. 33 of the transcript. The *Nathan Bailey* grounds were applied in *Conlan v University of Limerick*, Unreported High Court 4 February 1999 where the High Court held that the plaintiff had not been indirectly discriminated against in relation to the criteria applied for the selection of a professor of law.
48. The President has power under Article 26 of the Constitution of Ireland to refer a Bill to the Supreme Court if s/he has doubts about the Bill's compliance with the provisions of the Constitution.
49 The relevant sections were section 15 which provides for vicarious liability for employers in criminal proceedings; section 63 (3) which provides for certification as evidence of offences and section 16 and section 35 (4) which required that 'reasonable accommodation' be provided for disabled employees. Despite the inclusion of a provision for undue hardship, the Supreme Court found that the requirement was an unjust attack on the property rights of employers, as protected by Article 43 of the Constitution. See *In the Matter of Article 26 of the Constitution and In the Matter of the Employment Equality Bill, 1996.* Unreported Supreme Court 15 May 1997.
50. *In the Matter of Article 26 of the Constitution and In the Matter of the Equal Status Bill 1996*, Unreported Supreme Court 19 June 1997.

A (very slightly) amended version of the Employment Equality Bill was published in December 1997 and was signed by the President on 18 June 1998. Under the 1998 Act, discrimination is prohibited in relation to access to employment, conditions of employment, training or experience for or in relation to employment, promotion or regrading, or classification of posts.[51] Section 19 of the 1998 Act sets out the right to equal remuneration for 'like work'. This legislation applies to discrimination on the basis of nine grounds. These grounds are: sex, age, marital status, disability, family status, race, sexual orientation, religion and membership of the traveller community.[52]

The Act also includes, for the first time, a statutory prohibition on sexual harassment. The Act provides for the establishment of a new Equality Authority which replaces the existing Employment Equality Agency (EEA). The new Authority has a wider remit with responsibility for all nine grounds of discrimination named in the Act.

Although the prohibited grounds of discrimination are extended to nine grounds under the new Act, the definitions of discrimination and the general approach to the pursuit of equality remains as it was under the previous legislative framework. Thus, discrimination[53] occurs where, on any one of the prohibited grounds, a person is treated less favourably than another is, has been or would be treated.[54] The requirement of a comparator is retained throughout the Act.

Indirect discrimination is also prohibited by the 1998 Act. The 1998 Act contains four different definitions of indirect discrimination, two of these relate specifically to the 'gender ground' and two relate to the other eight prohibited grounds. Indirect sex discrimination is covered by section 19(4) — covering remuneration — and section 22 — covering access, conditions, training, promotion, regrading and classification of posts in employment. The approach adopted follows that set out by the Supreme Court in *Nathan v Bailey Gibson*[55] and is in line with the provisions of the Equal Treatment Directive. A claimant is required to show that the proportion of members of one sex disadvantaged by the suspect requirement is 'substantially higher' than those of the other sex and that this difference cannot be justified by 'objective factors' unrelated to sex.

---

51. S. 8 (1).
52. S. 6 (2) of the Employment Equality Act 1998.
53. 'Special treatment' for women in relation to pregnancy, maternity or adoption is exempted from the general prohibition on sex discrimination.
54. S. 6 (1).
55. Unreported Supreme Court 29 February 1996.

Under the 1974 and 1977 legislation, the main enforcement mechanisms are Equality Officers and the Labour Court and the statutory body, the Employment Equality Agency (the Equality Authority).

Equality Officers provide the first line of enforcement. These officers are civil servants whose role is to process discrimination claims at first instance. Both parties to the claim appear before the Equality Officer. The Equality Officer is limited to making a 'recommendation' which is not legally binding.[56] Either party can appeal the recommendation to the Labour Court within 42 days. The Labour Court consists of a Chair (presently a woman), two Deputy Chairs and seven ordinary members. The Court issues legally binding determinations in equality cases. Determinations may be appealed to the High Court on a point of law.

Although leaving these basic structures intact, the 1998 Act makes substantial changes to the existing enforcement mechanisms. Section 75(1) of the 1998 Act provides for a new independent statutory office of Director of Equality Investigations. The staff of the Director will include existing Equality Officers, and any additional appointees. The Director may also appoint Equality Mediation Officers.

The new forums for redress and the various enforcement mechanisms provided for in the Act have been described as 'labyrinthine'.[57] Complainants may refer allegations of discrimination directly to the Director of Equality Investigations.[58] The Director may refer a complaint to an Equality Officer for mediation[59] or may decide to carry out an investigation into the dispute. Complaints covered by the Equal Pay or the Equal Treatment Directive only (that is discrimination on the gender ground) may be referred directly to the Circuit Court.[60] No limit is set on the amount of compensation that may be awarded by the Circuit Court (although there is a general limit on Circuit Court awards of £30,000). While commentators have welcomed the removal of the existing ceiling on levels of compensation, some doubt the wisdom of introducing formal, lengthy Circuit Court procedures.[61]

It is too soon to say whether the 1998 Act will provide better protection against gender discrimination. However, given that the structural limitation imposed by the use of the comparator method is not removed, it is unlikely that the Act will make a real impact on the area of discrimination in employment.

56. S. 19 (4) (a) of the 1977 Act and s. 7 (3) of the 1974 Act.
57 Lynch Fannon I. (March 1999), *Annual Equality Lecture*, University College Cork.
58. S. 77 (1).
59. S. 78 (1).
60. Thus the structure of the Act seems to disallow recourse to court action in relation to discrimination outside the gender ground, except where the discrimination amounts to dismissal. See ss. 77 (2) and 77 (3).
61. Bacik, I. (1996), 'New Developments in Irish Employment Equality Law — The New Enforcement Procedures', Paper given to EIRI Conference, Dublin.

The Equal Status Bill

Almost two years after the Equal Status Bill, 1996 was found unconstitutional, the Bill was republished on 20 April 1999. It is difficult to understand the cause of the two year delay in republishing the Bill especially when the new Bill is very similar to the original Bill. The Equal Status Bill prohibits discrimination on the same nine grounds as those listed in the Employment Equality Act, 1998 in relation to a range of situations outside the employment context. These include the provision of services, accommodation and education and the membership of clubs and societies. The protections are enforced by the Equality Authority as set up by the Employment Equality Act, 1998.

Other Equality Legislation in Ireland

Other legislation essential for the achievement of equality includes legislation in the area of family responsibilities and legislation in relation to social welfare, pension provision and part-time workers.

There are three pieces of legislation dealing with attempts to combine work and family responsibilities. The Maternity Protection Act, 1994 provides protection for all pregnant employees, employees who have recently given birth or who are breastfeeding. Legal entitlements provided under the Act include, *inter alia*: 14 consecutive weeks maternity leave and the right to claim four weeks unpaid additional leave. The Parental Leave Act, 1998 was introduced in order to comply with Directive 96/34/EEC on Parental Leave. The Act provides for a leave entitlement of a total of 14 weeks for each parent that can be used up to any time before the child is five. Disappointingly, the leave is unpaid. The Adoptive Leave Act, 1995 provides for a minimum period of 10 weeks adoptive leave for female employees only. Adoptive leave is only available to an adoptive father if the adopting mother dies.

The approach of the Irish legislature to this genus of legislation has been minimalist to say the least. The length of maternity leave is among the shortest in Europe; the Parental Leave Act, 1998 does the least amount possible in order to comply with the Parental Leave Directive and the Adoptive Leave Act reinforces all stereotypes about the role of women as primary care-givers.

The Irish legislature's record in relation to social welfare and pension provision has not been any more inspired, although Irish legislation does comply with European requirements. Directive 79/7/EEC guaranteeing equal treatment in relation to social security systems was eventually implemented in Ireland — after considerable delay — by the Social Welfare (No.2) Act, 1985.[62] Part VII of the Pensions Act, 1990 implements Directive 86/378 on

62. See discussion of the extensive European case law to which the implementation of this Directive gave rise in Cousins, M. (1995), *The Irish Social Welfare System Law and Social Policy*, Dublin: Roundhall Press.

the Principle of Equal Treatment for Men and Women in Occupational Social Security Schemes. Finally, the Worker Protection (Regular Part-Time Employees) Act, 1991 provides limited rights to part-time workers.

Equality in Practice: The Economic/Social Status of Women in Ireland

Ireland's membership of the European Community contributed significantly to improving women's status as beneficiaries of public policy. Many of these reforms have been confined to the removal of formal legal barriers to women's participation in paid employment. Until recently there was little acknowledgement of the need for a more 'supportive' state to ensure women's participation in the labour force on an equal footing with men. Apart from legislative provisions for maternity protection and the inadequate Parental Leave Act, 1998, little has been done to enable workers to combine paid employment with family responsibilities.

In this context, one of the main barriers continuing to affect the achievement of real equality in the labour market has been the absence of childcare services for working parents. Under the fourth pillar on Equal Opportunities in Ireland's Empolyment Action Plan the State has undertaken to increase the level of good quality childcare in order to support women's entry and continued participation in the labour market.[63] However, childcare provision in Ireland is among the lowest in the EU.[64] A number of measures have recently been taken to address this problem. Under the agreement cemented in *Partnership 2000*, the Government established an Expert Working Group on Childcare. This Working Group published its findings in January 1999.[65]

Putting Gender onto the Law and Policy-Making Agenda

A wide range of bodies, governmental, statutory and non-governmental, have been established in an attempt to represent the many and diverse concerns of women in Ireland. The need for such bodies is reinforced by the continuing under-representation of women within parliamentary and government structures and the difficulties encountered by groups such as the NWCI in representing diverse groups of women.

63. See Government of Ireland (1998), *Employment Action Play*, Dublin: Government Stationery Office, pp. 44-9.
64. (1997), *Ireland's Combined Second and Third Reports under the United Nations Convention on the Elimination of All Forms of Discrimination Against Women*, Dublin: Government Stationery Office, p. 108.
65. (1999), *National Childcare Strategy Report of the Partnership 2000 Expert Working Group on Childcare*, Dublin: Government Stationery Office. See also Commission on the Family. (1998), *Strengthening Families for Life*, Final Report to the Minister for Social, Community and Family Affairs, Dublin: Government Stationery Office.

Department of Justice, Equality and Law Reform

The Report of the Second Commission on the Status of Women recommended the establishment of a Ministry for Women.[66] Although this recommendation was not taken up, in 1993, the Department of Equality and Law Reform was established. Following a change of government in 1997, Equality and Law Reform was merged with the Department of Justice to form a single Government Department. The Department is now headed by a Cabinet Minister holding the portfolio of Justice, Equality and Law Reform and a Minister of State (Junior Minister) with responsibility for Equality and Disability issues. The merger has further marginalised equality issues within Government. The Department is now responsible for a wide range of policy areas including policing, criminal justice, courts' administration, immigration and asylum, land registry as well as equality and disability issues. The Justice portfolio is one of the most demanding portfolios assigned to a Minister and there is little doubt that Equality and Law Reform is viewed as the junior partner within the Department. This dilution in status is confirmed by the loss of full Minsterial representation for equality issues at cabinet level. Given the significant institutional and policy reforms that are currently taking place in the field of equality, this move seems particularly ill-advised.

Joint Oireachtas Committee on Justice, Equality and Women's Rights

The First Joint Oireachtas Committee on Women's Rights was established in 1983. The Committee was charged with: (a) examining and proposing legislative measures affecting the interests of women; (b) identifying measures to remove obstacles to women's full participation in the political, social and economic life of the community; and (c) making recommendations to remove the specific economic and social disadvantages applying to women in the home. Following the election of the current (28th) *Dáil* in 1997, the Committee was reconstituted as the Joint Oireachtas Committee on Justice, Equality and Women's Rights. The present Committee is composed of 14 *Dáil* Deputies and five Senators (seven of whom are women). Committee members are appointed from across the political divide in proportion to party representation in the *Oireachtas*. The Committee is free to consider any issues of law or policy relating to gender equality, either on its own initiative or following a referral from the *Oireachtas*. Its meetings are held in public and both oral and written evidence are received.

The move towards addressing a broader range of equality issues, beyond gender, already presents a significant challenge for the Committee. The

66. Second Commission on the Status of Women, op cit, n. 20, para. 7. 5. 2.

addition of a Justice portfolio displays a lack of commitment on the part of Government and a lack of understanding of the many and varied mechanisms of discrimination and exclusion in Irish society.

The Commission on the Status of Women

To date there have been two Commissions on the Status of Women, both established by Government as a result of extensive lobbying on the part of women's groups. The First Commission was established in 1971 by the Minister for Finance. Its members were drawn from NGOs, trade unions and political parties. The Commission's First Report recommended a range of measures to address the problems of women in particularly disadvantaged groups.[67] This led to the introduction of a range of welfare measures to assist 'deserted wives', prisoners' wives and elderly 'spinsters'. Although these measures led to material improvements in many women's lives, the Report was criticised for reinforcing the prevailing presumption of female dependency within the social welfare system.

The Second Commission was established in 1990. Its nineteen members were appointed by the *Taoiseach* and again drawn from the Social Partners, the Community and Voluntary sector and political parties. In addition to reviewing progress made in implementing the Report of the First Commission on the Status of Women, the Commission was required to make recommendations on the means, administrative and legislative, by which women would be able to participate on equal terms and conditions with men in all aspects of society. Special attention was to be paid to the needs of women working full time in the home.

The Commission's final report contained a total of 210 recommendations covering all areas of political, economic, and social policy. Timetables and interim targets were set for the implementation of many of its recommendations. A Monitoring Committee — the Gender Equality Monitoring Committee — was established to oversee the implementation of the Report. The Committee's membership is drawn from Government Departments, the Social Partners, women's groups and the Employment Equality Agency.

To date, the Committee has published three Progress Reports. However, some dissatisfaction has been expressed with the Committee's work to date. Two key elements of an effective monitoring process were found to be lacking: (a) critical analysis of implementation and progress; and (b) effective use of targets and timetables.[68] Tensions have also arisen

67. First Commission on the Status of Women. (1972), *Report to the Minister for Finance*, Dublin: Government Stationery Office.

68. National Women's Council of Ireland. (1997), *Response to the Report of the Monitoring Committee of the Second Commission on the Status of Women*, Dublin: NWCI.

between representatives of Government Departments concerned to portray the Government as 'good implementers' and representatives of outside bodies seeking a more critical evaluation of progress.

The National Women's Council of Ireland (NWCI)

The NWCI is a non-governmental organisation funded by an annual grant from the Department of Justice, Equality and Law Reform and annual subscriptions from its affiliate organisations. The Council represents approximately 150 non-governmental organisations and an estimated 300,000 women, including members of national organisations, community groups, professional bodies and farming associations. Since 1997, membership is also open to individuals. The Council's main activities include:

- lobbying Government for legislative and policy reform;
- representing women's interests on various public and private bodies;
- liaising with European and international organisations;
- providing information and research services, organising seminars and training courses and providing support to affiliates.

With the expansion of social partnership, the Council has become directly involved in partnership institutions such as the NESF and was involved for the first time in 1996 in negotiations on the national agreement, Partnership 2000. It was successful in ensuring that commitments in relation to each of its policy priorities — the development of statistical methods to evaluate unpaid work, childcare and equality proofing, — were included in the final agreement.

The Employment Equality Agency/Equality Authority

The Employment Equality Agency is an independent statutory body. It was established under the 1977 Employment Equality Act to work towards the elimination of discrimination, based on sex or marital status, within the spheres of employment and vocational training. The Agency has both promotional and enforcement functions. It is represented on various public and private bodies, including the Expert Working Group on Childcare and the Gender Equality Monitoring Committee. One of its most important achievements to date has been the development of a range of 'soft law' measures, including the 1994 Code of Practice on the Dignity of Women and Men at Work (implementing the 1991 EC Recommendation and Code of Practice on Sexual Harassment).

From the very beginning, financial constraints have affected all aspects of the Agency's work. In carrying out its enforcement functions, the Agency has concentrated on providing advice and assistance. Its power to carry out formal investigations has rarely been invoked. Representation is provided only in a limited number of cases and on the basis of agreed priorities. In recent years these have included sexual harassment, pregnancy discrimination, treatment of part-time and other atypical workers, discrimination in promotion and in non-traditional areas of employment. The failure to develop the Agency's enforcement role is particularly disappointing given the heavy burden that is placed on individual complainants within the Irish tribunal system. The Agency has faced other problems. Despite its close links with Government – reinforced by rigid staffing policy — it has often had a relatively low profile when crucial decisions affecting women were being taken. Difficulties have also arisen in monitoring the impact of its work. The lack of gender disaggregated data in many areas has forced it to rely on general indicators such as trends in part-time work and low pay — in the words of one commentator, 'on impressions rather than objective data'.[69]

At the time of writing the Agency is in a period of transition. With effect from September 1999, it will become the new Equality Authority, with expanded functions across all areas of discrimination covered by the 1998 Employment Equality Act. Under the Act, the general functions of the Authority are to:

- work towards the elimination of discrimination in relation to employment;
- promote equality of opportunity in relation to matters to which this Act applies;
- provide information to the public on and to keep under review the working of this Act, the Maternity Protection Act, 1994 and the Adoptive Leave Act, 1995 and, whenever it thinks it necessary, to make proposals to the Minister for amending any of those Acts and;
- keep under review the working of the Pensions Act, 1990.

The Act makes provision for new enforcement powers. In addition to powers of formal investigation, the Authority can carry out Equality Reviews and design Equality Action Plans for businesses under review. These extended powers will go some way towards tackling broader structural obstacles to gender equality within the workplace. They may serve also to alleviate the burden on individual complainants under traditional enforcement mechanisms. Much will depend on the resources allocated to the Authority and its willingness to adopt a pro-active attitude to enforcement.

---

69. McGinley, M. (1996), *From Employment Equality Agency to Equality Authority*, Sixth Report to the Fourth Joint Oireachtas Committee on Women's Rights, Dublin: Government Stationery Office.

The expansion of anti-discrimination legislation and the increased powers of the Authority have generally been welcomed. However, some concern has been expressed at the range of discriminatory practices that will fall within the scope of the Authority's workload. It will be an enormous challenge for the Authority to continue to address gender discrimination while at the same time tackling previously unexplored areas such as race and disability discrimination. At the same time, the extended remit of the Authority will provide an opportunity to begin addressing the multiple disadvantages faced by women when factors such as gender and disability are combined.

Strategies to Improve the Situation of Women in Law and Policy-Making

Dissatisfaction with existing equality strategies has led, in recent years, to an increasing emphasis on the need to mainstream equality into all aspects of policy design and service delivery. Equality proofing procedures — administrative procedures to assess policies for their impact on equality — have been identified as essential to the mainstreaming process. One of the key elements of the equality strategy set out in the *Partnership 2000* agreement was the commitment to strengthen administrative procedures for equality proofing. The NESF has defined the essential features of an effective equality proofing procedure as:[70]

- identification of equality objectives and setting equality targets;
- development of data gathering processes adequate for monitoring the achievement of these targets;
- establishing the equality implications of any particular policy or practice prior to its implementation;
- development and implementation of strategies to achieve equality targets;
- creation of independent monitoring systems to analyse and review progress; and
- regular public reporting on progress.

To date a range of administrative procedures to 'proof' policies for their impact on women have been introduced. In 1998, as part of the National Anti-Poverty Strategy, a set of administrative procedures were introduced to 'proof' policies for their impact on poverty. Consideration is now being given to the introduction of a comprehensive system of equality proofing,

70. NESF (1996). *Equality Proofing Issues*, Dublin: Government Stationery Office, p. 28.

incorporating issues such as race, disability and sexual orientation into policy proofing.[71]

Gender proofing procedures — administrative procedures to assess policies for their impact on women — have been in place for some time. In 1991, the Second Commission on the Status of Women recommended that all Memoranda for Government should include a statement outlining the probable impact on women of the proposed policy change.[72] This recommendation was followed through and since 1993, all Memoranda for Government are required to include an assessment of their impact on women.[73] The supposed centrality and significance of gender proofing is highlighted as an example of 'good practice' in many Government publications. According to the *First Report on Implementation of the Platform for Action*, (setting out the progress to date on implementation of the Beijing Declaration and Platform for Action), there is now, 'a general recognition that policy proposals being made to Government need to be gender proofed, that is assessed for the differential effect they have on women and men'.[74] The Government, the Report states, 'systematically' considers the probable impact on women of any proposed policy change. Again, in *Ireland's Combined Second and Third Report under the UN Convention on the Elimination of All Forms of Discrimination Against Women,* gender proofing is identified as essential 'to overcome the potential for indirect discrimination and to contribute towards an integrated equal opportunities policy'.[75] The National Development Plan, 1994-1999 (setting out the framework for the current round of EU Structural Funds) identifies gender proofing as a 'socially desirable objective' and an important step towards achieving gender equality. Guidelines for gender proofing within the context of the EU Structural Funds have been developed and are likely to be incorporated into the next National Development Plan, 2000-2006.[76] A Working Group on Gender Proofing (chaired by the Department of Justice, Equality and Law Reform) is currently preparing detailed guidelines for gender proofing.[77]

Despite this apparent commitment to gender proofing, however, systematic changes in policy-making have not yet occurred. Many of the essential features of an effective proofing procedure are lacking. Additional

---

71. See Mullally, S. and Smith, O. (1999), *Guidelines for Equality Proofing*, Dublin: Department of Justice, Equality and Law Reform.
72. Second Commission on the Status of Women, op cit, n. 20, p. 508.
73. See Department of the Taoiseach, op cit, n. 2, p. 19.
74. Department of Equality and Law Reform. (1996), *UN Fourth World Conference on Women: First Report on Implementation of the Platform for Action*, Dublin: Government Stationery Office, p. 67.
75. Department of Equality and Law Reform, op cit, n. 63, p. 34.
76 See Mullally, S. (1999), op cit, n. 2.
77 Department of Justice, Equality and Law Reform, op cit, n. 2.

resources have not been made available to assist policy makers in carrying out gender impact assessments. Neither has any provision been made for training in gender analysis or gender planning. Consultation with outside bodies is not a requirement or even a general practice. Cabinet confidentiality requirements prevent impact assessment statements coming under public scrutiny, making it difficult to assess their adequacy and objectivity.

Despite these shortcomings, interest in policy proofing is growing. In 1998, a set of poverty proofing procedures were introduced, for all legislative and 'significant' policy proposals, including the National Employment Action Plan and Annual Budget Estimates.[78] These procedures have particular significance for women. Aimed at the 9-15 per cent of the population identified as being consistently poor, or at risk of poverty, they include households headed by a single adult or by someone engaged in home duties and lone parents. Women constitute a significant majority of these groups.[79] Poverty proofing is also underpinned by specific equality commitments:

- ensuring equal access and encouraging participation for all;
- guaranteeing the rights of minorities especially through anti discrimination measures; and
- reduction of inequalities and in particular, addressing the gender dimensions of poverty.

At the end of its first year of operation, many of the shortcomings of the gender proofing process have persisted within poverty proofing. Despite the fact that participation of target groups is recognised as being essential to any mainstreaming agenda, little has been done to make the proofing process a participatory one. Yet again, the failure to allocate additional resources to the proofing process has limited its transformative potential. Poverty proofing has been 'added on' to existing policy processes, doing little to transform those processes, much less mobilise them in pursuit of greater equality.

These failures are not unique to Ireland. Many of the same problems arose within the PAFT process in Northern Ireland. Reforming the PAFT has led to significant legislative changes.[80] Similar changes will be required in Ireland if policy proofing is to become more than a mere 'tick and dash' paper exercise.

---

78. Department of Social, Community and Family Affairs. (1998), *Guidelines for Poverty Proofing within the context of the National Anti-Poverty Strategy*, Dublin.
79. See Nolan, B. and Watson, D. (1999), supra, n. 6.
80. Northern Ireland Act 1998 s. 75. See Chapter Seven, this volume.

Conclusion

Recent years have witnessed an increasing awareness of the need to integrate a gender dimension into all aspects of the policy process in Ireland. As yet, however, this has not translated into systematic changes in the way in which such processes operate. Progress to date has not yet moved beyond the development of 'women-friendly' policies on an *ad hoc* and piece-meal basis. Women continue to be under-represented as agents in the formation and implementation of public policy. Although some moves have been made toward a more participatory approach to policy-making, much remains to be done if these changes are to translate into concrete improvements for women. Gender proofing has not yet developed into a systematic and effective mechanism for promoting gender equality. Women continue to be treated as an homogenous group and the particular interests of women from disadvantaged groups are often overlooked. The absence of gender disaggregated data in many areas and the failure to develop effective monitoring procedures makes it difficult to assess the impact of existing equality strategies. If we are to understand integrating gender as requiring that gender equality is actively and openly taken into account at all stages of the policy process and across all policy areas, then significant changes are still required.

3 Making Women Count in The Netherlands

MIEKE VERLOO

The Dutch state has been referred to as a woman-friendly state,[1] yet paradoxically the reality of Dutch gender relations rather contradicts this progressive image. Even if inequality between men and women has clearly decreased in the past 25 years, Dutch gender relations are characterised by vertical and horizontal segregation of the labour market and by a strong motherhood ideology.[2] The exceptionally high number of women working part-time (68 per cent) and the low number of female university professors (4 per cent) are good examples of continuing inequality. Emancipation stops with the one and a half earner household. The international visibility of the Dutch women's movement, of women's studies and of femocrats, in combination with the generally progressive image of the Netherlands are perhaps more responsible for the Netherlands' women-friendly reputation than the facts and figures of the day-to-day life of women and men.

This chapter, therefore, will examine the rhetoric and reality of Dutch equality policies, especially in the field of gender mainstreaming.

The Political and Legal Landscape in the Netherlands[3]

A constitutional democracy under a Parliamentary system was established in the Netherlands in 1814. The formal head of state is the monarch, currently

1. Gardiner, F. and Leijenaar, M. (1997), 'The timid and the bold. Analysis of the "woman-friendly state" in Ireland and the Netherlands', in Gardiner, F. (ed.), *Sex Equality in Western Europe*, London: Routledge, pp. 60-91.
2. Sociaal en Cultureel rapport 1998, SCP: Den Haag. See also: http://www.scp.nl/uk/defaultur.htm
3. Verloo, M., Fontein, E. and Krops, C. (1997), *State of the Art of Women in Political, Economic and Social Decision Making in the Netherlands*, Nijmegen: KUN. See also Kickert, W. and R. (1995), 't Veld. National Government, Governance and Administration', in Kickert, W. and van Vugt, F. (eds), *Public Policy and Administrative Sciences in the Netherlands*, London: Prentice Hall Harvester Wheatsheaf, pp. 45-63. And the official Dutch government site: http://www.minbuza.nl/english/Depth/c_stateeng.html

Queen Beatrix, while the Prime Minister is the head of the government. The office of Prime Minister has never been held by a woman. The executive is responsible to a bicameral Parliament, the States-general. The Upper House consists of 75 members who are elected indirectly by the members of the Provincial Councils. The Lower House numbers 150 directly elected members and elections take place every four years. The Netherlands consists of only one constituency. During the elections each voter is allowed to cast one vote. Each party compiles its own list of candidates competing for seats. Because of the low threshold of votes for gaining representation, a relatively large number of parties consistently win seats. Following each election, the leader of the party with the largest number of elected candidates is asked to form a Cabinet, with the support of other parties, which will have the support of a majority in Parliament. The Parliament controls the activities and decisions of the Cabinet.

The Cabinet consists of 14 Ministers, assisted by State Secretaries, who assume responsibility for some of the Minister's duties, but are not members of the Cabinet. The Prime Minister chairs the Cabinet and its system of decision-making is collective, with Ministers meeting in weekly councils. Ministers must have the confidence of Parliament. Once a government has been formed, the Prime Minister on taking office presents a statement of his government's policy to the Lower House, which then votes upon it. The government starts work after it secures the consent of Parliament. If the vote is lost new elections may be necessary.

No political party has ever won a Parliamentary majority. Cabinets are always coalitions. Since World War II, several parties have dominated Dutch politics. Until the elections of 1994, the *Christelijk Democratisch Appel* (Christian Democratic Appeal, CDA) dominated the Dutch Cabinet. Since then, there have been 'purple' cabinets, without the CDA, so named because of their mix of 'red' and 'blue' parties. The 'red' *Partij van de Arbeid* (Labour Party, PvdA) is the only mass-based left-wing party in the Netherlands. The 'blue' party is the *Volkspartij voor Vrijheid en Democratie* (Liberal Party, VVD) which has conservative overtones reminiscent of Britain's Conservative Party. To the left, there is also D66 (Democrats '66), a more leftist-liberal party and smaller parties such as *GroenLinks* (Green Left) and *Socialistische Partij* (Socialist Party). There are also some small right-wing religion-based parties.

Dutch government is open. In particular the Ministries are relatively open organisations, not only populated by civil servants, but also by many external consultants and scientists who contribute enthusiastically to policy and law-making.[4] It is important to keep in mind that the character of

4. Kickert, W. and R. (1995) ,'t Veld. National Government, Governance and Administration', in Kickert, W. and van Vugt, F. (eds), *Public Policy and Administrative Sciences in the Netherlands*, London: Prentice Hall Harvester Wheatsheaf, p. 56.

policy-making varies considerably across the Dutch government according to the subject matter and the issues. The departmental autonomy of officials is matched by the autonomy of Ministers in the Cabinet. The Dutch civil service is said to be relatively fragmented, sometimes being referred to as 'the kingdom of the disunited ministries'.[5] Civil servants are professional lifetime employees. Each Ministry is said to have its own legal and policy-making culture, due partly to different traditions and to the absence of a centralised recruitment system for civil servants.[6] In a number of areas, such as environmental policy, and to a lesser extent, equality policy, there have been close and functional relationships between civil servants, academics and movement activists, not unlike the 'iron triangle' described in the US between government departments, Parliamentary committees and interest associations.[7] Since 1991, the Law on Public Access to Government Information has allowed all citizens to request access to governmental documents.[8]

The Netherlands is often characterised as a consensus democracy.[9] Typically, the policy-making process is geared towards generally accepted agreements and regulations. The pursuit of compromise is deeply rooted in Dutch political culture. In order to reach this broad consensus a pluralisation of interests is taken into consideration in the policy-making process. Furthermore the Dutch political system is characterised by neo-corporatism. In the 1950s and 1960s an extensive corporate sector developed in which the defence of group interests took place through representation and the institutionalisation of networks of interest groups. These networks were often formally represented on official advisory bodies. Even though the number of advisory bodies has decreased dramatically, consultation with organisations representing interest groups is still often legally prescribed.[10] This policy style is celebrated in the Netherlands and has gained international attention as the 'polder' model.[11] This consociational style can also be traced

5. Toonen, T. A. J. (1988), 'The Netherlands: A Decentralised Unitary State in a Welfare Society', *Western European Politics*, 8 (10), pp.108-129.
6. van Waarden, F. (1995), 'Persistence of national policy styles: A study in their institutional foundations', in Unger, B. and van Waarden, F. (eds), *Convergence or Diversity*, Avebury, Aldershot, pp.333-372.
7. See Leroy, P. (1995), *Milieukunde als beroep en als roeping*, Nijmegen: Katholieke Universiteit Nijmegen, p. 38. Also Verloo, M. (1986), 'Emancipatie, de bouwbaarheid van een feministische visie', in Nelissen, N., Geurts, J. and de Wit, H. (eds), *Het verkennen van beleidsproblemen*, Zeist: Kerckebosch, pp. 201-231.
8. Korthal Altes, W. F. et al (eds), (1992), *Information Law Towards the 21st Century*, Deventer: Kluwer.
9. See Lijphart, A. *Verzuiling, pacificatie en kentering in de Nederlandse politiek*, Second Edition, Amsterdam: J. H. De Bussy
10. Kickert, W. and R. op cit, n. 4, p. 52.
11. A typical example can be found in Haverland, M. (1998), *National Autonomy, European Integration and the Politics of Packaging Waste*, a thesis completed at the Netherlands School for Social and Economic Policy Research, Utrecht.

back to the integrative strategies which prevailed towards contesting groups. To complete the picture, mention should be made of the tradition of sponsored pluralism in the Netherlands. Movements often receive financial funding from the Dutch State, even if it is usually on a temporary basis.

The Netherlands has codified law, developed deductively from principles elaborated in general rules, which are then applied to specific cases. Law follows practice and not the other way round. There is no judicial review of Parliamentary acts and the courts cannot invalidate Parliamentary acts. Under certain conditions, citizens can force organisations to comply with existing laws via the courts or can contest administrative acts.

Parliament, together with the Queen and the Ministers, exercises legislative power in the Netherlands. Parliament has, however, a significant role to play in the enactment of legislation and its primacy is apparent from two facts. The Netherlands has no constitutional court to review legislation in the light of the Constitution and the executive must enjoy the confidence of Parliament. Executive power is vested in the government, but it must account for its exercise of that power to Parliament. The two Houses of Parliament have four rights which enable them to scrutinise the executive's conduct of affairs: the right to set the budget, the right of interpellation,[12] the right to put questions to the Cabinet and the right of inquiry. The Lower House has also the right to amend bills and to initiate legislation. Legislation passed by Parliament is approved by a majority vote and normally is concerned to establish broad principles, leaving the practical details to be set out in an order in council. Specific matters are regulated by royal decrees.

The Constitution is the foundation on which the Dutch legal order rests. It contains a number of implicit guiding principles, dealing mainly with the monarchy, representative democracy, the rule of law and decentralisation. The principle of the separation of powers has applied in the Netherlands since the introduction of the 1848 Constitution, the independence of the judiciary being an important factor in this connection. The Constitution rules out jury trials and the imposition of the death penalty.

The Supreme Court is the Netherlands' highest court, in both civil and criminal matters. Its main task is to ensure the uniform application of the law. Supreme Court case law is an important source of law in the Netherlands. It is not, however, a constitutional court, as it has no power to nullify an Act of Parliament on the grounds that it is incompatible with the Constitution. The Supreme Court, like all other courts, may however decline to apply a statute on the grounds that it is incompatible with an international

12. This is the right to ask questions about factual or policy matters.

treaty. The primacy of those provisions of international law that are universally binding was enshrined in the Constitution as long ago as 1953. An amendment to the Constitution passed three years later added that universally binding provisions of treaties are directly applicable: that is there is no need for any action on the part of the Dutch legislative authorities. The Netherlands thus adheres to the principle of 'monism': the doctrine that national and international law together form a single legal order.

The Netherlands is clearly part of the larger international capitalist market economy, though the government also plays an important role in economic matters. Essentially the system is mixed. Opinions differ as to whether the system is more of an '*economie orientée*', where the government is steering only in a very general way, or whether it is better characterised as an '*economie concertée*', where the government, the private sector and the trade unions act in concert. The government aims at 'more market, less government', and acts accordingly. In the private sector different kinds of participatory democracy have developed (such as employees councils and representative advisory councils).

At the regional level there are 12 Provinces (*Provincies*) and approximately 600 municipalities. Each Province has a directly elected Provincial Council (*Provinciale Staten*), a Provincial Board (*Gedeputeerde Staten*) and a centrally appointed Queen's Commissioner. The local level consists of a directly elected Local Council (*Gemeenteraad*) which chooses the Alderman (*Wethouders*) from its midst. The appointed mayor chairs both the Council and the executive (*College van Burgemeester en Wethouders*).

Water authorities — public law bodies like the state, the Provinces and the municipalities — are one of the oldest forms of democratic government in the Netherlands, sometimes dating back to the Middle Ages. The water authorities are responsible for protecting the land against the water, obviously a matter of great importance given that over half the country lies below sea level. The owners of real property in its area elect the general council of a water authority, while central government appoints the executive committee and the chairperson.

In the Netherlands the representation of women on traditional political bodies has been possible from 1918 onwards, when male voters elected the first woman to Parliament. Women obtained universal suffrage in 1919. It took 30 years before women were appointed to the executive. The first woman Secretary of State was installed in 1953, the first woman Minister in 1956.[13]

13. Leijenaar, M. H. and Niemöller, C. (1994), 'Political participation of women: The Netherlands', in Nelson, B. and Chowdury, N. (eds), *Women and Politics Worldwide*, New Haven/London: Yale University Press, pp. 496-511

In the 1990s, women made up approximately one third of the membership of Parliament and the government. This represents considerable progress compared with the 1980s and earlier, when the percentage of women in Parliament was in the region of 15-20 per cent. The increase of women in political decision-making is connected with a concentrated effort by both the government and the political parties, which will be described later in this chapter.

Equality Legislation in the Netherlands

The first article of the Dutch Constitution contains a general prohibition on discrimination.[14] Article 1 states: 'All persons on Dutch territory are treated equally in the same circumstances. Discrimination on the grounds of religion, creed, political faith, race, sex or on any other ground is not permitted'.[15]

In 1977 the Dutch government started amending all legislation that made a distinction between men and women and between married and unmarried people. By 1991 there were only a few examples left in the context of family law and the law of persons and these too have now been removed. Equality policies in the Netherlands are not dominated by a legal framework. As *de jure* equality has largely been achieved in the Netherlands, the focus is on ensuring that equality is achieved *de facto* as well.[16]

The government aims to introduce legislation to prohibit discrimination against the disabled since surveys have shown frequent discrimination against them. This will be helpful to women since there are more women than men amongst the disabled and their position is often worse than that of men.[17]

There are three important legislative measures dealing with discrimination. The Equal Treatment Act (AWGB), which became law in 1994, covers discrimination, not simply on the grounds of sex, but also on other grounds (religion, belief, political opinion, race, nationality, sexual orientation or marital status). The prohibition on discrimination does not extend to indirect

14. Asscher-Vonk, I. (1995), *Equality in Law Between Men and Women in the European Community. The Netherlands*, Dordrecht/Boston/London: Martinus Nijhoff. See also (1999), *The Second Report of the Netherlands to the UN Committee for the Elimination of all forms of Discrimination Against Women (CEDAW)*, The Hague: Minstry of Social Affairs and Employment.
15. 'Direct discrimination includes discrimination on the grounds of pregnancy, confinement and maternity. Indirect discrimination means discrimination on the grounds of qualities other than sex, for instance marital status or family circumstances, which results in discrimination on the ground of sex', Article 1 Equal Treatment Act.
16. (1999), *The Second Report of the Netherlands to the UN Committee for the Elimination of all forms of Discrimination Against Women (CEDAW)*, The Hague: Minstry of Social Affairs and Employment, p.10.
17. Gorter and Winants, (1993), *Gehandicapt en vrouw*, The Hague.

discrimination which can be justified on objective grounds. Direct discrimination is prohibited unless the Act expressly makes an exception to this rule. Group action is possible.

The Equal Treatment (Working Hours) Act provides that part-time and full-time workers must be treated equally. Since most part-time workers are women, this legislation is relevant in combating indirect discrimination against women.

There is equal pay legislation in the Civil Code, which states that an employer may not discriminate between men's and women's terms and conditions of employment. The Equal Opportunities Act specifies that the employee with whom a comparison is made should work in the same enterprise and, even more restrictively, in the same branch within an enterprise. The government expressed the opinion in its last CEDAW report that this is not correct and intends to amend the law to allow for a comparison between people in the service of the same employer.[18]

There is specific legislation on sex offences, sexual harassment (as part of the Working Conditions Act 1994), on representation on Advisory Bodies (1997), Parental Leave (1997) and on Proportional Representation of Women in Managerial Posts in Education (1997).

The Equal Treatment Commission, an autonomous commission of nine experts, can investigate whether there has been unlawful discrimination. Anyone who believes that he or she has been discriminated against may file a petition free of charge. The opinion of the Commission is not binding, but, in practice, is usually accepted. The Commission can make recommendations to the person responsible for discrimination to facilitate a solution and does so regularly. The Equal Treatment Commission can apply to the courts for a binding decision, but in the period 1994-1996 the Commission has not done so. The majority of the 421 petitions in 1996 were petitions on the grounds of sex discrimination, followed by discrimination on the grounds of race and nationality (25 per cent).

In general, Dutch anti-sex discrimination law cannot be said to be heavily influenced by EU law or EU membership. Initiatives to eliminate discriminatory elements from existing law and the construction of the Equal Treatment Act (AWGB) were the result of long-term processes and pressure inside the Netherlands. In a number of cases the influence has been the other way round, for example in the case of sexual harassment. In 1984, the former Dutch Secretary of State for Emancipation, d'Ancona, who had introduced

18. Ministry of Social Affairs and Employment, op cit, n. 14, p. 72

the issue of sexual violence against women onto the political agenda, was appointed as rapporteur for the EU on sexual harassment. In addition, the Dutch government started to apply pressure at the EU level to make sexual harassment an EU policy issue and for an investigation to be conducted on the issue of sexual harassment. This study, by Michael Rubinstein, revealed that policies to combat sexual harassment were largely absent in the EU Member States and recommended action to prevent sexual harassment.[19] In response, the Commission produced a Code of Practice, with more symbolic than legal value.[20] Despite the efforts of the Dutch government to press for action at the EU level, no steps were taken on the national level to formulate specific regulations to prevent sexual harassment. In 1994, the Dutch government finally came up with a specific law to prevent sexual harassment. In this law sexual harassment is defined as a problem concerning labour conditions. According to the law, employers have the duty to protect their workers against sexual harassment. The law has had some effect as more than 50 per cent of collective labour agreements had a paragraph on sexual harassment in 1998.

Putting Gender onto the Law and Policy-Making Agenda

The Dutch government has had a well-developed emancipation infrastructure and policy since the 1970s.[21] In general, emancipation policy started as a two-track policy, aiming simultaneously at producing specific policies — called sector policies — and facet policy, the integration of emancipation as a cross-sectoral part of general policy. Since 1985 the central aim of emancipation policy has been:

> To promote the development of today's society — a society in which the differences between the sexes are still institutionalised to a great extent — into a pluriform society in which everyone has the opportunity — regardless of gender and civil status — to acquire an independent existence and in which men and women are able to realise equal rights, opportunities, freedoms and responsibilities.[22]

19. Rubenstein, M. (1987), *The Dignity of Men and Women at Work: A Report on the Problem of Sexual Harassment in the Member States of the European Community*, COM V/412/87.
20. Collins, E. (1996), 'European Union Sexual Harrassment Policy', in Elman, R. A. (ed.), *Sexual Politics and the European Union*, Oxford: Berghahn Books.
21. The Dutch term emancipation (*emancipatie*) will be used in this chapter, as neither equality nor equal opportunities is a correct translation.
22. English translation from Minstry of Social Affairs and Employment, op cit, n. 14, p.12.

Even with a previously dominant rhetoric about unequal power relations between men and women, emancipation policy in reality takes men as the point of reference. Women are seen as imperfect men, whose position needs to be improved by offering them equal access to employment. The result is an emphasis on economic independence and a lack of attention to caring responsibilities.[23] In the 1990s the focus of Dutch emancipation policy was slightly changed. More official stress was put on combining paid and unpaid labour. Since 1994, emancipation policy has been increasingly restricted to labour market policy, but its strength has increased. The general pursuit of economic growth is the explanation for this restriction. Some successes in other areas are connected to this concentration, such as the possibility of longer shop opening hours, the equalisation of the legal position of part-timers and full-timers and registered partnerships. The state has interfered more in the private sphere, obliging welfare mothers with children over five years old to apply for a paid job. This focus on increasing paid labour for women has been accompanied by an emphasis on the responsibilities of the social partners to remove the feminist problematic of how to combine paid labour and care, by providing child-care facilities as the obvious solution.[24]

Diversity as a new goal was introduced in 1997. The essence of this 1997 emancipation policy is formulated as 'the need to remove obstacles in the structure of society in such a way that diversity in terms of not just gender, but also of age, ethnic origin, sexual orientation and religion is seen and appreciated as a way of enhancing the quality of society'.[25] Apart from gender only ethnicity has so far attracted some attention.

The Dutch Emancipation Infrastructure

The Dutch infrastructure on equality can be found at several levels. The Equal Treatment Commission has a role to play in the implementation of legislation. Other important actors are the Department for the Co-ordination of Emancipation Policy (DCE) and the Interdepartmental Co-ordination Committee for Emancipation Policy (ICE) (administrative bodies), the Emancipation Council (ER) and TECENA (advisory bodies) and several state supported feminist institutions. In the 1980s, there was a Secretary of State for Emancipation. Later the emancipation of women became the

23. Keuzekamp, S. and Theunissen, A. (1990), *Emancipatie ten halve geregeld. Continuiteit en inenging in het emancipatiebeleid*, Den Haag: Vuga.
24. Outshoorn, J. (1998), 'Paars en de ommekeer in het emancipatiebeleid', *Socialisme en democratie*, 3, pp. 122-127.
25. Ministry of Social Affairs and Employment, op cit, n. 14, p.13.

responsibility of the Minister for Social Affairs and Employment, but since 1998 'work, care and emancipation policy' has been the responsibility of the Secretary of State for Social Affairs and Employment.

DCE, the key equality department since 1977, has been located in the Ministry of Social Affairs and Employment since 1981. DCE's function is to develop a framework for coherent emancipation policy. DCE was never strong due to its tense relations with the women's movement and the ER. Its power has been weakened further by the decline in support for equality among the political elite since the mid 1980s, its incapacity to develop an iron triangle except in a few areas like development co-operation and its lack of power over other departments, or even branches, within the Ministry of Social Affairs and Employment.[26] Next to the DCE there is the ICE. In this committee all Ministries have a representative. At the level of the Ministries there is often some internal body responsible for emancipation policy. The position, power, visibility and activity of these bodies varies widely.

Until the reorganisation of the advisory system in 1997 when the number of advisory bodies was reduced dramatically, the ER was the government's major advisory body on emancipation policy. In the reorganised system all advisory bodies are supposed to provide advice on emancipation matters when relevant to their own area. The effort that has been put into increasing the number of women represented on the new bodies has been successful, as the percentage of women is now around 45 per cent. The advisory bodies receive some guidance and support for their new task of integrating the emancipation perspective. The TECENA committee (four experts) is entrusted with this important task.

In the same period national support for other feminist institutions has changed considerably, resulting in reorganisations and mergers after the usual rounds of consultation. As of 1999, there are few institutions left: E-Quality, the expertise centre on gender and diversity; the IIAV, the archives of the women's movement; the Clara Wichmann Institute, experts on women and law; the *Vrouwen Alliantie*, an umbrella organisation of the women's movement; Toplink, a database of expert women and the Opportunity in Business Campaign. There is still a budget for projects.

In Parliament, the duties of the Parliamentary standing committee on emancipation policy that existed until 1994 have been transferred to the Parliamentary standing committee on social affairs and employment.

---

26. Prins, M. (1974-1989), *Emancipatie van vrouwen in beweging. Emancipatie als besturingsvraagstuk*, Groningen: PP&STYX. See also Outshoorn, J. (1995), 'Administrative Accommodation in the Netherlands. The Department for Coordination of Equality Policy', in McBride Stetson, D. and Mazur, A. (eds), *Comparative State Feminism*, London: Sage, pp. 168-186.

Gender Mainstreaming Strategies

The strategy of gender mainstreaming, which has received so much attention since Beijing as a 'new' strategy, is certainly not that new in the Netherlands. In fact, it can be seen as a progression from the strategy of 'facet policy' developed since the 1970s as one of the two-track equality strategies. The Netherlands has developed a special instrument for mainstreaming, called Emancipation Impact Assessment (EER). There is more mainstreaming experience in the field of development co-operation and in policies to increase women's participation in politics. This chapter tries to assess these different experiences in order to analyse their potential value, as well as the specific value of mainstreaming.

Mainstreaming will be defined as 'the (re)organization, improvement and development of policy processes in order to incorporate a gender equality perspective'.[27] Essentially, mainstreaming is characterised by two elements: target and the organisation of responsibility. The target of mainstreaming is every policy that can be relevant for gender relations. The responsibility for taking into account a gender equality perspective is always placed on the actors responsible for that policy area though it can involve equality agencies. (Re)organising policy processes so that these 'normal' actors are able to exercise the responsibility for gender is the quintessential point of gender mainstreaming.

Case 1:The Dutch Gender Impact Assessment Experience: The EER[28]

In 1998, Mr Ad Melkert, co-ordinating Minister for equality policies in the Netherlands, spoke at a conference on gender impact assessment at all levels of government. He admitted to having had serious doubts in the past about the Dutch instrument EER: too much trouble, too much time, too costly. However, he said he was converted and convinced by the fact that the instrument was apparently 'working', that it did what it was supposed to do: namely show how and where a policy, that was meant to be generally applicable and gender neutral, had an impact on gender relations. He was one of a good many politicians and policy-makers at that conference who were enthusiastic and positive about the instrument.

27. Definition of the Group of Specialists on Mainstreaming of the Council of Europe, (1998), *Gender Mainstreaming. Conceptual Framework, Methodology and Presentation of Good Practices*, Strasbourg: Council of Europe, p. 15.
28. This section is based on a lecture for the colloquium 'Predicting the Impact of Policy: a Model for Gender Auditing', Hulme Hall, Manchester, United Kingdom, 7 May 1999. See also Verloo, M. and Roggeband, C. (1996), 'Gender Impact Assessment: The Development of a New Instrument in the Netherlands', *Impact Assessement*, 14 (1), pp. 3-21.

The EER came about as a result of the policy goal of integrating of emancipation into all government policies. Emancipation policies in the Netherlands were never meant to be restricted to special or targeted policies for women only. Until 1994, however, there were no special instruments available to achieve integration. The EER was designed in 1994 to analyse *ex ante* the potential effects of new government policies on gender relations in Dutch society. Since then, the instrument has generated a little family of its own variations. Recently, a comprehensive evaluation study on the EERs at national level has been published. There is enough experience now to answer the question if is it true that the Dutch instrument, the EER, is a success.

The goal of any impact assessment is to analyse the potential effects of new policy plans or programmes before they are implemented. In general this type of assessment, known best in the field of environmental policy, is designed in five steps:

- description of the current situation;
- description of probable development without the new policy;
- description and analysis of the new policy plan;
- description of potential effects;
- evaluation of the positive and negative potential effects.

This is also the structure of the EER. There is a sixth step that is generally part of an impact assessment, but which was not initially part of the EER. This is 'the development of alternatives to avoid or to mitigate the negative potential effects'. The exclusion of the sixth step from the EER is the result of a compromise. At the time when the EER was developed, there were only a few people who believed in its potential. There were no previous examples. The policy depended on a high level of political commitment (on behalf of Elske ter Veld, the Secretary of State for Emancipation Policies), determination in the equality bureaucracy (Joke Swiebel, working at DCE and taking advantage of a power vacuum at the top) and two researchers determined to make it happen (it is incidentally not uncommon for these kinds of combinations to make policy innovation possible).

The development of a new policy instrument is a delicate process involving technical, theoretical and most of all strategic problems. It involves making compromises at all stages of the development process. The decision to use the basic impact assessment model solved not only a technical problem, but also made acceptance of the instrument easier, because of its connection with an existing and successful type of instrument. On the other hand this connection should not be stretched too far, because the terms of reference for the development of the gender impact instrument made it clear that the instrument should not be too demanding (in terms of costs, time or even expertise). There was simply no political support for an EER to be compulsory or highly sophisticated like its environmental sister. The use of gender experts to conduct the EER could be recommended, but could not be made a requirement. Along the same lines, the development of alternatives as a sixth step is recommended, but could not be included as a requirement. Some of the discussion partners at the Ministry would have preferred an instrument that was idiot-proof, that needed no expertise at all and could be applied in less than one day. The problem was how to combine that 'wish' with a reality where gender relations are very complex and any gender impact assessment would necessarily need a certain degree of sophistication. Introducing a theoretical framework that was based on firm academic knowledge, yet was also connectable to the existing emancipation policy history solved this problem.

The theoretical framework refers to three questions relating to three elements:

- where are the structurally unequal power relations between men and women to be found?
- how do they function? What are the mechanisms producing them?
- how are they to be evaluated?

The first element, structures, refers to the core of gender relations, showing which institutions and organisations are most important. The second element, processes, emphasises the formal theoretical level: what are the mechanisms that produce and reproduce gender relations? And the third element, criteria, is the normative element, necessary in order to be able to decide whether a certain situation is to be judged positively or negatively.

For a description of the most important structures a connection could be made with an 'analysis of the women's question' that had been produced for the government in 1982 (and was still considered valid). Building upon this analysis and more recent knowledge, the two main structures were described as first, the division of labour, and secondly, the organisation of intimacy and sexuality. The importance of differences between women was stressed, but not elaborated on.

To describe the operation of the mechanisms of gender relations, academic knowledge about mechanisms of power, primarily the work of Anthony Giddens, was utilised.[29] Here, luckily, there was an established definition in Dutch emancipation policies stating that there were 'unequal

29. Giddens, A. (1984), *The Constitution of Society*, Cambridge: Polity Press.

power relations between the sexes'. Two mechanisms were described, the first being the distribution of and access to resources, and the second being the rules (interpretations and norms) about or connected to gender.

For the third element, the evaluation, two criteria were used that had their history in different policy fields. The first criterion is equality in the sense of equality before the law and equal treatment in similar circumstances. To avoid equality in the sense of sameness, or adaptation to a male norm, account was taken of autonomy: 'the possibility for women to decide for themselves what is a good life'. The second criterion was that of pluriformity: a society where differences are not hierarchical.

This gave the EER a theoretical framework which was then combined with the basic impact assessment steps. This means that the current and future situation in a policy field has to be described for both structures (that is the division of labour and the organisation of intimacy), that the distribution of resources and the functioning of gender rules has to be described and analysed, and that the potential result of a policy plan then has to be evaluated in terms of equality, autonomy and pluriformity.

The development of this instrument shows the importance of making connections with existing policy frameworks. In the Netherlands policy frameworks on problem definition in terms of power could be found in the existing 'analysis of the women's question'. Policy frameworks for the criteria could be found too. The existing environmental impact assessment also enhanced political and bureaucratic opportunities.

As a result, the EER is not easily exportable. Not because of its qualities in an academic sense, but because of its qualities linking it to policy and political contexts, the qualities which make it accepted and used.[30] When Petra Meier and Allison Woodward were asked to develop a similar instrument for Flanders (in Belgium), they were critical of four aspects of the EER: the high degree of specialisation needed; the cost in time and money; the dependency on the quality of information and the omission of a requirement for the construction of alternatives.[31]

In Flanders the problem was that there was less expertise on gender available, less data on gender relations and less support for tackling the problem. In addition, the theoretical framework did not connect to the

30. Even if I would now add a few things to the theoretical framework. I would still defend its basic elements. See Verloo, M. (1998), 'Alle goede dingen in drieen', *Tijdschrift voor genderstudies*.
31. Woodward, A. and Meier, P. (1997), *Gender Impact Assessment: Tool in Mainstreaming or Tool to Begin Mainstreaming? A Comparison of Dutch and Flemish Approaches*, Paper for the ECPR Joint Sessions, Bern.

young policy history of Flanders. In fact, there was hardly any policy history on equality in Flanders. Meier and Woodward looked at other possibilities and decided to develop an instrument, that is much more educational, and process-oriented. This instrument, which drew on Canadian and New Zealand examples that were developed since the EER, would try to increase awareness on gender by asking questions at all stages in the policy process. Unfortunately, the Flemish instrument has not been used since it was completed in 1997.

The strength of the Dutch EER instrument is that it has been used. At the time when the evaluation report was written, seven EERs had been finished at the national level and two were in process.[32] The conclusions of that recent evaluation report are positive.[33] In principle, they say, it is a good instrument. It only needs more attention and further development, not to improve the quality of the instrument, but its context: its position in the policy-making process, its political support, the translation of its conclusions into alternatives and recommendations and guidelines for its use by the people who commission it. According to the evaluation report the four points of criticism mentioned earlier were not a problem in the Netherlands: there was enough expertise — often hired from outside — it was not too time consuming and/or costly, and, in reality, it nearly always did include recommendations or alternatives.

Two elements in the evaluation report are most important. It is stressed that the analysis of the policy plan should include a very precise analysis of its problem/solution combination. It should analyse not only the solutions proposed but also the problem-definition itself for its gender impact. As there is still a secret wish for a simple idiot-proof instrument in the hearts of many policy-makers, this emphasis on a high level of sophistication is important. The evaluation report warns against simplification of the instrument (on the basis of experiences at the local level with simplified checklists), saying that the gender perspective is easily lost, leading to 'sex without gender' evaluations which often revert to representations of women only as vulnerable victims.

The second point which arises from the evaluation report concerns the place of the instrument in the policy process. The report found a tendency to conduct the impact assessment at too late a stage, when policy plans can hardly be changed. Moreover, the report compared 'internal', 'external', and 'joint venture' teams. It concluded that 'joint venture' teams worked best, combining the advantages of distance (the external experts) and the power to define policy (the internal policy-makers). Next best was

32. Currently nine EERs have been completed and two are in process.

33. van de Graaf, H., Mossink, M. and Gröflin, J. (1998), *Van de EER geleerd*, Den Haag: Vuga.

an external team, as some distance proved necessary in order to develop critical focus.

Some reflections can be added to this. When developed, the EER was constructed as an instrument that could (and, ideally, would) be used for all policies that possibly had a relevance to gender. Now, five years later, nine EERs have been finished, two more are in process. During these five years probably more than a hundred new policies have been launched (this is a very low estimate). The process of selecting policies for an EER is therefore highly significant. If the EER is an instrument for gender mainstreaming, then it would be necessary to (re)organise the policy process in such a way that an EER will be undertaken for all the most crucial, the most important policies. So far, this has not been done. The instrument is supposed to sell itself. In fact, it did sell itself, but too slowly. Only the Ministry of Education tried to adopt a strategy whereby, in a pilot project, all parts of its organisation would use the instrument. This strategy failed for lack of supporters and expertise. Possible solutions for a better selection process are not hard to find, but depend on political and bureaucratic will. One solution would be an EER screening committee that would consider all policies and decide whether an EER is necessary or not (parallel to the procedure for an environmental impact assessment in the Netherlands). Another solution would be to institutionalise the use of a screening instrument such as SMART.[34]

A second reflection concerns the further development of a gender mainstreaming strategy. Much more will be needed for successful mainstreaming than simply the use of this first instrument. There is a need for improvement of the EER. What can be done to counter the criticism that it is only about gender and not about other structural inequalities? It is of course unacceptable to just 'say' that attention will be paid to other structural inequalities. The relationship between gender and ethnicity/or race, between gender and sexuality, or between gender and class, to name just three of the most important structural inequalities, is much too complex for that. In the Netherlands, the EER has been designed to point at the most important structures, mechanisms and criteria concerning gender. There is no reason to believe that exactly the same structures, mechanisms and criteria are the right ones when other structural inequalities are concerned. To give but a few examples: there are legal equal rights for both genders, but not for heterosexuals and homosexuals. The 'organisation of intimacy' can be analysed as a fundamental structure for gender inequality, but why should that be one of the structures of

34. SMART screens only if a policy is relevant to gender. See Council of Europe, (1998), *Gender Mainstreaming. Conceptual framework, Methodology and Presentation of Good Practices*, Strasbourg: Council of Europe, p. 62.

racial/ethnic inequality? People can escape some elements of homophobia and discrimination on the basis of sexuality by hiding in the closet, but people cannot escape racism and sexism in the same way, it is too hard to hide sex or colour. Therefore the analytical elements that are important for other structural inequalities should be established before designing a diversity impact assessment or any other mainstreaming strategy that can incorporate those inequalities.

A last reflection is on the possible place of the EER in a more comprehensive strategy for gender mainstreaming. Unfortunately, so far the Dutch government has not produced a comprehensive mainstreaming plan. Gender mainstreaming is not only about the screening of policy proposals by a technical instrument, it also involves a continuing need for the education of all policy-makers and procedures to allow for the consultation of both women and men. Further efforts could be made to integrate 'public-private contacts', such as 'Opportunity in Business', and 'TECENA', the committee that advises advisory committees in matters of gender, into the mainstreaming strategy.

Case 2: Gender Bias Guidelines: A Forgotten Instrument[35]

The Gender Bias Guidelines were commissioned by the Dutch government, and published in 1995. These guidelines are designed to help researchers that are (co)financed by the government, so that they can avoid gender bias in their research. The aim was to improve the quality of research and to ensure that research commissioned by the government adopted a gender perspective. Until now, only the guidelines have been published and no further action was taken. The original plan was to distribute the guidelines widely and to organise a workshop for all civil servants that are responsible for the commissioning of research, but this has not been done.

Case 3: Strategies on Women in Political Decision-Making Positions in the Netherlands

In the early 1990s the Dutch government decided to prioritise the policy of including more women in political decision-making. In general, the government's approach was not to force an increase in women's participation by law or regulations, but to set norms, targets and preconditions. Therefore, most of the policy instruments, such as information and communication, stimulation, steering, subsidisation, affirmative action policies and monitoring,

35. Verloo, M. and Hijmans, E. (1995), *Kwaliteit van onderzoe*, Den Haag: Vuga.

work in an indirect way. Examples include a report to Parliament once a year, the formulation of target figures, analysis and publication of results, subsidies for the projects of women's organisations, a gender impact assessment of a proposal for changes to the electoral system, a database for women candidates and direct discussion with and stimulation of political parties and other important actors. For the Dutch government the use of law enforcement, such as compulsory quotas for candidate lists, is not a policy option unless all other measures have failed. The only example of a legislative measure concerns the advisory bodies. In the new legislation on advisory bodies (*kaderwet Adviescolleges*) a stipulation has been included, which attempts to achieve the proportional representation of women and men in all newly installed advisory bodies. The target figures have almost been met: there are now 45 per cent women in the new advisory bodies.

Government policy is aimed especially at selection procedures as the obstacle primarily responsible for the underrepresentation of women in political decision-making. As selection for elected functions, such as Parliament and the municipality council, is relatively difficult to influence directly, the government has paid special attention to the appointment of mayors, Queen's Commissioners and women on district water boards, concentrating on increasing the number of female candidates, inspecting the selection criteria and guiding the selection committees.

The aims and goals of this policy are formulated in the form of targets and a set of concrete measures specifying what extra measures should be taken. A group, 'Women in Politics and Public Policy', has been created to implement them and it operates under the auspices of the Department of Internal Affairs. In addition, a network of contact persons has been established in all the Ministries which are involved in the selection procedures for appointments to advisory bodies and interdepartmental committees.

The Minister of Internal Affairs is responsible for the realisation of the government's aims, and has the task of reporting annually on the progress of the policy to Parliament and of disseminating the information to the public. The yearly reports, from 1993 onwards, consist of a summary of activities and quantitative data on women's participation in each project area. By demanding yearly reports, the government guarantees regular policy monitoring.

In the Netherlands, political parties play a crucial role in the recruitment, selection and nomination of candidates for political and public policy functions such as City Mayor and Queen's Commissioner. The government convinced them of the importance of women's participation and successfully persuaded them to consider their role and to develop programmes to integrate women into political functions. Probably this was partly due to the fact that the

Minister of Domestic Affairs personally showed his commitment by engaging in a dialogue with the political parties, and the political parties in turn advised the government on measures they thought the government should take in order to facilitate equal representation. One of these measures was to provide training for migrant women; another was to review the terms of employment regarding pregnancy leave for those in the political sphere and outplacement for ex-politicians.

Government stimulation of the political parties has had most effect at national level. The fact that the government's approach had much less effect at local and regional party levels suggests that the government's approach was too centralised.

Helped by the state, women's organisations have also taken up the issue of more women in political decision-making. The Action M/W 50/50, a working group of the Dutch Alliance of Women (*Vereniging voor Vrouwenbelangen, Vrouwenarbeid en Gelijk Staatsburgerschap*) ran a co-operation campaign between different women's organisations during the elections of 1994 to integrate emancipation issues into the electoral programmes of the political parties and to stimulate political parties to include more women on the candidate lists. These campaigns also encouraged voters to give a preference vote to a woman candidate.

An interdepartmental project group, Women in Decision-Making, based in the DCE, focused on the increase of women in social decision-making, identifying reasons why women are underrepresented as board members, stimulating research and developing activities, often in co-operation with non-governmental organisations.[36] Their final report identifies three roles for the government: providing stimulation, facilitating action and serving as an exemplar. The stimulation role includes monitoring and evaluating progress, signalling problems such as sectors that lag behind and providing information and advice. The facilitation role includes taking the initiative to perform and support experimental projects and financing useful initiatives taken by social organisations. Lastly, the government has to set an example by achieving its own target figures.

So far, these policy measures have had some results, particularly in changing attitudes towards women in political decision-making. The goal of more balanced representation is now accepted, and discussions are mainly

36 See Leijenaar, M., Niemöller, C. and Koster, A. D S. (1994), *Het maatschappelijk tekort: vrouwen in besturen van maatschappelijke organisaties*, Den Haag. Vuga. See also Nederland, T and Portegijs, W. (1996), *Bestuurders gevraagd: vrouwen en mannen over maatschappelijke participatie*, Den Haag: Vuga.

about the best strategy. The Women in Decision-Making position paper and its implementation have kept the problem of the underrepresentation of women in political decision-making on the public and political agenda. Moreover, some quantitative results are clearly visible.

As Table 1 shows, in 1994 target figures had been reached for the European Parliament, the Lower House, the Provinces and already existing external advisory bodies. The number of women mayors increased from 54 to 80. The percentage of women on municipality councils still lagged behind its target. The percentage of women in the interdepartmental committees did not reach the target figure of 20 per cent; staying instead at 1993 levels.

Table 3.1. Target figures and the results after the elections of 1994 (*Vrouwen in Politiek en Openbaar bestuur, Voortgangsrapportage 1995, Min. BiZa*)

	Total seats (end 1995)	Target Figure end 94	Women, end 94
European Parliament	31	9 (30%)	0 (32.3%)
Upper House	75	23 (30%)	19 (25.3%)
Lower House	150	45 (30%)	49 (32.7%)
Province	755	227 (30%)	216 (30.6%) (elections 1995)
Municipality Council	10948	3284 (30%)	2454 (22.4%)
Commissioners of the Queen	12	1 -	1 -
Mayors	608	100 -	78 -
External Advisory Bodies			
— existing ones	1421	213 (15%)	227 (16.0%)
— newly installed 1994	22	1 (50%)	2 (9.1%)
Interdepartmental Committees	773	155 (20%)	78 (10.1%)

According to Leijenaar 'the Dutch experience shows that positive action need not always involve quotas'.[37] The willingness to appoint and select women for high level political decision-making positions is due to the joint activities of the women's movement, the political parties and the Dutch government. All these initiatives have undoubtedly contributed to the present relatively high participation of women in the Cabinet and Parliament.[38] The joint activities fit well into the Dutch consociational tradition.

Case 4: Gender and Dutch development co-operation[39]

Policy formulation and institutional structure The starting point in 1990 for 'women and development' was that the integration of women's emancipation in development policy should be guaranteed and that obligations should be attached to its implementation. The adoption of the issue of 'women and development' as one of the four spearheads of the new development policy was a way to formally guarantee that policy-makers at all stages of the policy making process would pay attention to the issue. All relevant policy areas had to formulate emancipation targets. The central concept was women's autonomy, described as physical, economic, political and social-cultural autonomy. Specific policy issues were added afterwards, such as violence against women, women's circumcision and religion.

An organisational unit was established to realise the intended integration. The new unit had access to the highest level of decision-making, as it was allowed access to the weekly meetings of directors. The unit's tasks were undertaking preparation for decision-making, developing instruments, advising and training, overseeing the Women's Fund and making contact with women's organisations, donors, international forums and relevant institutions in developing countries.

Instead of creating a special organisational unit concerning women and development, the government could have chosen a network approach, which ensures better integration of gender equality in all policy departments. Instituting a unit means that expertise is concentrated, with the danger of 'ghettoisation'. The choice of a unit, however, fitted better into the existing institutional structure, as similar units had been established in connection with the other spearheads of the development co-operation policy. To prevent 'ghettoisation' of emancipation policy, the government gave the unit the

37. Ibid, p. 86.
38. Gardiner, F. and Leijenaar, M, op cit, n. 1, pp. 60-91.
39. (1998), *Women and Development. Policy and Implementation in Netherlands Development Cooperation 1985-1996. Evaluation Report*, Policy and Operations Evaluation Department, Ministry of Foreign Affairs: The Hague.

explicit task of integrating women's interests in the development co-operation programme as a whole.

Three years later the policy environment in relation to development co-operation was already undergoing change, although the policy objectives concerning women's emancipation did not change fundamentally. Collective security, emergency aid and conflict prevention became key words in policy formulation. Bilateral aid was weighed against other forms of aid, like multilateral aid and support for processes of transformation. The government did not consider what effects these policy changes could have on the issue of women and development. However, because bilateral aid was the main policy area relating to women and development, these policy changes could certainly have been expected to have had an influence on the progress of women's equality. Considering that 'women and development' was stated to be one of the central concerns of Dutch development co-operation, it was a major failure that the government did not analyse the possible impact of the proposed policy changes on women. The government evaluated the impact of individual projects in developing countries, but not its own policy changes.

An analysis of the impact on women of development co-operation policies was performed two years later, during the preparations for the Fourth UN World Conference on Women in 1995. The National Advisory Council for development aid (NAR), which performed the analysis, concluded that Dutch policy did not pay enough attention to issues of importance for women, such as education, employment, health care and the effects of macro-economic policy. After the Beijing Conference, some new policy areas were emphasised, such as women's participation in (political) decision-making, macro-economic policy, women and armed conflict, the girl child, heritage rights, reproductive health and violence against women.

In the course of restructuring Dutch foreign policy in 1996 a decentralisation of development co-operation policy was initiated, resulting in the creation of seven thematic directorates responsible for the development of policy in co-operation with regional directorates. The issue of women and development became the responsibility of the directorate for social and institutional development, together with programmes for health, water and sanitation, co-financing and children. The advisory tasks of the unit were transferred to the Dutch embassies. The unit's permission to attend the weekly meetings of directors was cancelled.

The repositioning of the issue of women and development under the authority of one directorate implied that it was limited to one sector; apparently the other six thematic directorates no longer had responsibility for the issue. It is hard to see this as an advance with regard to mainstreaming. Most probably, the thematic directorates will not be allowed to interfere in each other's policy sectors, which means that the integration of women's advancement in all development policy areas has become hard to achieve. The withdrawl of the unit's permission to attend meetings of directors makes integration of women's interests even less feasible.

Apparently even when gender equality is firmly integrated in the policy process, major reorganisations are a real danger when not accompanied by careful scrutiny of their gender impacts.

Policy instruments

In 1991, all available resources for women and development were amalgamated into the 'Women's Fund'. The Fund's targets were to strengthen the position of the women's movement, facilitate (international) networking and support innovative activities for women. In an effort to increase efficiency, part of the Fund was delegated in 1992 to sector specialists at the embassies, as the 'Local Women's Fund'. The sector specialists received guidance on how to improve women's economic, social, cultural and physical self-determination. The Local Fund can finance small projects for the preparation and development of policy, training and seminars, research, exchange programmes and small innovative projects to improve women's autonomy. Follow-up financing should be guaranteed. The sector specialist is responsible for identifying needs and monitoring results on a half-yearly basis.

The women's funds aim at promoting women's equality through different actors at several levels. As well as stimulating governments in developing countries and international organisations to integrate women's interests into their development policies, the funds support women's organisations and networks at local, national and international level. Both funds fit into the tradition of specific equality policies. Trying to involve more actors in the process is a first step towards more comprehensive equality policies.

Mainstreaming instruments

One of the main tasks of the 'women and development'programme was to elaborate new policy instruments. First, instruments were developed to ensure that gender relations and women's participation are considered in project proposals from the very beginning. Examples are the Women and

Development Screening Test and the Gender Assessment Study. The Women and Development part of the Development Screening Test (W&D-test) is meant to reject project proposals if they are unfavourable to women. The Gender Assessment Study (GAS) was developed to solve the problem of a lack of information about the situation of women in project areas. The GAS examines the situation of women by looking at the division of labour between the sexes, at women's access to and control over production means, services, gains and development results. Based on the results of the GAS, a project proposal can be adjusted in order to improve the prospects for women.

Next, instruments were developed to guarantee that expenditure is more directly aimed at the advancement of women. Examples are the DAC/WID criteria and target figures. The DAC/WID criteria were developed by the Development Assistance Committee (DAC) of the OECD and have the purpose of making visible which part of financial aid is likely to work to the benefit of women.[40] There are four points in the DAC/WID criteria:

- the needs and interests of women must be included in the project design either through direct consultation, or through the consultation of local women and development experts or documentation reflecting the views of women.
- women from the target group must be active participants during the implementation of the project.
- constraints on female participation in the project must be identified and conditions (including financial) must be created in order to enhance women's autonomy.
- women and development expertise must be planned, budgeted for and utilised throughout the project cycle.

In 1990, the Dutch government formally adopted the DAC criteria and combined them with a target figure. In the year 1998 at least 50 per cent of all Dutch expenditure on bilateral programmes that are of direct relevance for women had to meet with the DAC/WID criteria.

When applied, the Gender Assessment Study and the W&D test guarantee that women's advancement is considered as an important criterion from the very beginning of the policy-making process. Additionally, the DAC/WID criteria and target figures serve as guidelines for policy implementation.

40. Development Assistance Committee (1983), *Guiding Principles on Women and Development*, Paris: OECD.

One of the main conclusions of a 1998 evaluation study is that policies on women and development focus mainly on bilateral project-based aid, which is easier to steer and adjust to the benefit of specific target groups, in contrast to so-called 'programme aid'.[41] The term 'programme aid' refers to aid that consists of balance of payments support, co-financing with the World Bank (often in the form of structural adjustment programmes), budgetary support and debt release. Programme aid is much harder to adjust to the benefit of specific target groups, and therefore is not considered to be a suitable area for the implementation of a policy on women and development. This is problematic. Although less visible, programme aid does have a specific impact on women, if only because structural adjustment programmes harm poor people disproportionately, while disadvantaged groups usually consist of relatively many women. By not paying attention to gender in programme aid, the government neglects this negative impact on women.

The evaluation of the instruments shows that their significance is more symbolic than practical, as there was no subsequent monitoring of their practical application. Their main achievement has been to increase the visibility and salience of the issue. Sometimes the instruments have functioned as a reference for those preparing projects. Often the accent on women and development disappeared after the first phase, more specifically when the projects were taken over by consultants for further development. As for the Women's Fund and the Local Women's Fund, these have been quite effective.

It may seem strange that instruments with the specific tests and criteria described did not function well. The explanation is that, although the women and development target figure for 1998 seems very concrete, it is not. The DAC/WID criteria are too ambiguous to determine the share of projects that benefit women. Moreover, attempts to set up a monitoring system have faltered. Users were especially sceptical about the W&D Test, because between 1992 and 1995 not a single project was rejected because of an expected negative impact on women. In practice, the evaluation study concludes, the test was a paper tiger.[42]

41. Ministry of Foreign Affairs, op cit, n. 39.
42. Development Assistance Committee, op cit, n. 40, p. 153.

Conclusion

The quintessence of gender mainstreaming is allocating responsibility for gender equality within the policy process. The variety of experiences in the Netherlands can therefore be helpful in detecting both the pitfalls and possibilities of such a velvet revolution. The Netherlands is to date one of only a few countries to develop a special instrument for gender mainstreaming, and more important, is the only one to actually use the instrument. Though this in itself is some achievement, the Dutch experience has revealed some problems.

The first problem with the EER is that there is to date no systematic procedure to guarantee its use. In the 'kingdom of the disunited ministries' it is still apparently every Minister who decides for himself and unfortunately there is no procedure where salience, relevance and importance for gender relations are the criteria for a compulsory use of the EER or of any other mainstreaming strategy. It would be preferable if the Secretary of State, and hence the council of ministers decided this, informed by an expert advisor (from inside or outside the bureaucracy). The second problem is that the EER has been used at a rather late stage in policy development, so that its influence on the policies involved has so far been the exception rather than the rule. The evaluation report recognizes these problems and makes recommendations to solve them. As yet it is not clear if those recommendations will lead to any changes in practice. The potential of the EER is there, but it is still more a promise than a reality.

The different histories of two instruments: the gender impact assessment and the Gender Bias Guidelines show that mainstreaming involves more than devising an instrument. Whereas the first was promoted extensively by the DCE, by several local women's policy agencies as well as by some non-governmental organisations, the second was neither promoted nor supported and ended up in a desk drawer. The lesson to be learned from this is that it is not enough to have instruments available: the organisation of responsibilities for the instrument is crucial. Certainly in the beginning, promotion activities, such as workshops or articles in departments' newsletters, are necessary to 'seduce' civil servants who are new to questions of equality. The experiences from the Netherlands also show the importance of organizing mainstreaming at the top level. A clear commitment is necessary not only from political leaders but also in the policy formulation process.

Also, the experiences in women and development show that 'quick and dirty' instruments, such as the DAC/WID criteria have serious limitations. They are too vague and as a result their answers have no value. The idea of setting target percentages for the proportion of policy proposals to be screened for their gender impact is a good one, but the instrument needed to be more robust. Ideally, of course, all proposals would be screened, but to start with a few, and then set target percentages to increase the number every year, seems a more realistic option.

The experiences in the field of development point at another problem that is central to gender mainstreaming: the difficulty of organizing responsibility for gender equality in a context of continuing dynamism. It seems that structures and procedures in the Dutch bureaucracy are rather short-lived and the sad consequence for gender mainstreaming is that it is nearly impossible to give gender equality a 'safe' place within the structure. The women and development example shows clearly how a good attempt at mainstreaming can be frustrated as an unintended consequence of a policy reorganisation. In the beginning, the choice of bilateral aid was a good one. But this choice made the whole mainstreaming effort more difficult when that policy area over time became less important in the Ministry.

Finally the experiences in the field of political representation give a clear example of a mixed strategy that fits closely with the Dutch consociational political culture. Consensus building, a lot of talking, top level support and the engagement of all actors involved seem to be responsible for this success story.

On the question of the co-ordination of mainstreaming, there is a range of examples in the Netherlands. Monitoring can be in the hands of Parliament, as the example from the Ministry for Domestic Affairs shows. This, however, will work only if there is both clear political commitment and sound preparation at the bureaucratic level. Co-ordination is the biggest challenge. In the women and development field, the co-ordination was in the hands of a specialist unit, whereas in the Ministry for Domestic Affairs a network of contact persons was used. In practice, both seem to be sound options, although theoretically a network of contact persons fits better with the concept of mainstreaming. At the level of the Dutch government as a whole, there is both a unit (DCE) and a network (ICE). In theory, therefore, all prerequisites are met to make gender mainstreaming a success. It is now up to politicians and bureaucrats to make the Dutch promise a reality.

4 Making Women Count in Portugal

JOÃO CASQUEIRA CARDOSO

Due to its peculiar legal culture — a formal and, in one sense, a highly internationalised one — Portugal has managed to anticipate most of the legal changes promoted by international and European Union (EU) law in the field of equal opportunities. In fact, the Portuguese legal framework on equal opportunities may be said to be one of the most progressive in the EU. However, probably no other EU Member state needs, more urgently than Portugal, to develop its approach to equal opportunities between men and women.

This apparent paradox is not easy to explain. At the risk of over-simplification, it involves four observations. First, the Portuguese political and legal landscape shows that, although the Portugese Parliament has strong powers, only the government is allowed under the terms of the Constitution to take measures which have a *practical* impact on the respective situations of men and women. This is true of central and of local government. Secondly, the equality bodies created at governmental level have in practice little effective power to intervene in the preliminary stages of policy and law-making, despite their theoretical power. This might be explained by the politico-social context of feminism in Portugal. Thirdly, because of the 'formal law' culture that characterises Portugal, as in most *civil law* systems, common judicial courts and the Constitutional Court have a wide competence to supervise the principle of equal treatment and equal opportunities between men and women. However, as Portugal is a country where litigation levels are low, the court system is not as relevant as it could be as a tool for the assessment and revision of law and policy-making. As such, it is not possible to compare what cannot be compared, namely the Portuguese legal system, with other Member States belonging to the common law tradition. Fourthly, the political commitment to 'advanced' equality policies, such as positive action measures and mainstreaming, is relatively recent in the Portuguese context. The Global Plan for Equal Opportunities, the first comprehensive programme of commitment to equal opportunities of the government, dates only from 1997. It is, therefore, too soon to make any general evaluation of its success.

This chapter will focus on the most significant social, legal and institutional aspects of gender equality in Portugal, bearing in mind the relatively recent introduction of measures concerning mainstreaming.

The Political and Legal Landscape in Portugal

In Portugal, four sovereign bodies form the core of the government.[1] They are the President, the Assembly, the government and the courts. The President of the Republic is elected by direct, secret and universal ballot for a period of five years and, under the Constitution of the Portuguese Republic (CPR),[2] shares power with the Assembly of the Republic and the government of the Republic.[3] The most important functions of the President are guaranteeing the constitutional order, arbitrating between conflicting interests, supervising governmental actions and contributing to overcoming institutional crises.[4]

The Assembly of the Republic is elected by direct, secret and universal ballot for a period of four years. It is composed of at least 180 and at most 235 members who must be Portuguese citizens. The Assembly passes the majority of laws which are politically sensitive, that is contentious between the main political parties.

The government is 'the organ responsible for the conduct of the country's general policy' and the 'highest organ of public administration' (art. 182 CPR). It consists of the Prime Minister, Ministers and the Secretaries and Under-Secretaries of State (who are political appointees). According to art.

---

1. According to art. 110 of the Constitution of the Portuguese Republic (CPR).
2. 1997 Edition of the Constitution of the Portuguese Republic (the Constitution dates from 2 April 1976). See Gomes Canotilho, J. J. and Vital, M. (eds), (1997), *Constituição da República Portuguesa*, Fourth edition, Coimbra: Coimbra Editora.
3. The major constitutional functions of the President of the Republic can be divided into three discrete areas of power. First, the President exercises a range of powers that relate to the operation of other democratic organs (art. 133 CPR). Secondly, the President exercises a range of personal powers (art. 134 CPR) mainly the power to promulgate and order the publication of legislative instruments. Thirdly, the President exercises a range of powers which relate to the conduct of international relations (art. 135 CPR). The most significant of these is the power to ratify international treaties once they have been duly approved by the government. See Gomes Canotilho, J. J. and Vital, M. (1991), *Os poderes do Presidente da República*, Coimbra: Coimbra Editora; and Queiroz, C. (1992), *O Sistema Político e Constitucional Português*, Lisbon: Associação Académica da Faculdade de Direito de Lisboa.
4. Machado Horta, R. (1996), 'A Constituição da República Portuguesa de 1976 e o Regime Semi-presidencial', in Miranda, J. (ed.), *Perspectivas Constitucionais Nos 20 Anos da Constituição de 1976 Volume I*, Coimbra: Coimbra Editora, p. 531.

190 CPR, 'the government is responsible for its actions to the President of the Republic and the Assembly of the Republic'.[5] Also playing a significant role in government is the Council of Ministers which meets every week. The Council is composed of the Prime Minister, the Deputy Prime Minister (if any has been appointed) and Ministers. It adopts the general guidelines for government policy and its implementation.

The government possesses political, legislative and administrative powers. In light of the range of powers which the CPR places at the disposal of the government, their use has to be co-ordinated by some person or body. This task is divided under the CPR between the Prime Minister (together with his or her Ministers) and the Council of Ministers. The Prime Minister is responsible for directing the government's general policy as well as co-ordinating and guiding the action of all Ministers, while Ministers have to carry out the policies laid down for their Ministries and to maintain relations between the government and the other organs of the State in the area for which their Ministry is responsible (art. 201 § 1 and § 2 CPR). Hence the Prime Minister and his or her Ministers are responsible for initiating policy and laws to implement those policies. Thus a central role is played by the Prime Minister.

The Assembly may scrutinise the government at two main stages. In the first place, the Assembly may scrutinise the government's programme at the beginning of the legislature's term. Secondly, the Assembly may, on the initiative of one quarter of its members who are entitled to vote or on the initiative of any Parliamentary group, pass motions of censure on the government either in respect of the implementation of its programme or of any matter of national interest (art. 194 CPR). The conditions in the Constitution regulating the circumstances in which a vote on a motion of censure can occur are restrictive. According to art. 195 CPR, the government has to resign if 'a motion of censure is approved by an absolute majority of those Members of the Assembly entitled to vote'. Art. 193 CPR also makes provision for the government to ask the Assembly to pass a vote of confidence either on a statement of general policy or any issue of national interest. The government has to resign if 'a motion of confidence is not approved' (art. 195 (e) CPR).

5. The members of the government are bound by the government's programme, which states its political objectives and the measures to be adopted or proposed in the various areas of government activity. Rejection of that programme by the Assembly of the Republic will result in a government's dismissal. Moreover, according to art. 195 CPR, the government has to tender its resignation when 'a new legislative period starts'.

The fourth sovereign body according to the CPR is the courts and it lists four main categories (art. 209 § 1). First, the Supreme Court of Justice and the courts of law of first instance and of second instance;[6] second, the Supreme Administrative Court and other administrative and fiscal courts; third, the Court of Audit; and fourth, the Military Courts. The CPR guarantees the independence of the courts and provides that court hearings should take place in public, except in certain circumstances such as where this would not be in the interests of 'public morality'. The decisions of the courts are binding on all public and private bodies and prevail over decisions of all other authorities. The courts are also directed that, when reaching their decisions, they should not apply any rules which breach the provisions of the Constitution or the principles set out therein. By implication, therefore, the courts have the power to rule on the constitutionality of those laws that are relevant to any dispute they may be hearing. In this manner the way is open for an individual to assert in the course of a court hearing that a particular law, provided it is relevant to that hearing, is unconstitutional.

Apart from its four categories of courts, Portugal also possesses a Constitutional Court. The task of the Constitutional Court is to assess *inter alia* whether legal norms conform with the terms of the Constitution and the law (art. 223 CPR), although any court has the power to assess the constitutionality of those norms which are relevant to questions under trial (art. 204 CPR).[7]

Whilst Portugal is a unitary State, the Constitution recognises the existence of two kinds of local entities: the Autonomous Regions and local authorities. The Autonomous Regions are the archipelagos of the Azores and Madeira, which are part of the territory of Portugal. These two Autonomous Regions are self-governing entities not local authorities *stricto sensu*.[8] As such they enjoy a considerable degree of political power with regard to regional matters and possess legislative powers, albeit limited to matters which are relevant to the region. This autonomy means that those Regions have their own political and administrative statutes and are governed by their own institutions (art. 6 § 2 CPR). Such autonomy, however, does not

---

6. Law 38/87 of 23 December 1987 (as amended by Law 49/88 of 19 April 1988, Law 52/88 of 4 May 1988, Law 24/90 of 4 August 1990, Law 24/92 of 20 August 1992, and Law 33-A/96 of 26 August 1996, arts. 64 and 65).
7. See Cardoso Da Costa, J. M. (1992), 'A Jurisdição Constitucional em Portugal', in *Boletim da Faculdade de Direito de Coimbra — Número Especial Estudos em Homagem ao Prof. Doutor Afonso Queiró, Volume I,* Second Edition, Coimbra: Faculdade de Direito da Universidade de Coimbra. In English, see on the organization of the Constitutional Court: http://www.ci.uc.pt/cd25a/ospp-po/TRICONST.HTML
8. The CPR explicitly separates the sections on Autonomous Regions (Section VII) from those on local authorities (Section VIII).

permit any interference by the Autonomous Regions with central government initiatives in the fields of social and economic policy — including equal opportunities. Central government determines the policies, although the implementation of those policies *in concreto* is the responsibility of the local administration of the Autonomous Regions. As administrative entities, the Autonomous Regions enjoy legal personality and autonomous implementation powers.[9]

The CPR also creates 'categories of local authorities and administrative division' (art. 236 CPR). The local authorities on the mainland consist of parishes, municipal authorities and administrative regions. The local authorities on the islands of Azores and Madeira (the Autonomous Regions) consist of parishes and municipal authorities. Each local authority, including those of the Autonomous Regions, is composed of an elected assembly — elected by direct and secret universal suffrage of the resident citizens[10] — with decision-making powers and a corporate executive body responsible to the Assembly. In terms of law-making powers, the relationship between the local authorities *inter se* and between the local authorities and central government is a hierarchical one. Art. 241 CPR states that local authorities are bound, on the one hand, by the Portuguese Constitution and, on the other hand, by laws and regulations issued by higher ranking local authorities. The local authorities have their own powers to issue regulations within the limits set out in the Constitution, by law and by the regulations of higher ranking local authorities or authorities with supervisory powers. The administrative supervision of local authorities consists of verifying whether the law is complied with by the organs of the said authorities and is exercised in the cases and in the ways laid down by law. In practice, and according to the principle of subsidiarity implied in the CPR in relation to local authorities, the local authorities make their own policy and do not follow government policies except the general laws applicable both to the State (central level) and the local authorities. This makes local power effective in three main fields: town planning; public contracts for the provision of services or infrastructure for use by the local populations; and the regulation of private activities that could endanger the health, safety or well-being of inhabitants.[11] However, the two fields of health and education fall within the exclusive competence of the central administration and/or the autonomous regional government.

9. Caetano, M. (1984), *Manual de Direito Administrativo, Volume I*, Coimbra: Almedina, pp. 360-361.
10. In the case of the municipalities, the municipal assembly comprises the chairmen of the parish councils and at least an equal number of members elected by the voters in the municipal area.
11. See De Oliveira, A. C. (1993), *Direito das autarquias locais*, Coimbra: Coimbra Editora, p. 297.

The Law and Policy-Making Process

The terminology used to describe a law (for example laws or decree laws) merely indicates the source of that law — that is the Assembly of the Republic, the government or the Assembly of an Autonomous Region —and not its degree of importance. There are, however, exceptions to this general principle. In the first place, the laws in the CPR take priority over other legal instruments. In recognition of Portugal's so-called formal rights legal culture, the CPR puts considerable emphasis on fundamental rights and contains a list of them which are typically expressed in a very general fashion.[12] In addition to the laws set out in the CPR, there are other forms of superior law which laws, decree laws and regional legislative decrees must respect. These are:

- organic laws which are passed by the Assembly of the Republic and are within its exclusive legislative competence. They deal with such issues as elections, referendums and the organisation and operation of the Constitutional Court.
- laws delegating the power under which a decree law is made or containing the basic principles of the legal system which a decree law amplifies. When a decree law is made its terms must be in accordance with such legislative provisions.
- the general laws of the Republic, defined by the CPR as 'laws and decree laws, the purposes of which require their application without qualification to the whole of the national territory'. Regional legislative decrees must, as a general rule, respect such laws.

Where it is proposed that a law is made by the Assembly[13] it must first be debated in the Assembly. Here the government must rely on whatever political support it can muster in the Assembly. There is a first reading general debate and a second reading debate on detail. The second reading debate may take place in committee or in a plenary session of the Assembly. There is then a final vote on the measure by the Assembly. In certain cases, for example where the proposed law is an organic law, the CPR requires that a particular majority — here an absolute majority of the members entitled to

---

12. For example: 'Principle of Universality — All citizens enjoy the rights and are subject to the duties laid down in the Constitution', or 'Principle of Equality — All citizens have the same social dignity and are equal before the law'.
13. That is, from a member of the Assembly, one of its Parliamentary groups or the government.

vote — must be obtained on the final vote. Should a proposed measure be rejected by the Assembly, it cannot be reintroduced in that legislative session.[14] If, however, it is approved, the measure then goes to the President of the Republic for consideration.

The President has the power to promulgate and order the publication of laws. Under the terms of the Constitution (art. 136 CPR) the President must, within 20 days of receiving a proposed measure from the Assembly, either approve it or veto it. Should the President decide to veto it, then it is returned to the Assembly, together with a message indicating the President's reasons for urging reconsideration. The Assembly then has the option of either agreeing to that request for changes or re-affirming the original measure. If it takes the latter course of action then an absolute majority of the members entitled to vote must support[15] the measure which then goes back to the President of the Republic who has eight days to promulgate it.

If the proposal is that the government promulgate a decree law, it must first be given consideration by the government. The government cannot legislate on matters that are within the exclusive competence of the Assembly, on this the CPR is quite specific. The government's own legislative powers are: first, to make laws on matters not within the Assembly's exclusive powers; second, to make laws on those matters which the Assembly has chosen to delegate to it (this will depend on the degree of political power the government exercises in the Assembly); third, to make laws amplifying laws that set basic principles of the legal system; fourth, to make laws on matters within its own exclusive legislative competence. Essentially these are matters relating to the government's own structure and operation. When the decision is taken by the government to use its legislative powers then the decree law that results must be approved by the Council of Ministers. Since this body is made up of the Prime Minister and Ministers, this would appear to be a mere formality. The decree law in question is then published and takes effect.

Decree laws, other than those based upon the government's exclusive legislative powers, may be considered by the Assembly. Provided ten members of the Assembly petition for this to happen, the decree law in question will be debated by the Assembly which can refuse to ratify it or amend it. A refusal to ratify will mean that the decree law in question will cease to have effect, whilst a proposal to amend may result in the suspension

14. A legislative session lasts for one year beginning on 15 October. The Assembly normally sits from that date until 15 June.
15. A greater majority may be required in the case of certain laws such as organic laws or those dealing with elections to the European Parliament.

of the decree law. If there is no consideration by the Assembly, decree laws are sent by the government for promulgation by the President and he or she then has 40 days either to approve or veto it. If the decision is taken to veto a measure, there is no way the government can reverse the decision other than by proposing an identical measure.

In conclusion the legislative process in Portugal is both formal and highly complex. This situation is rendered all the more difficult by a lack of literature on the routes that law and policy initiatives follow in Portugal.[16] The government of the day clearly plays a central role, relying presumably on whatever majority it can muster in the Assembly to gain support for its legislative proposals. However the Portugese system of checks and balances means that those wishing to influence the law and policy-making process have to gain access to a variety of bodies if they are to be successful. In addition there is a very high turn-over rate among civil servants which produces a lack of continuity in developing and implementing policies.

These features present a considerable obstacle for women's groups seeking to make gains through the legal process. As long as women are poorly represented in the political parties and the administration, it is difficult to see how women will make their voices heard. Even the strategy of mainstreaming would seem likely to make little impact as it requires each of the bodies involved in law and policy-making in Portugal to be committed to advancing equal opportunities.

Role of The Economic and Social Council as a Consultative Body[17]

The Economic and Social Council (hereafter ESC) is the body responsible for consultation and co-ordination in the sphere of economic and social policies; the Council participates in the preparation of plans for economic and social development (art. 92 CPR). The ESC is organised as a plenary body (composed of representatives of the government, of workers organisations, of organisations representing economic and cultural activities, of the Autonomous Regions, and

---

16. Books on Political Science are rare in Portugal. Mention should, therefore, be made of a recent book containing a brief explanation of the 'legislative process' given in a chapter devoted to the Constitution of 1976. See Roboredo Seara, F., de Matos Correia, J. and Leite Pinto, R. (1995), *Ciência Política e Direito Constitucional*, Lisbon: Universidade Lusíada, Chapter V. For a brief guide also consult Fernando Loureiro, B. (1999), *Ciência Política — Guia de estudo*, Lisbon: Associação Académica da Faculdade de Direito de Lisboa.
17. The organisation and function of the ESC is regulated by Law 108/91 of 17 August 1991, completed by Decree-Law 90/92 of 21 May 1992. See Conselho Económico e Social. (1996), *O Conselho Económico e Social — Legislação e composição*, Lisbon: Conselho Económico e Social.

of the local authorities); as a permanent commission on social co-ordination, a tripartite body composed of representatives from the government, trade unions organisations, the Confederation of Portuguese Agricultors, the Portuguese Trade Confederation, and the Portuguese Industry Confederation; and as two specialised commissions on Economic and Social Policy and on Territorial Development and Administration.

The ESC has no power of initiative but in practice the permanent commission on social co-ordination plays an important and highly visible role in the field of socio-economic relations and labour programmes. It is a forum in which its members can exchange information and also criticise and discuss the global policy options of the government. It also negotiates non-binding agreements — called 'Strategic Social Pacts'. These agreements set out the main national social and economic options for the coming three or four years. 'Strategic Social Pacts' are worded in a rather general fashion. The most recent Pact (1996/1999, dated 20 December 1996), for example, refers in Chapter V (dealing with 'Productivity, Conditions of Work and Participation') to 11 aims in relation to labour law; one of which is the promotion of equal opportunities. The Pact does suggest changes to current labour law; however, it does so without specifying in great detail what those changes should be. For example, the Pact refers to a 'reform of the legal regime regulating the Commission for Equality at Work and in Employment' without indicating what kind of reforms are desirable.[18] Traditionally the Pact is signed by all but one of the nationally representative main Trade Unions Confederations.

Role of the Courts

Portugal has a Constitutional Court which plays a central role in the politico-legal system. If a law, decree law or regional legislative decree contains provisions that are in breach of a superior law then a ruling of illegality may be made by the Constitutional Court. As in Spain,[19] the existence in Portugal of a specific Constitutional Court does not preclude other courts from assessing the constitutionality of legislation — assessments which may lead to questions being forwarded to the Constitutional Court. But unlike Spain, Portugal has no avenue for individual challenge to the constitutionality of a law (*recurso de amparo*). There are, however, other grounds on which a ruling of illegality may be made beside the failure to observe a superior law.

18. Conselho Económico e Social. (1997), *Acordo de Concertação Estratégica 1996/1999*, Lisbon: Conselho Económico e Social, p. 109.
19. See for example Díez-Picazo, L. M. (1994), *Source of Law in Spain: An Outline*, EUI Working Paper Law 94/10, Florence: European University Institute, p. 9

More specifically, illegality can occur when a regional legislative instrument or an instrument made by a body with supreme authority breaches the provisions of the statute of an Autonomous Region (the statute of an Autonomous Region sets out the political and administrative framework for the Region).

The system of constitutional review in Portugal is both comprehensive and strict. It is comprehensive in terms of the potential objects of review — norms arising from international treaties and agreements, laws, decree-laws, regional legislative decrees, and regional regulatory decrees aimed at regulating general laws — and the possibility of anticipatory control. It is strict in the sense that the control of constitutionality is not automatic nor can it be initiated by the Constitutional Court *ex officio*,[20] and because the law regarding *locus standi* is restrictive.

In practical terms, the Constitutional Court may use four devices to assess constitutionality:

- anticipatory [pre-implementation] scrutiny of constitutionality
- supervision *in concreto* by the Constitutional Court of constitutionality and legality (art. 280 CPR);[21]
- supervision *in abstracto* by the Constitutional Court of constitutionality and legality (art. 281 CPR);[22]
- unconstitutionality by omission (art. 283 CPR).[23]

The importance of the Constitutional Court is demonstrated where it acts in relation to other tribunals. On the one hand the Constitutional Court is not bound by another tribunal's formulation of a constitutional question and can reformulate it.[24] On the other hand, the interpretation of the Constitution given by the Constitutional Court is not subject to any appeal and binds all other tribunals, including the Judicial Supreme Court and the Administrative Supreme Court.[25]

20. See De Matos Correia, J., Leite Pinto, R., and Roboredo Seara, F. (1997), *Direito Constitucional Português Vigente - Opúsculo temáticos I: A fiscalização da constitu cionalidade e da legalidade*, Lisboa: SPB Editores, p. 38.
21. That is where the legality or applicability of a legal measure has already been raised in proceedings before a common judicial court. Common judicial courts are organized according to Law 3/99 of 13 January 1999.
22. That is where a question of constitutionality or legality has been raised by the President of the Republic. See De Matos Correia, Leite Pinto, and Roboredo Seara, op cit, n. 20, p. 22.
23. That is where an omission in legislation that is necessary to implement the provisions of the Constitution may make such legislation in contravention of the Constitution.
24. Constitutional Decisions 27/84, 62/84 and 247/93.
25. Constitutional Decisions 516/93 and 163/95. See Cardoso Da Costa, op cit, n. 7, p. 19.

There are many constraints on the availability of information regarding the law and policy-making process in Portugal. The absence of clear communication between public bodies, the ineffectiveness of the co-ordinating structure, and the under-employment of information technology is to a large extent responsible for this state of affairs.

Even though Portugal was one of the advanced democratic regimes at the beginning of the twentieth century — a Republic in 1910 with an active and established feminist movement — five decades of administrative secrecy and closeness have built up a tradition that still characterises the current public administration. As Robinson demonstrates, in Portugal individuals feel powerless when dealing with the administration above the level of the parish or the Autonomous Region.[26]

Old and new elements combine to create tensions between formal and informal processes, with a contrast between the forms and the facts; between appearance and reality. Formal processes follow a relatively advanced democratic pattern; informal and actual use of institutional and legal tools is still characterised by extremely centralised, secretive and authoritarian patterns of decision-making. There is no formal restriction on access to information: the Official Secrets Act deals only with documents relating to defence (in this case, the information effectively belongs to the government and cannot be released).

Elected Members of Parliament (MPs) have no greater access to information than members of the public. All legal diplomas are published in the *Official Journal*. As regards other documents — for example comparative studies, theses, research — there is a tendency for the administrators of the main equality bodies (especially the Commission for Equality and Women's Rights) to retain information for as long as possible before it becomes public. The existing Freedom of Information legislation has no effect on such practices.

Women in the Law and Policy-Making Process

In 1931 some women were granted the right to vote but only those with a university degree or secondary school education. In 1968, political rights between men and women were almost completely equalised, the exception being at local level since only the 'head of the family' had the right to vote

26. Robinson, R. A. H. (1993), 'O Indivíduo e o Estado no Portugal Contemporâneo', in Brettell, C. B. (ed.), *Portugal — O Indivíduo e o Estado*, Lisbon: Editorial Fragmentos, p. 124.

in elections for the parish assembly.[27] It was not until 1974 (with the passage of Decree Law 621/A/74 of 15 November) that men and women were treated totally equally with respect to voting rights at national and local level.

The new Constitution of 1976 which was adopted after the revolution of 25 April 1974 led to important changes for women in relation to political participation, work and family life. In the field of family law, equality between men and women was provided for in the Civil Code in 1977, and divorce was permitted — once again. From the mid-1970s, the influence exerted by women in Portugal's social and economic life increased dramatically. Various professions have opened their doors to women, the last of these being the legal profession (it was not until 1975 that women were permitted to hold judicial office). Education is a sector where the democratisation that followed the revolution of 25 April 1974 created great hopes and had indirect consequences on the economic life of women: Portugal witnessed a substantial increase in the number of girls attending school — a process already initiated in the early 1970s.[28]

Nowadays, women are comparatively well-represented in key professions, in particular the judiciary. Women make up 33.1 per cent of all judges. However, the number of women in political positions is low. The Assembly of the Republic, as at 1 October 1995, comprised 12.2 per cent female MPs. However, three Parliamentary commissions (Economy; Work, Solidarity, Social Security and Family; and Parity and Equal Opportunities) are presided over by a female MP. Of 58 Ministerial offices, only five are held by women, namely the Ministry of Environment and Natural Resources, the Ministry of Health, the Secretary of State for Budget, the Secretary of State for Education and Innovation and the Secretary of State for Housing and Communication.[29] The concentration of political activity around the political parties is seen as one of the main reasons for the absence of any strong autonomous women's movement and, in turn, of the the under-representation of women in political life.[30]

---

27. Commission for Equality and Women's Rights. (1995), *Portugal — Status of Women — 1994*, Lisbon: High Commission for Equality and Family, p. 30.
28. Magalhães, M. J. (1998), *Movimento Feminista e Educação — Portugal, décadas de 70 e 80*, Oeiras: Celta, p. 98.
29. Comissão para a Igualdade e para os Direitos das Mulheres. (1998), *Situação das Mulheres*, Lisbon: Commission for Equality and Women's Rights, pp. 106-108.
30. Ferreira, V. (1998), *As mulheres em Portugal: Situação e paradoxos*, Coimbra: Oficina do CES, p. 25.

Equality Laws in Portugal

Equality laws in Portugal are based on the 1976 CPR, certain provisions of which were designed to repair the 'historical injustice towards women'.[31] However important constitutional provisions might be in providing a framework, past experience has proved that they are of little effect unless hierarchically inferior legal rules provide for their application in more detail. In Portugal, the great majority of legal rules applying constitutional equality provisions concentrate either on employment or on family rights (especially paternity and maternity). Paradoxically, legislation on equality has not been the result of social partner policy or lobbying,[32] but rather of government initiative. Equality laws should be seen as a *patchwork* of occasional government intervention, with little emphasis on advanced equal opportunities issues such as sexual harassment and positive action. The fact that the equality laws have not been supported by strong social movements — either from the social partners or from the women's movements — does not, however, explain the relatively low influence of EU legislation on Portuguese law, or the very low level of litigation. To explain that, certain structural aspects of the Portuguese legal system must be considered.

Existence of Constitutional Guarantees of Equal Treatment

Several articles in the CPR either explicitly outlaw sex discrimination or promote gender equality:

- art. 9 imposes a duty upon the State to promote equality between men and women;
- art. 13 affirms the principle of equal social dignity and equality before the law and asserts that no one shall be privileged, favoured, injured, deprived of any right or exempt from any duty because of his . . . sex . . .;
- art. 26 § 1 establishes the right to legal protection against discrimination;

31. Expression used in Decree Law 251/74 of 12 July 1974. On the new political philosophy that followed, see Pires, J. (1997), *Da Emancipação Juslaboral da Mulher*, Lisbon: Comissão para a Igualdade no Trabalho e no Emprego, Chapter 2.
32. Nunes highlights the low level of involvement of trade unions in equality issues, as far as collective bargaining is concerned. Nunes, M. C. (1996), *Equal Opportunities and Collective Bargaining in the EU — Exploring the National Situation in Portugal*, Dublin: European Foundation for the Improvement of Living and Working Conditions, Working Paper No: WP/96/57/EN.

- art. 36 § 3 affirms the equality of rights and duties of spouses regarding their civil and political capacities and the maintenance and upbringing of their children;
- art. 58 § 2 places a duty on the State to promote equality of opportunities in the choice of a profession or type of work, in order that there are no bars or limits, on the basis of sex, with regard to access to any responsibility, work or professional category;
- art. 59 § 1 states the principal rights of workers, including, *inter alia* their entitlement to the organisation of work that respects social dignity and permits the reconciliation of family and professional life;
- art. 59 § 2 makes it a duty for the State 'to guarantee conditions of work, salary and rest to workers so as to permit . . . special protection at work for pregnant women after giving birth';
- art. 67 and art. 68 concern 'paternity and maternity' rights;
- art. 109 states that the law shall promote equality in the exercise of civil and political rights and non-discrimination on the grounds of sex in relation to political responsibilities.

These constitutional provisions as well as those that indirectly touch on gender, have been expanded upon in legislation. As a result, equality legislation deals with two main subject areas: employment relations and family rights. There is very little legislation concerning equality in relation to social security (pensions or social benefits) beyond the family and employment contexts.

Employment Laws

Decree-Law n° 392/79 of 20 September 1979 is the basic legislative measure on equality between men and women at work. It guarantees women equality with men in respect of opportunities and treatment at work and in gaining employment. It also prohibits any form of discrimination — the concept of discrimination used by this regulation is extremely wide and includes implicitly indirect discrimination.[33] This legal instrument applies only to the private sector. The Labour Inspectorate is in charge of controlling the implementation of this law.

Decree-Law n° 426/88 of 18 November 1988 later extended its provisions to the public sector, the reason being that previously the public sector was

33. Machado Dray argues that it is indeed too wide. See Machado Dray, G. (1999), *O Principio da Igualdade no Direito do Trabalho — Sua Aplicabilidade no Domínio Específico da Formação de Contratos Individuais de Trabalho*, Lisbon: Almedina, p. 125.

assumed to respect the principle of equal opportunities between men and women. Decree-Law n° 426/88 on Equality of Treatment in Employment between Men and Women within the Public Administration guarantees women equality with men with respect to opportunities and treatment at work and in gaining employment at all levels (central, regional and local) of public administration. This legislation has two objectives: first, it extends the prohibition on discrimination, which already applies in the private sector, to the public sector; secondly, it enlarges the powers of the Commission for Equality at Work and in Employment (CEWE) which is the body given the task of implementing the legislation and hence power over the public administration (in conjunction with the Labour Inspectorate).[34]

To complete the picture, Law n° 105/97 of 13 September 1997 on the Guarantee of the Right to Equal Treatment in Work and Employment applies both to the public and the private sectors. Law n° 105/97 has reversed the onus of proof in cases of sex discrimination and gives competence to the Labour Inspectorate to investigate cases of alleged discrimination. It also provides a definition of the concept of indirect discrimination.[35] The CEWE is in charge of keeping a file on the case. Council Directive 97/80/EC of 15 December 1997 on the onus of proof in cases of sex discrimination was clearly the reason for the change to Portuguese law, though the Portuguese legislation came into being two months before the adoption of the Directive.

Decree-Law n° 491/85 of 26 November 1985 lays down the system of penalties for the violation of labour regulations and the sanctions applicable in the case of discriminatory practices relating to job advertisements, job descriptions and job assessments. The sanctions for either direct or indirect discrimination on the grounds of sex are set out in art. 8 of Law 105/97. They allow the imposition of a fine and the amount is 5 to 10 times the highest guaranteed weekly minimum wage for this particular form of employment.

---

34. The main provisions of Decree-Law n° 426/88 are as follows: any statutory or administrative act that has the effect of limiting in any way the access of women to any function or public office is void (art. 5); the principle of equal wages for 'equal work or work of equal value' is affirmed (art. 6 § 1); variations in wages are not discriminatory as long as they are based on objective criteria (art. 6 § 2); systems used to describe and evaluate job functions must be based on objective criteria common to both men and women (art. 6 § 3). These issues were addressed together in this way as a consequence of Portugal's accession to the European Union.
35. According to the law, *indirect discrimination* occurs where 'a measure, criterion or practice which is apparently neutral affects in a disproportionate way persons belonging to one of the sexes, with regard to civil or family status and which is not justified objectively by any other reason or necessary condition not related to sex' (art. 2 of Law 105/97) (my translation).

Decree-Law n° 4/84 of 5 April 1984 on the Protection of Maternity and Paternity is the source of the principal legal provisions regulating the family/gender nexus in Portugal. This Law has been amended and supplemented several times.[36] It applies both to the private and the public sector, though some related legal measures distinguish between these sectors and, on the whole, provide for more favourable treatment in the public sector. According to the Decree-Law, both parents have equal rights and duties with respect to the support and education of their children. All women are entitled to free health care during pregnancy and for 60 days after confinement. A pregnant worker cannot be dismissed on the grounds of her pregnancy. Women workers are entitled to 120 days maternity leave, 90 days of which must be taken after the birth. During this period of maternity leave there is no loss of employment rights and women workers receive their full salaries paid by the social security services. This is implementing, progressively, Council Directive 92/85/EEC of 19 October 1992 on measures to promote the safety and health of pregnant workers, those workers who have recently given birth or who are breast-feeding.[37] In certain circumstances in the private sector, namely on the occasion of the mother's physical or psychological incapacity or death, paternity leave may be taken by a child's father.

Pregnant workers have the right to time off work to attend medical consultations and during their child's first year mothers may be absent from work for two separate one hour periods a day to breast-feed. Workers are entitled to take leave of absence of up to 30 days per year to provide urgent care for sick children under 10 years of age, including adopted or stepchildren; in addition they are entitled to up to 15 days per year to provide urgent care in the case of the illness of their spouse or a family member over 10 years of age. These days absence do not involve any loss of employment rights. In the public sector a civil servant will continue to receive his or her salary, whilst in the private sector the worker is entitled to a daily subsidy. Hospitalized

---

36. Law 4/84 of 5 April 1984 was amended by Law n°17/95 of 9 June 1995 (supplemented by Decree-Law 332/95 of 23 December 1995) and by Law 102/97 of 13 September 1997, by Decree-Law 136/85 of 3 May 1985 (itself amended by Decree-Law n°333/95 of 23 December 1995), by Decree-Law 154/88 of 29 April 1988 (itself amended by Decree-Law 333/95 of 23 December 1995), by Law 194/96 of 16 October 1996 and by Law 18/98 of 28 April 1998.
37. Law 18/98 made the implementation of this period progressive: between 1 January 1999 and 31 December 1999, maternity leave will be for a period of 110 days. From 1 January 2000 it will be for a period of 120 days.

children are entitled to the permanent company of their father or mother. Working fathers and mothers can opt for unpaid leave (called 'special child-care leave') for a period of between 6 months to 2 years immediately following maternity leave. Workers having one or more children under 12 years of age are entitled to take up part-time work or flexible working hours in some circumstances.

There are two additional measures beside Decree-Law n° 4/84 on the Protection of Maternity and Paternity. The first, Decree-Law n° 136/85 of 3 May 1985 (as amended by Decree-Law n° 332/95 of 23 December 1995), regulates that part of Decree-Law 4/84 which is applicable to workers covered by an individual employment contract, including workers in agriculture and domestic service.[38] Decree-Law n°136/85 is itself supplemented by Decree-Law 154/88 of 29 April 1988 (as amended by Decree-Law n° 332/95 of 23 December 1995) which defines the system of financial benefits in respect of maternity, paternity, adoption and the care of minors for those workers covered by the general social security scheme — this includes those employed in the private sector (either full-time or part-time) as well as self-employed workers.[39]

The second complementary legal measure is Decree-Law n° 194/96 of 16 October 1996 which regulates that part of Decree-Law 4/84 dealing with parental leave as it applies to public sector workers. The scope of the Decree-Law 194/96 is wide: it covers any legal person constituted under public law, and applies to any worker employed under any form of contract of employment whatever their length of service or their working hours (art. 1 Decree-Law 194/96). In the public sector, paternity leave may be taken by the father by common decision of the parents, provided that the mother enjoyed 14 days leave after birth and if the father informs his employers of his decision at least 10 days before the commencement of leave and provided that the mother's employers have been informed of his decision (art. 3 Decree-Law 194/96). This provision anticipated Council Directive 96/34/EC of 3 July 1996 on parental leave.

---

38. The Decree-Law n°136/95, although it refers to 'domestic service', does not define it. According to the CEWE, 'domestic work' refers to work (often undertaken on a voluntary basis) whereby individuals offer their services in other persons' houses (most of the time these services will consist of caring and/or cleaning). It must be distinguished from work 'at home' or homeworking.
39. Decree-Law n°107/87 of 6 March 1987 extends the regulations laid down in Decree-Law 136/85 to employees of Caixas de Previdência [Welfare Funds] and Casas do Povo [Public Hostels].

Sexual Harassment

There is no specific legislation in Portugal dealing with sexual harassment, although such behaviour is subject to both criminal and general employment laws. The criminal law deals with the most violent behaviour, but its relevance for 'common' cases of sexual harassment is limited.[40] In the field of employment, particularly relevant are Decree-Law 494/08 of 24 November 1969 regulating the contract of employment and Decree-Law 64-A/89 of 27 February 1989 on the termination of the contract of employment and short-term contracts. None of these measures explicitly mentions sexual harassment. They state in general terms the duties of an employer, '... including the possibility of applying disciplinary sanctions, namely dismissal, to workers of both sexes who have by their conduct provoked or created a risk of demoralising their colleagues, especially women workers and minors' (art. 40 § 2 of Decree-Law 494/08).[41]

The Portuguese legislators simply ignored non-binding EU norms (resolutions and recommendations) on sexual harassment namely: Resolution 90/C 157/02 of 29 May 1990 and Recommendation 92/131/EEC of 27 November 1991 (protection of dignity at work). Despite this situation, the dominant *opinio juris* is that as far as sexual harassment is concerned, the Portuguese legal framework is not only sufficient but respects the spirit of EU law. Specifically, it is emphasised that the Portuguese have pursued a 'dignity at work' approach to sexual harassment which predates the adoption of such an approach by the EU.

Positive Action

There is no specific legislation dealing with positive action, although a general provision on employment relations is seen as allowing it. This is the interpretation given to Decree-Law 392/79 of 20 September 1979 which guarantees women equality with men with respect to opportunities and treatment at

40. Law 65/98 of 2 September 1998 amended the Portuguese Penal Code, so as to criminalise sexual harassment in the specific forms of sexual coercion and rape. Mouraz Lopes, J. (1998), *Os Crimes Contra a Liberdade e Autodeterminação Sexual no Código Penal*, Coimbra: Coimbra Editora, pp. 16-18.
41. Although of 'dubious validity' (that is possibly open to constitutional challenge) according to one author, this provision remains in force. Moreira, A. J. (1998), *Compêndio de leis do trabalho*, Coimbra: Almedina, p. 293, note 2. The possibility of dismissing the harasser (the legislation does not use this specific term, but refers instead to a person who committed acts of physical violence or had an injurious attitude) is retaken in Decree-Law 64-A/89, art. 9 § 2 (b) and 2 (i).

work and in employment. Article 3 § 2 of Decree-Law 392/79 specifies that 'temporary provisions establishing a preference on the grounds of sex and imposed by the necessity to correct factual inequality, as well as measures that are intended to protect maternity as a social value shall not be considered discriminatory'.

With regard to positive action, Portuguese legislators have ignored Council Recommendation 84/635/EEC of 13 December 1984 (promotion of positive actions in favour of women). The CEWE recently recommended the general use of positive action programmes for equal opportunities between men and women, but it has not clearly indicated guidelines or given examples of good and/or bad practice. This indicates that Portugal is likely to fall into an approach to positive action shared by certain other Member States whereby any positive action programme is regarded as good, whatever its contents.[42] Little attention has been paid to the requirements of EU law in this area.

Social Security

Due to their lower wage levels, women have traditionally been prejudiced by the low level of social protection afforded by the social security system especially the public pension scheme.[43] Decree-Law 329/93 of 25 September 1993 states the main principles of the public pension regime (old age and invalidity). One of its main points is that the normal pensionable age is 65 for both men and women. However, the regulation makes an exception for certain professions that may 'require a particular protection' (not defined), as well as for 'laborious' work (not defined) but in any event, pensionable age shall not be below 60. This regulation also provides a transitional period (between 1994 and 1996) during which old age pensions should progressively be equalised between men and women. Decree-Law 307/97 of 11 November 1997 extends to the sphere of occupational pensions the principle of equal pensionable age. The object of this regulation is to give effect to EU Directive 96/97/EC of 20 December 1996 (amending Directive 86/378/EEC).

42. Casqueira Cardoso, J. (1997), *Conceptions et Politiques des Mesures d'Action Positive*, Florence: European University Institute, pp. 197-242.
43. Silva, M. and Perista, H. (1995), *As Portuguesas e a União Europeia — Prospectivas para a Acção*, Lisbon: Comissão para a Igualdade e para os Direitos das Mulheres, p. 31.

In Portugal, the level of litigation is very low when it comes to cases of sexual discrimination. For instance, to date only three cases of sexual harassment have been ruled on by the Portuguese courts — none of them considering the question of sex discrimination as central to the issue. However, the figure of the *Ombudsman*,[44] inspired by Scandinavian legal systems, has been successfully imported into the Portuguese legal system where it acts as a quasi-litigation mechanism. However closer analysis reveals that the Portuguese Ombudsman has no judicial power and moreover cannot intervene directly in law and policy-making.

The office of the Ombudsman (*Provedor de Justiça*) is a State institution, responsible only to itself.[45] The holder of the Office has the rank of Minister. Citizens can complain directly — either individually or as members of collective entities — to the Ombudsman concerning the actions of, or omissions by, public authorities. The meaning of the term 'public authorities' is widely interpreted and includes public companies. A recent law — Law 30/96 of 14 of August 1996 — extends the powers of the Ombudsman to 'relations between private persons implying a special relation of power, within the domain of the protection of rights, freedom and duties' (art. 2 § 2 of Law 30/96). This 'special relation of power' refers to the relationship between a professional and a client in situations where the client is supposed to be particularly vulnerable, particularly in the fields of banking, insurance, and real estate.

Due to the increasing number of complaints that are made to the Ombudsman and the length of time the Ombudsman took to respond,[46] art. 29 § 4 of Law 30/96 set a deadline for the Ombudsman to reply to a claim which is within ten days of the receipt of the claim. In addition, art. 29 § 1 of Law 9/91 imposes a duty on any organ or official of a public body to co-operate with the Ombudsman. They must provide the Ombudsman with 'all the information and clarification that the latter might request from them'.

44. The office of Ombudsman is dealt with in the CPR under Part I, on 'Fundamental Rights and Duties'. Art. 23 § 1 CPR states that 'Citizens may present complaints concerning actions or omissions on the part of the public authorities to the Ombudsman who examines them without power of decision and makes such recommendations to the appropriate organs as are necessary in order to prevent or make good injustice'.
45. The Ombudsman is appointed by the Assembly of the Republic for a period laid down by law, namely four years which is renewable on one occasion only (art. 6 § 1 of Law 9/91).
46. See Reports of the Ombudsman for years 1988, 1992 and 1994, published in Diário da República, 2nd Serie-C, number 9, 11 December 1992, p. 42; *Diário da República*, 2nd Serie-C, number 33, 22 November 1994, p. 185; *Diário da República*, 2nd Série-C, number 23, 20 July 1996, p. 174.

The Ombudsman is entitled 'to order any civil servant, any official of any public body or any incumbent of any organ subject to the Ombudsman's control to appear at his/her seat or at any other place according to circumstances, with the object of co-operating with the Ombudsman as requested' (art. 29 § 3 of Law 9/91). Non-compliance with the duty to co-operate, if unjustified, amounts to a crime of disobedience and, where applicable, may be the subject of disciplinary proceedings.

Despite such comprehensive powers, which are unique in the Portuguese legal order, the impact of the Ombudsman on the law and policy-making process is limited. First, most interventions are after the event. Second, the Ombudsman has no power to issue binding decisions and can only make recommendations to the relevant bodies as to what actions they should take.[47] Third, the Ombudsman traditionally works with a relatively small staff.[48]

Impact of European Union Membership on Sex Discrimination Law

At a European level, Portugal was already a party to the European Convention on Human Rights (ECHR) and had recognised the right of individual petition to the European Court of Human Rights. To date the number of cases against Portugal dealt with by the European Court of Human Rights stands at 12. Most of these cases are relatively recent and in the majority the Portuguese State has been found to be in violation of the ECHR. Almost all of these violations concern Article 6 of the ECHR. The relevant authorities (tribunals in this case) have not acted in such a way as to ensure that the applicant received the effective benefit of his or her right, specifically because of the excessive length of proceedings.

In contrast with the situation in some other Member States, there has been little difficulty with the reception of EU law into the Portuguese legal system.[49] EU Law may be enforced in the national courts where the

47. Art. 29 § 4 of Law 30/96 strengthened the impact of the Ombudsman's recommendations, at least at the local level.

48. Lingnau da Silveira, L. (1989), 'O Provedor de Justiça', in Baptista Coelho, M. (ed.), *Portugal, o sistema político e constitucional 1974-1987*, Lisboa: Instituto de Ciências Sociais da Universidade de Lisboa.

49. In addition to measures already cited, Portugal has also transposed into Portuguese law Council Directive 75/117/EEC of 10 February 1975 on the approximation of the laws of the Members States relating to the application of the principle of equal pay for men and women; Council Directive 76/207/EEC of 9 February 1976 on the implementation of the principle of equal treatment for men and women with respect to access to employment, vocational training and promotion, and working conditions; Council Directive 79/7/EEC of 19 December 1978 on the progressive implementation of the principle of equal treatment for men and women in matters of social security; Council Directive 86/378/EEC of 24 July 1986 on the implementation of the principle of equal treatment for men and women in occupational social security systems; Council Directive 86/613/EEC of 11 December 1986 on the application of the principle of equal treatment between men and women engaged in an activity, including agriculture, in a self-employed capacity, and on the protection of self-employed women during pregnancy and motherhood.

national judge acts as an interpreter of EU law. Where Portuguese domestic law is not in line with EU law, the national judge will give priority to EU law as it is regarded as fully part of the Portuguese legal order.

However, because of a rather paradoxical chauvinistic reflex, the interface between EU law and Portuguese sex equality laws is limited. EU Directives have not been followed by any major legal changes in Portugal as most of the provisions enacted by the Directives are already present, at least formally, in Portuguese statutory law and, without the need for legislative intervention, in collective agreements. Many authors have argued in defence of the Portuguese position that EU legislation has produced little change, especially in the field of equality between men and women in employment, because the level of protection was already considered to conform to EU norms.[50] Others have indicated that in general, Portugal has maintained a low profile in response to EU Directives.[51] Although EU law provides a number of rights for working parents, their formulation in gender neutral terms has had the consequence of reproducing existing inequalities within the family and of reinforcing female absenteeism from employment. The concept of equality promoted through these laws is a notion of equality which aims at compensating women for the 'double-burden' of family and work which affects many of them. It is not a concept which aims at eliminating this double-burden.

There are two reasons why it is difficult to say whether Portuguese law could withstand any challenge in respect of its equal opportunities measures before the ECJ. First, there have to date been no cases. Secondly, Portuguese law contains many areas of doubt. However, most of them are purely 'internal', dealing with the equilibrium between national sources of law and the coherence of the various references to equal opportunities (for example, the question of positive action). Nonetheless, the question of the effectiveness of proceedings and sanctions — especially regarding issues such as indirect discrimination and sexual harassment — might be areas where a national judge could ask for an interpretation of EU Law (art. 234EC (177)). This

50. See for example Monteiro Fernandes, A. (1995), 'La réglementation du temps de travail au Portugal — Une approche de synthèse', European Forum *The Regulation of Working Time in the European Union — Gender Approach*, Florence: European University Institute.
51. Ferreira, V., Tavares, T. and Portugal, S. (eds), (1998), 'Positive action and employment segregation', *Shifting Bonds, Shifting Bounds — Women, Mobility and Citizenship in Europe*, Oeiras: Celta editora, p. 272.

might occur, as far as indirect discrimination is concerned, if improvements to the protection afforded to part-time workers become a reality in the foreseable future.[52]

Normative Effect of International and Community Law in Portugal

Portugal is party to a significant array of international or regional human rights agreements.[53] These affect Portugal's internal legal order in a number of ways. First, it should be noted that Portugal is a monist legal system which integrates a plurality of norms into its internal legal order (normative pluralism). Under the CPR, international treaties which have been ratified or approved become part of the Portuguese legal order as soon as they have been published in the *Official Journal* (*Diário da República*) (art. 8 § 2 CPR). In addition, norms issued by the international organisations of which Portugal is a member have immediate force of law within the Portuguese national legal order, as long as the statutes of the particular organisation so provide (art. 8 § 3 CPR).[54] This latter principle applies to EU law, where binding EU acts produce a legal effect in the Portuguese legal order as soon as they have been published in the *Official Journal of the European Communities* without any requirement that they be published in the *Diário da República*. In the case of both 'classical' international law and EU law, binding provisions are incorporated automatically into the Portuguese legal order (art. 8 § 1 CPR) and stand at an infra-constitutional and supra-legislative level in the hierarchy of norms.

---

52. So far, part-time work has not been very common in Portugal. A recent report of the Ministry of Labour and Solidarity (MTS) examines how part-time work has been dealt with in collective bargaining and other forms of collective labour regulation in Portugal. It appears from the study that part-time jobs made up a small proportion of all jobs (4.4 per cent). The use of part-time work as a tool of employment policy has only been timidly broached in Portugal, possibly because of the relatively low rate of unemployment and low rates of pay. In the period studied in the new MTS report (1986-96), the issue of part-time work appeared in a low percentage of agreements. Janeiro, M. J. (1998), *O trabalho a tempo parcial em Portugal e a regulamentação colectiva*, Lisbon: Ministério do Trabalho e da Solidariedade.
53. Since 1955, Portugal has been a member of the United Nations (UN) and has adopted the majority of general human rights instruments with relevance to sex equality. Portugal also approved and ratified a series of ILO Conventions with an indirect impact on the situation of women workers and undertook to enforce the Global Platform for Action (1995). For further details see Casqueira Cardoso, J. (1999), *Predicting the Impact of Policy: Gender-auditing as a Means of Assessing the Probable Impact of Policy Initiatives on Women. Country Report: Portugal*, Liverpool: Feminist Legal Research Unit, School of Law, University of Liverpool, Chapter Two.
54. Even non-normative instruments, such as the UN Universal Declaration of Human Rights, have been interpreted by the Consultative Council of the Office of the Attorney-General (Ministry of Justice) as having 'a supra-legal value, delimiting the interpretative solutions provided [in national law]' (Parecer 180/81) (my translation). See Procuradoria-Geral da República. (1983), *Pareceres, Volume I*, Lisbon: Ministério da Justiça, p. 328.

In theory, individuals can challenge national law using general international law sources — including binding EU law norms.[55] However, this is exceedingly rare for two reasons: first, because European and international legal instruments are often ignored by the litigants; second, because there is no appeal court where a question of the domestic interpretation of the international source could be invoked by individuals; hence there is no real incentive for Portuguese judges to take account of such measures. An exception is the European Convention on Human Rights which provides an avenue for appeal to the European Court on Human Rights. This may be the reason why the European Convention on Human Rights is referred to more frequently by Portuguese judges than any other international instrument, although there is no extensive research assessing this.

Putting Gender onto the Law and Policy-Making Agenda

In the Portuguese context, four bodies are in charge of securing equality between the sexes. The first is a Parliamentary body, the Parliamentary Commission for Parity, Equal Opportunities and Family. Then there are two governmental bodies, the Commission for Equality and Women's Rights, and the Commission for Equality in Work and Employment. A fourth body, the High Commissioner for Matters relating to the Promotion of Equality and the Family, plays an unclear role in the co-ordination of initiatives in the field of equality between men and women.

The Parliamentary Commission for Parity, Equal Opportunities and Family

Created in November 1995, the Commission for Parity, Equal Opportunities and Family replaced a sub-committee on women's questions that previously existed within the Commission on Constitutional Affairs. The Commission is the body within the legislative assembly where women's concerns may be voiced. The Commission has a membership of 22 MPs with the political parties being represented on the Commission in proportion to the number of seats each party holds in the Assembly (Hondt method).[56] Decisions are taken

55. Gonçalves Pereira, A. and De Quadros, F. (1997), *Direito Internacional Público*, Coimbra: Livraria Almedina, pp. 147-148.
56. The present composition of the Commission is as follows: ten MPs from the Socialist Party; seven MPs from the Social Democrat Party; two MPs from the Portuguese Communist Party; two MPs from the Centre-Right Party (CDS/PP); one MP representing minority parties (PEV).

by means of a simple majority of those voting. The Commission approves legislative initiatives on equal opportunities between men and women. It is also said to play a pedagogical function, by changing opinions on specific gender issues. The practical impact of the Commission's participation in the law-making process is limited.

The Commission for Equality and Women's Rights

The Commission for Equality and Women's Rights (CEWR), set up by Decree-Law 166/91 of 9 May 1991, is an historical survivor as it replaced the earlier Commission on the Status of Women which was created by Decree-Law no. 485/77 of 17 November 1977 only three years after the revolution of 1974, in an atmosphere of progressive transition to democratic institutions.

The CEWR is a government body attached to the Prime Minister's Office and it works under the authority of the High Commissioner for Matters relating to the Promotion of Equality and the Family. The CEWR consists of: a President, a Co-ordinating Committee and a Consultative Council, composed of an Interministerial Section, an NGO and an Administrative Section. The Chairperson of the Consultative Council is the President of CEWR.

The Consultative Council is a body which ensures the participation of government departments and non-governmental organisations in the pursuit of the Commission's objectives and contributes to defining and implementing policies on women and equality. The Consultative Council of the Commission ensures that Portugal is represented in the European Women's Lobby. The Consultative Council's four main activities are research, training, the provision of documentation, information and publications and legal matters. On this last issue, the CEWR has a Legal Division that has three main tasks: first, it is supposed to research, evaluate and prepare reports on the implementation of EU law. Second, the Legal Division prepares, when asked to do so by the Prime Minister's Office, reports in areas within the CEWR's competence. The third and main task of the Legal Division is to provide legal information and advice to the public.

The Interministerial Section of the Consultative Council is made up of representatives of government departments which are likely to be the source of policies that will have an effect on the status and situation of women and on the promotion of equality. These departments are identified by the member of government responsible for the Commission and the appointment of representatives is a matter for the Ministers responsible for those departments. The three main tasks of the Interministerial Section are:

- to ensure the co-operation of all sectors of government in the pursuit of the objectives of the Commission;
- to provide information, made available through their particular departments, on the situation of women, which will influence the promotion of equal rights and opportunities;
- to give its opinion on the annual programme of action of the Commission and on projects which have been submitted to it[57] and to follow up and evaluate the implementation of those policies on equality resulting from international commitments, particularly those arising as a result of Portugal's entry into the EU.

The law which established the CEWR gives the representatives of government departments on the Consultative Council the status of equal opportunities counsellors, and their respective departments are supposed to ensure that they receive the technical and logistic support necessary to carry out this task. According to a 1994 Resolution on Equal Opportunities those representatives also have to promote the adoption and implementation of specific equality measures in their respective departments.

The NGO Section of the Consultative Council consists of 43 national organisations with the same objectives as the Commission as well as organisations active in or with programmes for improving the living conditions and status of women or which promote equality. Organisations are granted membership of this Section by the President of CEWR once their terms of reference have been evaluated. The NGO Section helps to define policy on the situation of women and on rights and equal opportunities, and gives the views of the different organisations. It helps to implement policies which have been agreed on, by facilitating projects involving the member organisations and by mobilising women or women's groups to which the organisations have access. It gives its opinion on CEWR's annual programme of action and on projects which have been submitted to CEWR.[58]

The Commission for Equality in Work and Employment

The Commission for Equality in Work and Employment (CEWE), which was created in 1979, is part of the Ministry of Labour and Solidarity and that

57. The submission of a programme of projects allows the CEWR to indicate what amount of money it will need from the State budget in the following year.
58. The submission of a programme of projects of the CEWR to the NGOs helps the latter to adapt their projects to the CEWR programme.

Ministry exercises authority over it and is responsible for controlling it. CEWE's structure and powers are regulated by Decree-Law 392/79 of 20 September 1979, as amended by Decree-Law 426/88 of 18 November 1988. CEWE is a tripartite body involving the government and the social partners and it is composed of representatives of Ministries, trade union associations (CGTP and UGT) and employers' associations (CIP and CCP). The CEWE has no local or regional institutions.

The CEWE's mandate is to promote the application of Decree-Law 392/79, which 'aims to guarantee women equality with men as regards opportunities and treatment at work and in employment'. Its powers have been extended in respect of one specific issue: the dismissal of pregnant women, women having recently given birth or who are breast-feeding, by Law 17/95 of 9 July 1995.

In order to carry out its mandate, the CEWE produces research, handles complaints and gives opinions on matters relevant to women, particularly in the field of work, employment and training. More specifically, the CEWE's responsibilities include the following:

- making recommendations to the Minister responsible for labour for the adoption of legislative, regulatory and administrative provisions that will improve application of the regulations on equality;
- promoting studies and research with a view to eliminating discrimination against women at work and in employment as well as publicising cases of proven breaches of the legal provisions on equality;
- advising the bodies responsible for drafting collective agreements, with a view to establishing the correct correlations between the various occupational categories and their respective pay levels;
- issuing and approving opinions on equality at work and in employment. The recommendations the CEWE makes are on concrete cases concerning equality in the workplace and in employment.

The CEWE has considerable authority in relation to the assessment and handling of complaints about discrimination at work. It also regularly examines job advertisements for discrimination.[59] The CEWE has pointed to

59. The CEWE has found that, on average, some 50 per cent of advertisements in three national daily newspapers discriminate on the grounds of sex. This figure gives an idea of the extent of discrimination practised at the recruitment stage, indicating that advertising employers have a clear idea of the sex of the person they intend to recruit, without there being any objective reason for this.

the need for clauses to be prepared, in readiness for collective bargaining, which would give the Labour Inspectorate the right to obtain prior access to advertisements so that the Inspectorate could alert employers to any discrimination therein. The CEWE's advisory role and provision of services to those bodies responsible for collective bargaining has been reinforced by the Global Plan for Equal Opportunities.

Finally, the CEWE has one power in the field of employment which stands out in the Portuguese institutional landscape. According to Decree-Law 136/85 of 3 May 1985, it is compulsory for any employer to ask for an opinion from the CEWE before the employer dismisses a pregnant worker, or one who has recently given birth or is breast-feeding (art. 30). The dominant *opinio juris* considers that if the opinion of the CEWE were to be against dismissal, the dismissal would be void.

The High Commissioner for Matters relating to the Promotion of Equality and the Family

At government level, there is a High Commissioner for Matters relating to the Promotion of Equality and the Family who is responsible for taking decisions in a defined field of competence which includes several specific functions — for example help to poor children. and supervision over the CEWR. The High Commissioner's role and remit have been extended by the Global Plan for Equal Opportunities.

The Global Plan for Equal Opportunities 1997

The general law and policy-making framework in relation to women's issues in Portugal is intended to be significantly modified with the implementation by public bodies of Resolution 49/97 of the Council of Ministers, a Global Plan for Equal Opportunities (Global Plan), which was approved on 6 March 1997. It is the first government programme referring extensively to the promotion of equal opportunities in all sectors of policy-making. The Global Plan makes the High Commissioner for Matters relating to the Promotion of Equality and the Family responsible for encouraging the execution of those measures that form part of the Global Plan, by promoting its monitoring by the Interministerial Section of the Consultative Council of the CEWR. The Global Plan is binding on those Ministries which are involved in the execution of the actions and measures set out in the document. Responsibility for any financial charges also falls on those Ministries.

The Global Plan first recalls that the participation of women in political decision-making in Portugal is very limited and that the labour market suffers from strong sectorial and vertical segregation of female employment, with female employees concentrated in the health and education sectors and in lower or middle management positions within the employment hierarchy. The Plan then acknowledges the need to redress these inequalities affecting specific groups of women (adolescent mothers, older women and lone mothers). These social groups are extremely vulnerable to poverty and are at risk of social exclusion. Invoking demographic and economic arguments, but making no mention of EU law, the Global Plan refers to the objectives of the government and to the commitment assumed by the countries that signed the Platform of Action at the Fourth United Nations World Conference on Women.

The Global Plan contains one general objective: namely integrating the principle of equal opportunities between men and women into all economic, social and cultural policies. This general objective is to be realised by focusing on six specific objectives in the fields of violence against women, labour relations, conciliation between family and working lives, welfare regarding family and maternity, health and education, culture and science. The Global Plan does not include any specific measure for addressing women and poverty. Each objective is to be implemented by a particular body.

Mainstreaming, though not mentioned by name, is part of the general objectives of the Global Plan, namely Objective 1.5: 'to ponder [that is to integrate] gender considerations in the impact studies of the different measures and programmes of each government department in order to evaluate their effects on the living conditions of men and women'.[60]

The Global Plan also imposed an obligation on those Ministries involved in achieving the Plan's objectives to monitor its implementation. With this aim in mind, Equal Opportunities Counsellors (named 'Conselheiras' which is a feminine noun) have been established within the relevant Ministries. The concrete impact of this institutionalisation has been limited. One of the main reasons for this is the unwillingness of some Ministries to give a central role to the Counsellors. Another reason is the lack of efficiency in the communication networks: all the requests are

60. The Ministries responsible for the implementation of this measure are: the Presidency of the Council of Ministers; the Ministry for Home Affairs; the Ministry for Equipment, Planning and Land Administration; the Ministry of Justice; the Ministry of Economy; the Ministry of Agriculture, Rural Development and Fishing; the Ministry of Education; the Ministry of Health; the Ministry for Qualification and Employment; the Ministry for Solidarity and Social Security; the Ministry for Science and Technology.

centralised at the level of the cabinet of the Minister or Secretary of State. The research undertaken shows that Equal Opportunities Counsellors have little or no role in responding to requests for information on gender matters.

One of the innovations of the Global Plan (Objective 3.2) is the creation 'in the Commission for Equality in Work and Employment [of] an observatory to follow the question of equality in the instruments of the collective regulation of work, namely to detect and prevent direct and indirect discrimination and also to encourage the introduction of positive actions and of a new culture of equality in work environments, and to this effect to promote the sensitisation of trade-union and employer negotiators'. It is too early to assess the impact of this observatory.

The Global Plan imposes a duty on the High Commissioner for Matters relating to the Promotion of Equality and the Family to assess the result of this programme by March 24 1998. This assignment of responsibility has not been without its problems. The High Commissioner regards the CEWR as the entity responsible for executing the Global Plan (as it is in effect an executive body), and vice-versa. Whether the Global Plan will prove effective remains to be seen.

Conclusion

Portugal can be characterised as a country where the gap between law and reality is vast. Despite a 'modern' constitution and an institutionalised commitment to equality, the detailed laws and the institutions working on the ground appear to have very little impact on the day-to-day activities of employers and the state. In this context mainstreaming may be regarded as an opportunity to activate existing mechanisms, with a view to closing the gap between the sexes, as well as broadening the areas in which gender is perceived as a significant concern.

Despite the ambitious and, to a degree, innovative approach promoted in the Global Plan, the structures and processes of the existing Portuguese law and policy-making framework have remained largely unchanged. In particular, the equality bodies (CEWR and CEWE) has not been reformed and remain untouched. They have proved resistant to any superior intervention by the government and have survived despite their contradictory roles, duplication of work and, at the end of the day, inefficiency.

5 Making Women Count in Spain

FÁTIMA ARRANZ, BEATRIZ QUINTANILLA AND CRISTINA VELÁZQUEZ

As Spain has only had continuous democratic rule since 1975, formal government bodies and policies designed to incorporate gender issues into the law and policy-making process have been slower to develop than in other European states. However, there is now evidence of an evolving system of agencies, legislation and equality plans designed for that task. Several articles in the Constitution establish gender equality as a superior value to be pursued and protected. Since the early 1980s the principle of equal employment opportunities for men and women has been developed through a series of employment laws, and more recently Spain has legislated on the rights of workers with regard to pregnancy, adoption and family responsibilities. Legislation of this kind is complemented by the work of the Instituto de la Mujer (IM) which is formally charged with promoting public policies that would foster equality between men and women. The IM is responsible for preparing the Equal Opportunities Plans which set out Spain's gender equality goals and objectives over three year periods. The Third Equal Opportunities Plan 1997-2000[1] aims *inter alia* to promote better recognition of the contribution of women to the economy, to improve women's access to the labour market, to allow for greater participation of women in decision-making bodies, to encourage the equal sharing of responsibilities within the family and to tackle female poverty. It also introduces the concept of mainstreaming into the Spanish law and policy-making context.

However, it could be argued that to date the long term impact of these mechanisms has been restricted. For example, while women's participation in the labour market has been increasing since the 1970s,[2] socio-economic data reveals the persistence of discrimination in the kind of work that women undertake. Employment statistics show that 5.2 per cent of part-time

1. *Instituo de la Mujer. (1997), III Plan para la Igualdad de Oportunidades entre Mujeres y Hombres 1997-2000*, Madrid: Ministerio de Trabajo y Asuntos Sociales, Instituto de la Mujer.
2. As shown by Garrido, this increased participation has significant time periods: the first increase occurs between 1968 and 1974, and the second one develops from 1981 onwards: Garrido, L. J. (1992), *Las dos biografias de la mujer en España*, Madrid: Ministerio de Asuntos Sociales, Instituto de la Mujer.

workers are women, and only 31.1 per cent of women have full-time jobs. On the other hand, 38.1 per cent of all temporary contracts are filled by women, and only 34.87 per cent of women have permanent contracts. There is a significant gender pay gap: average monthly salaries for women amount to 73.2 per cent of those for men. As elsewhere many Spanish women bear the double workload of paid and unpaid labour.[3]

The following account will outline in more detail the various politicial and legal mechanisms that exist to incorporate gender into the law and policy-making processes in Spain and will assess the reasons for their limited effectiveness to date.

The Political and Legal Landscape in Spain

The Spanish State is a parliamentary democracy, defined by the Spanish Constitution (SC) as a social and democratic State based on the rule of law. The King (Juan Carlos I) is the Head of the State and, in constitutional theory, the highest representation of the State. However he has neither legislative nor executive power and requires the endorsement of other constitutional bodies in order to perform any act related to his office, among others, to sanction and promulgate laws.[4]

The Spanish Parliament (*las Cortes Generales*) is composed of two elected chambers: the Congress of Deputies (*Congreso de los Diputados*) — the Lower House — and the Senate — the Upper House. In the Spanish system, the Congress has primacy over the Senate:[5] bills are introduced and debated first in the Congress and then in the Senate. Afterwards, bills come back to the Congress, who can accept or reject the Senate's amendments by a simple majority, and overrule its veto by an absolute majority. Within each chamber, bills are studied and debated in the relevant Parliamentary Commission.[6]

3. (1998), *Panorama Sociolaboral de la Mujer en España*, No. 11, Madrid: Consejo Económico y Social.
4. Román Marugán, P. (1995), 'La Jefatura del Estado', in Román, P. (ed.), *Sistema Político Español*, Madrid: McGraw and Hill/Interamericana de España.
5. The organisation of the Spanish territory is the only matter within the exclusive competence of the Senate, this chamber being the constitutional body in charge of the territorial representation of the State.
6. Nowadays, most of the legislative activity of the Parliament takes place within these Parliamentary Commissions — subdivisions of the chamber which perform the ordinary functions of Parliament. As permitted by the Constitution, and in order to reduce the duties of the chambers (article 76, SC), most of these Commissions have complete power to legislate (via Commission laws), if so agreed by the Plenary Session of the chamber. The chambers, nonetheless, have the power to debate and vote on any bill previously delegated to the Commissions: Lucas Murillo de la Cueva, P. (1983), 'Los órganos constitucionales' in de Blas, A. (ed.), *Introducción al Sistema Político Español*, Barcelona: Editorial Teide p. 149.

The Commission then submits a report to facilitate debate and voting when the bill is considered in the relevant Plenary Session.

The Spanish Cabinet consists of the President, the Vice-Presidents and Ministers. Government and Cabinet are almost equivalent terms. However, even though the Cabinet is bound by collective responsibility, the President has final responsibility. In fact, the Spanish government has a distinctly presidential configuration: the President enjoys considerable discretionary power, and clear supremacy over the Ministers in the Cabinet, having the power *inter alia* to give directions about the specific policies to be developed within each Department.[7]

The number of members of the Cabinet is so large, and their responsibilities so wide, that the government has developed new solutions to permit the delegation of some issues to other bodies. The Delegated Commissions of the government, created by the government to deal with sectional issues, are restricted and specialised meetings of a limited number of Ministers. The General Commission of Vice-Secretaries is a meeting of all the Vice-Secretaries (*Subsecretarios*) from all the Ministries with the formal task of preparing the ground for the deliberations of the Cabinet. In practice, however, this Commission solves many of the issues formally assigned to the Cabinet. These meetings are important for the different Ministries as they offer an opportunity for gaining approval for their respective projects.[8]

Even though legislating is supposed to be the main function of the Parliament, it is the government which actually formulates and elaborates most bills and therefore determines the content of most legislation. This phenomenon occurs because of the government's control of the Parliamentary majority, and its greater access to technical and analytical resources, which mean that it is better able to foresee potential difficulties that may be encountered in the enactment of the law.[9]

The Spanish State is an 'Autonomic State', that is, a state with a territorial organisation in between that of a regional and a federal State. Article 2 of the SC acknowledges and guarantees the right to autonomy (that is self government) of those nationalities and regions that compose the Spanish State. According to the Constitution (article 137), the Spanish State is territorially organised into municipalities, provinces, and Autonomous Communities.[10] In 1981, the Spanish Constitutional Court defined an

7. Olías de Lima, B. (1995), 'El Gobierno', in Román P. (ed.), *Sistema Político Español*, Madrid: McGraw and Hill/Interamericana de España, 1995, p. 113.
8. Ibid, p. 117.
9. Sánchez de Dios, M. (1995), 'Las Cortes Generales', in Román P. (ed.), *Sistema Político Español*, Madrid: McGraw and Hill/Interamericana de España, pp. 87-89.
10. So far 17 Autonomous Communities have been constituted in Spain (only the provinces of Ceuta and Melilla are not included in any of the existing *Autonomias*).

Autonomía as a limited (and not sovereign) power that, without going against the unity of the State, manages its own territorial interests.

Contrary to the Anglo-Saxon tradition, judicial power in Spain is based on the Latin tradition where the judges apply a previously codified law that attempts to anticipate every particular case that could arise, leaving little room for the interpretation of the law.[11]

The Law and Policy-Making Process

The law and policy-making processes in Spain are mostly in the hands of the government and the bureaucratic apparatus. Most if not all of the possible control mechanisms by which other political forces and/or the citizenry can challenge the outcomes of the law and policy-making processes can be invoked only after the event — *a posteriori*. The most important of these mechanisms is an appeal to the Spanish Constitutional Court. The Spanish Constitutional Court (SCC) is the constitutional body in charge of determining the constitutionality of the laws making up the Spanish legal system: this is the only body within the State which can give an authoritative interpretation of the Constitution.

Three major forms of appeal can be heard in this Court.[12] First, there is the (abstract) appeal of unconstitutionality, which can be presented by either the President, the Ombudsman, 50 Deputies, 50 Senators, or the Assembly of any Autonomous Community affected by that law. Secondly, the question of unconstitutionality can be raised in relation to a concrete situation: that is, the constitutionality of a law can be challenged in the course of judicial proceedings by a judge or a party involved in the proceedings, in relation to a law that has to be applied in those proceedings. Finally, there is the Appeal of Constitutional Protection (*Recurso de Amparo*), which is designed to guarantee the protection of those rights and freedoms enjoyed by Spanish citizens. Individual citizens, the Ombudsman and the Public Prosecutor can formulate this kind of appeal.[13]

---

11. Sánchez de Dios, M. (1995), 'El Poder Judicial y la Jurisdicción Constitucional', in Román, P. (ed.), *Sistema Político Español*, Madrid: McGraw and Hill/Interamericana de España, pp. 137-138.
12. The SCC also has the power to decide matters regarding conflicts among Autonomous Communities or between these Communities and the State.
13. The fundamental rights invoked most frequently in this kind of appeal have been the principle of equality and the principle of effective protection of the law: Sánchez de Dios, op cit, n. 11, p. 158.

The Ombudsman is a constitutional institution linked to the Spanish Parliament and acting by virtue of powers delegated by the Parliament. His or her main duty is to control executive power — and, in particular, the performance of duties by the Public Administration — and to defend the rights and liberties of the citizenry. The Ombudsman can submit appeals of Constitutional Protection and abstract appeals of unconstitutionality to the Spanish Constitutional Court.

In addition to the Parliament, a legislative initiative can come from the following actors: the government,[14] the Autonomous Communities and the citizenry (via a popular initiative). In the Spanish system, the government is the body promoting most legislative initiatives, either directly by referring a bill to Congress, or indirectly, through the Parliamentary group supporting the government. The bills initiated by the government have priority over bills from other sources in their passage through Parliament.[15] These bills will have previously been agreed and discussed in each Ministerial office with the respective interest groups.[16] The material authorship of a bill is usually delegated to a wide range of bureaucrats, more or less sensitive to the interests of 'their' Administration.

In addition to these legislative initiatives, the government and the Administration also have the power, delegated by Parliament, to issue standing orders and decrees with the force of law: this allows the government a quicker and more streamlined procedure for the implementation of its programme. Even in cases where the Congress has to ratify or repeal any decree-law in the 30 days following its promulgation, the government may still decide to present the bill as a *proyecto de ley* since it can introduce further modifications afterwards. The simplicity of the procedure — requiring only the approval of the Cabinet — is one of the most important reasons why this instrument is used so often to regulate specific matters.

---

14. The legislative initiatives coming from the government are called *proyectos de ley* (projects of bill) and those coming from any other actors (including the chambers) are called *propuestas de ley* (proposals of bill).
15. The formulation of the Budget is an important tool of political management which gives priority to the legislative activities and initiatives of the government, given the relationship that it establishes between the government and any other institution or constitutional body. The government can oppose any Parliamentary proposal entailing any increase or decrease of the State's income: Olías de Lima, op cit, n. 7, p. 114.
16. Given the need or the desire to integrate other political forces into the decision-making processes, the acceptance of some amendments to these bills during Parliamentary debates is not unusual. This has the effect of broadening the consensus over and hence legitimising the bill.

Other Actors in the Law and Policy-Making Process

There are few non-institutional bodies within the Spanish political system which can influence the shape of policies and measures. With regard to those institutional bodies which could play a role in the law and policy-making process, there are two that may have a strong influence on issues related to women.

The Public Administration plays a very important role in the process of law and policy-making as a whole. In the first place, the Public Administration is an active actor in the limitation and channelling of demands coming from the public. It is also the body in charge of presenting possible solutions to a problem and of suggesting the most feasible alternative, according to the availability of resources and to the political ideology of the government charged with making the final decision. Finally, once a course of action is chosen, the Public Administration is the body responsible for implementing it.[17]

The Economic and Social Council (*Consejo Económico y Social*) is an autonomous body attached to the Ministry of Labour and Social Security that was created in 1991 to advise the government on socio-economic and labour matters. The Council has to issue reports on any Bill regulating socio-economic and labour matters and, at the request of the government, on any Bill considered by the government as especially relevant for the regulation of these matters. The government or any of its members can ask for reports on any other matter. The Council has the power to prepare reports on a wide range of issues, either at the request of the government and its members, or on its own initiative. In 1993, one of the three reports prepared by the Council on its own initiative was about the status of women in Spain. In this same year, the Council created a non-permanent Working Commission to deal with the social and labour status of women in Spain.[18]

Women's Participation in Politics

An analysis of trends in women's representation in various assemblies at the national, regional and local levels shows that overall progress has been made, but that the levels of representation achieved are hardly equitable. In

---

17. Ferri Dura, J. (1995), 'Las Administraciones Públicas', in Román P. (ed.), *Sistema Político Español*, Madrid: McGraw and Hill/Interamericana de España, pp. 179-180.
18. Consejo Económico y Social (1994), *Memoria de Actividades 1993*, Madrid: Consejo Económico y Social.

the early 1980s, women barely participated in politics, and were poorly informed about political issues. In 1980, only 15 per cent of women felt that they had a relatively high level of political awareness, while less than 25 per cent were members of a political party or trade union.[19]

During the first two legislatures, after democracy was instituted in Spain in 1978, only 6.3 per cent of Congress deputies and only 3 per cent of senators were women. In 1986, on average 6.4 per cent of members of regional parliaments were women; in 1983, 2 per cent of the mayors of all the municipalities existing at that time were women; finally, women's participation in the government and in the upper echelons of the Public Administration was insignificant — in 1982 there were only three women general directors, four (provincial) civil governors or government delegates and one woman Minister.

Women's rate of participation in the current legislature (1996-2000) and the European Parliament has, however, improved. Of the total current membership of the Congress of Deputies, 22 per cent are women; of the total membership of the Senate, women represent 14.9 per cent, and of the total number of Spanish Members of the European Parliament (MEPs), women represent 27.64 per cent. As for women's presence in senior posts in the Public Administration, women now constitute 10.57 per cent of the total.[20]

Information Policies

Information policies play an important role in Spain, where the public authorities utilise the media to disseminate and promote their policies, including the policies relating to women laid out in the *Plan para la Igualdad de Oportunidades de las Mujeres* (PIOM). The executive participates directly and indirectly in the control of the media: it exerts direct control where it administers parts of the media that are public property (*Televisión Española* and *Radio Nacional*); and it exerts indirect control by means of strategic political alliances with the communications corporations which are ideologically related to the government of the day.

It is the task of the *Instituo de la Mujer* (IM) to disseminate the government's information policies relating to women. The term 'information policies on women' refers both to the information that is directed at women

19. Instituto de la Mujer. (1994), *Spanish Women on the Threshold of the 21st Century. Report Submitted by Spain to the Fourth World Conference On Women, Beijing*, 1995, Madrid: Ministerio de Asuntos Sociales, Instituto de la Mujer.
20. Instituto de la Mujer. (1997a), *III Plan para la Igualdad de Oportunidades entre Mujeres y Hombres 1997-2000*, Madrid: Ministerio de Trabajo y Asuntos Sociales, Instituto de la Mujer.

(information is disseminated, for example, about women or about women's rights), and to information about women (for example facts or images which it is felt should be promoted through the media in order to promote positive images of women). The IM is also charged with acting on behalf of women, in particular, 'women in special need of help', and 'to receive and channel, within the Public Administration, women's complaints on concrete *de jure* or *de facto* cases of sex discrimination'.[21] The IM has created 10 centres of information on women's rights in various cities in Spain and reports:

> the main activity of the centres is the advising on different fields (legal, professional, employment, social resources, health and the right of association), also performing a series of complementary activities, such as participation in meetings with the media, as well as other activities of support.[22]

Equality Legislation In Spain

The Constitution

Several articles of the Spanish Constitution (SC) deal with gender equality, establishing it as a superior value to be pursued and protected. Article 9. 2 SC sets out the principle and value of 'equality' and illustrates the attempt of the Spanish State to pursue equality in real terms through the elimination of obstacles which may hinder the progress of particular individuals and/or social groups. Article 14 SC states that all Spaniards are equal before the law and may not in any way be discriminated against on account of birth, race, sex, religion, opinion or any condition or personal or social circumstances. The first clause is understood as requiring that like cases are treated alike, unless there is an objective reason for differential treatment, which then must be fair and proportionate. This clause is directed at public authorities and is directly related to the prohibition on arbitrary action by public authorities set out elsewhere in the Constitution.[23] The second part of Article 14 SC, outlawing discrimination, extends the duty to citizens (private parties) and hence also to the negotiating parties in collective agreements.

---

21. Articles 2. 11 and 2. 12 of Law 16/83 (24 October) of the creation of the IM.
22. Instituto de la Mujer. (1997), *Memoria del Instituto de la Mujer 1996*, Madrid: Ministerio de Asuntos Sociales, Instituto de la Mujer.
23. Cf. Article 9. 3 SC.

The effect of Article 14 SC is to establish that the principles of equality and non-discrimination form part of the 'reinforced protection area' whereby it is presupposed that particular groups or individuals have suffered disadvantage within the Spanish social system and that the 'system' (or Spanish society) has a responsibility to compensate for such disadvantage.[24]

This formulation of the constitutional prohibition on discrimination was drafted after the U.S. Supreme Court had ruled on race discrimination cases such as *Griggs*.[25] It allows for three types of discrimination to be differentiated: direct open discrimination, direct but hidden discrimination and indirect discrimination. Direct discrimination refers to a situation where the worker's gender constitutes the factor for their discrimination. Direct open discrimination refers to a situation where it is possible to single out specific factors responsible for the discrimination. Direct but hidden discrimination refers to a situation where specific factors are not evident or clearly responsible for the discrimination.

Indirect discrimination, on the other hand, refers to a situation where gender is no longer the determining factor that leads to the differential treatment of workers. Rather, the differential treatment (which may relate, for example, to age or strength) seems to affect women systematically as a group. Thus, the situation qualifies as indirect discrimination because the different treatment is not the result of gender differences but impacts on a specific gender group. In 1991 the Spanish Constitutional Court adopted an interpretation of indirect effect in which it recognised that indirect discrimination, as opposed to direct discrimination, does not require any motive but simply requires the existence of a policy which, whether consciously or not, has a detrimental effect on women, clearly evident in the result of its practice. The collective element of this type of discrimination, geared not towards an individual with determined characteristics but towards a group to which that individual belongs, is also recognised.[26]

This last feature of the prohibition on discrimination leads to a proven mandate, directly connected with the duties of public power as established in article 9. 2 of the SC, to remove those obstacles that prevent individuals

24. Goldman, A. H. (1979), *Justice and Reverse Discrimination*, Princeton: Princeton University Press, p. 171; Rodriguez Pineiro, M. (1986), 'Principio de Iqualdad y Derecho del Tradajo', in Rodriguez Pineiro, M. and Fernandez Lopez, M. F. (eds), *Iqualdad y descriminacion*, Madrid: Tecnos, pp. 1087-88.
25. *W. S. Griggs v Duke Power Company* 401 U. S., see also *Gaston County, North Carolina v U. S* 395 U. S.
26. Ruling 145 of 1991, Spanish Constitutional Court, BOE de 22 de Julio de 1991. Rectificaciones en BOE de 5 de Noviembre de 1991.

and groups from achieving real, as well as effective, equality and freedom. In this way, the principle of non-discrimination will not only justify but will also demand the establishment of particular measures and treatment in specific cases, necessary for the elimination of the previously mentioned obstacles. Thus 'positive action' is required to correct the particular disadvantages affecting groups identified by the factors enumerated in the second chapter of article 14 SC.

This approach requires that the list in article 14 SC must nowadays be approached from a different perspective than was previously the case. This is because once it is recognised that an intention to discriminate is no longer relevant, the factors enumerated in the list cease to constitute factors of discrimination; instead, they should be regarded as variables or characteristics which apply to the population and which allow the identification of specific groups which are in a disadvantaged situation: it is now perceived that the variables in the list are not the only ones relevant, merely those specifically identified by the drafters of the Constitution as in need of rigorous and concrete protection.[27]

Through interpretations of the Constitution such as this,[28] the right to equality and freedom from discrimination in the Spanish Constitution has evolved, in accordance with international and EU practice, from a concept of formal equality towards one of real and effective equality. In the Spanish context this has entailed a focus on the social factors which disadvantage particular groups, rather than on discrimination as experienced by a particular individual. The prohibition on gender discrimination is reinforced in other parts of the Spanish Constitution, noticeably in article 35 SC concerning the right to work.

Employment Law

The general principle of equal employment opportunities between men and women is set out in article 4. 2 of the Act 8/1980 of 11 March, which reads: 'workers are entitled, in respect of their work, to . . . suffer no discrimination in terms of employment . . . on gender grounds'. This general principle is developed and defined in further detail in article 17. 1 which stipulates that 'all regulatory precepts, clauses of collective agreements, individual covenants and

27. Rodriguez Pineiro, op cit, n. 24, p. 177 et seq.
28. See also Ruling 166 of 1988, Spanish Constitutional Court, BOE de 14 Octubre de 1988, which dealt with hidden discrimination, recognising pregnancy dismissal, where the employee could have been assigned to more appropriate tasks, as hidden direct discrimination.

employers' unilateral decisions shall be null and void . . . where they entail favorable or adverse treatment in terms of employment . . . on gender grounds'. The principle of gender equality in relation to conditions of employment is set out in articles 17. 1, 24 and 28 of the By-laws.

The first amendment to the Workers' By-laws was introduced by Act 3/89 of 3 March, whereby maternity leave was extended to 16 weeks and measures were introduced to favour equal treatment of women in terms of employment as a way of attaining the objective established in the First Equal Opportunities Plan of making the retention of a job compatible with maternity or paternity. It also established the right to return to the same job during the first year's leave of absence for child rearing, for either the father or the mother, as well as introducing measures to prevent sexual harassment. Similar standards are provided for civil servants. Act 8/1992 of 30 April amended the provisions of the By-laws and the Act on Measures to Reform Civil Service Rules on Leave. According to these new standards, leave for adoption of a minor between the ages of nine months and five years provided in the regulations may be taken, at the discretion of the employee or civil servant, either starting from the date of the administrative or legal ruling establishing custody, or from the date of the court finding on formal adoption.

Act 11/1994 of 19 May amended article 28 of the By-laws, substituting the term 'work of equal value' for the term 'equal work', pursuant to the terms of the Second Equal Opportunities Plan (1993-95). Finally, the 1994 Act also addressed briefly the issue of sexual harassment: Article 4. 2. f states that the worker has the right to the 'respect of his privacy and due consideration of his dignity, including the protection against verbal or physical offence of sexual nature'. In relation to this, article 96. 11 indicates that any action taken by an employer that would be against the respect of privacy or the due consideration of the worker's dignity would be a serious offence.

Enforcement

Act 8/88 of April 7 on Infringements of and Sanctions under Labour Law was passed in response to one of the objectives of the First Equal Opportunities Plan. This Act establishes that serious violations are committed in relation to employment when employers' acts infringe upon employee privacy or personal dignity or when employers' decisions entail gender bias with regard to emoluments, working hours, training, promotion and other conditions of employment, and in relation to on-the-job safety, health and hygiene when employers fail to observe regulations relating to leave for pregnancy and breast-feeding. Finally, the establishment of hiring conditions through publicity, circulation of job offers or any other means which would constitute gender-based discrimination is stipulated to be a serious violation on the part of the employer.

Act 7/1989 of 12 April, on Standards for Labour Court Proceedings stipulates that in labour disputes where the plaintiff alleges gender-based discrimination, it shall be incumbent upon the defendant to provide objective and reasonable justification of the fairness of the measures adopted, through submission of such evidence as he or she deems appropriate. This provision is in response to the above mentioned objective of the First Equal Opportunities Plan.

The Act on Labour Court Proceedings, approved under Royal Legislative Decree 521/1990 of 27 April, provides that when a question of discrimination based on sex arises in labour trials the Judge or Court may entreat competent Public Bodies to issue an official statement.

The 1990 Act also included for the first time in its article 96 the modification of the burden of proof in those procedures where sex discrimination is at issue. The Spanish Constitutional Court has, in fact, adopted such a practice since the early 1980s in those cases when there was a need to determine whether there was discrimination for trade-union membership or not, but there was not any law to deal with this matter. When the Spanish Labour Court Proceedings Law was being reformed in 1990, the draft Directive on the burden of proof already existed and was expected to be adopted. Accordingly, the Spanish legislator introduced an article on the subject into the new law, in order to avoid the need for an immediate amendment to the law after the Directive was adopted. The opposition of the United Kingdom then prevented the adoption of the Directive, but in Spanish law the modification of the burden of proof had already been secured. The recent Directive 97/80/EC of the Council of 15 December 1997, in relation to the burden of proof in cases of discrimination for reason of sex, does not demand any modification of Spanish law. It would, however, clarify Spanish law if the definition of indirect discrimination included in article 2. 2 of this Directive was adopted.

Social Security

Since the promulgation of the Spanish Constitution, it has not been permissible to establish differential treatment on gender grounds in respect of social security. Measures were taken to eliminate all such differential treatment existing under social security regulations, whether such discrimination affected men or women; in this regard, a Constitutional Court ruling eliminated discriminatory treatment of men with respect to payment of widower pensions.

Royal Decree Law 7/1989 of 29 December, replaced by Act 5/1990 on urgent budgetary, financial and tax measures, enabled spouses proving that they were employed by their husband or wife to qualify for social security. Act 26/1990 of 20 December, which deals with non-contributory social security benefits, introduced an important innovation with regard to benefits for dependent children, whereby a period of leave of absence for child rearing would not prejudice entitlement to social security, subject to the employee's entitlement to return to his or her job, so that workers exercising their right to this leave of absence are not penalized with respect to contribution periods; this provision contributes to enforcing the provisions of Act 3/1989 on the protection of maternity and paternity.

Until 20 February 1989, when the Constitutional Court ruled to the contrary, family units were under an obligation to file a joint income tax return, including the sum of the incomes of all members of the family. Act 20/1989 of 28 July, which amended personal income tax and property tax legislation to take account of the Constitutional Court ruling, recognized each family member's right to file a separate return providing that, where one member decides to do so, all other members also file accordingly. Finally, Act 18/1991 of 6 June on personal income taxes rectified the discriminatory treatment of persons with custody of their children under earlier regulations whereby they were obliged to declare the child support they received for their children as income. This Act provides that such income is tax-exempt, in response to one of the objectives of the First Equal Opportunities Plan.

Maternity Legislation

Article 26 of the Law 31/1995 of 8 November, on the Prevention of Labour Risks, incorporated Directive 92/85/EEC (the Pregnant Workers Directive) into Spanish law. The Directive required Member States to implement measures to foster improvements in health and safety at work and in security of employment for pregnant women, and women who have recently given birth or who are breast-feeding. The Directive establishes a minimum duration of fourteen weeks maternity leave, while in Spain the minimum duration of that leave has for a long time been sixteen weeks or eighteen weeks in cases of multiple births. The Directive indicates that working women should be guaranteed 'the maintenance of remuneration and/or appropiate benefits . . .'. In the Spanish regulations, access to maternity benefits is conditional upon the fulfillment of a number of requirements, such as the fulfillment of a previous quotation of work.

The Pregnant Workers Directive did have an impact on Spanish law in relation to women on part-time employment contracts or training contracts.

Initially, women on these sorts of contract could not obtain certain social security benefits, in particular maternity benefit. Once Directive 92/85/EEC was passed, the regulations governing such contracts were reformed to include protection for maternity, making it possible for working women on part-time or training contracts to qualify for these social security benefits.

Directive 92/85/CEE provides that once the risks to working women have been evaluated the necessary safety measures have to be adopted to eliminate these risks, or instead, women must be given a change of post/job, where possible; otherwise working women may be granted the right to stop working without loss of pay. This right has not been recognized in Spanish law. In addition, Spain has not acted in relation to the list in the Directive setting out agents, procedures and work conditions regarded as harmful to the health of the mother and the foetus.

It is expected that Spanish legislation will be harmonised with Directive 97/81/EC of the Council, of 15 December 1997, in relation to the framework agreement on part-time work in which the prohibition on discrimination between full-time workers and part-time workers is set out.

Spanish Equality Legislation and the European Union

In spite of the fact that Spain joined the European Communities in 1986, Article 28 of the Workers Statute was only amended in 1994, to state that: 'The employer must pay the same salary for work of the same value'. Prior to this, article 28 made reference only to equal pay for equal work, which was one of the main reasons why the Spanish courts permitted the existence of discrimination when work was not exactly the same or was not described in the same manner. With the 1994 amendment, Article 28 of the Workers Statute fell into line with what is contemplated in Directive 75/117/EEC (the Equal Pay Directive).[29]

In relation to both Directive 75/117/EEC (the Equal Pay Directive), concerning equality of pay and Directive 76/207/EEC (the Equal Treatment Directive), concerning the enforcement of the principle of equal treatment between men and women in relation to access to a job, training and professional promotion, and work conditions, Spanish law falls short. The relevant articles of the Workers Statute referring to this matter provide as follows:

29. In spite of the delay in amending article 28, the Constitutional Court has underlined that the equality of remuneration principle referred not only to equal jobs, but also to equivalent jobs. On this point Constitutional Court Ruling 145/1991 is particularly significant.

- that the principle of equality in access to employment will be guaranteed and no discrimination made by reason of race, sex, religion, opinion or any condition or personal or social circumstances (Art. 16. 2);
- that the criteria used to define categories and groups will employ common rules for workers of either sex (Art. 22. 4); and
- that the criteria for promotion in the company will employ common rules for workers of either sex (Art. 24. 2)

As can be observed, this wording refers to the need to make company practices employ common criteria for men and women. However EU law goes somewhat further than this, requiring that it is possible to value everyone. According to the jurisprudence of the European Court of Justice it is not enough to establish 'objective' criteria which are the same for everyone; these criteria must allow the valuation of the capacities and qualities of men and women, and besides must not be put into effect in a disproportionate way.

Putting Gender onto the Law and Policy-Making Agenda

In Spain, matters related to women's rights seem to be in the hands of the IM (and equivalent bodies in those Communities and municipalities that have created them). However, these bodies have very little autonomy to develop their own policies, because they depend on higher ranking bodies within the Public Administration.

The Instituto de la Mujer

The electoral victory, with a clear majority, of the *Partido Socialista Obrero Español* (P. S.O.E.) in 1982 can be regarded as heralding the inauguration of so-called 'institutional feminism' in Spain. The Socialist Party had placed feminist demands on its electoral programme in 1979 and 1982. However, during its twelve years in office, the Socialist Party's most significant deed with regard to public policies on women was the creation in 1983 of the *Institato de la Mujer* (IM), which would come to replace the former *Subdirección de la Mujer*, which had lesser rank in the organisational structure of the Spanish Public Administration. The IM is the only institution in Spain charged with securing equality between the sexes. The whole process of gestation of the IM took place exclusively within the P. S.O.E. The feminist movement and women's associations were hardly consulted, either about the desirability of founding an organisation for equality in Spain or about the way in which that organisation should function.

On the other hand, all the Autonomous Regions (CC. AA.) of the Spanish State, following the model established by the central government in creating the IM, began to equip themselves with organisations with the same characteristics as the IM. The IM itself collaborated with some of the CC. AA. in the establishment of these equality bodies and in the organisation and subsequent administration of some of their specific programmes. The IM and the various equality bodies of the CC. AA. have reviewed their relationships periodically through the Sectorial Conference.

According to the IM, its own design was such that there were opportunities to establish and strengthen the IM's relationships with other institutions. It could also be claimed, however, that this complex net of relationships (described below) served to develop an environment in which govermental responsibilities on women's issues could be either expanded or contracted.

The law creating the IM established that its governing organs would be its director and its Governing Council (*Consejo Rector*). The Governing Council consists of representatives from twelve Ministries, all with a rank no lower than that of General Vice-Director, designated by the relevant Ministers. The president of the Governing Council is the Minister of Social Affairs and the Vice-President is the director of the IM. According to the law setting it up, the Governing Council should hold meetings at least once every six months and a Standing Committee of this Council, consisting of fewer members, should meet at least once every three months.

Legal and Political Strategies for Improving Women's Status in Spain

The IM's founding law and regulations proposed that one of the main functions of this organisation was to act as a promoter of public policies that would be established by other institutions. After the creation of the IM in 1983 the number of legal reforms and measures on equality initiated was very high (certainly in comparison with other Western countries).

Since the IM became operational, there has been an attempt to involve most Ministries in the task of promoting equality for women. Until 1987 the way to realise this objective was through persuasion in the meetings of the Governing Council and, since 1988, this process has been formalised through the adoption of Equal Opportunities Plans. The stimulus for this came, without a shadow of a doubt, from Europe. As Gil Ruiz points out,

> the integration of Spain in the European Community has meant for Spanish women the application of the affirmative action policies and the Community regulations with regard to equality issues, being obliged, as a Member State, to reach the goals set out in the Social Charter, as well as those established by the different Community guidelines.[30]

However, despite all the laws and measures developed by public authorities over the past few years — from both within and outside the IM — to promote equal opportunities for men and women, some women still have the feeling that their problems tend to be considered as secondary. The significance of the role played by the IM in the context of Spanish public policy on women may be a good indicator of this feeling. As suggested by Valiente we have to consider two factors:

> The relevance of the measures formulated and implemented by the IM itself — in terms of staff and resources involved, and the number of women affected by these measures — is considerably smaller than the equality policies established by other institutions at the bidding of the Institute. . . . The starter role of the IM as an 'agenda setter' of equality policies contrasts, however, with its practically null function as an executor of the same, or as a controller in the process of putting them into practice.[31]

The Equal Opportunities Plans for Women in Spain

The IM prepared the First Equal Opportunities Plan for the years 1988-1990.[32] This Plan consisted of a set of legislative reforms and public policies that would have to be carried out by thirteen Ministries between January of 1988 and December of 1990.[33]

---

30. Gil Ruiz, J. M. (1997), *Las Políticas de Igualdad en España: Avances y Retrocesos*, Granada: Universidad de Granada, p. 188.
31. Valiente, C. (1996), 'El feminismo institucional en España: El Instituto de la Mujer, 1983-1994', *Revista Internacional de Sociología*, no. 13, p. 178.
32. Instituto de la Mujer. (1990), *Primer Plan para la Igualdad de Oportunidades de las Mujeres 1988-1990. Evaluación*, Madrid: Ministerio de Asuntos Sociales, Instituto de la Mujer.
33. In order to make this Plan viable, a certain strategy had to be followed. As Valiente shows, 'before the Plan was presented to the Commission of Undersecretaries and to the subsequent Cabinet Meeting, feminists had already negotiated with those Ministries in order to include in the Plan only those policies that they were really prepared to implement'. Valiente, op cit, n. 31, p. 182.

The First Equal Opportunities Plan for Women 1988-1990 consisted of 120 measures that could be grouped into six areas. The first group consisted of legislative reforms to bring to an end some of the discrimination between men and women that still existed under Spanish law (the Plan paid special attention to the private, tax, and penal juridical regimes). Without denying the relevance of these reforms, it has to be said, nevertheless, that the legal equality of citizens of both genders had already been granted by the Constitution and, hence, the only purpose of these measures was to bring the law into line with the Constitution.

The second set of equality policies was related to education and culture. The five general objectives in this area were: 'to counter sexist stereotypes conveyed through teaching aids and in school curricula; to foster change in faculty attitudes . . .; to guarantee equal opportunities for boys and girls in accessing all kinds of education and training . . .; to adjust continuing education to women's specific needs; (and) to promote a non-discriminatory, non-stereotypical portrayal of women in the media'.[34]

The measures included in the third area of the Plan, employment and working relationships, sought 'to improve knowledge on female working activity; . . . to promote greater diversification and qualification for the career options available for women; . . . to undertake actions to support female employment . . . fostering in the same way the quantity and quality of female entrepreneurial activity'.[35]

The two main objectives of the fourth section — involving health issues — were 'to improve women's health, focusing on those biological aspects that are peculiar to women and render as insufficient those health services shared with the male population, (and) to raise the level of health information and education, in order to improve their own health and that of all individuals who depend on these women, both biologically and socially'.[36]

The fifth and sixth areas of the Plan — the briefest ones — were concerned with actions to increase international co-operation in relation to projects relevant to women, and to promote female associationism in Spain, essentially by means of public subsidies.

The way in which the First Equal Opportunities Plan was adopted illustrates 'the deep conviction' of the socialist government of the time in relation to equality. As Valiente points out:[37]

---

34. First Equal Opportunities Plan, op cit, n. 32, p. 42.
35. Ibid, p. 56.
36. Ibid, pp. 81-82.
37. Valiente, op cit, n. 31, pp. 183-4.

the lack of a political figure fully identified with feminism in the meetings held by the Under-secretaries and the Cabinet where the approval of the equality plans was discussed, probably entailed that nobody defended such approvals vehemently enough during any of those meetings. Therefore, the Cabinet did not approve the plan. Instead, the Cabinet 'became acquainted' with the latter; that is, the Cabinet publicly announced that they knew of its existence, but that they did not regard it as a task for the government.

The First Equal Opportunities Plan proposed measures to formally give effect to the rule of non-discrimination on the grounds of sex: as Sensat and Varella note this rule is already established in the Spanish Constitution, and is in accordance with the European Community's rules on equality between the sexes.[38] Although this formal equality of the sexes before the law (rule of non-discrimination) entails some progress towards social justice, it does not acknowledge the inequality of material opportunities which exist between the sexes.

The Second Equal Opportunities Plan for Women, 1993-1995[39] was delayed in its preparation for two years beyond initial projections. Its ten main objectives were: 'to enforce and develop equal rights legislation; to promote women's equal participation in the processes of formulation and transmission of knowledge; to balance women's share in the labour force, in both quantitative and qualitative terms'; to portray a social image of women more in keeping with current realities; 'to promote an equal sharing of domestic responsibilities; to increase women's participation in society and politics; to contribute to women's access to decision-making positions'; to improve health care conditions specifically affecting women; 'to achieve social integration of groups of women in marginal situations'; and 'to integrate equality policies on an international scale'.[40]

Unlike the First Plan, the Second Plan was approved by the Cabinet on 15 January 1993. This seems to have occurred, partly at least, because the relationship between the IM and the Cabinet was closer than in 1987, due to the presence in the Cabinet of a woman as Minister of Social Affairs, a woman with wide experience in the realm of feminist activism.

38. Sensat, N. and Varella, R. (1998), 'Las políticas dirigidas a las mujeres: la acción pública para la igualdad entre los sexos', in Gomá, R. and Subirats, J. (eds), *Políticas públicas en España*, Barcelona: Ariel, p. 351.

39. Instituo de la Mujer. (1993), *Segundo Plan para la Igualdad de Oportunidades de las Mujeres, 1993-1995*, Madrid: Ministerio de Asuntos Sociales, Instituto de la Mujer.

40. Ibid, p 31.

The most relevant aspect of the Second Equal Opportunities Plan is its acknowledgement of the domestic responsibilities of women. The Plan stated that the sharing of such responsibilities is 'a necessary pre-condition to achieve equity in the public or market sectors, particularly in the access of women to posts of responsibility'.[41] The advancement of women to posts of responsibility, the defence of women's employment and the diffusion of a social image of women which accurately reflected current reality were also action priorities.

The Third Equal Opportunities Plan 1997-2000[42] was again delayed, being adopted two years after the completion date of the previous Plan. This Plan was the first to be approved by a government (*Partido Popular*) of a different political persuasion from that which approved previous Plans (*P.S.O.E*). Its objectives are summarised in ten categories:

- to promote women's equal access to all educational processes, and to develop an educational system that — from the conception of science and knowledge, to their transmission — is informed by egalitarian values;
- to promote an integrated approach to health, 'to influence — from prevention through to assistance — those specific aspects derived from sexual difference, as well as those derived from cultural and social conditions';
- in relation to the interconnected spheres of the economy and employment, 'in the former, to raise the visibility of women's contribution to the sector and to promote their access to social and economic rights; and in the latter, to foster women's incorporation into the labour market';
- to promote women to decision-making positions and to promote a better balance of power within the public realm as well as the equal sharing of responsibilities within the private realm, in order to make compatible and satisfactory both family and working lives;
- to co-operate in bringing about changes in image, particularly in the media, 'that will favour a more egalitarian society, considering the impact that the media has in the crystallisation of public opinion';

41. Sensat and Varella, op cit, n. 38, p. 351.
42. Instituo de la Mujer. (1997), *III Plan para la Igualdad de Oportunidades entre Mujeres y Hombres 1997-2000*, Madrid: Ministerio de Trabajo y Asuntos Sociales, Instituto de la Mujer.

- to promote women's participation in environmental programmes;
- to promote integrated measures to prevent and eliminate violence against women;
- to fight the feminization of poverty;
- to promote the development of women in rural areas;
- 'to integrate the dimension of equal opportunities in the policies of the public administration and public institutions and to foster co-operation with both non-governmental organisations and international organisations by mobilising all policies to attain equality'.[43]

The Third Equal Opportunities Plan insists on looking for factual equality between men and women. There is a concern for work in the public sector as well as on the private level: the family and employment fields remain the priorities, with a concern to promote equity between the two sexes in relation to production, reproduction and private areas such as leisure and rest.[44]

Even though there is a statement of intention in the Third Plan to put into place a mainstreaming policy, there is no evidence elsewhere in the document of either the philosophy implicit in this concept or the political measures needed to enforce it. In this regard Threfall comments that 'the Institute of Women's Equal Opportunities Plan was considered sufficiently 'vacuous' and 'lacking in operational measures' to be criticized in the editorial of a national newspaper' (*El País*, 9 March 1997).[45]

The general objective for each of the three Plans is summarised in the last Plan: 'If the First Plan was the one promoting legislative reforms for the existence of legal equality and the Second Plan was the one promoting the initiation and implementation of specific measures to promote equality of opportunities, the Third Plan is the first step towards involving and mobilising all general policies and measures with the purpose of attaining equality'.[46]

43. Ibid, p. 11.
44. Ibid, p. 42.
45. Threfall, M. (1998), 'State Feminism or Party Feminism?', *The European Journal of Women's Studies*, 5, p. 69.
46. To some extent, Gil Ruíz shares this opinion: 'the first distinctive aspect (between the First and Second Plan) lies in the special attention that the First Plan pays to perfecting the normative development of the constitutional principle of equality without discrimination on the grounds of sex; together with the attainment of better enforcement of current legislation in favour of women. The Second Plan, however, being aware of the fact that such legislative adaptation was important but not sufficient, and after acknowledging the achievement attained on this matter by its predecessor, preferred to concentrate on the areas of education and labour': Gil Ruiz, J. M. (1997), *Las Políticas de Igualdad en España: Avances y Retrocesos*, Granada: Universidad de Granada, pp. 26-7.

Conclusion

In Spain, the integration of gender into the law and policy-making process needs to be evaluated at two different levels. On the one hand, from a legal and political perspective, there seems to be the begining of a slow correction of inequality between the sexes. On the other hand, when the realities of everyday life are considered there seem to be a number of examples of resistance towards effective equality of rights and the correction of political and social discrimination based on gender conditions. This is especially pertinent with regard to many of those in charge of applying and implementing the laws, or with regard to those in charge of deciding on or implementing those policies that should favour women.

The following conclusions can be drawn: in the first place, Spain is in transition from a restrictive conception of equality and an absence of gender discrimination principles towards a more modern approach. Spanish laws frequently show a lack of precision and in many cases even contradict one another on the appproach to follow in relation to the elimination of sex discrimination and the design of positive actions that would prevent further discrimination and combat the disrimination that still exists. Therefore, it is imperative to pursue specific measures directed to the improvement of Spanish law, in order to achieve greater juridical rigour and greater clarity in relation to the law concerning equality between men and women.

Secondly, the Spanish model presents serious difficulties in terms of achieving the necessary autonomy for improving the position of women within society. First of all, the formulation of public policies for women — in particular the Equal Opportunities Plans — has been undertaken by femocrats, in the Spanish case individuals connected to the government's party or civil servants. There are no co-operative links — either formal or informal — between IM femocrats and feminist activists. Moreover, the role of the IM as an initiator, setting the agenda for equality policies, contrasts very strongly with its practically non-existent function as an executor of those policies, or as a controller in the process of their implementation. Last but not least, the position of the IM within the Spanish Public Administration (that is, under the aegis of the Ministry of Labour and Social Affairs) produces a problem of hierarchical rank when the IM comes to negotiate its own demands — first with its own Minister, and later with all the other Ministries.

It is difficult to assess the effectiveness of the Spanish Equal Opportunities Plans: a major problem is that there is no objective reference point for such an evaluation. On the contrary, all three Plans rely on self-evaluation of the implementation of their proposed measures. This lack of rigour in monitoring their implementation is a serious flaw.

A third observation is that the Spanish government's information policies on women do not seem to have had much impact. It appears that the privileged position of the government in relation to the media is not used, either direct or indirectly, to promote any real improvement in attitudes towards women or to acknowledge a plurality of role models for Spanish women. Information campaigns on women's rights in the media are either very rare or non-existent, and the defining features of the women who do appear in the media are still predominantly those features traditionally demanded of females.

Finally, the public policies on women's issues developed at the national, regional and local levels, have practically excluded the feminist movement. These policies have been formulated without taking account of the proposals and views of women other than those belonging at the relevant time to the ruling party in the central government, the different CC. AA. or the different town councils. So far, the contacts they have had with other groups have been very occasional.

6 Making Women Count in Sweden

MINNA GILLBERG

The Swedish law and policy-making landscape is characterised by a culture of framework laws and consensus building. Framework laws contain goals, general guidelines and principles to be put into practice by detailed regulations issued by government, public authorities or County Administrative Boards. It is up to these latter bodies how they go about developing such regulations. Such political issues are solved via an informal bureaucratic process of co-operation, negotiation and consensus building between recognised social partners. In many respects, such a system has developed a political and legal landscape that has been open, flexible and responsive to issues of gender equality and which is thought to be progressive in its approach to equality policies and legislation. The emphasis on participation and consensus building has helped to construct a well-integrated and decentralised network of equality bodies and a political landscape in which women are relatively well represented.

However, this system could be said to offer poor protection of formal civil rights. While Sweden does possess an Equal Opportunities Act, this single piece of legislation has required strengthening, through the issue of formal statements of what constitutes sexual harassment, for example, in order to be effective. The gender-neutral language in which this legislation is couched also fails to deal with the sexual specificity that underlies some forms of discrimination. The corporatist tradition which underpins Swedish politics could also be seen to have limited the opportunity to participate in decision-making to traditional and well-established organisational interests such as trade unions, rather than women's groups. As such, the positive impact that good levels of female representation can have in the political arena may be minimised by factors operating in the wider decision-making process.

Against this background this chapter will highlight key aspects of the law and policy-making landscape in Sweden with a view to emphasising recent moves by the Swedish government to develop a process-oriented, as opposed to a structural, approach to dealing with gender equality.

The Political and Legal Landscape in Sweden

Sweden is a country which, like many other European countries, has experienced a gradual shift of power from the King in Council to the people.[1] Today the Swedish constitutional system may be characterised as a parliamentary democracy with a state governed by law and a monarch as the representative head of state. The legal system is related to the European continental legal tradition which is characterised by a dependence on statutory law. The Constitution consists of four fundamental laws: The Instrument of Government[2] (1974:152) which regulates executive, legislative and judicial powers; the Act on Succession (1810); the Freedom of the Press Act (1949:105) and the Freedom of Expression Act (1991:1469).

The sovereignty of the Swedish people is manifested through Parliament which is the most prominent of the state institutions as *the* law-making body.[3] Parliament consists of a single chamber with 349 members who are appointed by free, direct and proportional elections (IG ch 3 sec 1).[4] In order to guarantee regional representation, the state is divided into 28 constituencies according to the Elections Act (1972:620). The government is elected by the Parliament based on a proposal put forward by the Speaker of Parliament (IG ch 6 secs 2 to 4). The Instrument of Government (ch 1 sec 1) provides that public power shall be exercised in accordance with the law. This is also manifest in ch 1 sec 8 and 9 which provide that for the administration of justice (the judicial power) there are courts of law[5] and for public administration there are state and municipal administrative authorities.[6] In addition there are a number of special courts, such as the Labour Court which is a bipartite court which adjudicates on employment law disputes, including sex discrimination cases.[7]

The Social Democratic Workers Party (*Socialdemokratiska Arbetarpartiet* founded in 1889) has, in co-operation with the Swedish Confederation of Trade

1. Cronhult, P. (1994), 'Introduction', in Tiberg, H. et al (eds), *Swedish Law. A Survey*, Stockholm: Juristförlaget, p. 37.
2. Hereafter referred to as IG.
3. Sterzel, F. (1994) 'The Constitution', in Tiberg et al, op. cit, n. 1, pp. 46-8.
4. The parliamentary period of mandate is four years and it runs parallel with the county and municipal council mandate periods. Since 1970 a system has existed which combines full national proportionality with a limit (4 per cent of the votes in the whole country, or 12 per cent in one constituency) inhibiting the proliferation of small parties (Cronhult, op cit, n. 1, p. 37).
5. There are three instances of general courts: 97 district courts, six courts of appeal and the Supreme Court.
6. There are 24 county administrative courts, four administrative courts of appeal and the Supreme Administrative Court.
7. Cronhult op cit, n. 1, p. 37.

Unions (founded 1898), been the most dominant force for change and legal reform during the twentieth century. Since the end of the Second World War the political balance has been stable and the Social Democrats have been, and still are, the largest party.[8] Since the general election in 1998 Sweden has had a Social Democratic government which attains parliamentary majority with the support of the Green Party and the Left Party.

Sweden is also a welfare state in which the public administration has the major responsibility for providing services to the public. Government administration is distinctively decentralised and it is possible to distinguish three different levels of administration: central, regional and local. When decisions have been made either by Parliament or the Government, the actual implementation and a large part of the financing is entrusted to the politically elected Municipalities (*kommuner*) and the County Councils (*landsting*). County Councils are to be distinguished from the County Administrative Boards (*länsstyrelse*) which are a state authority of great regional and local importance. According to the County Administrative Board Regulation (SFS 1990:1510), the Boards have four principal functions; (1) to carefully monitor the conditions and needs of the county, (2) to promote the development of the county and the best interests of its inhabitants, (3) to work towards the achievement at county level of national goals which have been established for various sectors, and (4) to exercise supervision and judicial functions concerning administrative appeals. The County Administrative Boards exercise general supervision in their county, but the principal bodies are the Municipalities and they bear the heavy operational and economic burdens of service provision. Most of the activities of the Municipalities and County Councils are regulated by the Local Government Act from which they obtain a so-called general competence. In principle this general competence can be seen as broad, but in practice there are a number of important limitations, both economic and legal, which restrict their leeway for independent action.[9]

---

8. The non-socialist parties have for a long time been three; the conservative Moderate Party (*Moderata Samlingspartiet*), the Liberal Party (*Folkpartiet Liberalerna*) and the Centre Party (*Centerpartiet*) with its roots in the old Farmer's Party. To the left of the Social Democrats there is the Left Party (*Vänsterpartiet*), which has its roots in communism and has, in recent years, been the third largest party after the Social Democrats and the Moderate Party. In 1988, a new party entered the Parliament for the first time in over half a century, The Green Party (*Miljöpartiet de gröna*). And in 1991 two other parties also managed to win Parliamentary seats, namely the Christian Democratic Party (*Kristdemokratiska Samhällspartiet*), and the new nationalistic and populistic party, New Democracy (*Ny Demokrati*). However, in the 1994 general election New Democracy lost all their seats.
9. Sterzel, F. 'Public Administration', in Tiberg et al, op. ci, n. 1,. pp. 75-82.

The number of central administrative authorities may be estimated at about 150. The authorities operate on the grounds that the Government issues broad initial instructions and then the agencies themselves make regulations concerning the functions entrusted to them, and their conduct of operations.[10] The result is a large administrative machinery with its own legal culture run by non-elected officials. Formal directives to the public authorities can only be given by the Government and it is not possible to control the administration or challenge administrative actions or decisions through, for instance, the general courts. Here, it should be noted that ministerial rule in its formal sense cannot be found in Sweden with regard to the relationship between Government and state authorities. The administrative authorities are accountable to the Government, but the individual Ministers have no powers to give detailed directives or interfere with the internal affairs of an authority. Most of the central state agencies are management organs and do not come into direct contact with the public to any great extent since they normally have their own regional organs whose primary function is management and to offer support to local government. Among these management tasks central agencies further issue binding regulations and general non-binding advices. Day-to-day operational functions are thus often taken care of by the Municipalities at the lowest level and by the County Administrative Boards at the regional level.[11]

Women's Representation in Parliament

As discussed earlier, the Social Democratic Party has a special ability to quickly integrate new trends and expressions of opinion into the party.[12] This capacity has at many times played a crucial role in enabling the party to remain in power. A recent example of this is when during the General Election in 1994 the so called *Stödstrumporna*,[13] a task force coalition of feminists from different spheres, managed to exert great pressure on the political parties by threatening to form a women's political party. The result was that the Social Democratic Party decided that every other candidate on

10. Ibid p. 77.
11. Ibid pp. 78-9.
12. For example Widerberg, K. (1980), in *Kvinnor, klasser, lagar*. 1750-1980, Helingborg: Publica p. 104.
13. *Stödstrumporna* was a political organisation which gained success in the Swedish General Election in 1994. A translation is difficult, but in Swedish the meaning of the word is 'support-stockings' (which in turn alludes to the so called red stockings, or red socks, the name of a group of feminists during the 1960s).

its election lists should be a woman. It also led to several measures being taken and implemented in favour of equality, both within the working processes of Parliament and through legislation. Since the mid-1990s the Social Democratic Party has claimed that equality is a highly prioritised Social Democratic project. Lately however, another political issue has surfaced to become the new primary question for the party, namely sustainable development. The Prime Minister, Göran Persson, is said to have turned away from the focus on equality issues. However, the implications of such a shift are not necessarily entirely negative as, for example, Agenda 21 adopted at the Rio Conference on Environment and Development, 1992 includes equality, along with economics and ecology, as a key dimension in the definition of sustainable development.

The question of female representation in Parliament (and on Municipal Councils) is central when analysing the equality situation in Sweden, partly because Parliament is the law-maker and partly because of the strong democratic tradition which views Parliament as a reflection of society's social categories. Today it is evident that the composition of party politics has changed fundamentally since women first entered Parliament (1922) and Government. The political scientist, Lena Wängnerud, states in her dissertation *Politikens andra sida* (The Other Side of Politics) that in 1960, the proportion of female MPs was about ten per cent, and after the 1994 General Election, female representation had risen to exceed 40 per cent.[14] Her study further shows that female MPs are more likely to single out women as a social category they choose to represent. In 1994, 54 per cent of female MPs regarded it as very important to personally represent women's interests/opinions. The corresponding figure for male MPs was six per cent.

Wängnerud also shows that female MPs are more positive towards the enhancement and enforcement of equality. Differences between women and men become more clear-cut when analysing who promotes gender equality issues in Parliament; almost all the MPs stating that they promote such issues are women. Her analysis also reveals systematic differences between women and men when it comes to arguing for reproductive and care issues on the political agenda: there is a higher propensity among female parliamentarians to promote such issues. Female politicians seem to increase the priority given to women's interests. However, Wängnerud further states that women will not stay forever within care-related policy areas, and that in the future women will most likely be represented in all political domains.[15]

14. Wängnerud, L. (1998), *Politikens andra sida. Om kvinnorepresentation i Sveriges riksdag*, Kungälv: Göteborg Studies in Politics 53, p. 207.
15. Ibid, p. 213.

In conclusion, it can be said that gender representation is relatively even within Government (50/50) and Parliament (43 per cent women). The picture does, however, look slightly different if one takes a closer look at the varying levels of male/female representation within these categories. An illustrative example of this is the staff composition of Prime Minister Göran Persson's office: during the electoral period 1994-1998 nine out of 12 political experts were men, whereas all nine assistants were women.[16] However, Wängnerud points clearly to the fact that women's presence in Parliament, at whatever level, has influenced the content of politics and enhanced the status of equality issues.

Women's impact on decision-making may, in turn, vary because of the nature of the law and policy-making process itself. However, before going on to discuss policy-making, it is necessary to complete the picture of Sweden's political and legal landscape by summarising its approach to freedom of information.

Formal Policy on Openness of Government

The principle of public access (offentlighetsprincipen) to information is laid down in the Freedom of the Press Act (SFS 1949:105) and is of great importance in Sweden in relation to access to public documents. The Freedom of the Press Act (hereinafter FPA) devotes a whole chapter (ch 2) to the public character of official documents. The emphasis is on written documents and the Swedish authorities are subject to wide-ranging duties to supply when requested complete documentation on matters being dealt with by the authority concerned. The FPA defines a 'document' as including 'any representation in writing, any pictorial representation, any other recording which can be read, listened to, or otherwise apprehended only by technical aids'.[17] This means that computer records are considered as documents. These provisions are far-reaching and letters which are personally addressed to a person holding office in a public authority are considered to be public documents if the letter relates to a case or any other matter resting with the authority. Incomplete working papers are not public documents, but in many cases it is possible to obtain the document if the paper has been despatched to and received by another authority and is therefore, by definition, a public document. The rules concerning

16. In total, 59 per cent of the governmental experts were men and of Parliament's 16 committees, only five were headed by women. As regards civil servants within the Ministries, 66 per cent were men. See Ulmanen, P. (1998), *(S)veket mot kvinnorna och hur högern stal feminismen*, Uddevalla: Atlas Förlag, p. 181.

17. Sterzel, op cit, n. 9, p. 87.

public documents apply to all authorities, whether municipal or state, including the government and Parliament without exception.

There are naturally certain documents whose disclosure could injure the public or a private person's lawful interest. These documents are exempt from the principle of public access in accordance with the Secrecy Acts (1980:100). The exemptions are rather extensive but do not (in most cases) undermine the principle of public access to information. If the Government, or an authority for some reason does not want to release a document it is common that they classify the document. The decision to classify a document can, however, be challenged in the administrative court, normally a very slow procedure, by which a case can take years to reach the final instance of appeal. However, it is not entirely unusual for the court to find that the document must be made public against the will of the government. The legal provision has proven to be effective at securing openness (transparency) and access to information in cases where 'classification' has been contested in court. However, since Sweden became a member of the European Union, 'classification' has been discussed with a renewed focus since it is not clear whether Sweden will be able to maintain this high degree of transparency regarding decision-making, in a European context. For example, several documents which are classified in Brussels can be obtained from the Swedish authorities as a result of the right of access to information.

The Law and Policy-Making Process

It is not an easy task to describe the Swedish policy and law-making process in a brief and concise way as it is a procedure which may look very formal on paper, but which in practice is determined by a highly informal process (as most political processes are). Therefore this section starts with an introductory account of the formal law-making route which is followed by an elaboration of the Swedish concept of framework laws (since this type of legislation dominates in Sweden and creates a legal landscape in which it can be difficult to influence the decision and policy-making process). Finally, the more informal process of law-making is discussed. This process is vital, particularly in relation to representation and information (or access and input), for the outcome of the formal law-making process.

All members of the Swedish Parliament have the right to present motions (IG ch 4 sec 3) during the two week general motions period in January and also in connection with government propositions.[18] A policy/law initiative, either from the Government or from a Member of Parliament, is referred to one of the 16 permanent committees which either supports or rejects the initiative. Parliament then makes a decision, usually in accordance with the committee's proposition. Parliament does, however, have the right to reject or amend the proposition. If the committee's proposition is approved by Parliament, the Government normally appoints an independent investigation commission (*Statens Offentliga Utredningar*).[19] The Government can, however, choose to delegate the issue directly to a Ministry, authority or to an already existing investigation commission.

When an investigation commission is appointed it usually involves Members of Parliament and individuals from interest groups who are going to be affected by the legislation. In the commission's report, all its proposals and reasoning must be clearly set out. The commission's report is then sent to all authorities, organisations and other concerned parties for consideration. This process of referral creates the opportunity for a range of views to be expressed concerning the proposal. The law-maker assumes that this process will provide a certain guarantee of acceptance of the proposal by Swedish society. The proposal is finally formulated at Ministerial level on the basis of the commission's report. The work carried out by the Ministry often consists of finding an acceptable compromise between conflicting interests. The proposal is then referred to the permanent Council on Legislation[20] which makes a statement, if it finds it necessary. The Council on Legislation, normally reviews and pronounces on, amongst other things, the constitutional legality of the more important legislative amendments or proposals, and the

18. Sterzel, op cit, n. 3, p. 49.
19. The Government issues a so-called directive for all commissions and investigations, indicating the work to be undertaken and guidelines to be followed. Every committee publishes a report in one of two series: *Statens Offentliga Utredningar, SOU* (The Public Inquiries of The State) or *Departementsserien, Ds* (The Ministry Publication Series).
20. The Council on Legislation is a Swedish institution which is comprised of members of the Supreme Court and the Supreme Administrative Court. Several legislative councils can work at the same time; each council has three members. The Council on Legislation gives out opinions on five different aspects of proposed legislation, including the implications for the Constitution and the legal system in general, its effects in relation to the requirements of due process and whether it is formulated in a manner which it can be assumed will fulfil the required purpose (Ch. 8 sec. 18).

opinion of the Council weighs heavily in any investigation.[21] As a last step the proposal is brought back before Parliament and again referred to a committee which supports or declines the proposal in a recommendation to Parliament. Parliament then votes on the proposal, usually deciding according to the Parliamentary committee's recommendations.[22] The Act of Parliament is accompanied by an 'expressed will' in which Parliament, to afford guidance in the application of the law, develops and clarifies the objective of the enactment and the meaning of its wording. Particularly during the introductory phase, before any established practice has been formed, these written opinions are of great importance as a source of law. When applying and interpreting the law, the Swedish courts pay great regard to the legislator's expressed will.[23]

The general view among the established political actors is that the decision-making process is characterised by open, rational and direct mutual understanding. This is due to the fact that the government in the preparatory stages of the legislative process encourages the parties and actors concerned to take part in or to try to influence the decision-making process. The traditional spirit of consensus and mutual understanding often creates a situation where the different parties can unite behind a proposal.[24] However, many changes suggested by the working groups to the government's propositions, are the result of informal negotiations between the government side and one or more of the opposition parties. In many cases the government has made concessions to the opposition before they outline the proposition to be presented to Parliament.[25] Thus, what appears to be different steps and repeated efforts in the formal process of decision-making in fact constitutes an informal and united process, where the same interests and actors meet over and over again.[26]

Framework Laws

The formal power to enact law and issue other forms of regulation is based on three levels in Sweden. The highest level is Parliament, which according to the Instrument of Government (ch 1 sec 4) enacts the laws. The second level is government. Government also has a third tier, which in practice is

21. Sterzel, op cit, n. 3, p. 55.
22. Hydén, H. (ed.) (1987), *Rättsregler*, Lund: Studentlitteratur, pp. 60-2.
23. Sterzel, op cit, n. 3, p. 55.
24. Larsson, T. (ed.) (1993), *Det svenska atatsskicket*, Lund: Studentlitteratur, p. 401.
25. Sannerstedt, A. and Sjölin, M. (1994), *Den moderna demokratins problem*, Lund: Studentlitteratur, p. 99.
26. Larsson, op cit, n. 24, p. 404.

important: the public authorities. Both state and municipal authorities can issue a number of regulations through the use of so called framework laws and delegation of powers.[27] One of the most important trends of modern Swedish legislation is the increasing resort to framework laws. Such laws are based on a principle whereby the legislative power of Parliament can be delegated, and in practice limited, if the Parliament only lays down legal rules in a very general manner. A framework law contains goals, general guidelines and principles to be elaborated on and put into operation by detailed regulations issued by the government, public authorities or by the County Administrative Board.[28] Thus the Instrument of Government and its rules concerning the legislative powers of Parliament can be set aside in certain respects and this has been a common practice since the 1970s.[29] As a result there are around 1,200 laws in Sweden, compared to some 15,000 regulations issued by government and public authorities. Examples of important framework laws are the Law on the Working Environment, the Environment Protection Law, the Social Welfare Law and the Health and Social Security Law.

It is the Social Democratic Party which has been foremost in delegating political issues to the administrative system through the use of framework laws. This strategy plays an important role in upholding the Swedish culture of consensus (see below). However, from a critical perspective it could be said that in this manner controversial political questions are transformed into technical matters and solved as bureaucratic problems. And since the administrative system, which constitutes a decision-making institution and process, is more or less closed to communication with actors outside the administration, there is no critical discourse regarding the use of framework laws in Swedish society. In a sense it can be claimed that the consensus culture (conflict avoiding) has thus been transformed into Swedish legislation, through the use of framework laws.[30]

Another aspect of framework laws concerns access to information and the administrative system's decision-making process. The character of the

---

27. Sterzel, op cit, n. 3, pp. 52-5.
28. Sterzel, op cit, n. 3, p. 54.
29. This occurs when Parliament delegates powers to the Government or to a public authority. In some areas the Government may issue regulations without any delegation of powers by the Parliament. In two areas, it has independent powers (IG ch. 8 sec. 13): One relates to provisions which are necessary for the implementation and enforcement of enactments, the other for regulations applicable to matters where the IG has not specifically designated certain items as for decision by Parliament. Bruun, N. et al (eds), (1992), *The Nordic Labour Relations Model*, London: Dartmouth.
30. Gillberg, M. and Hydén, H. (1998), 'Environmental Decision-Making in Sweden', in Weidner, H. (ed.), *Alternative Dispute Resolution*, Berlin: Zigma.

framework law, in itself a continuous decision-making process, creates a situation where it is difficult to establish channels for inputs, or outputs, of information concerning the decision-making process as the administrative system is rather anonymous and closed. The use of framework laws creates a situation where it is extremely difficult to establish a public discourse regarding decision-making. These laws (there are more than 15,000) do not always comply with the principle referred to as the *rule of law* and Sweden has lost several cases in the European Court of Human Rights because of the framework law system and the poor protection of civil rights such a system at times offers.

Informal Law-making

Sweden has a long political tradition of co-operation and consensus-seeking which has its roots in the labour movement. Since the turn of the century, different interests from the the political and economic sectors have been co-opted into policy-making, as an efficient means of conflict avoiding/solving and as a neutralising mechanism. The political actors, especially the Social Democrats, have been skilful and tactical in absorbing different well-established organised interests into the formal decision-making process. As mentioned earlier, politically recognised organisations — such as the employers organisation, labour unions and the farmers union — are drawn into the formal policy-process either by being appointed as members of the public investigation or through the system of referrals (*remissförfarande*).

A distinguishing trait of this process is its *informality*. In practice the process is coloured by undocumented informal communication and input of information which eventually results in a formal decision. The question of whom and what information to include in the process is decided solely by the Government and public authorities involved. This corporatist tradition has given the opportunity to participate in the formal (informal) decision-making process almost exclusively to traditional and well-established organisational interests, such as employers organisations and trade unions. For example, environmental NGOs and women's organisations (non-political) have not, until recently, been represented in this process to any wide extent.

Finally it is necessary to emphasise again the influence the labour unions have had on Swedish society. Legislation regulating labour issues, for example, has to a very large degree been developed and adopted with the co-operation and consent of the major labour market organisations (including unions and employers) and the Social Democratic Party. The political consensus has not included the dimension of factual or formal equality, until rather recently.[31] The parties of the labour market have above all been represented by men and these men have not been particularly devoted carriers of values that promote equality between women and men. However, at the end of the 1990s there are signs that several large unions are beginning to integrate and prioritise the issue of gender equality more seriously into their political agenda. This is a change of attitude which can partly be explained by the fact that today more women than men are active in the unions. There are also expectations that the mainstreaming directive (1994:124), if properly enforced, will improve the situation concerning information inputs and outputs on gender and equality issues to and from public investigations and committee work (see below). Indirectly this might result in the inclusion of women's representatives and thus give more room for gender-related input into the formal and informal decision-making process.

Equality Legislation in Sweden

The Constitution

The Swedish Constitution provides through the Instrument of Government (SFS 1974:152) that all administrative authorities and others exercising functions within the public administration must observe the principle that everyone is equal before the law and maintain objectivity and impartiality. The wording in IG ch 1 sec 2 refers to respect for everyone's equality, the individual's freedom and value, the individual's personal, economic and cultural welfare as basic goals, and to equal rights between women and men *inter alia*.[32] However, the Swedish Constitution is a great disappointment to those who expect to find a well-phrased declaration of equality and inalienable human rights independent of state authority. A peculiarity with the Swedish

31. Nielsen, R. and Halvorsen, M. (1992), 'Equality Laws', in Bruun, N. et al (eds), *The Nordic Labour Relations Model*, London: Dartmouth, pp. 185-186. The 1948 United Nations Declaration on Human Rights (Article 23 sec. 2) states the right to equal pay for equal work. Article 2 of the declaration states that the Member States must promote and ensure, by appropriate means, the principle of equal pay. In Sweden, 14 years passed before the Convention was finally ratified in 1962. Though the commitment to the principle of equal pay was restated upon ratification of the 1966 United Nations Convention on Economic, Cultural and Social Rights, no significant redistribution of wages between women and men took place. Women's salaries improved in comparison with men's but only very slowly. It was not, and still is not, unusual for women to receive less pay than men for exactly the same job (on average women earn 80 per cent of men's earnings).
32. Sterzel, op cit, n. 9, at pp. 75-6.

Constitution is the fact that it is based on the idea that fundamental rights exists as a result of it [the Constitution] and only to the extent laid down by it. As Parliament in Sweden has the exclusive power to change the Constitution, it means that Parliament can also restrict fundamental rights and that the Constitution itself cannot be challenged in a Swedish court (Sweden does not have a Constitutional Court). The purpose of the Swedish system is to provide legal rules that can be invoked in national courts and in relation to national authorities.

Despite the early progressive approach to the development of equal opportunities in Sweden, it was not until 1976 that the Instrument of Government was changed to include a prohibition against sexual discrimination. As of 1976 Paragraph 2:16 in the Instrument of Government states that laws and regulations must not, as a consequence, result in citizens being unfairly treated on the grounds of sex (Prop. 75/76 209). Some exceptions are allowed for legal regulations which have the intention to create and enhance equality between women and men, as well as for çertain regulations regarding military service and other obligatory duties. Thus, the IG allows legislation which is not gender neutral if its purpose is to enhance and create a further degree of equality in society. So, for example, the Equal Opportunities Act (see below) does allow positive discrimination in situations where a woman and a man apply for a job and they both have the necessary qualifications; the employer is legally allowed to choose the woman, if women are the under-represented sex in the workplace (or vice versa regarding men). To choose the under-represented sex is not a legal obligation but rather a legal option for the employer to enhance equality in the workplace (this is a legal obligation, but it is left to the employer to decide on the means to employ). It is interesting to note that the Swedish provision allowing quotas is formulated in a gender-neutral way, and thus differs from the Germanic laws which have been subject to interpretation by the European Court in the cases of *Kalanke* and *Marschall*.[33] The Equal Opportunities Act states, in paragraph 9, that an employer, when employing new personnel, must make special efforts to find employees of the 'underrepresented sex, if there is a major imbalance between the sexes in the workplace. It is expected that employers shall strive to increase the percentage of the under-represented sex'.[34]

---

33. Case C-450/93 *Kalanke* and C-409/95 *Marschall*. See also Lundström K. (1997), 'Women Caught in a Logical Trap in EC Law: An analysis of the use of quotas in the Kalanke Case', *Statsvetenskaplig Tidskrift*, no 1.

34. Special treatment is also allowed if based on differences between the sexes which are of a bodily character, such as women giving birth. In this case the investigation specifically referred to the legislation concerning pregnancy benefits and the Act on Abortion which states that the woman alone has the right to request that a pregnancy be terminated. As the investigation wished to maintain compulsory male military service in the future, this exception was included in the paragraph (the reasoning behind this exception was however not made explicit).

The Equal Opportunities Act

The first Equal Opportunities Act came into effect in 1980 and some minor amendments were adopted in 1985. In 1991, a new Equal Opportunities Act (1991:433) was adopted which introduced the positive action measures which had been left out of the Act of 1979.[35] The new Act was drafted to conform with corresponding EC law.[36] It is notable that the only addition 'forced' by EC law at this point was a provision on direct discrimination. Legislation in Sweden today is, on the whole, basically gender neutral, even in those Acts concerning questions of positive measures to create and enhance equality in the workplace. Instead of using a terminology that singles out women or men, the legal text talks of 'the under-represented sex'. The wording was chosen to create more 'legal flexibility', so that, for instance, men could be given priority in a workplace dominated by women and vice versa.[37]

The Equal Opportunities Act (1991:433) aims at promoting equal rights for women and men regarding employment, conditions of employment and other conditions of work, such as opportunities for personal development (sec 1). The Act protects both women and men, but 'aims primarily at improving women's conditions in working life' (sec 1). The Act contains two set of rules: one concerns active measures to promote equality; and one stipulates prohibitions against discrimination. The first part (active measures) has more of a goal-oriented character and, for example, regulates the employer's obligation to introduce a plan on equal opportunities for both women and men. The second part provides clear rights and rules for protection against discrimination.

The active measures are aimed at combating and abolishing all and any gender related differences in working life and bringing about an equal distribution of various tasks at all places of work. Employers are legally obliged to make systematic efforts to realise these goals. As part of their statutory obligations, employers with ten or more employees must present an annual equality plan which lists necessary measures and when they are

35. Nielsen and Halvorsen, op cit, n. 31, p. 187.

36. Article 119 of the Treaty of Rome and Directive 75/117/EEC on Equal Pay.

37. Examples of exceptions, where gender neutral legislative language is not used, can be found in the rules about pregnancy benefits in the Law on General Social Insurance, LAF, (1962:381, paragraph 9 and 9a) and in the law regulating the right to Parental Leave (Law 1963:115, paragraph 4). In a number of the provisions on, *inter alia*, assault and sexual crimes in the Penal Code, the words 'he', 'his' or 'him' are used to refer to persons of both sexes. These words are to be modified in favour of expressions such as his or hers or similar. The Government attaches importance to gender neutral language as a whole in the Penal Code and any other legislation.

to be executed. Employers also have to audit and account for the previous year's plan. Since 1994, there has been a similar obligation in the Act concerning the existence of salary differences between women and men (SFS 1994:292). An employer who fails to comply with his or her statutory obligations can be ordered to do so (on the initiative of the Equal Opportunities Ombudsman via the Equal Opportunities Commission and as a final instance by the Labour Court (see below). The Court can impose fines on those who fail to comply (Equal Opportunities Act, Paragraph 32, 35, 42 and 44). If an employer is found guilty by the Labour Court of discrimination against an individual, the employer is liable to punitive damages and can also be liable to financial damages. An example of how the Swedish law and the Labour Court works in reality is that a discriminatory decision to hire one person in preference to another of the opposite sex, can at the most result in symbolic punitive damages.[38] No order to vacate the decision and replace it by a non-discriminatory one is possible under Swedish law. Thus the person discriminated against cannot obtain the job.

The other set of statutory rules in the Equal Opportunities Act deals with direct or indirect discrimination in individual cases. Gender discrimination is considered to exist when someone is treated improperly provided that there is a direct or indirect connection between such improper treatment and the sex of that person. For example, the Act limits an employer's prerogative to hire, promote or select an employee for training with a view to promotion on the basis of the employee's sex. The law is limiting only in the sense that a better qualified person of one sex has priority over a less qualified person of the other sex, never in the sense that a less qualified or equally qualified person of one sex has priority over persons of the opposite sex. However, affirmative action (positive discrimination) to promote equality at work is permitted provided that it is deployed in a consistent and systematic way. Another instance deals with differences in pay or other conditions of employment for work objectively considered to be the same or of equal value. Such differences are illegal unless the employer can show that any discrepancy is due to differences in the employee's objective qualifications or not related, directly or indirectly, to the employee's sex.[39]

38. As the law entered into force when this was written, it is difficult to estimate the size of future punitive damages. However, they are not likely to exceed the ones awarded by the Labour Court in other matters where the figure rarely has exceeded SEK 80.000 (ECU 7000).

39. Fahlbeck, R. (1994), 'Labour Law', in Tiberg, H. et al (eds), *Swedish Law. A Survey*, Stockholm: Juristförlaget p. 265.

The Equal Opportunities Act of 1991 contained a provision which prohibited harassment by an employer of an employee who has rejected sexual advances on the employer's part (paragraph 22). However, this was only the provision on sexual advances which gave rise to liability for compensation. The Equal Opportunities Ombudsman raised the question of the way in which sexual harassment in the workplace was to be regulated (in view of the fact that the prohibition contained in paragraph 22 of the Act did not deal with sexual harassment *per se*). In addition, the 1991 Act did not include a definition of sexual harassment which was in accordance with the EC Recommendation and the Code of Practice on Protecting the Dignity of Men and Women at Work. Therefore the Ombudsman proposed[40] to the Government that the Act ought to be strengthened and supplemented by a rule which holds the employer responsible in certain situations, if a woman is subjected to any form of sexual harassment by her colleagues. Furthermore, the Equal Opportunities Ombudsman had for years worked to introduce a legal definition of sexual harassment and insisted that Sweden's membership of the European Union (1994) and the EC Recommendation on sexual harassment lent legal support to the case for such a definition to be introduced. In 1997 the Ombudsman initiated an investigation into sexual harassment, and its findings came to serve as a blueprint for the government proposal which finally followed.[41]

On 22 April 1998, Parliament decided to accept the government's proposal (based on the suggestion by the Ombudsman) regarding a supplement to the Equal Opportunities Act. The proposal entered into force on 1 July 1998 and strengthened the Act (SFS 1998:208). The following definition of sexual harassment has been inserted into the Act under Paragraph 6;

> By sexual harassment is meant unwelcome behaviour of a sexual nature or other unwelcome behaviour based on sex (gender), that violates the employee's integrity at work.

The change to the Act makes it clear that every employer is obliged to take active measures to prevent an employee from being exposed to sexual harassment. The employer must make it clear in a general staff policy statement that sexual harassment involving employees cannot in any way be tolerated. This policy must be made known to the employees. It is equally important that routines

40. The Ombudsman has no formal right to make proposals to the Government but has the right to participate in the public debate and make suggestions.
41. Sexual Harassment and the Responsibility of the Employer, Dnr A97/3077/JÄM.

are devised for dealing with alleged or actual harassment. The employer who does not fulfil his or her obligations runs the risk of a fine, which can be imposed at the initiative of the Ombudsman.

Furthermore, an employer who receives information that an employee has been exposed to sexual harassment by another employee must investigate the circumstances surrounding the alleged harassment (paragraph 22a). Where necessary, the employer must take such steps as can be reasonably required to prevent the continuation of sexual harassment. An employer who fails to fulfil these obligations will be liable to pay damages to an employee who has been exposed to sexual harassment (paragraph 27a). Damages will be payable for violations following from the neglect of these duties. In cases where the employer is sexually harassing an employee, the rules in the Penal Code concerning molestation or sexual molestation are also applicable. An individual can take action by addressing the employer, the union or the Ombudsman. If the Ombudsman wants to act in a specific case, authorisation is required from the person who has been harassed; should the union decide to act, the Ombudsman must step down in favour of the union in Labour Court proceedings.

The Equal Opportunities Ombudsman

It is the Ombudsman for Equal Opportunities who initiates, directs and supervises efforts to promote equality, and who ensures compliance with the Equal Opportunities Act, together with the Equal Opportunities Commission.[42] The Ombudsman is head of the government authority bearing the same name: the Office of the Equal Opportunities Ombudsman. This Office was established in 1980 under the auspices of the Ministry of Industry, Employment and Communications.[43] As with other Swedish authorities, the Ombudsman has an independent status which means that the Office reaches its own decisions in all individual matters.

An employee who claims to have been a victim of discrimination on the grounds of their sex can, first and foremost, obtain help from his or her trade union. The Swedish trade unions play an important role as they have priority in representing their members in disputes concerning sex discrimination.

---

42. Fahlbeck, op cit, n. 39, pp. 264-265. The Ombudsman's duties are not only governed by the provisions of the Equal Opportunities Act. European Community law on equality also governs the interpretation and application of the Swedish Act. Frequently, the Ombudsman must also take into consideration other employment legislation, for example the Employment Security Act, when investigating an allegation of sex discrimination.
43. *What is JämO?* (1997), Stockholm: Jämställdhetsombudsmannen, p. 3.

This means that if an individual makes a complaint to the Ombudsman, and that person is a member of a trade union (as a great majority of Swedish employees are) the Ombudsman will always ask the union concerned whether it desires to represent its members in the dispute. If the union chooses to represent its member, the Ombudsman still keeps the matter under scrutiny. The matter is not considered to be concluded until it has been resolved. However, in most cases the Ombudsman co-operates successfully with the union concerned.[44] Employees who are not union members or those who do not receive sufficient help from their union can turn to the Equal Opportunities Ombudsman. If a dispute cannot be settled or if an employer refuses to comply with the Ombudsman's instructions, the Ombudsman is entitled to file proceedings at the Labour Court in cases concerning sex discrimination or go to the Equal Opportunities Commission in cases involving equal opportunities in the workplace.[45]

Overseeing the preparation and implementation of equality plans (an employer with ten or more employees is obliged to establish such a plan) is one of the major activities of the Equal Opportunities Ombudsman. Random check-ups are carried out within different branches and sectors of the economy. The Ombudsman also carries out checks on equality plans in several specific counties as means of enforcing compliance with the Equal Opportunities Act. This has proved efficient and effective: in many cases it has been sufficient to forewarn that such a check is about to take place to secure compliance — the warning has worked as a catalyst, initiating the establishment of equality plans.[46] The fear of penalties combined with the fear of negative publicity which could accompany any failure to establish an equality plan, works effectively as an enforcement mechanism.

Another efficient way for the Ombudsman to ensure compliance is to pursue a case by using a communicative strategy (for instance offering assistance) which gives an employer an opportunity to comply with the law and 'repent', as happens in most instances, before the case progresses. A total amount of 38 equality cases have been argued in the Labour Court and most of these have been initiated by the Equal Opportunities Ombudsman. In only 11 of these 38 cases did the Labour Court rule in favour of the opinion of the Ombudsman. However, it must be noted that in cases where an employer had not established an equality plan it was only in two or three cases that the Ombudsman had to refer the matter to the Equal Opportunities

44. Ibid, p. 14.
45. Ibid, p. 4.
46. (1998), *JämOs Nyhetsbrev*, No 5, June.

Commission. And only once has a penalty been imposed in such a case. This low number can be attributed to the successful 'communication-consensus strategy' of the Ombudsman, as a majority of the cases that the Ombudsman takes on are never brought to court. Thus, the Ombudsman does not pursue a strategy of forcing compliance by threats or sanctions, except in a few extreme cases.

The Ombudsman also plays an important role as a *guardian* of equality in the public sphere by actively taking part in public discourse. The Equal Opportunities Ombudsman is often engaged in public investigations and committee work. In the course of these activities the Ombudsman can act as both an informal and formal messenger, disseminating information via its general activities and various publications (including a newsletter). Thus the Ombudsman can play an important role with regard to inputs and outputs of information. At the end of the 1990s the educational role of the Ombudsman has been emphasised and resources have been allocated by the government to increase such activities, since true equality is a matter of changing societal norms and behaviour through knowledge.

The Equal Opportunities Commission

The Equal Opportunities Commission is a governmental body which was established in 1980. The Commission consists of nine members (lawyers, representatives of the social partners and experts on labour market and equality issues). The Commission can order an employer to take active measures to promote equality between the sexes in the workplace. The Commission has the task of deciding questions regarding 'conditional fines' (see below) in accordance with paragraph 35 in the Equal Opportunities Act. The procedure is for the Ombudsman to request the Commission to require an employer 'on pain of the imposition of a conditional fine' to follow the provisions of the Equal Opportunities Act (paragraphs 4-11) on active measures. The Commission will consider the Ombudsman's request and if it is approved, the employer is required to comply with the Ombudsman's directions. These can include the preparation of an equal opportunities plan or the improvement of an existing one. If the employer does not comply with the decision, the Ombudsman is entitled to apply to the District Court to have the fine imposed.[47] The Ombudsman can then return to the Commission with a

47. The district court shall apply the Acts on Litigation in Labour disputes (SFS 1974:371) which in most cases requires that the parties negotiate about the dispute before going to court.

request for a new order combined with a higher conditional fine.[48] If the employer still does not comply, the Ombudsman or the trade union turns to the Labour Court.

The Labour Court

The Labour Court came into existence in 1928 and it is a court which adjudicates on employment law disputes. It is legally defined as a court but it functions more like an arbitration board as it is a tripartite body where members representing the labour market always form the majority.[49] Disputes in relation to sex discrimination can be brought before the Labour Court by trade unions on behalf of their members and also by the Ombudsman. The Labour Court can award damages for discrimination and can declare void collective agreements which breach the provisions of the Equal Opportunities Act. Court decisions are reached through a simple majority and the court is the last instance of appeal. A private individual is unable to commence proceedings before the Labour Court, but can have recourse to the District Court instead. This normally only happens if the union or the Ombudsman chooses not to act in the case, or if no amicable settlement is reached during the 'compulsory pre-court negotiations' and if the union then declines to bring the case to the Labour Court. Employees who are not members of a union may also turn to the District Court in cases where they fail to reach an agreement with their employer. A judgement of a District Court can, however, always be appealed to the Labour Court.[50]

Other Relevant Legislation Concerning Equality and Women's Rights

The Swedish Social Security System is universal and individual, which means that everyone legally resident in the country is individually insured through the Law on National Insurance (paragraph 3 and 4, SFS 1962:1368). As most of the benefits are paid through the principle of salary-reduction (as an example the unemployment benefit (SFS 1973:370) amounts to 80 per cent of salary, up to a certain maximum level of income),

---

48. *What is JämO?*, op cit, n. 43, p. 13.
49. The court normally works with seven members, three of whom are 'official appointees' and represent society; the Chairman and Vice-Chairman who are lawyers and an expert who is well versed in labour market issues. The remaining four members are representatives from the parties of the labour market, that is, two persons from the trade unions and two from the employers' associations.
50. *What is JämO?*, op cit, n. 43, p. 14 and Swedish Law p. 268-269.

actual access to social security benefits is based on having employment and an income. Persons who have been unemployed for a long period must turn to the social welfare system.

A pregnant woman is entitled to Pregnancy Benefit if her capacity to work is reduced by at least 25 per cent and she is unable to be transferred to a less strenuous task, or if the Working Environment Act (SFS 1977:1160) does not allow her to work or to be transferred. Pregnancy Benefit is paid from the sixtieth day before the planned time of birth and, at the most, to the eleventh day before the expected time of birth.[51] The allowance is the same as for Sick Benefit, that is 75 per cent of the lost income.

In accordance with chapter 4 in the Law on National Insurance parents have a right to parental allowance during a total period of 450 days which can be used until the child starts school. The father is also guaranteed an additional 10 days which must be used within 60 days of the birth of the child. The parents can divide the 450 days between themselves as they please. However, there are 30 days that are ear-marked for each parent, namely the so called 'fathers' month' which was introduced in 1995 in order to encourage fathers to take care of their children (SFS 1994:1568). If a parent does not make use of these ear-marked days they cannot be used by the other parent. In conjunction with information campaigns this provision has resulted in an increase by four per cent in fathers who have made use of the parental allowance: in 1994, 28.3 per cent of men used parts of the allowance while in 1998 the number was 32.4 per cent (it should be noted that these figures are not final since the parents can use the allowance until the child starts school). Payment amounts to 75 per cent of the parent's normal income during a period of 360 days and during the 90 days remaining the parent gets a guaranteed amount of 60 SEK/day. In addition a special parental allowance is paid for the care of sick children under the age of twelve, up to a maximum of 60 days per child per year. Investigations have shown that more fathers would stay at home if the family could afford the loss of income. A majority of Swedish men have higher incomes than their spouse/partner, on which the family is dependent.

There is also a Child Benefit which is paid to all Swedish children, via the parents (irrespective of the parents' income). The law also includes children who have been living in Sweden for at least six months (SFS 1947:529) and the benefit amounts to SEK 7.680 per child per year until the child is 16 years old.

---

51. Among others see SFS 1963:381, SFS 1973:349 and SFS 1997:562.

Putting Gender onto the Law and Policy-Making Agenda

Since 1994, the Swedish Government has assumed a collective responsibility for achieving the established gender policy objectives. Each Minister is responsible for the promotion and enhancement of an equality and gender perspective in his or her specific policy area. However, it is the Minister of Equality Affairs who holds the co-ordinating responsibility for equality issues and the development of the Government's mainstreaming policy. The Minister of Equality Affairs is assisted by a state secretary, political advisors and the Equality Affairs Division.

The Equality Affairs Division

At the end of the 1970s equality issues had become increasingly politically important, therefore the Government established an Equality Secretariat within the Government Office. In 1994, the Equality Secretariat was replaced by a separate Equality Affairs Division which in 1998 was located in the Ministry of Industry, Employment and Communications. Among its tasks, the Division supports the Minister of Equality Affairs with information and research. It also initiates efforts to promote equality at national and regional levels, to develop methods for the integration and implementation of a gender perspective in all policy areas and aims to achieve equal representation of women and men in various bodies in the state and public sector. Another vital task is to review government proposals and committee work in order to ensure the gender perspective has been included in accordance with Directive 1994: 124 (see below). In addition, the Division is responsible for training the entire Cabinet Office and other governmental authorities regarding equality issues and government policy. The Division also administers the budget and appropriations issues relating to the Equal Opportunities Ombudsman and the Equal Opportunities Commission, as well as matters involving the Equal Opportunities Act. It is also responsible for co-operation with the European Union, Nordic countries and other international organisations with regard to equality issues.[52]

The Council for Equality Issues

The Council for Equality Issues is an advisory body to the Minister of Equality Affairs and was established in 1994. Its 30 members represent various political and private interests, including women's organisations, political parties, and

52. Ministry of Industry, Employment and Communications. (1999), *Fact sheet: National Machinery for Equality between Women and Men*, February.

employer and employee organisations. The Council meets four times a year to exchange information and discuss equality issues. In practice the Council has no influence on policy-making but serves as a forum where the Equality Minister informs members about government initiatives and discusses 'work in progress'.

Regional Bodies with Responsibility for Equality – The Equality Expert

According to a Parliamentary resolution, County Administrative Boards were given an enhanced role in relation to equal opportunities in 1994. Since 1995 every County Administrative Board has been required to have an Equality Expert.

The primary tasks of the regional Equality Experts are as follows:

- to follow up on all the national equality goals set by Parliament and thus coordinate and support national, local and regional activity and initiate activities in order to increase the knowledge in the field.
- to develop, in co-operation with representatives from the County Administrative Board, strategies, methods and models so that women's as well as men's situations, conditions and needs are analysed in all proposals for measures and strategy documents.
- to act as a support mechanism and offer services to the companies and places of work in the region in the matter of equality.
- to co-operate with the national authorities which are represented in the various counties and municipalities, and also with the unions, companies, other organisations and citizens. The co-operation can mean that the Equality Experts take part in meetings and education at places of work. The Expert can be involved in initiating University courses since it is a national goal to enhance equality through all forms of education.

Furthermore, the Expert shall cooperate with the Equal Opportunities Ombudsman in questions concerning equality in working life.[53] When it comes to the Equal Opportunities Act, it is only the Ombudsman who has the authority to request that a company submit their equality plan, but the Equality Experts can at times assist the Ombudsman, by offering their services to

53. Jämställdhetsstrategi för Göteborgs och Bohus län Regionalekonomiska avdelningen 1996:3, Länsstyrelsen i Göteborgs och Bohus län, January 10 1996, p. 5.

companies to assist in the establishment of an equality plan. In 1998, there was an ongoing discussion whether the Equality Experts should be given an extended authority in the matter of control and enforcement of equality plans and be given a supervising responsibility.[54]

Swedish Mainstreaming Strategies

A majority of the Swedish work on equality issues has been, and is still, organised through *ad hoc* projects outside the everyday work of the government. However, in the early 1990s the government experience was that these projects did not substantially contribute to reforming the societal structures which uphold and maintain gender inequality. New tools had to be developed to change these normative structures, and mainstreaming was such a tool.[55] Since 1994 the Social Democratic Government has declared in the government's annual statement that a gender equality perspective must permeate all aspects of government policy. To indicate this change in equality strategy the Government introduced the concept of 'gender mainstreaming'. The Swedish meaning of the concept is that all governmental (political) and administrative work shall be permeated by a gender perspective at all levels and in all areas. Mainstreaming means the integration of a gender perspective into all policy fields. It should be noted that this is not the same as 'the integration of women'. The latter approach often makes the conditions that are peculiar for women less visible or even invisible, if it is assumed that women are to be integrated into existing organisational structures, obeying existing formal and informal behaviour codes. Thus, 'the integration of women' approach often problematises the women rather than the existing structures.[56] From a Swedish perspective mainstreaming should be defined as the integration of a gender perspective into structures and processes; hence, mainstreaming can be understood as an umbrella term for various strategies and methods for achieving gender equality objectives. However, it is impossible to describe all of the mainstreaming measures that have been undertaken. Therefore the following sections will discuss only some of the most influential strategies.

---

54. S. Lindsten, Equality Expert at Vaestra Goetalands County Administrative Board, Interview 4 July 1998.
55. Ibid.
56. Lundkvist, H. and Thoursie, A. (1997), *Report on the Swedish Part of the Project Mainstreaming Gender Equality in Local Government*, Swedish Association of Local Authorities p. 5.

Directive 1994:124

In order to enhance and promote equality the Ministry of Social Affairs issued a general mainstreaming directive in 1994 to all committees and those in charge of various investigations. In accordance with Directive 1994:124 all committee and investigation reports and proposals should have an analysis and a report on the consequences of the suggested policy from an equal opportunities and gender perspective.

However, it appears that compliance with the Directive is not satisfactory since most committees and investigations have not taken the instructions and demands of Directive 1994:124 seriously. An evaluation of the Directive which was carried out by the Equality Affairs Division in 1997 showed that only 33 per cent of investigations had included a thorough gender perspective in the written report.[57] This poor result has been attributed to a lack of knowledge about equality issues and to the lack of effective implementation mechanisms, such as supporting structures, review mechanisms and enforcement sanctions if the Directive is not properly applied by an investigation. Another consequence for the Equality Affairs Division is that they are forced into the role of 'policing investigations' instead of concentrating their resources on pro-active and supportive measures. In other words, the result clearly indicates the need for a proper *Gender Impact Assessment* model. Consequently, the Government initiated an investigation in 1999 with the task of finding ways to enhance compliance and thus strengthen the Directive.[58] The Equality Affairs Division has presented a proposal for a simple model which currently is being tested in different Ministerial divisions. This model for Gender Impact Assessment (or analysis) consists of the following four questions:

1. *Does the document affect one or more target group(s)?* If the answer is yes, a gender perspective should be applied in the analysis.
2. *What are the conditions for women and men respectively in the policy area in question?* This requires a review of the representation in decision-making bodies and the distribution and access to resources and an investigation of rights, obligations and responsibilities from a gender perspective.
3. *What are the different/similar conditions for women and men in a particular area?* Structures, norms and organisation must be analysed.
4. *What assessable measures have been planned in order to achieve the established gender policy objectives?*

57. Evaluation of Directive 1994:124, The Equality Affairs Division, 10 November 1997.
58. Interview with Katarina Scmidt, the Equality Affairs Division, 11 January 1999.

Some interesting practical research concerning local government and mainstreaming has also been undertaken. These local projects exemplify a process-oriented approach to equality work which aims at changing the prevailing norms that have dominated the way societal structures work. Furthermore, the alternative projects constitute a shift in Swedish equality policy by turning away from the previous exclusive focus on legislation and active measures. In several of these local projects whole Municipalities are engaged in striving towards equality goals and since 1994 an annual award has been given by the Ombudsman to 'the most equal' Municipality in Sweden. The first Municipality to receive the award was Växjö; it is mentioned here as a good example of how a Municipality can approach equality issues. Växjö has an extremely active Equality Committee which raises issues of equality directly with Municipality leaders. The Committee is a part of the so-called Municipal government, and has an equal number of women and men as representatives. The Committe functions formally as a board with a budget of its own. The Municipality has an equality programme in which it is established that the social order of society is patriarchal and that equality issues concern both men and women. This Municipality has successfully managed to establish a consensus which cuts across the political divisions on equality questions.

The result of the Committee's work is very positive — for example, parental leave is divided equally between both parents. It is also the official policy of the Municipality that the number of administrative managers and managing directors should be equally distributed between the sexes. Another interesting change is that public transport has been adjusted to suit both women's and men's working hours. In addition when applications for management positions are considered within the jurisdiction of the Municipality, parental leave is considered as a merit. Furthermore, the Municipality has established a goal regarding gender based wage differences which should be levelled out by the year 2000. Here the Municipality of Växjö has noticed that the foremost factors which hinder the achievement of this goal are located centrally, as it is the social partners who settle wage levels.[59]

59. *Dagens Nyheter*, 15 February 1998.

JÄMKOM

In 1995 the Government allocated SEK 2 million to a project initiated by the Swedish Association of Local Authorities. The intention of the JÄMKOM[60] project was to develop a concrete method with the capacity to both analyse and promote equal opportunities within local government. In other words, the objective was to create an efficient and practical tool for the integration of a gender perspective into local government.[61] With regard to methodology, the researchers of the project noted that a close connection between theory and practice was crucial, that the development of method must take place *in situ*, that is, as an integrated process within the municipal activities, and that the actual implementation should take a bottom-up approach.

The method which evolved is called the '3R-method'. The three 'Rs' stand for *Representation*, *Resources* and *Realia* and constitute the pillars of a method which builds upon gender related knowledge, experience and practice. The first variables *Representation* and *Resources* are quantitative and directed towards answering questions concerning features of the decision-making process. The method measures the extent to which women and men have access to decision-makers (Representation) and how resources are allocated between women and men (Resources); it also provides a qualitative assessment of how products (services) are delivered (Realia) The method can answer questions like: how are women and men represented on different levels? What does the 'power' structure look like? Are there informal networks which influence the decision-making process? How are resources such as time, money and space distributed between women and men? The two first variables, *Representation* and *Resources* provide a basis for *Realia* which is the qualitative variable. Realia can be said to stand for the content of the activities that the local government engages in. The research project also gives examples of other vital aspects which can be detected by the use of the method: for instance what are the norms that have influenced the content of a certain activity? Who influences the 'right to formulate what the problem is and where the problem is to be found'? Can a 'target person' be identified — if so, who decided the characteristics of this 'target person'?

60. The word is difficult to translate directly as it combines the beginning of the Swedish word for equal opportunities (*jämställdhet*) with the word for municipality (*kommun*).

61 The Swedish research project was also a part of a study commissioned by the Equal Opportunities Commission (United Kingdom) on Mainstreaming in Local Government. It was partly funded by the European Commission as part of the Fourth Action Programme on Equal Opportunities for Women and Men. The Swedish part of the study was carried out by Helen Lundkvist and Anna Thoursie.

The primary objective of the 3R method is to obtain new knowledge of how the division of power, structures and norms must change in order to create activities that provide women and men with truly equal opportunities.[62] So far, one of the most important findings of the Swedish project is that the implementation of the variables *Representation* and *Resources* have given rise to the development of a range of indicators to assess the quality of equality (in this local context the quality of the services offered to the users by local government). Moreover, the project also demonstrates the importance of developing equality indicators that can be used at national, regional and local levels and the need to establish and implement procedures to review equality policies at all levels.[63] The JÄMKOM project also illustrates how important it is that individuals in key positions become involved in the process of furthering equality issues at local level. However, the project did stress the danger of an approach that relies too much on individuals in comparison to lasting structures and processes. It appears to be extremely important to establish a lasting process that continuously promotes mainstreaming, so that the driving forces behind mainstreaming do not disappear together with the 'equality champion', who may, for example, leave for another job.

In addition, there are several projects which have focused on using the market's self-regulating mechanisms to enhance equality, drawing experience from the environmental field of procurement, eco-labelling and environmental management systems.

Public Procurement as a Future Option to promote Equal Opportunities

Through the procurement of goods and services, even a small Municipality which wants to enhance equality, can support suppliers who promote equality issues in their organisation. As an example, the Municipality can ask for a company's equality plan and statistical information on differences in salaries between women and men. However, the Swedish Board of Public Procurement[64] has established that such factors may not formally be taken into consideration when a Municipality awards a contract. However, it is not

---

62. Lundkvist and Thoursie, op cit, n. 56.
63. Equal Opportunities Commission. (1997), *Mainstreaming Gender Equality in Local Government, Synthesis Report*, Manchester: Equal Opportunities Commission.
64. The Board of Public Procurement (Nämnden för Offentlig Upphandling) is a central government agency which supervises the observation of the Public Procurement Acts (Lagen om Offentlig Upphandling, SFS 1992;1528). The Board also gives general advice and comments on how the procurement regulations shall be interpreted.

forbidden to ask whether a company complies with Swedish legislation, which includes the Equal Opportunities Act. Hence, it is possible for the Municipality to make a subtle inquiry. In several cases a simple question about a company's equality work has proved to be an efficient strategy since few companies, when asked, dare take the risk of leaving out aspects of equality when submitting an offer to a public purchaser.[65] At present several Municipalities are successfully carrying out projects concerning public procurement and social and environmental demands.[66]

Equality Labelling and Equality Management Systems

In 1998 there were several ongoing projects in Sweden which investigated the possibilities for equality labelling of products and organisations. This labelling would work in the same manner as eco-labelling which is extremely successful in Sweden. By using consumer power (ethical preference) and exploiting the market's self-regulating mechanisms, such labelling could help to enhance equality, particularly in the private sector of production. Another possibility which has been examined is the development and integration of an equality standard which would be compatible with the management systems of EMAS and ISO. An equality management system could be an efficient tool allowing the organisation to address equality issues in a systematic and continuous manner at all levels. Furthermore, as the environmental management systems have shown, it would most likely lead to a continous improvement in the equality situation in the organisation beyond the requirements of the law.[67] In the autumn of 1998 the Government presented an investigation called *Jämställdhetsmärkning — konsumentmakt för ett jämställt samhälle* (Equality Labelling — Consumer Power for an Equal Society)[68] and in early 1999 the Government issued instructions for

---

65. Dagens Nyheter, February 15 1998.
66. In the EU Commission's Green Paper, *Public Procurement in the European Union: Exploring the Way Forward*, the inclusion of social and environmental aspects on procurement are considered as a future option (Communication adopted by the Commission on 27 November 1996 on the proposal of Commissioner Monti, DG XV). The economic importance of public procurement in Europe is considerable: public authorities and public utilities subject to Community rules spend some ECU 720 billion each year on goods and services, equivalent in 1994 to 11.5 per cent of the GDP of the 15 Member States of the Union which equals some ECU 2000 per citizen of the Union. To follow up on the Green Paper's discussion regarding procurement from the perspective of improving equal opportunities constitutes an interesting opportunity and challenge.
67. Gillberg, M. (1999), 'From Green Image to Green Practice. Normative Action and Self-regulation', in *Lund Studies in Sociology of Law*, No 6, Lund: Lund University.
68. Gillberg, M. (1998), in *Jämställdhetsmärkning – konsumentmakt för ett jämställt samhälle (Equality Labelling – Consumer Power for an Equal Society) Ds 1998:49*, Stockholm: Fritzes Offentliga Publikationer, p. 49.

another investigation to draw up a final proposal for Parliament. However, a government initiative might have been side-stepped by the labour union LO, and the employers organisation TCO, who in May 1999 decided to co-operate in the development of their own scheme for equality labelling.

Conclusion

Sweden is in general regarded as a society in which there is a relatively high degree of equality between women and men. Reference is often made to the high percentage of women's representation in government (50 per cent), in Parliament (43 per cent), in County Councils (48 per cent) and in Municipalities (41 per cent). Swedish women also have a relatively high employment rate (70 per cent), giving them good possibilities of supporting themselves. Both women and men also have ample possibilities to combine employment with parental and household responsibilities due to Sweden's well developed child-care system.[69] In many areas, however, there still remain considerable imbalances in the power relations between women and men. Since 1994, a number of measures and investigations to promote equality have been introduced by the Government. The so called Women's Power Commission was part of this effort and was launched by the Government in 1996. The task of the Commission was to map and analyse, from several aspects, the actual distribution of economic power and economic resources between women and men, and the forces behind this. The final report was presented in January 1998 (SOU 1998:6) and concluded that Swedish equality, to a large extent, is still only formal and not factual. The Commission came to the following conclusions regarding the Swedish gender imbalance:

- an academic education in general pays off less for women than for men, both in the matter of wages and careers (women earn between 70-80 per cent of the earnings of men).
- professions dominated by women have lower wages than male-dominated professions.
- three out of four managers are men, and the Commission indicated that the informal traditional 'quota of men' should be abolished.
- women lose considerably in terms of future wage increases if they give birth to children.

69. SFS 1985:1100 and SFS 1997:1212 (chapter 2a).

- men who make use of parental leave lose more of their income than women, as they normally earn more.
- the public sector exploits women by offering low wages, part-time work, poor opportunities for personal development and very low pensions.

The investigation also emphasised that a strong indicator of the remaining power imbalance between women and men is the high level of men's violence against women. The Swedish experience thus tells us that there is a great difference between formal (legal) gender equality and informal social gender equality. A feminist critique of the Swedish law and policy-making process could therefore partly consist of a critique of the law's gender neutral language, which in the present light can be seen as a serious obstacle. 'Official' gender neutrality can sometimes effectively conceal conditions which are grounded on prevailing behavioural norms in a society. As described, the Swedish consensus process of decision-making has in itself a gender imbalance and can be considered as a relatively exclusive and closed system, when it comes to the representation of societal interests.

Since the mid-1990s the Swedish Government has recognised that equality is not something which can be achieved solely through legislation. The mainstreaming policy approach is an attempt to attack the fundamental problem, namely the prevailing norms in society which uphold gendered inequality. Swedish mainstreaming recognises the necessity of changing societal norms and emphasises process rather than structures, and the importance of a bottom-up implementation approach. Hence, the government has supported several projects to promote this approach, for instance local government mainstreaming and alternative measures such as equality labelling.

A general awareness must be developed regarding the norms and behavioural patterns which do not promote gender equality. The Swedish case has shown that a proper mechanism or process must be developed which illuminates the normative and fundamental dimensions of gender equality, especially in the political decision-making process. The main-streaming Directive 1994:124 is a step in the right direction. The Government initiated an investigation in 1999 to find ways to enhance compliance and thus strengthen the directive.[70] It remains to be seen whether the model for Gender Impact Assessment currently being tested will prove effective.

70. Interview with Katarina Scmidt, the Equality Affairs Division, 11 January 1999.

7 Making Women Count in the United Kingdom

FIONA BEVERIDGE, SUE NOTT AND KYLIE STEPHEN

This account of law and policy-making in the United Kingdom is intended to draw attention to the numerous mechanisms which exist for the explicit purpose of integrating gender into the law and policy-making processes. This task is complicated, however, by the far-reaching changes currently being made to constitutional arrangements in the United Kingdom. Those changes include the process of devolving certain legislative powers to regional assemblies in Scotland, Wales and Northern Ireland. Devolution has provided a focus for political action that will undoubtedly have long-term effects on the legal and political landscape of the United Kingdom and may bring more open and innovative political structures which could make a difference to the representation of women's interests. Such changes include new methods of election for the devolved assemblies, the introduction of new 'family friendly' operating practices for the devolved assemblies and the construction of new equality machinery such as the Equality Commission in Northern Ireland.

The current Labour government in the United Kingdom is also committed to a programme of 'modernising government' to ensure that decision-making is more integrated and that government provides high quality and efficient services to the public. The programme to modernise government aims to make decision-making more open, accountable and democratic. Such an agenda may, in turn, offer opportunities for women's organisations and individual women to be involved in the process of policy and decision-making in a manner not previously possible. There is also a commitment on government's part to the development of new processes for addressing gender equality such as mainstreaming and gender impact assessment mechanisms (specifically the statutory obligation to assess policies for their gender impact in Northern Ireland).

Whether these changes will affect women for better or worse is hard to say at this point because the new systems and structures are still in their infancy. But what is clear is that in reforming its existing policy-making structures and processes, the United Kingdom is changing the way in which it approaches equality issues.

The Political and Legal Landscape in the United Kingdom

When compared with other states, the United Kingdom is exceptional in not possessing a written constitution. Written constitutions often describe the chief actors in the law and policy-making process, their powers and their relationships to one another. In the United Kingdom this information has to be extracted from a mass of laws, conventions[1] and judicial decisions.[2]

There are two forms of legislation — primary and secondary — and the power to make legislation is vested in the Westminster Parliament and the monarch, though the latter plays a purely formal role.[3] Parliament consists of two chambers — an elected House of Commons and the unelected House of Lords. Parliamentary elections must be held at least once every five years. It is a matter for the Prime Minister when he or she requests a general election.[4] The United Kingdom uses the 'first past the post' system of voting in Parliamentary elections. The country is divided into 659 constituencies and whoever secures the most votes in a constituency is elected as that constituency's Member of Parliament (MP). This system of voting invariably guarantees that one party[5] will win an overall majority in a general election. The party which wins a majority of the seats in the House of Commons is the party whose leader will be invited by the sovereign to form a government. It also means that the government of the day controls the House of Commons because of its majority in that chamber.

---

1. A constitutional convention is a practice or an understanding which becomes accepted over the years by those who are affected by its existence. A convention is not legally binding though it may be regularly observed. Once a convention is ignored by those whose behaviour it regulates then it ceases to exist as a binding convention.
2. Some commentators argue that this is sufficient to constitute a constitution. See Hood Phillips, O. and Jackson, P. (1987), *Constitutional and Administrative Law*, Seventh Edition, London: Sweet and Maxwell. Other commentators disagree. See Ridley, F. F. (1988), 'There is no British Constitution: A Dangerous Case of the Emperor's Clothes', *Parliamentary Affairs*, p. 41.
3. As a matter of law the sovereign can refuse to give her assent to proposed legislation. The last time this happened was in the eighteenth century. Since that date a constitutional convention has developed to the effect that the sovereign automatically gives her assent.
4. The sovereign has formally to grant that request by dissolving Parliament.
5. There are two major political parties in the United Kingdom — the Labour Party and the Conservative Party. Other political parties exist, such as the Liberal Democrats and the Scottish Nationalist Party, but they normally secure far fewer seats in the House of Commons.

The number of women MPs is still small despite the fact that women have had the vote since 1918.[6] Women represent approximately 18 per cent (121 of 659)[7] of the membership of the present House of Commons. While a relatively small number, this represents a 100 per cent increase on the previous Parliament where only 9.2 per cent of MPs were women.[8] Attempts have been made by some political parties to increase the numbers of women MPs. For example, at the last general election the Labour Party committed itself to increasing the number of Labour women MPs by preparing all-women short-lists in certain Parliamentary constituencies. This policy was abandoned, however, because of a successful challenge to it on the grounds that it constituted sex discrimination.[9]

The House of Lords is an unelected chamber consisting of hereditary peers, life peers and bishops from the Church of England and senior members of the judiciary. As an unelected chamber the power of the House of Lords to veto legislation is very limited. Under the terms of the Parliament Acts 1911 and 1949, legislation can be approved without the agreement of the House of Lords after the passage of one year.[10] Currently the role of the House of Lords is under scrutiny. The decision has been taken to abolish the voting rights of hereditary peers,[11] though this will have little effect on women's representation in the Lords. In the long-term, however, the decision to change the composition, and perhaps functions, of the House of Lords, could offer an opportunity to secure greater representation of women.

The government of the day exercises executive power. Members of the government are appointed by the Prime Minister and must be members of either the House of Commons or the House of Lords. Holders of one of the senior positions in government, such as Chancellor of the Exchequer, are normally members of the House of Commons in order to ensure their accountability to the electorate. Those holding senior positions in government will be members of the Cabinet. The Cabinet consists of the Prime Minister

---

6. Only women over 30 years of age were granted the right to vote at this time.
7. In the 1997 elections, 120 women were elected to office. Since that time there has been a by-election and there is now an additional Conservative woman Member of Parliament.
8. Figures come from the Labourwomen webpage: http://www.labour.org.uk/views/women/mp.html
9. *Jepson and Dyas-Elliott v The Labour Party* [1996] IRLR 116. By the time this policy was abandoned it had already had the desired impact.
10. There have been only four occasions when the Parliament Acts have been invoked. The most recent example of legislation passed in this manner is the European Parliamentary Elections Act 1999.
11. House of Lords Act 1999.

and between 18 and 24[12] senior Ministers such as the Foreign Secretary. The Cabinet meets every week and discusses any immediate problems that the government is facing as well as the government's legislative programme and the economic situation. Most detailed discussion regarding government policy on particular issues takes place in Cabinet committees. These committees, which may be permanent or temporary, are made up of Ministers not all of whom will be Cabinet members. The committees are concerned with specific aspects of government policy such as defence and overseas policy. Their task is to discuss and take decisions in respect of that particular area of policy. Those decisions, depending on their importance, may require confirmation by the Cabinet.

The Cabinet has a crucial role to play in co-ordinating government business and integrating government policy-making. Thus it would seem essential that women's interests need to be given adequate representation at this level of decision-making to ensure that they are fed into the policy-making process at the earliest possible stage. Whether this happens is difficult to say. In 1999 there were five women in the Cabinet; the highest number ever for a British government.[13] There is also a Cabinet Sub-Committee on Women as well as a Women's Unit based in the Cabinet Office. The strategic role played by these bodies and whether their existence means that women's needs are being addressed in a comprehensive and co-ordinated fashion will be considered later in this chapter.

The judicial system in England and Wales[14] consists of a hierarchy of courts namely in civil matters the county courts, the High Court, the Court of Appeal (Civil Division) and the House of Lords and in criminal matters, the magistrates courts, the Crown Courts, the Queen's Bench Division Court, the Court of Appeal (Criminal Division) and the House of Lords. There is also a body known as the Judicial Committee of the Privy Council which in the past has simply heard judicial appeals from Commonwealth countries. This body has now assumed the role of determining disputes between the Scottish Parliament, the Welsh Assembly and the Westminster Parliament on questions of competence.

---

12. There is no set number. This is purely a matter for the Prime Minister of the day. There is, however, a limit of 20 on the number of salaried Cabinet posts. See Ministerial and Other Salaries Act 1975.
13. This is compared with 17 men in Cabinet.
14. For an account of the similar but distinctive judicial system in Scotland see Walker, D. (1992), *The Scottish Legal System: An Introduction to the Study of Scots Law*, Edinburgh: Green.

In the United Kingdom a system of precedent operates whereby the lower courts are bound by the decision on a point of law of a higher court. The courts also regard the will of Parliament as sovereign and themselves as bound by legislation agreed by Parliament even though it might be inconsistent with the United Kingdom's international obligations.[15] The only exception is if a conflict occurs between national and European Community law. In such a situation the courts will do their best to interpret United Kingdom domestic law in a manner that is compatible with Community law. If this is not possible then the courts will give any piece of Community law[16] with direct effect priority over domestic law.[17]

Most courts, with the exception of magistrates courts which in the main try minor criminal offences, are staffed by professional, as opposed to lay, judges. The judiciary in the United Kingdom is dominated by men. Women are grossly under-represented at all levels of judicial work. There are no women judges in the House of Lords and one, as compared with 34 men, in the Court of Appeal. Seven High Court judges are women as compared with 90 men.[18] The composition of the judiciary can and does have concrete effects on the way in which equality issues are incorporated into law and policy-making.

The courts' task is to interpret legislation and the common law. Hence their policy toward statutory interpretation — whether to give words a literal or a purposive interpretation — is crucial. Even if the courts are prepared to look at what harm a particular piece of legislation was meant to address (purposive approach) there is no guarantee that their view of its purpose corresponds with that of the Minister who introduced it.[19] In the same way a literal approach to the interpretation of legislation gives the courts considerable power since there is no objectively discoverable meaning to a particular set of words. In this manner the courts' policy on interpretation can allow them to remodel the policy which the legislation was meant to put into practice.

15. See *Cheney v Conn* [1968] 1 All ER 779 where a challenge to the Finance Act 1964 on the basis that it was in breach of the Geneva Convention (set out in a schedule to and given effect in part in the Geneva Conventions Act 1957) to which the United Kingdom was a signatory was rejected.
16. See *Pickstone v Freemans plc* [1989] AC 66.
17. See *R v Secretary of State for Transport* ex parte Factortame Ltd [1990] 2 AC 85 at p. 140, *R* v *Secretary of State for Transport* ex parte Factortame Ltd (No 2) [1991] 1 AC 603 at p. 659.
18. Figures for 1998 taken from Government website: http://www.open.gov.uk/lcd/judicial/womapp.htm
19. After the House of Lords decision in *Pepper v Hart* [1993] AC 593 it is permissible for a court to refer to Hansard (the verbatim account of proceedings in Parliament) to discover what a Minister's intention was in introducing legislation.

In the past the court's interpretation of the legislation designed to promote equal opportunities, and in particular the anti-discrimination legislation, has been extremely unsympathetic[20] with many judges believing that it imposed an unwarranted burden on industry.[21] Legislation was given its literal meaning with scant attention being paid to the purpose behind that legislation. As the years have passed the United Kingdom courts have undoubtedly become more tolerant of the legislation — a stance that may have been forced on them by the more sensitive approach taken by the European Court of Justice.

The Law and Policy-Making Process

The development of policy is the responsibility of the government or more specifically, government Ministers, their departments and Cabinet committees. Who should be consulted when developing policy is a matter for Ministers. Consultation may be informal or formal. A Minister may, for example, issue a consultation paper (Green Paper) outlining various policy options and inviting responses from anyone who cares to comment. Alternatively the government may publish a White Paper which will contain recommendations for changes to the law. Although the government may invite comments on a White Paper, it is unlikely at this stage to radically modify its proposals. In many cases, though, no formal consultation process will be undertaken though Ministers may choose to consult publicly or in confidence with interested parties.

Details of how the policy-making process works are sketchy because few studies have been undertaken into policy-making practice. The lack of available evidence may be explained in large part by the cult of secrecy, described by many as obsessive, which historically has characterised government and administration in the United Kingdom.[22] Legislation has been in place from the start of the twentieth century which is cast in wide terms to 'give greater protection against leakages of any kind of official information whether or not connected with defence or national security'.[23] Even after reforms in the 1980s,[24] drawing more tightly the classes of information

20. See for example *Turley v Allders Department Stores* [1980] IRLR 4.
21. See *Grimsby Carpet Company v Bedford* [1987] IRLR 438 at p. 440. See also Morris, A. and Nott, S. (1995), 'The law's engagement with pregnancy', in Bridgeman, J. and Millns, S. (eds), *Law and Body Politics*, London: Dartmouth.
22. For an historical account see Birkinshaw, P. (2nd 1996), *Freedom of Information. The Law, the Practice and the Ideal*, London: Butterworths, Chapter Three.
23. *Report of the Committee on Reform of Section 2 of the Official Secrets Act 1911*, (1972), Cmnd 5104, vol. I, London: HMSO, para 50.
24. For example, the Official Secrets Act 1989.

covered by criminal interdict, there was no general expectation of freedom of information. The release of information about how policies had been arrived at, about studies and/or consultations underway or about policy options under consideration was still controlled by government and entirely discretionary. Though in recent years some efforts have been made by government to introduce greater elements of openness to the workings of government there is still no general right of freedom of information in the United Kingdom. The government retains a wide degree of discretion in relation to information. Since 1994, however, there has been a *Code of Practice on Access to Government Information* which, along with its *Guidance on Interpretation,*[25] regulates public rights of access to government-held information in the absence of a legal right or statutory entitlement. In relation to policy-making the Code commits government departments, agencies and public bodies to disclose information used in decision-making, except where disclosure would not be in the public interest.

Essentially there are two forms of disclosure: publication and disclosure in response to a specific request. In relation to the former the commitment is made 'to publish the facts and analysis of the facts which the Government considers relevant and important in framing major policy proposals and decisions'.[26] In relation to the latter there is a commitment 'to release, in response to specific requests, information relating to their policies, actions and decisions and other matters related to their areas of responsibility'.[27] Thus individuals (including MPs), interested groups and organisations can request the release of information from the relevant department on any subject matter; there is a presumption that it will be disclosed, subject to the exemptions provided for in the Code, and a decision not to disclose can be challenged.[28] Part II of the Code contains the exemptions from the commitment to disclose grouped into 15 headings. Of particular relevance to policy-making is the second heading 'Internal discussion and advice': here confidentiality can be maintained where disclosure would 'harm the frankness and candour of internal discussions'.

A Freedom of Information Act is currently under consideration by the Government and is likely to be introduced during its term of office.[29] It is

25. Open Government. (1997), *Code of Practice on Access to Government Information and Guidance on Interpretation,* Second Edition, Part V.
26. *Code of Practice*, op cit, n. 25, Part I, 3.1.
27. Ibid.
28. A decision not to disclose may be reviewed internally and then, if this does not produce results, by the Parliamentary Commissioner for Administration.
29. The Government's proposals for a Freedom of Information Act were first put forward in December 1997 in the White Paper entitled *Your Right to Know*, Cmnd 3818, London: HMSO. A Freedom of Information Bill [H.L.] was introduced into the House of Lords on 10 December 1998 and the Government's paper, *Freedom of Information: Consultation on Draft Legislation,* Cmnd 4355, London: HMSO, was presented to Parliament by the Secretary of State for the Home Department in May 1999.

anticipated that any new Freedom of Information Act will retain exemptions for the policy-making procedure. This culture of secrecy has obvious implications for those both inside and outside government who would seek to influence policy-making and has important ramifications for mainstreaming initiatives. Women's groups and others (including 'inside' agencies such as the Women's Unit) are not guaranteed any right to be consulted about or to comment on new proposals in their intial stages. Though the Women's Unit itself has explored some new ways of allowing women's voices to be heard in the policy-making process,[30] more is required to meet the government's stated desire to make government more open and accountable.

Once a policy is agreed, then the form it should take will be determined. The government may use legislation (hard law) or a soft law measure such as a circular to implement a policy. Legislation is used where it is important that a particular policy is observed by all those affected and where there is a need to bind those who are external to government. Many policies are, however, implemented through a soft law measure, such as a government circular, rather than legislation. Soft law is not binding on officials in the same way as hard law but it cannot be ignored by decision-makers: the courts have regarded it as a factor which has to be taken into account in relevant circumstances.[31]

One of the most significant recent developments within the policy-making framework of the United Kingdom has been the development of regional assemblies in Scotland, Wales and Northern Ireland. The Scotland Act 1998 established a single chamber Scottish Parliament consisting of 129 members. The members of the Scottish Parliament are elected by a combination of simple majority voting and proportional representation. Elections are held once every four years. The Scottish Parliament can legislate on any matter that is not specially reserved for action by the Westminster Parliament. Reserved matters include economic and monetary policy, social security, immigration, defence and consumer protection. Equal opportunities legislation is also a reserved matter despite a campaign that the issue be devolved. Any measure of the Scottish Parliament which deals with a reserved matter or is incompatible with the European Convention on Human Rights or EU law is not law. A Bill which, in the opinion of the Presiding Officer of the Scottish Parliament, is outside the competence of the Scottish Parliament may not be introduced. It is also possible for a Bill to be referred to the Judicial Committee of the Privy Council for a ruling on whether or not it is outside the Scottish Parliament's competence.

---

30. For example, women's juries and the use of the Internet. For further discussion of these innovations see Chapter Nine, this volume, p. 240.
31. *R v Home Secretary* ex parte Khan [1985] 1 All ER 40; *R v Secretary of State for the Environment*, ex parte Tower Hamlets L.B.C. [1993] Q.B. 632.

As well as the Scottish Parliament, the 1998 Act makes provision for the establishment of a Scottish administration, including a Scottish executive. The executive consists of a First Minister, other Ministers appointed by the First Minister and the Lord Advocate and Solicitor General for Scotland. It is the role of the Scottish Parliament to establish committees to scrutinise the actions of the Scottish executive. The Scottish executive is funded in the main by grants voted by the Westminster Parliament. The Scottish Parliament does, however, possess some limited powers to raise revenue. It can vary the rate of income tax set by the Westminster Parliament by up to three pence in the pound.

The first Scottish Parliament was elected in May 1999. Women are well represented in this new body with 37.2 per cent of the seats (48 out of 129). This is because there has been a long-standing campaign for equal representation if and when a Scottish Parliament was established. In the event it was left to individual political parties to secure the equal representation of men and women in the first Scottish Parliament. Only the Labour Party, however, adopted a specific mechanism to ensure gender balance among its candidates. As well as the campaign for equal representation, pressure has been brought to bear to ensure that the Scottish Parliament takes account of women's interests when conducting its business. A standing committee on equal opportunities has been established and the Parliament has been urged to adopt family-friendly working practices. There is a commitment to the mainstreaming of equality in the work of the Parliament though it remains to be seen whether or how this will be realised.

As well as the Scottish Parliament, a National Assembly for Wales has been established.[32] It consists of 60 members elected by a combination of simple majority voting and proportional representation. The powers of the Welsh Assembly are very different from those of the Scottish Parliament. It has no power to pass primary legislation. Responsibility for this remains with the Westminster Parliament. Provision is simply made for the Secretary of State for Wales to consult the Welsh Assembly regarding the government's legislative programme. What will be transferred to the Welsh Assembly are powers to make secondary legislation and responsibility for matters such as agriculture, education, health and the environment which currently rest with the Secretary of State for Wales. The Assembly is financed by grants from Westminster and has no power to raise taxes. Most of the business of the Assembly is to be dealt with in subject committees. The chairs of those committees together with the First Secretary[33] form an Executive Committee which is meant to give political direction to the Assembly.

32. Government of Wales Act 1998.

33. This is the leader of the group with the largest number of seats in the Assembly.

In the first Welsh Assembly elections held in May 1999, 40 per cent of the seats were secured by women (24 out of 60). Whilst this is an excellent result, there has not been the degree of campaigning on gender issues in Wales to match that in Scotland. This may be linked to a general lack of enthusiasm in Wales regarding the Assembly and what it can be expected to achieve. The Assembly is, however, committed to equal opportunities[34] and, as a first step, has established an equal opportunities committee.

The Government of Ireland Act 1920 gave Northern Ireland its own executive and Parliament with the power to pass primary legislation on certain matters. With the advent of civil unrest in Northern Ireland these arrangements were suspended. The Northern Ireland Constitution Act 1973 made provision for a new Assembly and a power-sharing executive. This initiative failed and as a consequence there was direct rule of Northern Ireland by the Secretary of State for Northern Ireland in relation to all matters previously devolved to the Northern Ireland Assembly. Most recently the Good Friday or Belfast Agreement provided, among other things, for the election by means of proportional representation of an Assembly with devolved powers in Northern Ireland. This Assembly is a 108 member power-sharing body with Ministers appointed and decisions taken on a cross community basis. It was, however, suspended after only a few months because of political disagreements over other aspects[35] of the Good Friday agreement. The tensions within Northern Ireland mean that increasing the representation of women in any devolved Assembly has not attracted much attention. Only 12.96 per cent of those elected to the Assembly are women (14 out of 108). One of the parties represented in the Assembly is the Women's Coalition.

The radical changes, such as devolution, that are currently re-shaping the United Kingdom's institutional landscape may have significant consequences for women's representation and their ability to influence political decision-making overall. The attention paid to equal opportunities in the establishment of the devolved assemblies is encouraging, but it should be remembered that central government retains responsibility both for equal opportunities legislation and for many significant areas of policy. The absence of any Parliamentary machinery dedicated to equality at Westminster is increasingly anomolous. Small changes are occurring at the administrative level. Efforts are being made to alter the composition and

---

34. S. 48 of the Government of Wales Act 1998 requires the Assembly to have due regard to equal opportunities in the conduct of its business and to make appropriate arrangements to that end.
35. Most particularly the decommissioning of weapons and explosives.

working practices of the civil service.[36] Similarly, targets have been set to secure the appointment of more women to non-departmental public bodies (NDPBs).[37] These are bodies created either to perform specific functions or to offer advice to the government and their capacity for independent policy-making varies greatly depending on their task and the manner in which they are constituted. Although usually accountable to a Minister, the duty of these bodies to promote equality and to take into account women's interests and views is usually left unclear.

One area of government where women are relatively well represented is local government. Currently one in four local councillors are women. Local councils are elected bodies which have limited power to impose local taxes (council tax which is a property tax[38]) in order to finance the services they provide. Although they have the ability to raise revenue, the majority of their income comes from central government and their competence to raise money via the council tax is capped (restricted) by central government.[39] They are responsible for providing a range of important services such as education, but the relevant policy will usually be dictated by central government. The domination of local government by central government has important consequences for women because if local authorities were allowed to raise revenue freely and to spend it in implementing policies that they themselves decided upon the likelihood is that women would benefit considerably.

Over the years many local authorities have given a high priority to promoting equal opportunities among their own workforce and also insisted that those from whom they bought goods or services did the same. They would refuse to award a contract unless the firm in question could demonstrate its commitment to equal pay and promotion prospects. This became particularly significant when central government forced local authorities to contract out specified services, such as the provision of school meals, to firms in the private sector. Central government reacted by outlawing contract compliance in relation to sex (though not race) discrimination in the Local Government Act 1988.

---

36. See the report by the Cabinet Office, Office of Public Service - Development and Equal Opportunities Division. *Equal Opportunities in the Civil Service 1995-97*. p. 4.
37. The Office of Public Service, Machinery of Government and Standards Group, outlined in the paper, *Quangos: Opening up Public Appointments* an action plan for individual Departments setting out specific goals and objectives for increasing the representation of women and members of the ethnic minorities on the boards of public bodies, during the period 1998-2001. Progress against those plans will be monitored annually by the Public Appointments Unit.
38. Local Government Finance Act 1992 s. 1.
39. Local authorities receive a general grant (revenue support grant) as well as specific grants for services such as transport.

Equality Legislation in the United Kingdom

The United Kingdom has not (until very recently) possessed a Bill of Rights and has not to date developed a strong rights culture. Citizens in the United Kingdom can act as they please provided their actions are not contrary to the law. The significance of this situation to United Kingdom jurisprudence is that citizens have no clear understanding of what their 'rights' are and how those 'rights' may be eroded by legislation. This situation, however, will shortly change as a consequence of the Human Rights Act 1998. This legislation forces public authorities to observe certain rights set out in the European Convention on Human Rights (ECHR) and its protocols. These so-called Convention rights will be incorporated into United Kingdom law and it will be unlawful for public authorities to act in a manner that is incompatible with them.[40] Should an individual believe that a public authority has acted in this unlawful fashion, she or he will have the opportunity to seek judicial review in the courts. A further consequence of incorporating Convention rights and the jurisprudence surrounding them is the need for primary and secondary legislation to be interpreted, so far as possible, in a manner compatible with those rights.[41] Any declaration that primary legislation is incompatible with Convention rights will not have the effect of rendering the law in question void,[42] rather it is hoped that this will prompt the government and Parliament to change the law and eradicate any incompatibility. The Human Rights Act also introduces a new procedure to make the human rights implications of proposed government legislation more transparent. The responsible Minister will be required to provide a statement that any proposed legislation is compatible with the Convention.[43] Finally neither the Scottish Parliament, the Northern Ireland Assembly nor the Welsh Assembly has the competence to legislate in a manner that is incompatible with the ECHR.

This decision to give certain provisions of the ECHR the force of law in the United Kingdom may well signal the development of a much stronger rights culture. Its effect on women is much harder to predict, but at first sight appears limited. This is because while those rights protected by the ECHR are, under Article 14, to be exercised without discrimination, there is no article prohibiting discrimination *per se*.[44] Furthermore, like the UN

40. Human Rights Act 1998 s. 6.
41. Ibid, s. 3.
42. Ibid, ss. 3 and 4. Secondary legislation can however be set aside if it is incompatible.
43. Ibid, s. 19.
44. O'Donovan, K. (1998), *Engendering Human Rights*, p. 3. (Paper delivered at the conference of the Society of Public Teachers of Law, 1998.)

International Covenant on Civil and Political Rights, the ECHR, and hence the Human Rights Act, is oriented towards protecting the civil and political rights of the individual from interference by the state, and not by other individuals. The text thus has limited application in relation to women's concerns for protection from domestic violence and other violations or restrictions imposed by individuals. While the United Kingdom is signatory to international human rights instruments such as the United Nations Universal Declaration of Human Rights and the Convention on the Elimination of All Forms of Discrimination Against Women (CEDAW) and hence has, on paper at least, a broad commitment to gender equality, such instruments have a limited capacity to promote active measures to eliminate discrimination against women.

In the context of Northern Ireland, however, the situation is somewhat different. In view of the province's troubled history, the decision has been taken to establish a Northern Ireland Human Rights Commission. It will deal with the effectiveness of Northern Ireland law in protecting human rights, promote an understanding of human rights and in certain situations support individuals who wish to bring actions alleging breaches of the Human Rights Act. In addition an Equality Commission has been set up to promote equality in a variety of contexts. The Northern Ireland Act 1998 dissolves the four existing Northern Ireland statutory equality agencies[45] and replaces them with a single agency, the Equality Commission, which began work in October 1999. It consists of 20 commissioners who were appointed for a three year period with effect from 2 August 1999.[46]

A Working Party[47] was set up in November 1998 to devise the best possible structure for the new Commission. Its report which was published in February 1999 stated that a unified Commission was preferable to a body composed of separate Directorates. The Working Party proposed that, in the early stages of the new Commission, work should be done through separate Directorates to ensure continuity at the change-over.[48] This is the current working practice of the Commission. It has been suggested that women will suffer as a consequence of the decision to scrap the independent Northern Ireland Equal Opportunities Commission and incorporate it into the new

45. The Fair Employment Commission, the Equal Opportunities Commission for Northern Ireland, the Commission for Racial Equality for Northern Ireland and the Northern Ireland Disability Council.
46. See Northern Ireland Office press release 22 July 1999 at http://www.nio.gov.uk/990722b-nio.htm
47. The Working Party consisted of the heads of the four equality agencies and was chaired by Joan Stringer, principal of Queen Margaret College, Edinburgh.
48. See 'Creating a Unified Equality Commission — the challenge ahead', *Equal Opportunities Review*, 83, Jan/Feb 1999, pp. 21-27 and 'NI equality body proposals', *Equal Opportunities Review*, 84, March/April 1999, pp. 6-7.

Equality Commission. The fear is that a hierarchy of discrimination will develop with the greatest emphasis being placed on religious and political discrimination, with the result that fewer resources will be devoted and less attention paid to combating sex discrimination. It is too early to judge whether the fears of of those with an interest in gender equality will materialise.[49]

Anti-Discrimination Legislation

There are two major pieces of general legislation in the United Kingdom designed to outlaw sex discrimination. The Equal Pay Act 1970, despite its name, is concerned with ensuring that the terms of a woman's contract of employment, which will include those dealing with rates of pay, are no less favourable than those of a man's. In order to obtain the modification of a term in a woman's contract of employment the following conditions have to be satisfied:

- it must be possible to identify a male 'comparator', that is, an actual man in the same employment as the woman in question. The male comparator does not have to work in the same place as the woman, rather they must have the same, or an associated, employer. If they are employed at different establishments, then common terms and conditions of employment must be observed at those establishments.[50]
- the woman must show that she and her male comparator are performing either broadly similar jobs even though his job title may be different from hers or work rated as equivalent in a job evaluation scheme or work of equal value.[51]
- the difference in her treatment as compared with that of her male comparator must be based on sex and not on some other material factor such as the possession of superior qualifications or greater experience.[52]

---

49. The potential impact and significance of these changes are discussed in more detail in Chapter Nine, this volume.
50. See *Leverton v Clwyd County Council* [1989] ICR 33, *British Coal Corporation v Smith* [1994] IRLR 342. Common terms and conditions of employment meant in *Leverton*, for example, that where a nursery nurse working at one establishment compared her job with that of a clerical officer working at another establishment, she had to demonstrate that nursery nurses working at the comparator's establishment would have broadly the same terms and conditions of employment as herself. United Kingdom law envisages that the female worker and her male comparator will be employed at the same time. Under the terms of Community law, this need not be the case: See *Macarthys v Smith* 129/79 [1980] ICR 672.
51. S. 1(2), Equal Pay Act 1970 as amended by SI 1983 No 1794.
52. Ibid, s. 1(3).

There are many shortcomings associated with the Equal Pay Act. Firstly, it is complex to administer and the time taken to resolve a single claim is usually very long. Secondly, job evaluation schemes (used when determining an equal value claim) are not totally gender-neutral and certain skills, particularly those identified with women, are under-valued whilst others identified with men are over-valued.[53] Thirdly, when faced by an equal pay claim an employer can use the defence that one employee is paid more than another because of legitimate reasons for doing so. The courts in the United Kingdom have shown themselves remarkably sympathetic to such claims by employers.[54]

Despite these shortcomings the Equal Pay Act has secured for some women substantial increases in pay. Relying on the market, it has been said, will never secure equal pay for women. There has to be some independent mechanism for securing this objective. Whilst the current mechanism may be flawed it is better than no equal pay machinery whatsoever. Indeed the trade unions and the Equal Opportunities Commission have recognised the potential of the equal pay legislation and have done their best to exploit it for the benefit of their members and for specific groups of workers such as part-timers.

The Sex Discrimination Act 1975 makes it unlawful to discriminate against women[55] and men[56] on the grounds of their sex, discriminate against married persons on the grounds of their married status (but only in relation to employment),[57] or discriminate by victimising those who assert their rights under the Act or help others to do so.[58] The Sex Discrimination Act does not outlaw discrimination whenever and wherever it occurs. Its impact is limited to discrimination occurring in employment,[59] education,[60] and the provision of goods, facilities, services and premises.[61]

Under the terms of the legislation discrimination can be either direct or indirect. A woman will be directly discriminated against if, on the grounds of her sex, she is treated less favourably than a man is, or would be, treated.[62] Direct discrimination simply requires that a woman compares her treatment

---

53. In the past, job evaluation schemes were used as a justification for paying men and women different rates of pay. See Morris, A. and Nott, S. (1995), *All My Worldly Goods*, Aldershot: Dartmouth, p.73.
54. See *Enderby v Frenchay Health Authority and Secretary of State for Health* [1992] IRLR 15, 127/92 [1993] ECR 1-5535.
55. Sex Discrimination Act 1975, s. 1.
56. Ibid s. 2.
57. Ibid s. 3.
58. Ibid s. 4.
59. Ibid s. 6.
60. Ibid Part 111.
61. Ibid s. 29.
62. Ibid s. 1(1)(a).

to that of a hypothetical man. The intention or motive of the person who directly discriminates is irrelevant.[63] Hence a person cannot argue that she or he discriminated in order to protect a woman or to save money or because of customer preference.

Indirect discrimination is a more complex notion but it has the potential to tackle those more insidious forms of discrimination, such as conditions regarding age, height or hours of work, which on their face appear gender neutral but in reality work against the interests of women because of women's inability to comply with such conditions. Indirect discrimination occurs when a condition or requirement is applied to a woman which applies or would apply to a man but:

- the proportion of women who can comply with it is considerably smaller than the proportion of men who can comply; and
- the person applying the condition cannot justify it irrespective of the sex of the person to whom it is applied; and
- it is to a woman's detriment because she cannot comply with it.[64]

The Sex Discrimination Act has, however, had a limited impact in promoting equal opportunities for a number of reasons. In the first place, issues, for example pensions, were deliberately excluded from the scope of the legislation though most of these have now been tackled in other legislative measures. Secondly the interpretation given to the legislation by the United Kingdom courts has often been exceedingly unsympathetic, particularly the requirement that a woman compares her situation to that of a man.[65] The problem is that this test of discrimination does not bring about any substantive changes in the composition or organisation of the workplace since it uses male standards to

---

63. See *R v Birmingham City Council* ex parte EOC [1989] IRLR 173, *James v Eastleigh Borough Council* [1990] IRLR 288 at p. 295.
64. Op cit, n. 51, s. 1(1)(b). The same definitions of direct and indirect discrimination are used when dealing with discrimination on the grounds of marital status. See s. 3(1)(a) and (b).
65. See, for example, in *Turley v Allders Department Stores* [1980] IRLR 4 where the Employment Appeal Tribunal (EAT) refused to accept that a claim of direct discrimination could be brought by an employee dismissed because she was pregnant, arguing that the 1975 Act required a woman to compare her treatment with that of a man. In *Hayes v Malleable Working Men's Club and Institute* [1985] IRLR 367 the EAT modified their approach by accepting that a pregnant woman, who had been treated less favourably than a sick man, might allege discrimination. In *Webb v EMO Air Cargo (UK) Ltd* [1993] IRLR 27 the House of Lords did concede that in principle to dismiss a pregnant woman was direct discrimination. In that particular case, however, the House of Lords referred the issue to the ECJ since they did not believe that the female employee had been dismissed because she was pregnant. The ECJ held that the dismissal did amount to sex discrimination—32/93 [1994] IRLR 482. This was then confirmed by the House of Lords - [1995] IRLR 645. The position of pregnant workers has been strengthened by the Pregnant Workers Directive 92/85 which was implemented in the United Kingdom. See now the Employment Rights Act 1996.

evaluate whether women are fairly treated. Thirdly the complexity involved in proving indirect discrimination means that it is seldom used even though the concept is intended to tackle those discriminatory practices which can represent such barriers to women. Finally, the pursuit of other policies by government, such as privatisation and deregulation, has had the effect of undermining the anti-discrimination legislation as a whole.[66]

Related Equality Measures

A variety of other measures have been adopted in the United Kingdom to supplement the anti-discrimination legislation. Some are designed to eliminate sex discrimination in areas that were excluded from the scope of the original anti-discrimination legislation. One of the most significant of these areas is discrimination in the context of retirement. There have been a variety of legislative measures over the years to ensure that state and occupational social security schemes observe the principle of equal treatment.[67] Other measures have been designed to cope with experiences that are a source of discrimination for women alone, such as pregnancy. The Employment Rights Act 1996 deals with pregnant workers and guarantees them maternity leave, maternity pay and protection from dismissal.[68] This legislation has, however, been criticised as paternalistic,[69] complex and limited in scope.[70]

---

66. For example, the abolition of the Wages Councils (s. 35, Trade Union Reform and Employment Rights Act 1993) which set minimum wages for certain occupations such as hairdressing and the clothing trade. This was done on the basis that employers should be allowed to offer and employees to accept whatever wages the market would bear. The government argued that the lack of regulation would create new jobs. The current government has reversed this policy by making provision in the National Minimum Wages Act 1998 for a minimum wage covering, with few exceptions, all employment sectors as well as a wider range of workers, including home and agency workers. See also the study carried out by the Equal Opportunities Commission (EOC) into the impact on women of compulsory competitive tendering. This policy required local authorities to put certain services, such as rubbish collection, out to tender rather than providing those services themselves. EOC. (1995) *The Gender Impact of Compulsory Competitive Tendering in Local Government*, Manchester: EOC.
67. Such as the Social Security Act 1980 which implemented Directive 79/7 guaranteeing equal treatment in relation to state social security systems. The legislation contained a great many exceptions to this principle which limited its potential impact.
68. The Act implements the Pregnant Workers Directive 92/85, [1985] OJ L348/1. The present government has amended the Employment Rights Act (s. 7 Employment Relations Act 1999). This will, it is hoped, simplify the law relating to maternity leave. The 1999 Act also makes provision for parental leave as well as leave for domestic and family reasons.
69. Morris, A. and Nott, S. (1995), 'The Law's Engagement with Pregnancy', in Bridgeman, J. and Millns, S. (eds), *Law and Body Politics*, Aldershot: Dartmouth, pp. 53-78.
70. This is because the legislation offers no protection beyond the period of pregnancy and maternity leave.These limits can be seen in *Handels-og Kontorfunktionaerernes Forbund I Danmark v Dansk Arbejdsgiverforening* 179/88 [1991] IRLR 31 and *Handels-og Kontorfunktion Aerernes Forbund I Danmark v Dansk Handel* 400/95 [1997] IRLR 643. See also Szyszczak, E. (1997), 'Community Law on Pregnancy and Maternity', and Kilpatrick, C. (1997), 'How long is a piece of string? European regulation of the post-birth period', in Hervey, T. and O'Keeffe, D. (eds), *Sex Equality Law in the European Union*, Chichester: Wiley.

Changes to the law have on occasions been forced on the United Kingdom in order to comply with a ruling of the ECJ.[71] The courts in the United Kingdom have demonstrated an increasing willingness to interpret, where possible, United Kingdom law in a manner that is consistent with EU law.[72] If this has not been feasible the courts have been prepared to acknowledge the supremacy of EU law with direct effect.

Finally, positive action is a strategy adopted in some countries as a way of improving the situation of women in society. In the United Kingdom the more radical forms of this strategy, such as the use of quotas making it obligatory for an organisation to employ a certain number of women, are illegal, since the requirement not to discriminate applies equally well to a man as it does to a woman. The Sex Discrimination Act 1975 does, however, permit some forms of positive action. Section 48 allows an employer to give female employees access to training facilities in order to encourage them to take up particular forms of employment provided no or comparatively few women were performing that work in the past twelve months. Training bodies are also permitted to offer training to women only to equip them to take up certain forms of work which no or comparatively few women were performing in Great Britain or a region of Great Britain in the past twelve months. The legislation also allows certain organisations, such as trade unions, to reserve seats on that organisation for women and to train or encourage female members to take up posts in the organisation. Positive action initiatives can be taken in respect of men as well as women.

Putting Gender onto the Law and Policy-Making Agenda

Apart from the equality legislation and its associated measures, other strategies have been adopted in the United Kingdom in an attempt to promote equal opportunities and force decision-makers to take account of gender.

---

71. As originally drafted, the Equal Pay Act 1970 was found to be in breach of Community law since it did not permit a woman to claim equal pay on the basis that her work was of equal value to that of a man. See *EC Commission v United Kingdom of Great Britain and Northern Ireland* 61/81 [1982] ICR 578. As a consequence of this case the Equal Pay Act was amended by the Equal Pay (Amendment) Regulations 1983, SI 1983 No 1794.
72. Contrast the position in *Duke v Reliance Systems Ltd* [1988] AC 618 where the Court of Appeal refused to interpret the Sex Discrimination Act 1975 in a manner which was consistent with the Equal Treatment Directive 1976 with the House of Lord's approach in *Webb v Emo Air Cargo (UK) Ltd* [1995] IRLR 645 where they did just that.

Equality Bodies

Equality bodies have developed in the United Kingdom in a piecemeal fashion often to meet a specific need such as overseeing the operation of the anti-discrimination legislation. Part VI of the Sex Discrimination Act 1975 provided for the setting up of the Equal Opportunities Commission (EOC). The EOC has offices in Manchester, London, Glasgow and Cardiff and is financed by the government[73] which also makes certain key appointments, such as the Chair of the EOC. There is a separate Equality Commission for Northern Ireland with the statutory power to enforce the Sex Discrimination (Northern Ireland) Order 1976[74] and the Equal Pay Act (Northern Ireland) 1970. The Equal Opportunities Commission has a range of tasks assigned to it in the Sex Discrimination Act to enable it to fight sex discrimination. Those tasks are:

- to work toward the elimination of discrimination;
- to promote equality of opportunity between men and women generally;
- to review the working of the Sex Discrimination Act 1975 and the Equal Pay Act 1970 and, when they are so required or otherwise think it necessary, draw up and submit to the Secretary of State proposals for amending the legislation;
- to keep under review those provisions in health and safety legislation which require men and women to be treated differently and to make proposals for reform as well as submit reports on specified matters when required to do so by the Secretary of State;
- to produce an annual report which is presented to Parliament.

In order to carry out these duties the EOC is given a number of specific powers in the Sex Discrimination Act. These include:

- the power to undertake or to assist research or other educational activities;
- the power to carry out formal investigations;[75]
- the power to issue codes of practice in relation to employment;[76]

73. On 2 February 1998, Andrew Smith, Minister for Employment, Welfare to Work and Equal Opportunities, announced that the DfEE would be supporting the EOC with grant-in-aid in 1998/99 of £5.792m. See website: http://www.coi.gov.uk/coi/depts/GDE/coi7360d.ok
74. This order provided that rules governing sex discrimination virtually identical to those in the Sex Discrimination Act 1975 would apply in Northern Ireland.
75. Op cit, n. 51, ss. 57-61.
76. Schedule 4 of the Race Relations Act 1976 inserted this power in the Sex Discrimination Act 1975, s. 56A.

- the power to assist individuals to bring sex discrimination claims;[77]
- the power to bring legal proceedings in the name of the EOC;
- the power to issue a non-discrimination notice or to make recommendations at the conclusion of a formal investigation.[78]

While it would appear that the EOC possesses a formidable array of powers with which to eliminate sex discrimination and to promote equal opportunities, in practice it has not fulfilled initial expectations. Commentators have argued that the EOC's litigation strategy lacks coherence and that the EOC has failed to liaise with women's organisations who might bring suitable test cases to its attention.[79] Yet the EOC's power to assist individuals has allowed it to support a series of test cases which have done a great deal to clarify the United Kingdom's law relating to sex discrimination and its relationship with European law. It has also given its help in a great many of those cases which have found their way to the European Court of Justice (ECJ), such as *Macarthys v Smith*[80] and *Johnston v Chief Constable of the Royal Ulster Constabulary.*[81]

Critics of the EOC's record on formal investigations, that is its powers to investigate potential discrimination either in a particular industry or by a named organisation, also argue that there is no evidence of a coherent strategy or ability to plan and conduct investigations. In reality judicial interpretation of these powers has imposed stringent conditions on investigations which limits their usefulness.[82] Some commentators have, however, remarked that faced with the same problem the Commission for Racial Equality (CRE) has still managed to undertake a considerable number of formal investigations.[83]

The Women's National Commission (WNC) acts as an advisory body to government and channels the views of women in the United Kingdom into government. Its membership consists of women's organisations which include the women's sections of the major political parties, trade unions,

77. Op cit, n. 51, s. 75.
78. Op cit, n. 51, s. 67.
79. Lovenduski, J. (1995), 'An emerging advocate: The Equal Opportunities Commission in Great Britain', in Stetson, D. M. and Mazur, A. (eds), *Comparative State Feminism*, London: Sage, p. 122.
80. 129/79 [1980] ECR 1275.
81 222/84 [1986] ECR 1657.
82. See, for example, *R v Commission for Racial Equality*, ex parte Prestige Group plc [1984] ICR 473.
83. Bourn, C. and Whitmore, J. (1993), *Race and Sex Discrimination*, London: Sweet and Maxwell, p. 300.

religious groups, professional women's organisations, voluntary bodies and other organisations broadly representative of women.

The WNC defines its role as follows:

> The Commission provides members' organisations with a forum from which to influence policies and practices of importance to women. From the perspective of government, the WNC offers ministers and officials a vital conduit to the informal opinions of a wide cross-section of women.[84]

The WNC's work involves meetings, conferences and working groups to discuss issues of particular concern to women. It regularly carries out in-depth studies on issues of importance to women and small *ad hoc* working groups undertake research and prepare reports which are then submitted to government Ministers and are widely circulated. It produces policy papers and participates in consultation exercises by circulating policy proposals to its membership and representing their views.

The WNC, however, seems to exert little influence. It lacks the ability to ensure that its views are acted upon by government. At present there would also appear to be a lack of proper consultation between itself, other women's groups and government. In the WNC's own recent (1998) review of its activities, it acknowledged that it needed to raise its membership to involve more organisations and expand its public profile. The WNC would appear to be so little known and its activities are so little publicised that it has not been the subject of detailed research. It would also appear that, while Whitehall should consult the WNC on all policy initiatives that affect women, such consultation is somewhat patchy at the moment; the WNC probably sees only one tenth of what passes through the Women's Unit. Thus from the perspective of both member organisations and government the WNC fails to fulfil its remit.

Since coming to office in 1997, the Labour government has established a whole new system of governmental bodies to deal with gender equality issues. They have set up the post of Minister for Women which is currently filled by the Leader of the House of Lords, Baroness Jay of Paddington.[85] She is in turn supported by the Minister of State at the Department of Health, Tessa Jowell MP, who is Minister for Women in the House of

---

84. WNC. (1994), *A Direct Line Between Women and Government: 25 Years of the Women's National Commission,* London: WNC p.3.
85. Originally Secretary of State for Social Security, Harriet Harman, and Parliamentary Under-Secretary of State, Joan Ruddock, were appointed as Ministers for Women but they were removed from this position in the July 1998 Ministerial reshuffle

Commons.[86] The role of Minister for Women is seen as one of co-ordination and initiation.[87] The Minister for Women is charged with driving forward the government's key policy initiatives on family friendly employment, a national childcare strategy and domestic violence. She is also responsible for co-ordinating a cross-departmental approach to initiatives for women and equal opportunities.

The Minister for Women also oversees the work of the Women's Unit, which acts to promote women's issues across Whitehall and often provides other departments with information and advice on equal opportunities. It may even provide equal opportunities training to members of staff in other departments. The Women's Unit has two key tasks. First, it initiates policy on gender related issues. It sees itself as the prime mover in taking forward the government's policy priorities for women and in addition it is responsible for co-ordinating the government's mainstreaming strategy, developing an effective cross-departmental approach to women's issues and opening up a dialogue between women and government. Secondly, the Women's Unit analyses policy for gender bias. As a matter of course, virtually all draft government policy documents are reviewed by the Women's Unit for gender impact. Where problems exist the Unit will contact the Minister responsible and indicate how he or she can go about tackling them.

The Cabinet Sub-Committee on Women is a (permanent) standing committee, bringing together Ministers from different Departments to discuss issues of concern to women that cut across government Departments.[88] It co-ordinates action on the women's agenda across government. The Labour Government has indicated that the Cabinet Sub-Committee on Women will be the focal point of the Government's policy to incorporate women into decision-making. It is believed to meet once every two months.[89]

It is perhaps too early to assess the implications of this set of structural changes or the success of the Minister for Women or the Women's Unit in pursuing their agenda. There has been very little written analysing these new developments or even describing how they operate and what their purpose is. The creation of a Minister for Women (or two) is a new development yet

86. In addition to these two Ministers there are other Ministers with responsibility for women's interests and equal opportunities: for example, there is the Minister for Employment, Welfare to Work and Equal Opportunities.

87. Press release Department of Social Security, 97/080, 3 June 1997.

88. The composition of the Committee can be drawn from information on the Cabinet Office website: http://www.cabinet-office.gov.uk/cabsec/1998/cabcom/hs_w.htm.

89. *Equal Opportunities Review*, 77, Jan/Feb 1998.

little if anything is known about this position. No Ministry is attached to the post and this could be said to leave the issue of the location of support and the lines of responsibility unclear. The fact that after 12 months the first incumbents of the post were replaced for reasons unconnected with their handling of this portfolio demonstrates that the government's commitment to this area will be subject to overriding political objectives.

The Women's Unit appears to have a somewhat vague remit that is susceptible to change to meet the political circumstances of the government of the day. For instance, it is not clear what the priorities of the Women's Unit are. Under the first Ministers for Women, the areas of domestic violence, childcare and family friendly work practices were emphasised, yet on the appointment of new Ministers 12 months later it was announced that new key policy areas would include issues that affect teenage girls, poverty in old age and investigating the pay gap. At the same time, the Women's Unit has grappled with mainstreaming, seeking to establish guidelines for government Departments (see below). Overall the impression is one of a Unit struggling to set its own agenda and unsettled in its appraisal of what constitute key issues for women and how to approach these issues.

On a day to day basis the Women's Unit would also appear to be overcome by the volume of work associated with analysing policy for gender impact which is done through Policy Appraisal for Equal Treatment (PAET), a process which is supposed to be carried out in every department but which is in practice very often referred back to the Women's Unit. This would seem to suggest that as yet there is no clear view in government as to what mainstreaming entails or ought to entail in a United Kingdom context. For the most part, though, the emphasis is still on gender-proofing, as opposed to proper consultation with women on policy development. Practice appears to fall short of what is required to successfully implement an approach to policy-making that fully integrates gender issues into all aspects of the policy-making process.

The Cabinet Sub-Committee on Women, potentially a powerful force in government due to its position at the heart of the policy-making machinery, operates under the blanket of secrecy which shrouds policy-making in the United Kingdom. Exactly what it does and how it interacts with the other bodies mentioned in this section is unknown. In the light of these efforts on the part of government to take account of women's concerns, it seems anomalous that Parliament has not shown a similar commitment to advancing women's interests. There is an All Party Group on Sex Equality made up of MPs and peers from the three major political parties. The Group's principal objective is 'to keep sex equality issues before Parliament by keeping members informed of relevant and topical issues related to sex equality, giving members the pointers to scrutinise relevant Bills at relevant stages, and getting members to put down Parliamentary questions as appropriate'.[90] The low profile of this Group and its limited remit mean that it is no substitute for a Select Committee on Equal Opportunities which would question the government on how well its current policies are working.

Procedures for Scrutinising Proposed Policy Measures for Their Gender Impact.

There have been two long-standing initiatives in the United Kingdom to address gender impact within the policy-making process: Policy Appraisal for Equal Treatment (PAET) and Policy Appraisal and Fair Treatment (PAFT). PAFT was the better known of the two and was used exclusively in the Northern Ireland Office. It consisted of a set of guidelines with the aim of ensuring that issues of equality informed policy-making and the delivery of services to the public. A PAFT assessment was meant to be undertaken in relation to all new policies and whenever existing policies and services were reviewed. The process identified a number of areas where there was potential for discrimination or unequal treatment to occur: gender, age, ethnic group, religious belief or political opinion, married and unmarried people, people with or without dependants and people of differing sexual orientation. The procedure appeared to have started out as a means of identifying direct and indirect discrimination against one of the target groups[91] but developed into a wider appraisal to eliminate unfairness. The PAFT guidelines also offered advice on monitoring and training.

Departments in the Northern Ireland Office took responsibility for assessing their policies in accordance with the guidelines and were required to submit reports outlining their actions in implementing PAFT. An annual report containing a list of the policies and services for which an appraisal was conducted, its outcome and any amendments was then produced.

As a procedure, PAFT was criticised for a number of reasons.[92] First, whilst PAFT seemingly developed into a mechanism for eliminating unfairness,

90. As stated in the Group's terms of reference according to correspondence with Kevin Marsh, Director of Marketing at the EOC (Manchester).
91. CCRU. (1995) *Policy Appraisal and Fair Treatment Annual Report 1994*, Belfast: CCRU p. 15.
92. For more detailed analyses of PAFT see McCrudden, C. (1996), *Mainstreaming Fairness — A Discussion Paper on PAFT*, Belfast: Committee on the Administration of Justice; Nott, S. (1999), 'Mainstreaming Equal Opportunities', in Morris, A. and O'Donnell, T. (eds), *Feminist Perspectives on Employment Law*, London: Cavendish.

there was no clear and consistent notion of how that term should be defined. Secondly, uncertainty persisted over when a PAFT appraisal should be undertaken and what bodies were expected to observe the guidelines apart from Departments in the Northern Ireland Office. Thirdly PAFT appraisals took place behind closed doors and, apart from the annual report, there was no indication of how well or how badly the procedure was working. Indeed, there was strong suspicion that PAFT was simply an 'add on', that is a hurdle that had to be negotiated before a particular policy could be implemented. This was fuelled by the fact that, in the annual report, policies with definite adverse consequences for women were said to have no PAFT implications.

The PAFT guidelines have now been superseded in Northern Ireland by a new statutory procedure set out in the Northern Ireland Act 1998. This requires public sector bodies in Northern Ireland to ensure that their day-to-day functions are carried out with due regard to the need to promote equality of opportunity in relation to religion, political opinion, gender, race, disability, age, marital status, dependants and sexual orientation. Each public body has to draw up its own appraisal system, including consultation with interested parties and its compliance with that will be monitored by the new Equality Commission. Some commentators have argued, however, that it remains unclear as to what extent an alleged failure to comply would be subject to independent legal action.[93]

In the rest of the United Kingdom a procedure known as Policy Appraisal for Equal Treatment (PAET) was used by government Departments which they tailored to suit their own needs and conditions.[94] PAET identified a number of areas where there was potential for discrimination or unequal treatment to occur: gender, age, racial group, religious belief or political opinion, married and unmarried people, people with or without dependants, people of differing sexual orientation and women who are pregnant or on maternity leave. The idea was that:

> at every stage in the life of a policy or programme, the potential impact on different groups of the population is actively considered, and amendments are made where necessary. It applies to reviews of existing legislation, services or policies as well as to new developments.[95]

93. For an extensive review of the new proposals see McCrudden, C. (1999), 'Mainstreaming equality in the governance of Northern Ireland', *Fordham International Law Journal*, 22, pp. 1702-1780.
94. CCRU. (1997), *Policy Appraisal and Fair Treatment Annual Report 1996*, Belfast: CCRU, p. 4.
95. Ibid, p. 1.

In 1998 these guidelines were revised by the Women's Unit, circulated to all Departments and made publicly available on the Women's Unit Website.[96] The revised guidelines emphasise:

- that all policy proposals must include an impact analysis which sets out the effect a policy may have on different sections of the population, such as men and women;
- that Departments may consult with non-governmental organisations, such as the Equal Opportunities Commission, over likely differences in impact;
- that Departments should make use of existing statistics and data in determining the impact of a policy, even commissioning new data if no appropriate figures are available;
- that if a policy has a differential impact on women it must be amended if that impact would constitute unlawful discrimination;
- that, if a policy with a differential impact is lawful, a decision must still be taken on whether it is appropriate to proceed with it.

The PAET guidelines represent an attempt to develop a policy appraisal mechanism. There are, however, significant weaknesses in the PAET process which need to be addressed if it is to succeed. The guidelines give only the vaguest direction on what PAET's purpose is — to avoid breaches of the law or the pursuit of substantive equality — or how PAET appraisals are to be conducted. A great deal of discretion is given to government Departments on how they employ PAET and no machinery is put in place to monitor their decisions or progress in general. Whilst the intention is there to take account of women's interests as well as those of many other groups, the details are lacking and, as is often remarked, 'the devil is in the detail'.

Conclusion

On the face of it, substantial gains have been made under the present government to integrate gender into the law and policy-making processes in the United Kingdom. So far, the returns are limited but at least part of the explanation for this may be that some of the mechanisms discussed are so

96. Women's Unit. (1998), *Policy Appraisal for Equal Treatment*, London: Central Office of Information for the Cabinet Office.

recent that it is impossible for them to have made an impact at this stage. The flaws of established agencies (such as the EOC) and procedures (such as PAFT and PAET) have been discussed above. There are, however, a number of features which characterise law and policy-making in the United Kingdom and which need to be addressed if a long term commitment to equality and mainstreaming is to be secured.

Firstly, government in the United Kingdom is highly centralised and dominated by a relatively small group of influential policy-makers, thus the priorities of government are subject to political whim. In addition, government lacks transparency. While the present government may appear committed to equality, this commitment is not institutionalised in the United Kingdom's constitutional arrangements. Moreover, the Westminster Parliament has little opportunity to force such concerns on government, and the current PAET guidelines will not ensure that policy-making becomes transparent, accessible and responsive to women's situations. Nothing that has so far emerged under the 'modernising government' initative has the capacity to actually transform the way in which law and policy is made to ensure that equality is a central concern of present and future governments.

Secondly, it should be noted that the improvements which have been secured in the Welsh and Scottish assemblies have come about as a consequence of political opportunism rather than as a product of any secure commitment to equality or to mainstreaming. Thus while constitutional change has acted as a catalyst to improve the way in which women's issues are addressed, it also demonstrates the instability of existing arrangements and the ease with which they may be replaced or abandoned.

Thirdly, the evolution of mechanisms and procedures for addressing inequality in the United Kingdom has proceeded very much on an *ad hoc* basis without any clear direction or objective. Although it is possible to list equality agencies and describe procedures for gender impact assessment it is harder to detect any overall plan for promoting women's interests. This raises the question as to whether efforts have been directed to maximum effect.

Alongside the equality agencies and gender impact mechanisms stands the anti-discrimination legislation. For a considerable period of time its impact has been undermined by a determination on the part of government to resist changes to the legislation that would make it more efficient. In this respect EU law has been indispensable in forcing reform on an unwilling government, though the limits of a litigation strategy underpinned by notions of formal equality must also be noted. The current government is more open to legislative reform than its predecessor. However, its legislation on the minimum wage and on parental leave show a reluctance on its part to place additional financial burdens on employers. Successive governments in the United Kingdom have been unwilling to grasp the nettle that the market can contribute to structural inequality and to impose the 'costs' of equality on employers. Yet inequality also imposes a cost of which the government is undoubtedly aware. Once again this highlights a barrier to progress, namely the unwillingness of politicians to alienate certain sectors of the community, particularly business interests. This perhaps demonstrates the limits of the government's commitment to tackling inequality.

8 Same Song — Different Tunes: A Lesson in Harmony Singing?

FIONA BEVERIDGE

Introduction

There can be no doubt that the EU adheres to the mantra of equality between men and women. Through the inclusion of Article 141EC (119) in the original Treaty of Rome, its subsequent interpretation by the European Court of Justice (ECJ) and the legislative initiatives in the fields of equality, maternity and parental rights, the EU has done as much as most developed democratic states in addressing inequality between men and women. In some respects this should come as no surprise. The Member States of the EU also subscribe to the equality mantra and have acted on it in fields outside the competence of the EU, for instance in relation to civil rights and family matters. All are parties to important international conventions such as ILO Conventions No. 100 on Equal Pay and No. 111 on Discrimination in Employment and Occupation and to the UN Convention on the Elimination of all Forms of Discrimination against Women (CEDAW). Given this common core of commitments to equality ideals, it seems appropriate that the Member States of the EU have chosen to act in concert where equality issues have been perceived to intersect with the 'core' business of the EU, that is economic integration. After al'. it was precisely to address this interface between equality policies and economic competitiveness that Article 141EC (119) was included in the Treaty of Rome in the first place.

It is, however, clear that in relation to equality issues the EU has been more than merely a forum in which like-minded states could co-ordinate their mutual interests to act on the equality ideals to which they subscribed. The institutions of the EC have assumed a significant role in furthering and shaping that commitment. As commentators have noted,[1] this commitment has taken the form of a rights discourse, whether or not this was the intention

1. Ward, I. (1996), 'Beyond Sex Equality: The Limits of Sex Equality Law in the New Europe', in Hervey, T. and O'Keeffe, D. (eds), *Sex Equality Law in the European Union*, Chichester: Wiley, p. 370.

of the framers of the Treaty or of subsequent legislation:

> . . . encouraged by the Court, there is now much talk about rights to this and rights to that, and sex equality is very much part of this rights-talk.[2]

Moreover, within the evolving EU legal order, equality law has its own dynamic and indeed has made its own contribution to the evolution of the EU legal order.[3] Indeed the commitment to equality between men and women has become, arguably, part of the constitution of the new Europe.

The purpose of this chapter is to explore this apparent harmony between the EU and the states whose equal opportunities strategies have been discussed in earlier chapters. Whilst the EU has been active in developing first and second generation equality strategies, the focus of this chapter will be primarily on the former, that is rights based and anti-discrimination strategies. The intention is to explore the nature and extent of the EU's guarantee of equality and its attempts to eliminate sex discrimination. The chapter will then go on to consider the degree to which the EU's commitment to equality has had an impact on those states featured in *Making Women Count*. More specifically, it will examine the extent to which particular features of the national landscapes disrupt the harmony which EU law seeks to promote.

Equality Law in the EU

Sex equality law in the European Union has it roots in two places: the formal guarantee of equal pay for equal work in Article 141EC (119) and the legislative powers vested in the Community institutions which have evolved through successive Treaty negotiations to enable those institutions to enact measures in the social field with a direct or indirect bearing on equality issues.

---

2. Ibid, at p. 375.
3. Jacobs has commented: 'many principles of fundamental importance to the Community legal system are to be found in the Court's case-law on sex equality, including the use as an exceptional judicial technique of the prospective ruling, the spelling out of the conditions in which directives may produce direct effect, the elaboration of the duty of national courts to interpret and apply national legislation in accordance with relevant directives, and the developing principle of the duty of national courts to provide all remedies necessary for the full enforcement of Community rights' Foreword in Ellis, E (2nd 1998), *EC Sex Equality Law*, Oxford: Clarendon Press, vii-viii.

Article 141EC (119), requiring Member States to enact a formal legal guarantee of equal pay between men and women, was originally included in the Treaty as a consequence of political lobbying by women in some Member States and in response to pressure from states, such as France, which already had such a guarantee in its domestic law and feared opening up their markets to manufacturers and service-providers in other Member States who were not subject to such a requirement and who might hence gain a competitive edge.[4] As has been noted elsewhere,[5] the binding obligation and tone of Article 141EC (119) stands in marked contrast to the other social policy articles, which originally were only aspirational.

The subsequent treatment by the European Court of Justice (ECJ) of Article 141EC (119) gives rise to two significant observations. The first is that the Court, from an early stage, treated the equal pay principle as a constitutional principle in European Community law; the second is that despite this 'constitutionalisation'[6] of Article 141EC (119), the ECJ remained constrained to some extent by its perception of the Article's economic origins and foundations.

The Constitutionalisation of Article 141EC (119)

The constitutional character ascribed by the ECJ to the equal pay principle is related to the ECJ's view of the Article as embodying dual objectives: in the words of the Court in the *Defrenne Case*:[7]

> Article 119 pursues a double aim. First, in the light of the different stages of the development of social legislation in the various Member States, the aim of Article 119 is to avoid a situation in which undertakings established in States which have actually implemented the principle of equal pay suffer a

4 Barnard, C. (1996), 'The Economic Objectives of Article 119', in Hervey, T. and O'Keeffe, D. (eds), supra note 1, p. 321; Hoskyns, C. (1996), *Integrating Gender, London*: Verso.

5. See e.g. Beveridge, F. and Nott, S. (1995), 'Women, Wealth and the Single Market', in Mayes, D. (ed.), *The Evolution of Rules for a Single European Market*, Cost A7 Vol. 5, Part III, Brussels: Office for Official Publications of the EC; Shaw, J. (1994), 'Twintrack Social Europe — The Inside Track', in O'Keeffe, D. and Twomey, P. (eds), *Legal Issues of the Maastricht Treaty*, Chichester: Wiley, p. 295; Szyszczak, E. (1994), 'Social Policy: A Happy Ending or a Reworking of the Fairy Tale?', in O'Keeffe and Twomey (eds), ibid, p. 313.

6. The term is Weiler's: c.f. Weiler, J. H. H. (1991), 'The Transformation of Europe', 100 *Yale Law Journal*, 2403. It is applied to Article 141 EC (119) by Flynn: c.f. Flynn, L. 'The Body Politic(s) of EC Law', in Hervey and O'Keeffe (eds), supra note 1, p. 301 at 302.

7. Case 43/75, *Defrenne v. SABENA* (No. 2), [1976] ECR 455 paras. 8-10.

competitive disadvantage in intra-Community competition as compared with undertakings established in States which have not yet eliminated discrimination against women workers as regards pay. Secondly, this provision forms part of the social objectives of the Community, which is not merely an economic union, but is at the same time intended, by common action, to ensure social progress and seek the constant improvement of the living and working conditions of their people, as is emphasised by the Preamble to the Treaty.

In doctrinal terms this meant that the equal pay principle embodied in Article 141EC (119) was stated to be fundamental, was interpreted widely and was given a purposive meaning.[8] From this it should also follow that the equal pay principle cannot easily be displaced when it has to be balanced against other considerations; for instance, where discrimination can be justified only where objective differences can be shown between men and women which affect their suitability for a particular job.[9]

The *Defrenne* ruling also established the social dimension of the equal pay principle, which, by focusing on the situation of women workers, rather than on the economic needs of employers, may have been important in establishing that some 'substantive' as opposed to 'formal' notion of equal pay was the objective. This to an extent may have helped the ECJ to develop wider interpretations of the equal pay principle,[10] and later the equal treatment principle,[11] than might otherwise have been the case.

In addition the ECJ recognised, as Ellis stresses, that Article 141EC (119) has a dynamic element, such that its scope would require further clarification and development in the future: this, she argues, allowed the ECJ in later cases to extend the equality obligation beyond the field of equal pay into equal treatment and equal opportunities more generally.[12]

---

8. Ellis, E. (1998), supra note 3, at pp. 63-4.
9. See for example Case C-243/95 *Hill and Stapleton v Revenue Commissioners* [1998] ECR I-3739. See also Case C-13/94 *P v S* [1996] ECR I-2143, where the Court reiterated the fundamental character of the principle of equality. This case involved a transsexual. Note, however, the refusal of the Court to follow this approach in relation to gay and lesbian couples in *Grant v SouthWest Trains*: Case C-249/96 [1998] ECR I-621.
10. Case 12/81 *Garland v. British Rail* [1982] ECR 359; Case C-342/93 *Gillespie v. Northern Health and Social Services Board* [1996] ECR I-475; Case C-262/88 *Barber v. Guardian Royal Exchange Assurance Group* [1990] ECR I-1889.
11. See for instance the rulings in *Dekker* and in *Webb v EMO* that pregnancy dismissal does constitute sex discrimination contrary to the Equal Treatment Directive: Case 177/78 *Dekker v. Stichting Vormingscentrum voor Jonge Volwassen* [1990] ECR I-3941; Case C-32/93 *Webb v EMO Air Cargo (UK) Ltd.* [1994] ECR I-3567.
12. Ellis supra note 3, p. 63.

However, the 'equality' principle elevated to constitutional status by the Court, however widely interpreted, is at root a non-discrimination principle — it is a negative right *not* to be subjected to discrimination on grounds of sex, with a corresponding *no-right* of others to discriminate on grounds of sex. The right to equality constitutionalised by the ECJ is not a right which gives rise to any corresponding *duty* on anyone else to promote equality; indeed, as will be seen in Chapter Ten, this non-discrimination right at times seems to militate against the establishment of any such duty. Meanwhile the negative right not to be discriminated against on grounds of sex will be examined more closely.

The Non-Discrimination Principle

It is inescapable that Article 141EC (119) has been used to advantage by those seeking improvements in the legal protection of women in many Member States and that the ECJ has played a very prominent role in its development. In the first place, the ECJ developed the important doctrines of supremacy and direct effect which ensured that EC law had to be given priority over national law in the Member States and that it had to be recognised and given effect to by national courts so as to give remedies to individuals appearing before them. Moreover rights of action and adequate means of redress had to be provided, by the courts if necessary. As can be seen in relation to the UK[13] and Ireland[14] these developments served to activate the litigation route for individual complainants who had suffered discrimination on the grounds of sex.

As noted above, the ECJ was also responsible for the 'constitutionalisation' of the non-discrimination principle. This refers both to the weight attached to the non-discrimination provision, and to the willingness of the Court to define discrimination widely Of major importance from the 'equal rights' perspective have been the development of the concept of indirect discrimination[15] and the eventual reversal of the burden of proof in this area.[16] Indirect discrimination occurs where in the allocation of a benefit of some sort (recruitment to a job, setting of a rate of pay, giving preferential access to a service) a requirement is imposed or a practice followed which, though not

13. See Chapter Seven, this volume.
14. See Chapter Two, this volume.
15. See e.g. Case C-317/93 *Nolte v Landisversicherungsanstalt Hannover* [1995] ECR I-4625.
16. See e.g. Case 109/88 *Handels-OG Kontorfunktionaerernes Forbund I Denmark v Dansk Arbejdsgiverforening (acting for Danfoss)* [1989] ECR 3199.

actually employing sex as a determining criterion, has an adverse impact on men or women as a group. Such discrimination is not regarded as unlawful, however, if the adverse impact can be objectively justified by reference to factors unrelated to the sex of the disadvantaged group. Through a succession of cases the ECJ eventually reached the position that the prohibition on indirect discrimination did not depend on there being any intention to discriminate;[17] moreover, if the adverse impact of a practice was shown there was no need to identify the discriminatory aspects of the requirement or practice in question — instead, the burden of proof would then lie on the other party (for instance, the employer) to show that the adverse impact flowed from objectively justifiable criteria unrelated to the sex of the disadvantaged group. While in the first place the burden of proof was reversed in this way to take account of the particular problem faced in establishing discrimination in the face of non-transparent pay systems,[18] later cases have developed this line of jurisprudence so that it is now necessary only to demonstrate through 'significant statistics' a *prima facie* case of indirect discrimination.[19]

In most of the Member States examined in this study, the ECJ's rulings on Article 141EC (119) had had a major impact on national 'equal opportunities' laws, which effectively had to change to accommodate developments in the ECJ's jurisprudence (see further below). The difficulties with which this was achieved in some Member States[20] are a testament to the innovation of the ECJ: clearly national judges, even when faced with a broad 'equality' provision in a national constitution or in legislation would have had difficulty in reaching the same result. While the ECJ has often moved ahead of and educated the legislator, the pattern has often been the reverse in the national context, with the courts lagging behind even their own national legislator.[21]

Feminist critiques of the ECJ's jurisprudence on Article 141EC

Despite the improvements in equality law attributable to the ECJ and notwithstanding its 'constitutionalisation' of the equal pay principle and its recognition of the dual purpose served by that principle, it has been argued that the ECJ has been constrained in its interpretation of Article 141EC (119) by its perception of the Article's economic origins and foundations.

17. Ellis supra note 3, pp. 109-117.
18. Case 109/88 *Handels-OG Kontorfunktionaerernes Forbund I Danmark v. Dansk Arbejdsgiverforening (acting for Danfoss)* [1989] ECR 3199.
19. Case C-127/92 *Enderby v Frenchay Health Authority* [1993] ECR I-5535.
20. See further, for instance, Chapter Two (Ireland) and Chapter Seven (United Kingdom), this volume.
21. Ibid.

Fenwick and Hervey, for instance, after an examination of four cases (*Habermann-Beltermann*,[22] *Webb*,[23] *Enderby*[24] and *Neath*[25]) in which the Court had to address a range of economic justifications for discrimination, concluded that the Court was equivocal in its apparent pursuit of substantive, rather than formal equality:[26]

> the concept of sex discrimination in EC law is premised upon a particular market-related philosophy; thus furtherance of equality in the context of market forces creates a contradiction . . . choice will tend to arise between formal and substantive equality. To choose substantive equality may be to create a more severe disruption of 'natural' market forces, and the Court seems to be indicating its reluctance to make such a choice.

For some commentators these limits are implicit in the market context in which EU equality law operates: Mazey has argued that EU equality law has done nothing to tackle the job segregation which flourish on gender discrimination,[27] while Hervey queries whether the aim of EU equality laws is the completion of the internal market or the correction of social inequalities *caused by* the market.[28]

An important element of the ECJ's jurisprudence in this regard is its own perception of the scope of EC law, or the 'domain' of the EU, leading it to rule, as in *Hofmann*,[29] that the Equal Treatment Directive 'is not designed to settle questions concerning the organisation of the family, or to alter the division of responsibility between parents'.[30]

Fredman echoes the Court's own sentiment in her critique of the principle of indirect discrimination which, she argues, suffers from two inherent limitations:[31]

---

22. Case C-421/92 *Habermann-Beltermann v Arbeiterwolfahrt, Bezirksverband Ndb./Opf. eV* [1994] ECR I-1657.
23 Supra note 11.
24. Case C-127/92 *Enderby v Frenchay Health Authority and Secretary of State for Health* [1993] ECR I-5535.
25. Case C-152/91 *Neath v. Hugh Steeper Ltd.* [1994] ECR I-6935.
26. Fenwick, H. and Hervey, T. (1995), 'Sex Equality in the Single Market. New Directions for the European Court of Justice', 32 *Common Market Law Review* 443 at 469.
27. Mazey, S. (1988), 'European Community Action on Behalf of Women: The Limits of Legislation', 27 *JCMS* 63.
28. Hervey T. (1988), *European Social Law and Policy*, London: Longman, Chapter 1.
29. Case 184/83 *Hofmann v Barmer Ersatzkasse* [1984] ECR 3047.
30 Ibid at para. 25.
31. Fredman, S. (1992), 'European Community Discrimination Law: A Critique', 21 *ILJ* 119 at 125.

> Firstly, disproportionate impact does no more than establish a *prima facie* case of indirect discrimination. The employer is still permitted to defend indirectly discriminatory practices by arguing that they are justified for reasons which are not due to the sex of the worker. In effect then, the anti-discrimination principle is not a 'fundamental right', as it is frequently proclaimed to be, but merely a presumption which can be trumped by other considerations. Second, in its practical application, indirect discrimination does not make sufficiently radical inroads into the male norm . . . it does not demand a resolution of the underlying structural problems which disadvantage women in the workplace.

Scheiwe, examining the Court's approach to the equal treatment directives, concludes that there is an ideological division drawn by the ECJ in its jurisprudence between the public and private spheres of market and family:

> [a] rigid separating line between two spheres, the market and the family, has been erected in case law and used by the Court to justify a narrow interpretation of the intended purpose of the equal treatment directives.[32]

Thus the 'non-discrimination' approach taken by the Court is criticised because it measures equality in relation to a male norm, which in itself is underpinned with liberal assumptions about the individualism of workers and an untrammelled capacity to contract:

> The Community's formula for sex equality is . . . abstract, narrow and rigid: it is conceptually incapable of eradicating all but the most superficial inequalities faced by women. It helps only those women workers who are already well-assimilated to men; it reinforces inequalities based on gender differences; it restricts the use of positive action; and it masks the fact that many of women's inequalities at work are intimately related to their role in the family.[33]

At times even the ECJ's commitment to the formal non-discrimination principle is questioned. The recourse by the Court to prospective overruling,

---

32. Scheiwe, K. (1994), 'EC law's Unequal Treatment of the Family: The Case Law of the European Court of Justice on Rules Prohibiting Discrimination on Grounds of Sex and Nationality', 4 *Social and Legal Studies* 243 at 261. See also: Cullen, H (1994), 'The Subsidiary Woman', 16 *Journal of Social Work and Family Law* 407.
33. More, G. (1993), '"Equal Treatment" of the Sexes in European Community Law: What Does "Equal" Mean?', 1 *Feminist Legal Studies* 45 at 64.

for instance in relation to pensions,[34] the practice of the Court in permitting levelling-down to eliminate discriminatory employment practices,[35] and not least the rulings of the Court in positive discrimination cases[36] are seen by some to undermine the ECJ's insistence that the non-discrimination principle is 'fundamental' under Community law.

A legislative approach to equality between the sexes

The same basic non-discrimination approach has informed the bulk of EU legislation on equality. Indeed the weight placed on the non-discrimination principle by the ECJ may have played a role in legitimising pressure on the EC institutions to develop further legislative measures to tackle inequality between men and women.

Like the judicial version of the non-discrimination principle, the legislative interventions in this field were constrained in important ways by the market context in which they developed. In the first place there were difficulties with the legal base for such measures. The original Article 94EC (100) permitted the adoption of directives for the approximation of laws directly affecting the common market,[37] and required unanimity in the Council of Ministers, as did the supplementary Article 308EC (235) which ascribes to the Council power to take other measures necessary to attain the objectives of the EC and which also required unanimity. Basing their action on these provisions, the EC did enact Directives in the 1970s and 1980s on Equal Pay,[38] Equal Treatment[39] and on Equality of Treatment in Social Security,[40] in Occupational Pension Schemes[41] and in relation to self-employment.[42]

---

34. See e.g. Case 262/88 *Barber v. Guardian Royal Exchange* [1990] ECR I-1889, where the ECJ ruled that its judgement would only have prospective effect, except in the cases of those who had already initiated legal proceedings or raised an equivalent claim under national law: ibid at 1956.
35. See e.g. in relation to pensions: Case C-408/92 *Smith v Advel Systems Ltd* [1994] ECR I-4435.
36. See further Nott, Chapter Ten, this volume.
37. See Article 94EC (100) and Article 308EC (235).
38. Directive 75/117/EEC, *OJ 1975 L45/19*, based on Article 94EC (100).
39. Directive 76/207/EEC, *OJ 1976 L39/40*, based on Article 308 EC (235).
40. Directive 79/7/EEC, *OJ 1979 L6/24*, based on Article 308 EC (235).
41. Directive 86/378/EEC as amended by Corrigendum 1986 L283/27, *OJ 1986 L225/40*, based on Article 308 EC (235).
42. Directive 86/613/EEC, *OJ 1986 L359/56*, based on Article 308 EC (235).

Buckley and Anderson attribute this period of activity to a 'happy coincidence' between Second Wave feminism and the development of the EC as a body politic.[43] Cunningham has argued that they coincided with a perceived need to bring the EC closer to the citizens of the Member States; to develop a human face for the Community.[44] Hoskyns adds to this that equality issues fitted the bill because they were perceived as marginal and without great cost implications, and hence were areas on which concessions could be made.[45] Generally, this raft of measures adopted and promoted the non-discrimination approach to equality issues referred to earlier, providing a remedy only for those women whose situation was comparable to that of a man, and which could be invoked only by the economically active.[46] Moves to develop a more specific commitment to a social policy for the EC were fraught with difficulties in the 1980s and early 1990s, partly, but not entirely, due to the presence in the UK of a government which was trenchant in its opposition to such a development.[47]

New Directions for the EU in Equality Matters?

When the Single European Act of 1986 introduced a new legislative competence in respect of the 'working environment', Article 138EC (118A), it was restricted in its scope and hedged by conditions: moreover, although 'qualified majority voting' could be used in connection with Article 138EC (118A), it was not available where the issue at hand concerned 'the rights and interests of employed persons', a major restriction as far as equality legislation was concerned. The new competence to legislate in relation to the 'working environment' was similarly limited and unclear in its scope. The impact of these restrictions and of the divisions in legislative competence on maternity legislation has been considered elsewhere.[48]

---

43. Buckley, M. and Anderson, M. (eds), (1988), *Women, Equality and Europe*, London: Macmillan; see also Lovenduski, J. (1990), 'Feminism and Western European Politics: an overview', in Urwin, D. W. and Paterson, W. E. (eds), (1990), *Politics in Western Europe Today*, London: Longman.
44. Cunningham, S. (1992), 'The Development of Equal Opportunities Theory and Practice in the European Community', 20 *Policy and Politics* 177 at 180.
45. Hoskyns, C. (1992), 'The European Community' Policy on Women in the Context of 1992', 15(1) *Women's Studies International Forum* 21 at 22.
46. See for instance Scheiwe, supra note 32.
47. It has been argued that the opposition of the UK to social policy developments allowed other states to engage in 'cheap talk': supportive populist statements on which they knew they would not have to deliver: c.f. Lange, P. (1992), 'The Politics of the Social Dimension', in Sbragia, A. (ed.), *Euro-Politics: Institutions and Policy-Making in the 'New' European Community*, Washington: Brookings Institute, p. 242.
48. Beveridge and Nott supra note 5, at pp. 59-64; Morris, A. and Nott, S. (1992) 'The Legal Response to Pregnancy', 2 *Legal Studies*, 54-73; Muffat-Jeande, D. (1991), 'The Proposed Pregnancy and Maternity Directive', 20 *Industrial Law Journal* 76.

Wrangling over the proper role of the EU in relation to social policy led to a somewhat unsatisfactory set of compromises in the Treaty of European Union (TEU) which came into force in 1992. The existing Treaty bases for legislation remained largely unaltered, changing only to reflect the development of new decision-making powers, particularly in relation to the European Parliament. Noticeably the greater involvement of the Parliament was not extended to areas under Article 138EC (118A) which involved the 'rights and interests of employed persons'.

However the Social Protocol attached to the Treaty did permit the adoption of new legislation in this field by the Member States excluding the UK. Significantly, a full role for the social partners — employers and employees — was institutionalised in the Social Protocol, reflecting the approach taken to labour market issues in most Member States other than the UK. Subsequent activity under the Social Protocol demonstrated the importance of this, as the collective agreement was utilised to forge a new consensus on areas such as parental leave, to be followed by legislation on the same subject which reflected closely the normative content of such collective agreements.[49] Noticeably, however, the Social Charter on which the Social Protocol was based is confined to the employment sphere, thus reaffirming the public/private divide of which feminist commentators have complained. In response to this, there has been a call for the representation of women as economic actors in Community law to be replaced by representations which recognise, on the one hand, the sociological and political reality of women's lives[50] and, on the other hand, the diversity of women's situations.

The Treaty of Amsterdam, which came into force in 1999, introduces two major initiatives in relation to equality law. First it amends the central 'equal pay' provision to introduce a significant new legislative competence in the field of equality between men and women. The new Article 141(3)EC (119) reads:

---

49. See e.g. Directive 96/34/EEC, OJ [1996] L145/4 (on parental leave); Directive 97/81, OJ [1998] L14/9. For an account of the development of social dialogue see e.g. Ross, G. (1995), 'Assessing the Delors Era and Social Policy', in Liebfried, S. and Pierson, P. (eds), *European Social Policy: Between Fragmentation and Integration*, Washington: Brookings Institute, p. 357 at p. 373 et infra.

50 Ackers, L. (1994), 'Women, Citizenship and European Community Law: The Gender Implications of the Free Movement of Persons', 14 *Journal of Social Welfare and Family Law* 391; Fredman, S. (1992), 'European Community Discrimination Law: A Critique', 21 *Industrial Law Journal* 119; Ward, I. (1996), 'Beyond Sex Equality: The Limits of Sex Equality Law in the New Europe', in Hervey and O'Keeffe (eds), supra note 1, p. 369.

> The Council, acting in accordance with the procedure referred to in Article 251EC (189b), and after consulting the Economic and Social Committee, shall adopt measures to ensure the application of the principle of equal opportunities and equal treatment of men and women in matters of employment and occupation, including the principle of equal pay for equal work or work of equal value.

This allows the adoption of any type of act and permits the adoption of any measure ensuring equality of opportunity (not merely measures outlawing discrimination). Whereas the old Article 119 dealt only with pay, the new competence extends to all issues of equal treatment, though it remains confined, of course, to 'matters of occupation and employment'. As Ellis notes:

> [t]he important issue of how far it will be permitted to extend to equal treatment outside the traditional world of paid work will depend on the policy adopted by the ECJ in relation to the interpretation of the word 'occupation'.[51]

The second major innovation of the Amsterdam Treaty was the insertion of a new provision, Article 13EC (6a):

> Without prejudice to the other provisions of this Treaty and within the limits of the powers conferred by it upon the Community, the Council, acting unanimously on a proposal from the Commission and after consulting the European Parliament, may take appropriate action to combat discrimination based on sex, racial or ethnic origin, religion or belief, disability, age or sexual orientation.

This Article, though restricted to measures to tackle discrimination (thus excluding measures promoting equality of opportunity in the wider sense), could be used to tackle multi-factored discrimination. Moreover its ambit is not restricted to the employment sphere and this is reflected in the law-making route to be followed by initiatives under this provision — the consultation procedure indicated gives only a limited role to the European Parliament, requires the Council to act unanimously and gives no formal role to the Economic and Social Committee.[52]

---

51. Ellis, supra note 3, p. 5.
52. See further Barnard, C. (1999) 'Article 13: Through the Looking Glass of Union Citizenship', in O'Keeffe, D. and Twomey, P. *Legal Issues of the Amsterdam Treaty*, Oxford: Hart Publishing, p. 375.

A third major development was the dropping of resistance by the UK to the Social Chapter, thus allowing the obligations assumed by other Member States under these provisions to become operable in the UK and, perhaps, opening the door for further developments in this sphere.

Together these three developments represent the potential to move beyond the non-discrimination principle. The earlier legislative initiatives cited above have been supplemented, subsequent to these amendments to the treaty base, by the Pregnant Workers Directive,[53] the Directive on Part-time Work[54] and the Parental Leave Directive.[55] The focus of each of these measures is still the labour market, and each has its own limitations, particularly in relation to the distribution of financial burdens. However, they do perhaps represent a small step forward in the EU's approach to equality issues in that each of these pieces of legislation embodies some recognition of the social situation of many women as mothers and/or carers and reflects the reality experienced by many women of fractured work patterns and unpaid caring responsibilities. As Hoskyns observes: '[v]ery slowly, the domestic and the sexual are creeping up on the EU, and the barrier between the public and private is becoming harder to maintain'.[56]

The adoption of further legislation which might give legal shape to a broader understanding of equality will, of course, depend on commitment in the political sphere. The new provisions on equality in the Treaty of Amsterdam provide one indication of the current state of that commitment. The need for unanimity in most areas may well act, in any case, as a brake on future legislative action in this field. But for indications of how the political commitment represented might be translated into future policy or legislation the activities of the Commission, in particular of Directorate-General V, should be noted.

The European Commission and Equality

Despite its place at the heart of EU policy-making the European Commission has always been somewhat constrained in relation to social policy:

53. Directive 92/85/EEC, *OJ [1992] L348/1*, based on Article 118A (now 138).
54. Directive 97/81/EEC *OJ [1998] L14/9*, based on the Social Policy Protocol.
55. Directive 96/34/EEC, *OJ [1996] L145/4*, based on the Social Policy Protocol. One further piece of legislation secured during this period was the Directive on the Burden of Proof, Directive 97/80/EEC, *OJ [1998] L14/6*.
56. Hoskyns, supra note 4, at p. 201.

> Constitutionally, the Commission can propose policy only in areas permitted by EC/EU treaties. Next, it can propose only what member states are likely to entertain, given that governments in the decision setting of the Council constitute the EU's legislature. Finally, it must itself have the capacities to find and exploit those limited opportunities that treaty prospects and the intergovernmental context do allow . . . The simple truth is that these three factors rarely combined positively in social policy.[57]

To a large extent the fortunes of equality policy, and policies of significance to women, have merely followed those of social policy more widely construed. Thus gender issues were largely ignored up till 1973. From 1973 to 1983 the Commission was extremely active in proposing Directives on social policy which were then frequently blocked in the Council. This was the fate that befell *inter alia* measures on work hours and on prorated (proportionate) social benefits for those working less than full time, measures to accommodate work and family obligations, a memorandum on working conditions, a draft Directive on equality in social security and a draft Directive on positive discrimination.[58] As noted earlier, this period did, however, see the adoption of five equality directives conforming to the non-discrimination mould.[59]

During this period the Commission also drew up a series of action programmes on equal opportunities which the Council did adopt.[60]

Broadly, the first action programme (1982-86) concerned measures to consolidate the impact of the existing equality directives and proposed the introduction of further directives. In addition, studies, discussions and research were initiated which would inform future action.

The second action programme (1986-90) continued this work but with the emphasis less on the legal sphere, and more on the examination of the social realities outside the paid employment sphere which affected women's participation in the workforce. Thus for instance the issue of childcare was prominent in the work of the Commission during this time, culminating in the adoption of the Recommendation on Childcare in 1992.[61]

---

57. Ross, supra note 49 at p. 358.
58. Ostner, I. and Lewis, J. (1995), 'Gender and the Evolution of European Social Policies', in Leibfried and Pierson (eds), supra note 49, p. 159 at 163.
59. Supra, notes 38-43. The last two of these were adopted in 1986.
60. See e.g. Ostner and Lewis, supra note 54 at p. 164; Nielson and Szyszczak (2nd 1993), *The Social Dimension of the European Community* Handelshojskolens Forlag; Commissioner Diamantopoulou has promised a fifth framework programme for the period 2001-2005
61. Council Recommendation 92/241/EEC of 31 March 1992 on childcare *OJ (1992) L 123*. See further Hoskyns, supra note 4, pp 156-7.

The third action programme (1990-95) ties equality issues more closely to the EU's structural policy and general socio-economic policy. There is a new focus, for instance on integration of women into the labour market, through vocational training, positive action measures and female entrepreneurship and on the participation of women in decision-making more generally. The third action programme also announced a substantial raft of measures intended to achieve its objectives including draft Directives and the targeting of funds.[62]

The fourth action programme (1996-2000) makes gender mainstreaming a central focus, and this is reflected in the Commission communication on the same subject in 1996.[63]

These action programmes have been significant in a variety of ways. Their very existence demonstrates some level of commitment to equality between men and women at the EU level and thus opens the door for lobbyists, European parliamentarians and others to seek action in respect of this commitment. In addition, acceptance of the political commitments contained in the action programmes may have shortened the distance between existing and proposed legal measures in a number of cases, making the adoption of binding legal measures easier than might otherwise have been the case. The political commitment to issues addressed in the action programmes has also helped to establish an EU interest in areas previously regarded as outside the EU's sphere of competence, and may have contributed to the eventual extension of competence into those fields.

Steps taken in furtherance of such action programmes have also had some important consequences: for instance, the Commission has developed new approaches to policy-making[64] and has secured the adoption of measures of soft law (recommendations and communications) which have subsequently played a role in shaping Community action in the legal sphere. In the field of equal opportunities, much of the ideological development regarding equality

62. Council Resolution of 21 May 1991 on the third medium-term Community action programme on equal opportunities for women and men (1991-95) *OJ (1991) C 142, p. 1*: for a detailed account see Roelofs, E. (1995), 'The European Equal Opportunities Policy', in van Doorne-Huiskes, A., van Hoof, J. and Roelofs, E., *Women and the European Labour Markets*, London: Chapman, p. 122 at pp. 135-7.

63. COM (96) 67. See further Nott, Chapter Ten, this volume. An important development which serves both to highlight the mainstreaming approach and to give it some impetus is the production by the Commission since 1996 of an Annual Report on Equal Opportunities for Women and Men in the European Union: e.g. Commission of the European Communities *Annual Report on Equal Opportunities for Women and Men in the European Union 1998*, 5th March 1999, COM (1999) 106 final.

64. Such as the tripartite approach to law-making in the employment sphere, now fully integrated into the legal arrangements for social policy-making, as noted above.

measures which has informed more concrete measures, and much of the bridge-building which has preceded the extension of the equal opportunities remit into hitherto unaffected fields, can be attributed to Directorate-General V of the Commission and traced through the action plans and other non-binding measures.

It can be concluded that in this policy-shaping role the Commission has exercised more influence in relation to EU equality law and policy than, for instance, in its enforcement role, though it has not been idle here either. It should be noted, though, that the range of participants in this policy-making process has changed over time, as the role of the 'social partners' in the employment field has received more explicit recognition in the EC Treaty. It remains to be seen whether the Commission's policy-making style will be further altered by the need to reform the Commission to introduce greater openness and accountability.[65] It also remains to be seen what the Commission makes of the new competences established by the Treaty of Amsterdam: as noted above these do not create any duty to bring forward legislation in the future but merely provide a legal base. The need to maintain a broad consensus among the many actors involved in the policy-making process and the need to maintain and defend a balance between social protection on the one hand and competition and sound public finances on the other may act as major constraints: '[t]he "all things to all people" approach may have the benefit of securing apparent agreement from many policy actors. However, it does run the risk of failing to deliver concrete or enforceable legal provisions'.[66]

The Role of EC law in the Member States

EC law can be seen to have played a significant role in each of the Member States studied. However it is not the only influence — most of the Member States featured here had some form of commitment to equality before their accession to the EU, and all have furthered their commitment to equality in areas outside the competence of the EU as well as within it. Moreover, as noted above, all of the states examined in the preceding chapters have subscribed to international instruments such as ILO Conventions on *inter alia* Equal Pay and Discrimination in Employment and to the UN Convention on

---

65. For a discussion see e.g. Curtin, D. M. (1999), 'The Fundamental Principle of Open Decision-Making and EU (Political) Citizenship', in O'Keeffe, D. and Twomey, P. *Legal Issues of the Amsterdam Treaty*, Oxford: Hart Publishing, p. 71.
66. Barnard, C. and Hervey T. (1998), 'European Union Employment and Social Policy Survey 1998', 18 *Yearbook of European Law* 613.

the Elimination of all forms of Discrimination Against Women (CEDAW). Thus at both the political and the legal level each of these states has been exposed to a wide range of ideas, concepts and strategies concerning equality.

Alongside this it is clear from the preceding chapters that each state is heavily influenced in its approach to equality matters by its existing legal and political culture and institutional arrangements. For instance, those states which traditionally left the regulation of employment matters to the social partners — labour and management — usually left matters concerning equality in the employment sphere to be addressed through the collective bargaining process. Indeed, in the case of Sweden, bad feeling emerged between the labour movement and the ruling Social Democratic Party when the government proposed the introduction of equal opportunities legislation in 1978/79.[67] In contrast states which typically left the employment relationship to be regulated through the medium of private contract addressed issues concerning equality in the employment sphere by enacting legislation which imposed new parameters on the freedom of these parties to contract.

Finally it should be borne in mind that the Member States and the EU are not mutually exclusive bodies — the development of ideas, policies, legislation and jurisprudence at the EU level comes about as a result of myriad forms of interaction between the political representatives, the officials, the populace and the cultures of the Member States and the EU institutions. While a small number of states have been the source of the vast majority of references to the ECJ on equality issues and hence have, in a somewhat unwitting sense, acted as the drivers of the development of law by the Court, others have undoubtedly been much more active in seeking the setting of higher standards of protection in legislation and through the policies of the Community, in keeping with their own national perspectives and policies. Such states may have been able to influence to a significant degree the approach taken at the EU level to the issues in question, though such an assertion is admittedly very difficult to verify.

EU laws and policies are therefore as much influenced by the laws, policies and cultures of the Member States as national laws and policies are a product of EU laws and policies, though the precise equation is ever-variable, and perceived differently by different actors at different times.

Given these factors it is no easy task to discern the role and influence of EU law in any of the states examined, and more difficult still to draw general conclusions.

67. See further Chapter Six, this volume. Also: Gillberg, M. (1999), *Predicting the Impact of Policy: Gender-Auditing as a Means of Assessing the Probable Impact of Policy Initiatives on Women, Country Report: Sweden*, Liverpool: Feminist Legal Research Unit, School of Law, University of Liverpool, p. 21

The role of national constitutions

Each of the Member States considered in this volume has a written constitution, with the exception of the UK. These constitutions reflect changing attitudes and legal approaches to equality. The national constitutions examined gradually gave recognition, through the end of the nineteenth and the beginning of the twentieth century, to the concept of equality between men and women in the civil and political spheres. This usually entailed a move from gender-specific to gender-neutral provisions;[68] the notable exception is the Irish Constitution which in many areas continues to endorse the notion of 'separate spheres' for men and women.[69]

With this exception it can be said that these constitutions reflect a liberal approach to equality and endorse the gender neutral approach to law and rights which is a fundamental feature of their legal systems. However the Spanish Constitution, drafted in 1978 and apparently influenced by civil rights litigation in the United States, appears to an extent to move beyond the gender neutral approach: it promotes a (gender neutral) concept of equality before the law alongside a non-discrimination principle which is understood as presupposing the disadvantage of certain groups and requiring compensation.[70] That is, gender is specifically recognised as a factor in disadvantage which the Spanish state must therefore address. Although more sophisticated than most constitutional provisions on equality, the Spanish provisions referred to do not appear actually to embrace a positive duty to tackle inequality. Only one of the states examined had such a provision in its constitution: the Portuguese Constitution was amended in 1997 to impose a duty on the State to promote equality between men and women.[71] It is not clear what effect, if any, this may have had within Portugal or what its potential effects are.

---

68. See for instance Sweden, where until 1909 the Constitution barred women from higher offices in most professions. At the same time that such restrictions were removed, the regulation of women's employment was removed from the scope of the constitution to be dealt with in general laws instead, see *Country Report: Sweden*, supra note 67, p. 19 et infra.
69. Donnelly, M., Mullally, S. and Smith, O. (1999), *Predicting the Impact of Policy: Gender-Auditing as a Means of Assessing the Probable Impact of Policy Initiatives on Women, Country Report: Ireland*, Liverpool: Feminist Legal Research Unit, School of Law, University of Liverpool, pp. 64-69.
70. See Chapter Five, this volume and references cite' therein.
71. Article 9, Constitution of the Portuguese Republic, 1997 edition.

Constitutional challenges by individuals

It was noticeable that in the two states — Ireland and Spain — where individual citizens could raise actions based on the alleged unconstitutionality of laws or government actions, the Constitutional Court had played a major role in shaping the legal principles of equality and non-discrimination laid down in the respective Constitutions. In the case of Spain this had on the whole been helpful, allowing a creative and progressive Court to move from a formal equality perspective (held in the early eighties) to a wider perspective recognising hidden direct discrimination (pregnancy dismissal) and indirect discrimination. Moreover the Spanish Constitutional court has increasingly looked at the results of actions rather than the intention behind the acts, so that a more substantive concept of equality is promoted and one which appears capable of tackling 'gender-plus' discrimination situations. In the case of Ireland, however, the role of the judges of the Supreme Court has not always been so positive. While there have been some rulings favouring women and promoting equality between the sexes, the Supreme Court has generally been unwilling to use the Constitutional provision guaranteeing equality before the law as the basis for any decisions, and has restricted its material scope so as to render it inapplicable in the labour market context.[72] In Portugal, individuals also have the right to raise the issue of the constitutionality of laws or acts, including their compatibility with the 'Fundamental Rights and Duties' protected under the Portuguese Constitution, but such actions are rare, reflecting the fact that litigation levels are already low and the rights in question are expressed only in very broad, general language.[73]

Where individuals had no right of constitutional challenge, there was a very mixed pattern. In Sweden, where levels of litigation were low and the employment sector historically was not regulated through the legal sphere, actions based on the Constitution played a very limited role. But in the United Kingdom, where litigation did play an important role both generally (in determining legal obligations) and particularly (in the employment sphere), constitutional-type litigation played an important and prominent part, despite the absence of any national constitution or substantive 'right to equality': the provisions of EU law were simply invoked to fill this gap.[74]

72. See *Country Report: Ireland*, supra note 69, pp. 64-68.
73. Such an action may be raised in any court of justice or administration and an appeal lies to the Constitutional Court: see Casqueira Cardoso, J. (1999), *Predicting the Impact of Policy: Gender-Auditing as a Means of Assessing the Probable Impact of Policy Initiatives on Women, Country Report: Portugal*, Liverpool: Feminist Legal Research Unit, School of Law, University of Liverpool, pp. 11 and 22-3.
74. See Chapter Seven, this volume.

This would seem to have been a product of political rather than legal circumstances: many of the cases could have been avoided by a government committed to furthering equality objectives and commitments.

Influence of EU law on National Law

EU law has fulfilled a number of roles in the Member States examined; however it has not fulfilled the same roles in every state. As noted above, EU law has played an extremely prominent role in the United Kingdom, satisfying at times a constitutional function in the context of litigation; it has also provided, as noted in Chapter Seven, the basis for much of the United Kingdom's equality legislation. Similarly in Ireland, Portugal and Spain there has been a noticeable alignment of national law with EU law (although it is only in Ireland that compatibility between national and EU obligations is regularly tested before the courts).

The Dutch example provides an interesting contrast: here the high level of political commitment to equality policies meant that Dutch legal provisions were usually ahead of those of the EU, so that EU law played very little role in the formation and enactment of equality obligations. The Netherlands does however seem to embrace the 'rights talk' of EU law in conceptualising and enforcing equality obligations, and the law does play an important role in remedying individual grievances concerning discrimination: thus, though the influence cannot directly be seen, there is a strong match between Dutch and EU equality law. The Netherlands may simply be ahead of and influencing the laws of the EU, rather than responding to or anticipating changes in EU law. In Sweden, on the other hand, there is less 'rights talk' altogether in relation to equality, and this is reflected in the more consensus-oriented grievance procedures; additionally there has been less emphasis on giving effect to EU law which is largely regarded as irrelevant in the Swedish context, in favour of the 'active' measures to promote equality in the workplace established in the Equal Opportunities Act of 1992.[75]

Thus in discussing the relationship between national and EU law it should be borne in mind that the relationship, and the way in which it is perceived, varies between different Member States.

In those Member States where EU law has played a prominent role, it has provided the impetus for a widening in the scope of the gender-neutral equality laws which are commonplace in the Member States. Notably the

75. *Country Report: Sweden*, supra note 67, pp. 23 et infra.

ECJ has brought about a widening of the definition of key concepts such as 'equality' and 'pay'. Protection has been widened in a number of distinct ways. First, centring on 141 EC (119), the concept of pay has been broadened to include elements such as occupational pensions and redundancy pay.[76] Secondly, the concept of indirect discrimination, previously non-existent or underdeveloped in many Member States, has been given a broad and effective interpretation by the ECJ, so that many forms of systematic discrimination in which gender played an important role could be tackled.[77] Thirdly, the sphere of protection has been widened beyond the traditional sphere of employment relations, principally through the adoption of the Equal Treatment Directive and measures requiring equality of treatment in the social security field.[78]

A second role played by EU law has been the establishment of a minimum floor of protection in areas of particular concern to women, notably in relation to the treatment of pregnant workers and in the field of parental leave.[79] In theory at least this deprives employers of arguments against the basic entitlements established by the EC measures based on costs and competitiveness with other EC-based firms. Similarly governments are obliged to accept the minimum entitlements established as an irreducible core of social protection. However, it must be borne in mind that the intention behind the pertinent Directives was merely to establish minimum standards and that in real terms the level of protection provided, particularly in relation to pregnant workers, was not high: indeed the danger was that many employers would level down the protection previously offered to some or all women workers to the minimum required under the new provisions, at least where Member States' legislation permitted. Another danger was that Member State governments would abandon attempts to maintain higher standards, either generally or in the public employment sector, effectively treating the minimum as a norm, though this was in some instances ruled out.[80]

A third area where EU law has also made a notable contribution is in ensuring that the domestic laws of the Member States provided adequate remedies for breaches of sex equality law. It is arguable that this is an area where there has been a spillover into the equality field from an agenda which

---

76. Supra, p. 196.
77 Supra, pp. 197-8.
78. Supra, p. 201.
79. Supra, p. 205.
80 See for example the Pregnant Workers Directive supra note 49, Art. 1(3), providing that where levels of maternity pay higher than that stipulated in the Directive were required by pre-existing Member State law, that should be protected.

is played out on another plane — the ECJ's quest to establish the supremacy of EU law over national law. As was noted above, this is an area where equality cases have played an important role in shaping EU obligations more generally. In cases such as *Von Colson*[81] and *Marshall (No. 2)*,[82] both involving Article 6 of the Equal Treatment Directive, the Court acknowledged the discretion which the provision gave to Member States in relation to the development of a system for effective implementation of the equal treatment principle, but insisted that Article 6 required that the victims of discrimination be able to seek full redress through a judicial process and that full redress would, for instance, include interest on sums due. In cases on provisional measures and on other forms of relief, the ECJ has similarly emphasised the need for 'effective' protection of rights derived from EC law. It seems likely that there will be further litigation exploring the ramifications of these rulings in the equality field in future.

The establishment of higher normative and procedural standards in relation to remedies is clearly seen in those states where individual litigation is favoured in the employment sphere: in both Ireland and the UK, litigation played a prominent role in securing legal change. This effect was particularly marked in the UK where the Equal Opportunities Commission, although not in favour with the Conservative government between 1979 and 1997, was nevertheless able to adopt a litigation strategy to expose flaws in the existing UK legislation. But although such gains are important, and high-profile cases can play a significant educative role more generally, there are obvious inherent and practical limitations to this type of action.

A contrast can be drawn with states such as Portugal and Sweden where great faith is placed on collective bargaining between the social partners to implement broad general expressions of the right to equal pay and equal treatment. In both states the possibility of individual litigation does exist but there is no regular resort to national courts to test the legality of current employment practices. It is difficult in this context to be clear about whether EC law is fully respected in the labour market, particularly where collective agreements reflect and perpetuate vertical or horizontal segregation. Moreover it is unclear whether the requirement of an adequate remedy for breach of the non-discrimination requirement is met in some states, again because the point has not been tested.

81. Case 14/83 *Von Colson and Kamann v. Land Nordrhein Westfalen* [1984] ECR 1891.
82. Case C-271/91 *Marshall v. Southampton and South-West Hampshire Area Health Authority* [1993] ECR I-4367.

EU law and the common law tradition — the devil in the detail?

There are at times tensions between the law and policy-making traditions and understandings of the EU and the Member States. These seemed particularly acute in the two common-law states examined, Ireland and the United Kingdom. In a general sense, the teleological reasoning of the ECJ, by upsetting commonly-held perceptions of what existing legal obligations might entail, is problematic in any system of law, and indeed this is indirectly recognised by the ECJ when it resorts to, or considers, prospective overruling. But beyond that, Ireland and the United Kingdom in particular, seem regularly to have 'trouble' over the transposition of the requirements of EU Directives into national law. To what extent this is attributable to the requirements of the common law tradition of certainty and predictability, and to what extent political factors are at work, is not clear. However, the need to commit to detail the rights and obligations of, for instance, employers and employees, has led to trouble on a number of occasions.

For instance, following a similar pattern, the UK Equal Pay Act 1970 and the Irish Equal Pay Act 1974 introduced the concept of the 'comparator', compared to whom the claimant's treatment had to be shown to be less favourable to prove discrimination. The comparator had to be in the same employment and the sex of the claimant or his/her marital status had to shown to be the causal element in the discrimination. In the case of the UK it was established in legislation that this did not admit of a hypothetical comparator, nor of a comparator employed during a different period (e.g. immediately before or after the claimant). Irish law, on the other hand, required an actual comparator in relation to direct discrimination relating to pay, though a hypothetical comparator could be used in relation to indirect discrimination and discrimination on the basis of marital status which was covered by different legislative provisions.

Similar complexities were introduced in both systems in relation to the concept of indirect discrimination: in the UK it is necessary to show that a condition or requirement is applied with which a considerably smaller proportion of women than men can comply (or vice versa), which cannot be justified, irrespective of the sex to which it is applied and which is to a woman's (or man's) detriment because she cannot comply with it.[83] In Ireland the question of indirect discrimination was at first regarded as falling under section 2(c) of the Employment Equality Act, 1977. Under this provision indirect discrimination could be established where it had been shown that a

83. Sex Discrimination Act 1975, s. 1(1) (b).

condition had been imposed (e.g. on recruitment) which was not an 'essential requirement' of the job and with which a 'substantially higher' proportion of one sex than the other was able to comply. However in 1996 the Supreme Court delivered a judgement stating that this provision did not cover cases of indirect discrimination, and set out a new judicial test for indirect discrimination which conforms broadly to EC law on the matter.[84]

The approach of specifying such matters in detail within the primary legislation, though an integral feature of the constitutional and legal system in these states, produced both negative and positive effects. The detailing of the precise requirements of equality provisions has led to unhelpful (narrow) definitions, particularly where the courts have been called upon to give interpretations. The complexity of legal provisions has also made enforcement difficult at times from the point of view of employees, employers and the relevant statutory bodies. And the laws themselves have had to be amended repeatedly to bring national law in line with ECJ rulings. There have also been many periods where substantial uncertainty has existed, particularly where the scope of ECJ rulings has been left unclear. Thus a feature characteristic of the common law tradition and justified as promoting clarity and predictability has often had the opposite effect when combined with the approach of the ECJ, to which it is almost diametrically opposed.

The problem is compounded where EC law itself allows exceptions or justifications to general principles to be made: in Ireland and the UK, both in the Anglo-American common law tradition, national legislators have sought to flesh out the justifications to give them the sort of detail and the accompanying appearance of legal certainty which is a feature of law-making in those jurisdictions, only to see these provisions become the subject of protracted and confusing rounds of litigation before the courts. Thus, as Fredman has argued, the very existence of the possibility of justification undermines the effectiveness of the law as a tool for tackling inequality.[85]

Contrasts can be drawn with both the framework law system in Sweden, where only the general principles will be established in primary legislation, leaving the details to be developed through administrative practice and detailed regulation,[86] and the Dutch legal system where law tends to follow practice.[87]

---

84. *Country Report: Sweden*, supra note 67, pp. 31-4.
85. Fredman, supra note 31, at p. 125.
86. *Country Report: Sweden*, supra note 67, p. 6.
87 See Chapter Three, this volume.

The diversity of national responses

It was very noticeable in the equality laws of the states featured in this book that even when responding to or anticipating legal change at the EU level, the Member States' responses were heavily influenced by national political, legal and institutional cultures. Thus despite superficial similarities at times between the instruments enacted to give effect to EU measures, these measures varied enormously in terms of their normative content, the methods by which they would be acted upon and implemented and their overall effectiveness in bringing about in practice the changes which the EU measure was designed to secure. One significant variable referred to previously is the extent to which formal legal rights, rather than collective bargaining, are relied on to effect change in the labour market. Where the latter approach was used, the influence of the social partners (employers and employees) was evident at other stages too, for instance in the negotiation of legislation and policy more generally and in the resolution of disputes, reflecting a social market approach, rather than a free market approach, to labour market regulation. This distinction can be traced through to the treatment of particular issues such as sexual harassment in the workplace. Sexual harassment does not easily fit into the 'free market' paradigm and has been 'accommodated' only by treating harassment in severe cases as the cause of constructive dismissal i.e. by reading a contractual meaning onto what is patently not in essence a contractual matter.[88] Beyond this, criminal law might be used, but this is then seen as taking the matter outside the employment context (though the employer may choose to ensure that consequences follow for employees found guilty of a criminal offence).

In states where a social market approach was followed, it was common to tackle the problem of sexual harassment through the 'dignity at work' approach developed and favoured by the ILO, under which the situation of the worker as a human being working in an atmosphere created and maintained

88. See for instance *Country Report: Ireland*, supra note 69, pp. 38-40; Beveridge, F., Nott, S. and Stephen, K. (1999), *Predicting the Impact of Policy: Gender-Auditing as a Means of Assessing the Probable Impact of Policy Initiatives on Women, Country Report: United Kingdom*, Liverpool: Feminist Legal Research Unit, School of Law, University of Liverpool, p. 45. In Ireland problems have been encountered in establishing the responsibility of an employer for acts carried out by an employee, since in perpetrating such acts the employee has clearly been acting outside the course of his employment. Similarly, in the United Kingdom an employer can escape liability by demonstrating that the actions in question were not done in the course of the employee's employment, or that he took reasonably practicable steps to 'prevent the employee from doing that act, or from doing in the course of his employment acts of that description'.

by the employer is central. Under this model sexual harassment at work can readily be conceptualised as falling within the responsibility of the employer, and as a matter therefore to be regulated through agreement with the social partners.[89]

Another area in which there were distinct differences between different states was in the law-making role played by litigation. In both Ireland and the United Kingdom, there was relatively frequent resort to litigation in respect of equal opportunities matters. A number of different observations, both negative and positive, can be made. On the negative side this undoubtedly reflected the choices made by the governments in those two states to rely on an individual rights strategy, backed up by the threat of court action, as a main plank of their enforcement strategy in relation to equal opportunities. In the two states in question no other really effective strategy was in place. There was little attempt to institutionalise any consensus-building mechanisms, for instance between employers and employees, or between service-providers and clients and consumers, in relation to equal opportunities. Under such a strategy the burden of tackling discrimination falls upon women and no responsibility is placed, apparently, on society in general to address inequality between men and women. Individual court cases are portrayed as further instalments in some interminable 'battle between the sexes' and the plaintiffs as the 'victims' of discrimination. Moreover, the lottery of litigation pits the plaintiff on the one side against the hurdles of judicial conservatism, complicated and sometimes uncertain legislation and the evidentiary burden — a formidable challenge by any standards.

Yet on the positive side the litigation culture has led to substantial gains in equality law in both the United Kingdom and Ireland, particularly the former where, as noted above, EC equality provisions were invoked in a quasi-constitutional role within these states by equality advocates and agencies acting strategically to challenge unduly restrictive legislative and

89. See for example *Country Report: Portugal*, supra note 73, pp. 37-8; Arranz, F., Quintanilla, B. and Velázquez, C. (1999), *Predicting the Impact of Policy: Gender-Auditing as a Means of Assessing the Probable Impact of Policy Initiatives on Women, Country Report: Spain*, Liverpool: Feminist Legal Research Unit, School of Law, University of Liverpool, p. 20. Under Portuguese law employers are duty-bound to apply disciplinary sanctions (including the possibility of dismissal) to employees who have provoked or created a risk of demoralising their colleagues, especially women and minors. Employees who are the victims of offences against their physical integrity, freedom, honour or dignity perpetrated by colleagues are regarded as having 'just cause' for the termination of their employment contacts and a claim for compensation, equivalent to redundancy. Under Spanish law the worker is entitl ı to respect for his privacy and due consideration of his dignity, including protection against verbal or physical offences of a sexual nature.

remedies. Through this process and referrals from other EU Member States (notably Germany), many provisions of EC equality law were further developed and clarified. It also seems that such cases, in attracting media attention, have an important role in educating others — employers and legal advisors as well as those who suffer unlawful discrimination. However there has perhaps been something of an assumption that with the courts playing an active role in the enforcement of EC and national law, resort to other mechanisms for change is not required. This clearly ignores both the inherent and practical limits of litigation as an implementation strategy and the problem of structural inequality which the concepts of direct and indirect discrimination, as currently operated, do little to tackle.

Member States with a less dominant litigation culture, by contrast, may seem to have developed institutions and processes which have greater capacity to tackle structural inequality. Of the countries studied here Sweden would appear to be the exemplar, with the institution of the Equality Ombudsman and the process-oriented mechanism of requiring the preparation of annual equality plans illustrating a greatly contrasting approach to litigation as a means of enforcement.[90]

Renewal and Modernity

In several of the Member States examined, major developments in the State's approach to equality had been secured as part of a wider process of constitutional reform. This occurred most dramatically in Spain with the adoption of the new Constitution in 1978, and in Portugal with the revolution of 25th April 1974, followed by the adoption of a new constitution on 2nd April 1976. In the latter case, for instance, the authoritarian Constitution which had been in place since 1933 provided for equality before the law 'except, in the case of women, [due to] the differences inherent in their nature and in the interests of the family',[91] whereas the 1976 Constitution explicitly outlawed sex discrimination and promoted gender equality in a number of separate provisions. In a less dramatic way, in the United Kingdom the devolution of power to national assemblies in Scotland and Wales was seized as an opportunity to push forward equality demands,

90 These mechanisms are discussed in Chapter Six, this volume.

91 Constitution of the Portuguese Republic 1933, Article 5 Under the authoritarian regime significant gains were made towards equal political rights, but generally speaking the legal regime promoted a 'head of family' or 'paterfamilias' legal model: *Country Report: Portugal*, supra note 73, pp. 31-2.

though equality legislation itself remains within the domain of the Westminster government.[92] In Northern Ireland too, the devolution arrangements stemming from the Good Friday Agreement have had a significant effect on equality provisions. In Ireland, there is great pressure for constitutional change which, if effected, would almost certainly included significant gains for the equality lobby.

However, such major changes tend to be highly politicised and it is also evident that despite the general commitment of governments to furthering equality, this issue does not receive much attention at times of such radical change. In the United Kingdom any gains were opportunist, rather than planned and the Westminster government's commitment to mainstreaming was not a major influence on the negotiation of devolution.

A similar pattern is seen in relation to the implementation of large-scale change at lower levels in government. In the case of the Netherlands it was seen that a major restructuring of foreign policy in 1996 was carried through with scant attention to equality responsibilities,[93] while in similar mode government reorganisation in Ireland led to a reduction in the status of the Minister responsible for Equality and loss of full representation at Cabinet level.[94]

There is clearly no place for complacency about equality issues at times of constitutional change where, depending on the direction of change, either clever opportunism or determined vigilance may be called for. Bureaucratic changes, which may be carried out without much notice or consultation and which are much easier to effect, are similarly threatening to equality mechanisms.

Negotiating Equality

While it is generally the case that the EU and the Member States accept the need for equality laws, policies and machinery this does not automatically produce any consensus as to what should be done to further equality goals. The difficult negotiations at EU level over social policy generally and over particular instruments such as the Pregnant Workers Directive and the Parental Leave Directive are well documented and it is clear that despite the

92. See further Beveridge, F., Nott, S. and Stephen, K. (2000) 'Mainstreaming and the Engendering of Policy-Making: A Means to an End?', 7(4) *Journal of European Public Policy* (forthcoming).
93. See Chapter Three, this volume.
94. See Chapter Two, this volume.

renewed and extended commitment to equality in the Treaty of Amsterdam, there will still be difficulties in securing pro-equality measures. In the Member States examined in this volume, similar difficulties regularly manifested themselves at national level with regards to the implementation of EU laws and policies, even where the intention of those measures was to establish minimum levels of protection. While the problem was particularly acute in the United Kingdom under the Conservative government (1979-97),[95] reluctance or lack of enthusiasm for EU measures can also be seen in Ireland (e.g. in relation to the implementation of the Parental Leave Directive), and Spain (in relation to Article 11 of the Pregnant Workers Directive).[96] While in some cases there may genuinely be room for debate over the requirements of the EU measures in question, the cases cited attest to political strains, usually a reluctance on the part of the government to place the financial burden of equality policies on employers. They indicate the continuing need for well-organised and active lobbying at the national level: although the EU may have 'occupied the field' in terms of securing legislation or establishing minimum standards, satisfactory implementation cannot be presumed and needs still to be addressed at the national level. In each of the cases cited, of course, the ECJ has been or can eventually be called upon to adjudicate on the effectiveness of the implementation measures: Member States persist in 'watering-down' Community norms even in the face of the threat of legal action.

The pattern of responses to soft law measures indicates extremely wide variations and the absence in any of the states examined of a systematic approach. No state, for instance, seemed to routinely allocate responsibility to consider the matters raised in a Recommendation to any particular Ministry or to prescribe any form of response, still less its shape or content. In relation to sexual harassment, for instance, the EU Resolution and Recommendation on Sexual Harassment[97] called on states to take action to promote awareness of the problem of sexual harassment (Article 1), to take action in the public sector to implement the Commission's Code of Practice (Article 2) and to encourage employers' and employees' representatives to develop measures to implement the Code of Practice (Article 3).

The responses of states ranged widely: in Portugal there existed a belief that the existing Portuguese legal framework was within the spirit of EU

95. This is evidenced most clearly in relation to the Parental Leave Directive where the UK 'opted-out' under the terms of the Protocol on Social Policy.
96. The article related to the right of Pregnant Workers faced with health and safety risks to cease work with pay, where no suitable alternative employment exists.
97. Resolution 90/C 157/02 of 29/05/1990 and Recommendation 92/131/EEC of 27/11/1991 respectively.

law and the Recommendation itself was ignored in favour of an established 'dignity at work' approach which had its roots in ILO instruments. In the Netherlands, though the Dutch had played an active role in securing the adoption of a Recommendation, no action was taken immediately at the national level. In the UK the Recommendation and Code of Conduct appear to have been largely ignored by government, whereas in Ireland the EU measures fed into an important ongoing debate about sexual harassment, which led in 1994 to the adoption of Ireland's own Code of Practice and later to a statutory prohibition on sexual harassment.[98] The influence of the EU measures in that debate, however, is difficult to judge.

Conclusions

The EU has been an important driver of equality laws and policies within the Member States but its achievements have been varied, a very direct impact being evident in some States and virtually none being visible in others. In accordance with its 'constitution', the EU is able to exert its influence in only certain fields, though its area of competence in relation to women has expanded significantly through successive Treaty amendments. Predominantly the EU has focused its attention to date on the 'core' economic area of the labour market and there is little indication that this will change in the short term.

In the Member States the 'gender agenda' has not stagnated in areas outside the EU's sphere of competence — Member States have evolved new laws and policies to tackle matters of family and social welfare, domestic violence and sexual harassment and overall these developments have attempted to address the situation of women. Common to both the EU and the Member States is a shift in the focus of attention from the formal law towards the policy sphere — all the Member States examined and the EU had declared their political commitment to mainstreaming and had taken some steps towards concretising this commitment.

It might be concluded that within the scope of its (expanding) competencies the EU has served instrumentally as the conduit through which equality claims have been directed, and at times has offered a better conduit than was

98. Employment Equality Act, 1998, S.23. Excluded from the definition, however, is same-sex harassment or harassment based on sexual orientation: c.f. Smith, O., Mullally, S. and Donnelly, M. (2000), *Case Study: Ireland's Legal and Extra-Legal Responses to the European Commission's Recommendation and Code of Practice on Protecting the Dignity of Women and Men at Work* Liverpool Feminist Legal Research Unit, School of Law, University of Liverpool.

available in some Member States. But national law and policy-making has also continued to develop new responses to gender-based claims. The EU does not hold a monopoly on issues concerning equality and fairness for women and in certain periods has been constrained by its economic orientation and concerns, and by the Treaty provisions in which these are manifest.

Different Member States stand in distinctly different relationships to the EU in relation to equality laws and policies, playing different roles and influencing policy or being influenced by policies differently. Where the EU does command influence over an issue, for instance where it issues a Directive which necessitates legal change in a number of Member States, those states, though generally accepting the imperative to give effect to the Directive, will develop distinctly 'national' responses to this imperative. This response will reflect their political and legal culture in general, and the historic approach to the particular policy and legal issues in question. Although plainly evident in relation to binding measures, this was particularly true of soft law measures, which at times produced little or no direct response, though the issues raised may have been pursued eventually and/or indirectly.

The question of enforcement of equality rights raised particular problems. The ECJ has nailed its colours firmly to the mast in requiring individual recompense for breaches of rights flowing from EU obligations and in requiring full and effective remedies. However in the equality sphere this serves to draw a line between states where the individualistic and litigation-centred approach has figured in labour market relations, and those where it has not — in relation to the latter group (here Sweden, Portugal and, to an extent, Spain) there were doubts as to whether the more collectivist enforcement traditions would withstand a challenge to the ECJ. Yet there is no suggestion that the more collectivist methods are intrinsically any less effective, and the collectivist approach has been endorsed in relation to *law-making* within the EU, as evidenced by the formal inclusion of the social partners in the legislative process relating to the social policy field. It remains to be seen how the ECJ will strike a balance between national approaches and the growing *acquis communitaire* in the sphere of remedies generally.

Finally the recent attention paid to mainstreaming has not and does not detract from the importance of established equality laws and enforcement mechanisms, and this appears to be accepted in the EU and in the Member States. Mainstreaming initiatives do, however, increasingly turn attention to structural barriers and disadvantages faced by women, matters which equality laws in the liberal tradition, based on formal rights, have been inadequate to address. In this regard some of the collectivist approaches to enforcement and duty-based approaches to the promotion of equality identified above seem increasingly relevant and attractive. It therefore remains important to highlight the weaknesses and structural limitations of existing equality strategies as part of an ongoing process of improvement and renewal. Enforcement solutions which seemed promising twenty or even ten years ago may be viewed differently now, while the imposition of obligations, for instance on employers, which seemed unduly onerous twenty years ago have shown themselves to be workable in specific contexts.

9 Catalysts for Change? The Effectiveness of State Agencies in Promoting Equality

KYLIE STEPHEN

Each of the states featured in *Making Women Count* possesses a sophisticated array of agencies or other institutional machinery for eliminating sex discrimination and promoting gender equality. The form of such bodies varies widely being shaped to a degree by the legal and political landscape of which it is a part as well as by the state's gender equality policies. In Sweden, for example, there is a Minister of Equality Affairs, an Equality Affairs Division, a Council for Equality Issues, an Equal Opportunities Ombudsman, an Equal Opportunities Commission and a range of regional equality bodies. In Spain, however, there is a single national equality agency, the Women's Institute. The purpose of this chapter is not to describe these individual bodies and their specific contributions to promoting equality since this has already been dealt with in those chapters devoted to national practice. Instead the analysis which follows will address the range of tasks these bodies perform in order to promote gender equality and the factors that influence their ability to.

What tasks do equality agencies perform?

It is important to say at the outset that the agencies evaluated in this chapter are state bodies. They are state bodies in the sense that they are either part of government or are agencies which, although they are 'independent' of government, are either financed by government or have their terms of reference determined by government or have their members appointed by government. This study does not address the role of grassroots 'women's groups' that either make representations to government on behalf of women in general or, more commonly, organise around specific issues, for example better childcare or preventing domestic violence. This is deliberate since

Making Women Count is concerned with the effectiveness of those mechanisms adopted by states in order to secure equality between the sexes and one of these mechanisms is to create equality machinery. Since, however, women's groups represent grassroots opinion it is important to consider the relationship between them and state agencies and whether those agencies can and do act as a conduit for channeling grassroots opinion into the law and policy-making processes.

There are a variety of reasons why states establish equality agencies. First, some agencies are given a key role to play in respect of a state's equality legislation. They may be entrusted with the task of keeping that legislation under review and proposing changes in the law to government. Alternatively they may play a direct or indirect role in the enforcement of the equality legislation. Furthermore they may provide help and advice to individual women who feel that they have been the victims of sex discrimination. In the United Kingdom, the Equal Opportunities Commission has a statutory duty to keep under review the anti-discrimination legislation, to advise those who believe they had been the target of sex discrimination and, in certain circumstances, can provide litigants with financial aid. Jämo (Sweden), the Joint Oireachtas Committee on Justice, Equality and Women's Rights (Ireland), and the Commission for Equality at Work and in Employment (Portugal) perform a similar task. They keep their state's equality legislation under review, ensuring that the law is observed and dealing with complaints regarding its breach.

Secondly equality agencies, in the form of central government departments or units, may be given responsibility for developing and over-seeing a state's entire gender equality policy. Such bodies may determine policy objectives, identify key issues which require immediate action, establish equality targets and provide the focus for a state's approach to equality. Bodies such as these are 'agenda setters' and occupy a position at the heart of government.

In some countries, a single body may perform this role. In Ireland, for example, this central coordinating role has been entrusted to the Department of Justice, Equality and Law Reform. In other countries this role is shared among a number of government agencies. In the United Kingdom there are three organisations which are supposed to work together to co-ordinate gov-ernment policy on women and gender issues. They are:

- the Ministers for Women who are charged with driving forward the government's key policy initiatives and for coordinating a cross-departmental approach to initiatives for women and equal opportunities;

- the Women's Unit[1] which supports the Ministers for Women and promotes women's issues across government, often providing government departments with information, advice and training on how best to promote equal opportunities; and
- the Cabinet Sub-Committee on Women which co-ordinates action on the women's agenda and acts as the focal point of the government's policy to incorporate women into decision- making.[2]

Equality agencies which are part of government may also represent the public face of a state's concern for gender equality to regional and/or international bodies, such as the European Union and the United Nations. The Commission for Equality and Women's Rights (CEWR) represents Portugal, sometimes in conjunction with other government bodies, on a range of international bodies including the Council of Europe's Steering Committee for Equality between Women and Men and the OEGD's Working Group on the role of Women in the Economy. In Ireland, the Department of Justice, Equality and Law Reform prepares the Irish report as required by the UN Convention on the Elimination of All Forms of Discrimination Against Women. It also played a key role in the preparations for the 1995 UN Fourth World Conference on Women (Beijing). In possessing a body of this nature, a state may be regarded as fulfilling its international human rights obligations, to be in compliance with any international treaties outlawing sex discrimination to which it might be signatory (for example CEDAW)[3] and appear as though it is taking active measures to eliminate discrimination against women.

Thirdly, equality agencies are set up by government to advise it on women's issues or 'represent' women's views in the policy-making process. Such bodies often have discrete budgets and, at least theoretically, are regarded as independent of government. The Women's National Commission in the United Kingdom and the Women's Council of Ireland (NWCI) are just such organisations. These bodies are meant to be representative of the diverse range of women's needs and interests and exist to channel the

1 Set up by the Labour Government at the same time as the Ministers for Women in 1997.

2. There is also an All Party Group on Sex Equality which essentially keeps sex equality issues before Parliament and provides a pipeline to the decision-makers for other groups working on sex equality.

3. Those countries who are signatory to the Convention on the Elimination of all Forms of Discrimination Against Women are theoretically obliged to pursue policies in accordance with it. They must file periodic reports with the Committee on the Elimination of Discrimination Against Women on the 'legislative, judicial, administrative or other measures which they have adopted to give effect to the provisions' of the Convention (Article 18).

views of women and grassroots bodies into government decision-making. They may be consulted by government on a wide range of policy issues and may put forward recommendations or lobby government on certain policy proposals. The notion of a 'representative body' can, however, be quite problematic. The NWCI has expressed its concern at the difficulties inherent in representing a wide and diverse range of women's organisations. It is hard for one body to represent so many interests. This problem is compounded, the NWCI notes, by women's continued absence from decision-making and leadership positions at government level.[4]

Fourthly, equality agencies can be given the task of conducting research on women's status in society. Feminists have long argued that the ideology of promoting equal treatment between the sexes cannot, on its own, attack gender hierarchies and produce widespread substantive gender equality.[5] Pressure from feminist or women-centred activism has demanded new and better structures which can deliver substantive social and political equality for women. This has provided the impetus for the setting up of equality bodies that examine women's status in society such as the Women's Institute in Spain and the Women's Unit in the United Kingdom. Research carried out by bodies of this nature has acknowledged that men and women lead different lives premised on socially constructed notions of appropriate male and female behaviour and therefore that policies impact upon men and women differently. There is a recognition that social differences between men and women may undermine any benefit derived from specific equal treatment laws or indeed may actually be reinforced by such laws. By their research, equality bodies can highlight the need to develop, promote and monitor state gender equality policies which accommodate differences between men and women.

Finally, in some countries, equality agencies are given an educative role in relation to gender equality. It is their task to encourage good practice on the part of employers, public bodies or service providers. They may do this either by undertaking research into what actions might best promote equality or by publicising initiatives taken by a company or a public body that have proved particularly successful. Many of the equality agencies featured in this book act as an information exchange. Sometimes this is a proactive function

4. See 2 *In Focus* March/April 1996. See also Chapter Two, this volume.
5. See for example Lister, R. (1990), 'Women, Economic Dependency and Citizenship', *Journal of Social Policy*, 19(4), pp. 445-467; Walby, S. (1994), 'Is Citizenship Gendered?', *Sociology*, 28(2), pp. 379-395; Pateman, C. (1988), *The Sexual Contract*, California: Stanford University Press, and Young, I. M. (1991), *Justice and the Politics of Difference*, Princeton: Princeton University Press.

with the agency deliberately setting out to promote good practice. On other occasions an agency may offer advice only when specifically approached. Another aspect of this educative role may involve representatives of an equality agency appearing on television or in the media to publicise new legislative initiatives or existing equality laws. Making women aware of their rights may help to ensure that they take advantage of them.

The states featured in *Making Women Count* had a variety of bodies performing some or all of these tasks. Equality machinery, however, does not remain static and in some countries quite considerable changes had taken place over the years with new agencies being created or existing agencies undergoing some form of metamorphosis. These changes often took place in response to shifts in gender equality policies or more general political change. In some states attitudes towards securing 'equality' have shifted from a focus on equal treatment to alternative strategies such as positive action and mainstreaming. Mainstreaming fits well with established feminist views that women's social, political and economic disadvantage stems from an integrated system of public and private oppression and that, as a consequence, an integrated network of institutional arrangements which address all aspects of law and policy-making is required to tackle the biological, cultural and power differences between the sexes. Many states have now adopted a mainstreaming approach to equality: that is 'the reorganisation, improvement, development and evaluation of policy processes, so that a gender equality perspective is incorporated in all policies at all levels and at all stages, by the actors normally involved in policy-making'.[6]

The move towards mainstreaming may be prompted in part by the realisation that traditional equality laws and the equality bodies which complemented it have had limited impact on the promotion of substantive gender equality. Mainstreaming recognises that gender equality issues transcend traditional areas of gender policy and represents a broader and more integrated approach to tackling inequality which avoids the limitations identified with specific legislation[7] and specialised agencies (see later in this chapter). But established equality bodies may not be well-equipped to respond to such changes: for instance, where previous efforts have focused on the employment sphere, they may not be able to deal with inequality which has its origins outside the labour market, and may require root and branch reform if they are to actively contribute to mainstreaming policies.

---

6. Council of Europe (1998), *Gender Mainstreaming: Conceptual Framework, Methodology and Presentation of Good Practices*. Strasbourg, May, p. 15.
7. See Chapter Eight, this volume.

It is not clear in the countries featured in this volume that such matters have always been given full consideration. Mainstreaming may necessitate the development of a new generation of equality agencies to ensure that gender concerns are properly integrated into all policy areas and that all relevant actors properly integrate gender into their policy activities. Sometimes, however, the arrangements which have been made to accommodate mainstreaming initiatives have a very *ad hoc* feel about them. In both Ireland and the United Kingdom, for instance, there has been a proliferation of bodies but with no clear sense of co-ordination between them.

Analysing effectiveness

Most analyses of the effectiveness of state equality agencies focus on individual agencies. There has been almost no attempt to look at a range of state equality bodies and isolate those factors that will determine whether or not they prove effective. It could be the case that the outstanding success or failure of a particular agency may be attributable to exclusively local factors. It is, however, also true that if a body has a particular task or tasks to perform then there will be certain conditions which have to be complied with if it is to succeed. For example, in Portugal gender assessment is by law the responsibility of the Commission for Equality and Women's Rights (CEWR). Yet as has been pointed out,

> [I]t is common ground that the Government forgets the consultative functions of the CEWR. The absence of any sanction for failure to consult with the CEWR may be part of the reason for this discrepancy between what the legislation says and what happens in reality.[8]

If, therefore, an equality agency is effectively to assess policies for their gender impact then it stands to reason that there has to be some monitoring or enforcement machinery in place to ensure that it is not bypassed.

The influence exerted by equality agencies and their contribution to improving women's substantive equality may, however, not be easy to measure. A recent study of the impact of specific agencies was carried out by Stetson and Mazur.[9] Their focus is on women's policy machinery which

8. Casqueira Cardosa, J. (1999), *Predicting the Impact of Policy: Gender-Auditing as a Means of Assessing the Probable Impact of Policy Initiatives on Women. Country Report: Portugal*, Liverpool: Feminist Legal Research Unit, School of Law, University of Liverpool, p. 50.
9. Stetson, D. M. and Mazu., A. (1995), 'Introduction', in Stetson and Mazur (eds), *Comparative State Feminism*, London: Sage Publications.

they define as 'any structure established by government with its main purpose being the betterment of women's social status'.[10] In their book, *Comparative State Feminism*, individual state structures in a range of countries were evaluated to determine the extent to which they advanced feminist goals. From the results of this study, Stetson and Mazur suggest that women's policy machinery best promotes a feminist agenda when it simultaneously attains high levels of policy access and policy influence.

The aim of this chapter, however, is not to compare and contrast a single equality agency from each of the states featured in *Making Women Count*. Instead the intention is to examine integrated systems for addressing equality issues and analyse how they fit within the broader law and policy-making framework of that state. More importantly, this chapter aims to assess the effectiveness of such machinery against a background of evolving equality strategies.

The relative success or otherwise of any gender equality machinery would seem to depend on a number of interrelated structural factors. These are:

- the location of the equality body within the broader policy-making framework;
- the degree of political commitment to equality;
- the role and remit of the equality body;
- the differentiation between a gender equality body's functions as an agenda setter for policies, an executor of those policies and as a policy monitor;
- the degree of fit between a state's attitude towards equality and the tasks assigned to equality bodies;
- the relationship between equality bodies and other social actors; and
- the composition of equality bodies.

Location within the Broader Policy-Making Framework

How equality bodies relate to, or are integrated into, the overall government decision-making process is important on two counts: firstly, in terms of the influence these bodies can have on the decision-making process; and secondly in terms of the relative integration of the equality agenda into all policy and legislation that is developed. The position, power and visibility

10. Ibid, p.3.

of equality bodies will always vary. Clearly, however, access to the highest level of decision-making will significantly impact on their relative effectiveness.

The placement of an equality body either at the heart of or on the periphery of decision-making depends on a number of factors. First equality issues become politically important or hold political currency at different times. This centrality is influenced by social movements such as second wave feminism. In addition political parties vary in the degree of priority they give to what are often referred to as 'women's issues'. As a consequence the proximity of equality agencies to the heart of government also varies. The states examined in *Making Women Count* indicate that left-wing governments are more likely to contribute to the creation of centralised equality agencies than right-wing governments. For example, as equality issues became politically more important in Sweden during the 1970s, it was the Social Democratic Government that situated the Equality Secretariat within the Governmental Office in order that the Social Democratic Party could influence it. Nowadays, the overall governmental responsibility for equality between women and men rests with the Minister of Equality Affairs, at present located in the Ministry of Labour. A separate Equality Affairs Division (which replaced the Equality Secretariat) was established at a central governmental level in 1984. This Division supports and initiates efforts to promote equality at national and regional levels, developing methods for the integration and implementation of a gender perspective — mainstreaming gender in all policy areas.

Secondly, if priority is given to gender analysis of policy and the co-ordination of cross-departmental initiatives, this will often result in a the location of an equality agency within the central coordinating agency of government. This may mean that a self-standing Department or Ministry may not be established for fear that it will lack political clout and access to crucial government submissions and decision-making forums. Rather, an equality unit located within a supporting Ministry will be favoured. What needs to be kept in mind is that where the associated Ministry is seen as secondary or junior in ranking or political importance (generally those related to social and cultural affairs) the relative centrality of the equality agency can be undermined. This appears to be nearly always the case when it comes to national machinery responsible for gender equality. For example, the Women's Institute (IM) in Spain was founded as an autonomous administrative organisation under the aegis of the Ministry of Culture. The Institute won some proximity to the Government in July 1988 when it was incorporated into the new Ministry for Social Affairs (this was a smaller department with a more focused remit). The relationship between the IM and the Government was also considered to be close on the basis that its director was directly accountable to, and dependent on, the Minister for Social Affairs (as opposed to being dependent on an under-secretary). Now, after a recent reshuffle, the position of the Institute has fallen back because of its dependence on a bigger Ministry (following the merging of two ministries). This example clearly shows that equality machinery is vulnerable, or susceptible, to the reorganisation of the political decision-making structure. Moreover, equality units which are dependent on the support of larger Departments always run the risk of being political footballs and misadventures or exile in low-ranking portfolios can be financially and politically debilitating.

Even where a body is central to the policy and decision-making processes of government, a lack of political commitment to the goals of such agencies can eliminate any perceived strategic advantage. For example in Portugal, the CEWR is supposed to play a central role in scrutinising all policy or law-making initiatives from the Government or the Assembly for their differential impact on men and women. The CEWR is, however, prevented from exercising this function effectively because of a lack of co-operation by the government and/or the Assembly. By law the CEWR 'shall be consulted on any project of regulation having an effect on the issue of women and of equality'.[11] However, in reality this does not translate into any systematic or effective procedure. The CEWR is not used frequently or systematically as a forum for discussion and clarification before government initiatives are taken. The absence of any sanction for failure to consult with the CEWR may be part of the reason for the discrepancy between what the legislation says and what happens in reality.

Political commitment to equality issues is therefore important because it helps to determine the degree to which formal and informal channels of influence are open to the groups concerned. It is also important to have within government a minister who is 'feminist' in the sense of being willing to 'take a stand' and promote gender policies, defend equality commitments and protect equality agencies and machinery from short-term political pressures. In the United Kingdom, while the current Minister for Women refuses to call herself a feminist, the political climate is one that incorporates equality issues into a broader political agenda of 'modernising government' that includes the devolution of decision-making.[12] With a government that is therefore focused on delivering greater democracy to the people there is currently a high level of (rhetorical at least) political commitment to equality issues.

---

11 Decree-Law 166/91 of 9 May 1991, Art. 3 § 2.

12 For more details on 'modernising government' see Chapter Seven, this volume.

While a centralised body is important for co-ordinating a state's overall approach to equality, an extensive yet integrated system of regionalised bodies is also useful for meeting specific women's needs and delivering a cohesive and comprehensive package of reforms for women. An integrated system of regionalised equality bodies ensures the integration of gender equality into all levels and all aspects of government policy-making, greater participation by women and feminist groups in policy-making and that ideas or proposals are publicised effectively.

The states examined in this text have mixed experiences with respect to the regionalisation of women's policy machinery. Sweden is well known for its extensive regional equality bodies. As a result of a parliamentary resolution, County Administrative Boards were given an enhanced role in relation to equal opportunities in 1994 and currently every County Administrative Board must have an equality expert. The Boards co-operate with national authorities which are represented in the various counties and municipalities, and also with unions, companies, other organisations and citizens. This fits in with the existence of strong local authorities and the general devolution of decision-making with respect to framework laws in Sweden.

More recently, all the Autonomous Regions (CC.AA.) of the Spanish State, following the example of central government in creating the Women's Institute (IM), have equipped themselves with organisations possessing similar characteristics in their configuration and functions to those of the IM. Local and provincial bodies have the power to perform in conjunction with other public bodies activities related to the promotion of women.[13] The IM has signed agreements with the Spanish Federation of Local and Provincial Bodies (FEMP) to give force to local policies designed to improve the situation of women and to develop programmes in order to share information between these bodies. The IM has also signed agreements with different municipalities and provincial deputations all over Spain in order to create Information Centres on Women's Rights and to set up homes for battered women.

Problems associated with a non-regionalised system of equality bodies are exemplified by the Portuguese experience. In Portugal, of the two main public institutions in charge of the promotion of equal opportunities between men and women, only the Commission for Equality and Women's Rights (CEWR) has a second branch (in Oporto[14]), but this branch does not possess the power to take autonomous decisions. The lack of regional

13. According to section 2 of the law 16/83 of 24 October and sections 28 and 31 of the Law 7/1985 of 2 April (Regulation of the Basis of Local Government).

14. Its head office is in Lisbon. Comissão para a Igualdade e para os Direitos das Mulheres. (1998), *Situação das Mulheres,* Lisbon: Commission for Equality and Women's Rights, p.134.

offices means that issues and problems at ground level are not heard by the Lisbon institutions. It also means that Lisbon institutions and initiatives are not necessarily known in the more remote parts of the country, especially the Northern regions, where a substantial part of the population lives.

A regionalised network of equality bodies avoids the development of 'equality ghettos'[15] whereby gender expertise is centralised in special organisational units given the explicit task of working on gender equality. It is often feared that specialised gender equality units become the waste-paper baskets for women's problems and an alibi for gender-blind policy in the rest of government. This is not to say that in some circumstances specialised equality units are not useful. The centralisation of responsibility for specific issues, such as labour/employment, women and leadership may be useful in effectively targeting specific areas of concern to women and perhaps making the case to government for new legislation. For example, the Commission for Equality in Work and Employment (CEWE) in Portugal, which was created in 1979, is part of the Ministry of Labour and Solidarity. CEWE's mandate is to guarantee women equality with men as regards opportunities and treatment at work and in employment.[16] The CEWE's responsibilities relate specifically to the promotion of gender equality in the workplace.

However, the positioning of the issues of 'gender equality' under the responsibility of a specific department or unit gives the impression that equality issues are limited to one sphere of society (in this case employment) and/or that equality can only be legitimately pursued by government in relation to specific issues, for example paid labour, and not other issues like unpaid labour, domestic violence or the division of labour in general. Further, the setting up of specific equality units in specialised areas does not bode well for the integration of equality across policy areas, as it is not as likely that such units will be able to influence each other's policy-making in the same manner that a fully mainstreamed approach to policy-making might allow.

A decentralised network approach to the development of equality machinery would appear to fit better with the contemporary emphasis on mainstreaming, whereby gender issues are fully integrated into all policy-making processes. However there still needs to be a system of accountability which may require a centralised 'equality' authority to co-ordinate and/or monitor work. Essentially, the choice of a more or less centralised approach

15. See Chapter Three, this volume.

16 As set out by Decree-Law 392/79 of 20 September 1979 (as amended by Decree-Law 426/88 of 18 November 1988).

to equality issues will be determined by the existing institutional framework of a state. There is little point in adopting a system of dealing with equality issues that is not in keeping with existing attitudes and patterns of policy-making. As Verloo[17] points out, this means that less progressive measures which fit existing structures of policy-making are more often than not chosen for implementation.

The Role and Remit of Equality Bodies

Equality agencies can be said to play a number of different roles with regard to gender equality. Equality bodies may variously be responsible for:

- the enforcement of legislation;
- the promotion of gender equality policies;
- providing advice to government;
- representing grassroots or non governmental organisations;
- setting the agenda for equality issues and coordinating or steering policy on that agenda;
- monitoring the implementation of policies and/or legislation.

These roles do not all demand the same skills or resources. Where there exists a plurality of roles for women's policy machinery there also exists a plurality of demands for:

- gender expertise;
- access to decision-making bodies and processes;
- links to other social bodies;
- a degree of distance from central government to ensure objectivity;
- independence;
- power and/or authority to impose their view;
- high level support for their key objectives; and
- penetration (both horizontal and vertical) into the decision-making process.

Not all these roles can be discharged by one body because it may not be capable of fulfilling all the demands associated with these tasks. An equality body may not be able simultaneously to provide advice to government and

17. See Chapter Three, this volume.

enforce equality legislation because it may lack the gender expertise or independence required to do either or both of these tasks. Further, not all roles can be fulfilled by one body because they may at times be contradictory. It may not be possible for the policy agenda setters to monitor and review the implementation of the equality policies without being accused of a lack of objectivity or accountability. To work well, each body needs an appropriate remit and corresponding staffing and resources to fulfil its allotted task.

An equality body's remit or its terms of reference impinges directly on its capacity to act and achieve goals. The scope of the remit is important, for if it is drawn too widely then an agency may have problems with over-extended resources and decreased levels of effectiveness and efficiency. Some of the equality agencies that feature in *Making Women Count* appear to have been given quite strong powers to achieve gender equality but are then unable to use them fully because of their lack of resources. Originally, the Irish Employment Equality Agency was assigned both a promotional and an enforcement role in relation to equal opportunities in employment between women and men. In carrying out its enforcement functions, the Agency can provide advice and assistance to complainants of discrimination, it can undertake formal investigations into discriminatory practices and it can issue 'non-discrimination notices'. Commentary on the work of the Agency to date has generally been favourable; however, commentators note that the Agency has been unable to fulfil many of the tasks assigned to it, because of severe institutional and financial constraints. Because of the Agency's limited resources, representation cannot be provided in all cases; formal investigations have rarely been undertaken; and research is carried out only when finance is secured, but the future of such support is never guaranteed. The proposed new Equality Authority[18] will retain many of these powers; however, its effectiveness or otherwise will depend largely on the resources committed to it. It is feared that without a sufficient commitment of resources and staffing, the Authority will be unable to fulfil an effective role in *any* area of equality protection.

How the dilemma of matching remit and resources is worked out in practice depends on the substantive understanding of equality employed by the decision-makers of the day. What a government sees to be the goal of equality policy[19] will determine what it perceives individual bodies should do and how they should act. The evolution from an equal treatment to a positive action to a mainstreaming approach to addressing gender equality

---

18. See Chapter Two, this volume.
19. See Chapter One, this volume.

raises questions about the role and remit of equality bodies. Some of the present role confusion may be attributable to evolutions in understandings of equality, leading to old equality bodies being required to take on new functions without any real consideration being given to what their existing resources are, or whether they are appropriately constituted or possess the appropriate attributes to perform the newly assigned functions.

This trend is most evident at present in Ireland and the United Kingdom. In Ireland for example, the terms of reference of the first Joint Oireachtas Committee on Women's Rights reflected a concern to address the status of women as both 'clients' of law and policies and as 'partners' in decision-making procedures. Following the election of the 28th Dail in 1997, the Joint Oireachtas Committee was reconstituted and renamed the Joint Oireachtas Committee of Justice, Equality and Women's Rights. This move followed the merger of the Department of Justice with the Department of Equality and Law Reform. Furthermore, the Irish Employment Equality Agency will presently be transformed into a single Equality Authority dealing with a much wider range of equality issues including discrimination on the grounds of race, religion, age and sex. While the proposed extension of the prohibited grounds of discrimination (section 6 of the Employment Equality Act, 1998) has been welcomed, the increased workload that this will entail has provoked anxiety in certain quarters. The Authority will, for the first time, be dealing with discrimination outside the workplace in relation to such matters as education and the provision of services. The structure of the proposed new Authority is, therefore, of crucial importance.[20]

Concerns have also been expressed over the establishment of a new Equality Commission in Northern Ireland, as provided for in the Northern Ireland Act 1998, to implement and ensure compliance with the statutory obligation requiring all public sector bodies to promote equality of opportunity. The former Fair Employment Commission, Equal Opportunities Commission for Northern Ireland, Commission for Racial Equality for Northern Ireland and Disability Council for Northern Ireland will be merged as of 1 October 1999. The proposal to collapse the four existing anti-discrimination agencies into one has created much debate on the institutional arrangements to be set up.[21]

---

20. A report commissioned by the Joint Oireachtas Committee on Women's Rights has recommended that the Authority's work should be divided on a category basis in order to make best use of staff expertise. Categorisation could take place in numerous ways - work/non work, group based categorisation, sections dealing with enforcement and promotion/publicity. See McGinley, M. (1996), *Sixth Report to the Fourth Joint Oireachtas Committee on Women's Rights. From Employment Equality Agency to Equality Authority*, Dublin: Government Stationery Office.
21. See Chapter Seven for more detail.

On the one hand, these moves have generated concern amongst women's organisations that the extension of each body's terms of reference, or the creation of a single equality body, to address broader justice issues may detract from questions of gender inequality. Non-governmental organisations (such as the NWCI) have expressed their concern that the significance of gender as a factor in social exclusion and inequality may no longer be prioritised where the remit of an equality body is so extended as to include all forms of inequality. Concern was expressed by groups such as the Standing Advisory Commission on Human Rights (SACHR) that the new Equality Commission in Northern Ireland would be submerged in 'procedural wrangling' and 'riven with infighting' as the different representatives for the socially excluded — religion, gender, race and disability — fight for funding and prominence within the amalgamated body.[22]

On the other hand, some critics have argued that anti-discrimination theory as a whole is impoverished by its failure to recognise the plurality of some women's oppression and its tendency to treat race and gender, for example, as entirely separate categories of experience.[23] What are perceived as singular and discrete forms of discrimination may actually be experienced cumulatively, and where individual bodies are given the task of addressing discrete forms of discrimination (such as the Equal Opportunities Commission and the Commission for Racial Equality in the United Kingdom) there is a failure to appreciate and deal effectively with the ways in which many women are treated. The existence of separate equality bodies, for race and gender for example, 'creates a conceptual and institutional hurdle before those, such as black women, whose experience of discrimination straddles the boundaries of the regulatory agencies'.[24] Complainants alleging race and sex discrimination cannot appeal to a single body which could adopt an 'holistic' approach to multiple discrimination and a broader understanding of equality.

Evolution of thinking about equality would appear to be unavoidable and is most generally welcomed; however, none of the states examined in this volume appeared to have any blueprint for how associated women's policy machinery should evolve in harmony with thinking about equality.

---

22 McCrudden, C. 'A British notion of responsibility on equality', in *The Sunday Business Post* Online, March 16 1998.

23. Ashiagbor, D. (1999), 'The Intersection between Gender and "Race" in the Labour Market: Lessons for Anti-Discrimination Law' in Morris, A and O'Donnell, T. (eds), *Feminist Perspectives on Employment Law*, London: Cavendish Publishing, pp. 139-160.

24. Ibid, pp. 155-156.

The general trend in considering issues of gender inequality to be part of a broader problem of social exclusion is reflected in the evolution from specialist equality agencies to a more decentralised system of women's policy machinery. However, it would appear that greater thought needs to be given to the form of machinery required to ensure that gender is integrated into all areas and to whether gender needs to be considered alongside other equality issues such as race, religion and class.

The Composition of Equality Bodies and their Links to Other Social Actors

The broader relationship between equality agencies and other women's groups/feminist bodies is essential for proper consultation in the law and policy-making process. The existence of integrated networks of equality bodies with high levels of policy authority is important. If, however, they have little contact with women's and feminist groups then they may be seen as irrelevant or unrepresentative. The degree to which equality agencies can act to further women's status and rights within the social and political context of a state will depend partly on the extent to which they develop opportunities for society-based actors to have access to the political process. It would appear that in almost all the states examined, the level of access and consultation between women's policy machinery and other social actors has been less than impressive.

In Sweden, Jämo is perceived to have done little to empower feminist activists or organisations. It has failed to bring in feminists as staff or advisors, and has also resisted calls from autonomous feminist groups to expand its purview to sex inequality outside the workplace. It has, however, worked with feminist activists in the political parties and through parliamentary groups in trade unions embracing a state inspired notion of what would advance women's status by focusing on gender-neutral notions of equality.[25]

In Spain, women's associations were hardly consulted in the creation of the Women's Institute (IM), either about the suitability of founding an organisation for equality or about the way in which any future organisation should be organised. Informal relationships between the IM's staff and activists in women's associations have always been infrequent. Participation in the *Consejo Rector* (governing council of the IM) is the only formal way that leaders of the feminist movement can obtain access to the IM's decision-

25. Stetson and Mazur supra note 9, p. 281.

making process and this has been very restricted. Since its establishment in 1985, the *Consejo Rector* has included only six members from 'among individuals with a reputable personal or professional development in favour of equal gender rights'.[26] However, as Valiente suggests, 'these members cannot be considered as representatives of the movement in the *Consejo Rector*, since their appointments were a function of their individual contribution to equality between genders and not of their active membership in women's organisations; they were not elected by the array of associations'.[27]

Feminist collectives were also not invited to help formulate or to participate in the tasks of monitoring and implementing the Spanish National Plans, except for the failed attempt in 1988, when the IM pressed for the consultative committee for the monitoring of the First Equality Plan to be exclusively made up of feminist militants. This proposal was frustrated, but it did result in access to the *Consejo Rector* for three members representing nation-wide (hence more inclusive) feminist associations as well as one more member from each of the Secretariats or Women's Departments of the Trade Unions *Comisiones Obreras* (CC.OO.) and *Unión General de Trabajadores* (U.G.T.). Thus the IM could be said not to have played a very active role in helping society-based groups to get involved in the policy-making process.

In Ireland growing disillusionment with the central government, and its failure to represent those groups that have traditionally been excluded from political activity in the Irish State, has resulted in a significant recent growth in organised community-based women's groups. This disillusionment has led to a search for new mechanisms to combat social exclusion and to the development of alternative political forums concerned with community development and community survival. The growth of organised women's groups, throughout both rural and urban Ireland, has been seen as a response to the erosion of traditional forms of community. The significance of this kind of politics; decentralised, communalist, responsive to local demands and needs which had been increasingly marginalised within a women's movement dominated by middle-class, highly-educated urban women, was highlighted by Mary Robinson in her term of office as President.[28]

26. Article 2 of the Order 7 May 1985 of the Ministry of Culture. This matter is also included in article 5 of the New Regulation of the Women's Institute, Royal Decree 774/1997 of 30 May.
27. Valiente, C. (1996), 'El feminismo institucional en España: El Instituto de la Mujer, 1983-1994', in *Revista Internacional de Sociología,* 13, p. 189.
28. See (1997), *Ireland's Combined Second and Third Reports under the United Nations Convention on the Elimination of All Forms of Discrimination Against Women,* Dublin: Government Stationery Office, p. 42.

This is contrary to what is happening in other countries, such as the United Kingdom, where a new approach to public sector management has evolved that makes it difficult to sustain the structures needed for long term projects such as improving the status of women. One of the most important functions of women's policy machinery is to make resources available to enable community organizations to gather information and gain access to the policy-making process. Today governments often express doubt that community organizations are really representative of women and prefer to engage in market research to test women's attitudes towards government policies. For example, in the United Kingdom the government has made use of what are termed 'women's juries'. These are:

> small groups of women, selected to give a cross-section of experience, who meet to deliberate upon a policy-question. They are informed about the issue by taking evidence from witnesses and cross-examining them. . . . Juries provide an opportunity for women whose voices are not normally heard to contribute to the democratic process.[29]

How much emphasis is given to the views of the 'women's juries' remains a mystery as the rhetoric of 'listening to women' needs to be strongly supported by economic backup and delivery on policy goals. But within the new commercial product format and the focus on public sector service delivery, this approach may result in a devaluing of expertise in gender analysis and a reluctance to extend links between formal women's policy machinery and other social groups interested in promoting gender equality.

The location of equality agencies within a central policy area may also have unexpected drawbacks in terms of feminist process. The confidentiality of policy advice at central policy level may cause tensions with non-government organisations expecting more sharing of information. Policy success is certainly most likely when there is a joint partnership from inside and outside government, but this is often frustrated or discouraged by bureaucratic red tape and notions of confidentiality.

In this respect, the development of 'social partnerships' may be a means of opening up informal channels for consultation and negotiation and be important to the development of integrated equality machinery. Social partnerships often involve the coming together of interested social and economic parties (employers organisations, trade unions, government and other interest groups) to jointly negotiate social and economic programmes

29. See http://www.womens-unit.gov.uk/dialog.htm

to achieve, for example, economic growth, low levels of unemployment, improved health and education and a reduction in inequality. For example, in 1996, the National Women's Council of Ireland was involved, for the first time, with the negotiation of the national agreement for government, *Partnership 2000 for Inclusion, Employment and Competitiveness.* As the NWCI's role in policy formulation was a relatively recent development, the NWCI Executive Board adopted a strategic approach to the negotiations. In an attempt to respond effectively to its role in the extended social partnership, the NWCI established a Policy Unit with the specific aim of increasing their effectiveness as participants in the social partnership process. In addition to participating in the social partnership process, the Council also participates in various policy-development working groups (it is presently involved, for example, in the Inter Departmental Working Group on Abortion) and regularly submits reports and discussion documents to various governmental bodies and Departments. This national programme provides an important mechanism for ensuring greater participation by women and other excluded groups in the policy-making process. As a result of the widening of the concept of social partnership, bodies such as the NWCI have been involved for the first time in negotiating the programme for national development. This has led to an increased emphasis within such bodies on policy development and participation in decision-making structures.

The composition of and theoretical background to these social partnerships is, however, extremely important. This is exemplified by the Swedish experience where the welfare state institutionalised a pattern of corporatist decision-making involving key interest groups and bureaucratic agencies, rather than political parties and legislatures, in which women are generally more active.[30] Sex segregation in the workplace, therefore, limited women's influence in these corporatist channels, since trade unions and businesses (whose leaders are men) tend to dominate this system. Thus social partnerships of this kind will not work to women's advantage if women are not well represented in the partnerships themselves.

The composition of equality bodies in general is important as it has an impact on their degree of independence and the extent to which equality bodies can interpret and act on their remit. On the one hand, partisan bias in appointments to those bodies may be beneficial in that it may allow greater access to information and the policy-making process in general. Policy-makers and civil servants are more likely to co-operate with insiders as opposed to those from outside the public service. However, this would have

30. Stetson and Mazur, supra note 9, p. 7.

to be accompanied by the clarification of the relationship between a body's agenda setting, policy enforcement and policy monitoring tasks. Partisan bias in appointments can muddy the waters in terms of the functional role of the equality agencies in question. How can an independent executive agency objectively monitor the implementation of government policies when staffed by party political appointments? Confusion over tasks or the inability to separate executive and regulatory functions, because of partisan appointments, can result in the overall ineffectiveness of equality bodies and lead to claims of a lack of objectivity.

This problem is clearly exemplified in the case of the Second (National) Commission on the Status of Women (Ireland) which recommended the establishment of a Monitoring Committee to oversee implementation of the recommendations in its Report.[31] A committee was established under the aegis of the Department of Equality and Law Reform, comprising representatives of government departments, the social partners, women's organisations and the Employment Equality Agency. However, some dissatisfaction has been expressed with the progress reports published to date[32] and more generally with the role of the Monitoring Committee. The NWCI, for example, has argued that the reports have focused more on proving that the government and others are 'good implementers' than on engaging in any kind of critical assessment of 'progress' made. Donnelly, Mullally and Smith[33] have suggested that problems have arisen because of the dual role of some of the committee members — those who are representatives of government departments combine responsibility for implementation of the recommendations with a monitoring role and have tended to be more reluctant to criticise the work of government departments and to pursue their colleagues for necessary information.

Partisan bias in appointments to women's policy machinery may also detract from the development of *bipartisan* support for women's policy structures. For example the Department of Justice, Equality and Law Reform (Ireland) liaises with the National Women's Council of Ireland and the Employment Equality Agency. Representatives of the Department participate in various working groups with both bodies, as part of a general trend to promote greater 'partnership' between state and civil society and develop bipartisan support for equality policies. However, the Employment

---

31. Recommendation 0.7.2
32. To date, two progress reports have been published by the Committee.
33. See Donnelly, M., Mullally, S. and Smith, O. (1999), *Predicting the Impact of Policy: Gender-Auditing as a Means of Assessing the Probable Impact of Policy Initiatives on Women. Country Report: Ireland*, Liverpool: Feminist Legal Research Unit, School of Law, University of Liverpool.

Equality Agency is treated for staffing purposes as a section of the Department. This has considerably restricted the pool from which staff of the Agency are appointed. The movement of staff forward and backwards between the Agency and the Department has led to difficulties in building up a body of expertise within the Agency. The rigidity of this staffing system has created difficulties for the Agency and has been the subject of some criticism.[34]

In contrast to the partisan approach to equality bodies is the option of establishing an independent commission to tackle gender inequality, enforce equality legislation or provide advice to government on issues that affect women. Nearly all the countries examined in this volume had created some such body: for example the Equal Opportunities Commission in the United Kingdom; the Commission for Equality in Work and Employment in Portugal and the Employment Equality Agency/Equality Authority in Ireland. While, theoretically at least, these bodies have a greater capacity to criticise government policy, bodies of this kind are often less accountable than those directly responsible to a department or ministry. They have no constituency to answer to and are quite often characterised as having poor links with other social and/or women's groups (as already discussed in this section). If this type of structure is to be utilised to any great extent, a careful balance needs to be established and maintained between their independence and accountability both to some kind of monitoring body above them and to those to whom they owe a duty of representation.

The dual problems concerning equality bodies of bipartisanship and accountability may be solved through the strategic use of parliamentary select committees. These are committees composed of representatives from all parties represented in Parliament which investigate the affairs of a particular area of government.[35] The Parliamentary Commission for Parity, Equal Opportunities and Family in Portugal is one such example. However there is little evidence to date that any such parliamentary select committee has adequately filled this void in decision-making in relation to issues of equality.

34. See McGinley, M. (1996), *Sixth Report to the Fourth Joint Oireachtas Committee on Women's Rights. From Employment Equality Agency to Equality Authority*, Dublin: Government Stationery Office, p. 8. Criticisms of these staffing arrangements have been taken into account in drafting proposals for a new Equality Authority, to replace the Agency following the coming into force of the Employment Equality Act, 1998.

35. For a discussion of the role of parliamentary committees see Unit for the Study of Government in Scotland (1988), *Mainstreaming Equal Opportunities*, Report to the Consultative Steering Group to the Scottish Parliament, University of Edinburgh.

Conclusion

The equality bodies analysed in this chapter do not lend themselves easily to categorisation as they are complex and adapted to fit the needs and political context of each individual country. They vary in their organisation, authority and power and their links to other governmental and non-governmental agencies. However, it is plain that they have played an important role as public voices for change. Whilst there were disparities in how particular bodies operated, a number of key issues emerged that need to be considered in the development of a policy-making framework that is responsive to women's diverse needs and interests.

First and foremost, the location of equality bodies within the broader policy-making framework of a state is very important. A balance needs to be struck between the development of a centralised body or bodies with the role of agenda setting and/or monitoring policy progress and a system of decentralised bodies charged with ensuring the integration of equality across all policy areas. Whether centralised or decentralised, equality bodies require political clout and the ability to ensure that women's views are acted upon by government. This includes committed and extensive resources to carry out their task of promoting equal opportunities; resources which fit with the tasks assigned to the equality agency in question. Otherwise, the level of effective gender input into intergovernmental policy arrangements is minimised. As such, equality bodies need to be seen as central to the policy-making process rather than a sideline.

Secondly, the existence of equality bodies represents a potential means to ensure that equality issues do not move out of the public domain. The remit of such bodies should therefore allow them the chance to consult and contribute to issues of importance to women, for example sex discrimination legislation or the promotion of family-friendly work policies. However, clear lines of responsibility and accountability need to be established. The demarcation between the agenda setters, the policy/programme implementers and the policy monitors needs to be established so there can be no implication that equality agencies have been constrained by the government agenda.

Thirdly, while there is an obvious need for the location of equality bodies within the central policy coordinating agencies of government, as 'inside agents for change', the expertise and independence offered by 'outsiders' to the processes of government is just as important. There needs to be proper consultation between equality bodies and other women's groups and government. The work of each of these groups needs to complement each other. Most partner states had some mechanism in place to evaluate laws and/or policies for their gender impact and high levels of consultation with individuals and agencies with relevant gender knowledge was essential for their success. This requires that greater emphasis should be placed on contacts between groups and the co-ordination of initiatives. Equality bodies should more fully embrace the role of supporting greater co-ordination amongst non-governmental women's organisations. The fact that to date many have not developed a high profile in this regard needs to be addressed most urgently.

Fourthly, an expansion of the remit of some equality bodies may encourage women's groups to use their resources more fully. However, in some countries there was a growing trend to give a single agency the task of promoting not just equal opportunities between men and women but equal opportunities for other discriminated groups such as the disabled and ethnic minorities. This has signalled potential problems in terms of access to resources, the allocation of responsibility for specific areas of equality and the fear of an equality hierarchy developing. What is required is a clear state blueprint indicating how gender equality bodies are to evolve in harmony with a state's approach to dealing with inequality and promoting equality.

Finally, it was observed earlier that this general trend in considering issues of gender inequality to be part of a broader problem of social exclusion is reflected in the evolution from specialist equality agencies to a more decentralised system of equality bodies. This has most recently evolved into a policy of *mainstreaming* equality into all aspects of policy-making. Mainstreaming requires continual effort and monitoring in order to keep pressure on bureaucrats to integrate gender equality issues into all parts of policy development. Without a substantial institutional basis the mainstreaming strategy can be ignored as institutional dynamics can make or break policies. Thus greater thought needs to be given as to the form of machinery required to ensure that gender is integrated into all areas and, as suggested in the previous point, whether gender needs to be considered alongside other equality issues such as race, religion and class.

10 Accentuating the Positive: Alternative Strategies for Promoting Gender Equality

SUE NOTT

The promotion of equal opportunities is often conceived simply as a matter of eliminating sex discrimination and ensuring that men and women receive equal treatment. The accepted way of securing these goals is to put in place legislation outlawing sex discrimination in the public sphere, more specifically in the workplace, to provide guarantees of equality in the constitution and to eliminate systematically any laws, that for no good reason, treat men and women differently.[1] As is apparent from the chapters detailing national practice, each of the states featured in *Making Women Count* has employed these strategies only to discover that they are part of, but not the whole answer to, eliminating gender inequality. There are numerous shortcomings associated with these strategies and the most fundamental is the concept of equality which they employ, namely equality as equal treatment. The best that such a concept of equality can do is remove some of the more glaring examples of unequal treatment that women experience. Equality as equal treatment promotes formal but not substantive equality between the sexes.

What is needed, therefore, is an equality strategy that addresses the deep-rooted causes of inequality. These rest on the fact that men and women experience life in very different ways because of the social construct of gender. Gender refers to the manner in which society perceives the roles of men and women, such as the belief that women should raise and care for children or that men are better suited to certain forms of employment such as those requiring physical endurance. This social construction of the roles of men and women is learned, can change over time and can vary between societies. It is also value-laden affecting everyone's perceptions of what is and what is not acceptable, including those of women. Finally it has also proved to be very deep-seated, permeating culture, social organisation, language and the

1 For example laws which deny women certain civil and political rights, such as the right to vote, or which restrict the times and hours when women, but not men, may work.

psyche, so that it has immense power to resist change sought through legal or political means.

The ability of laws based on the concept of equal treatment to tackle gender inequality is very limited. Equal treatment demands that women should not be treated less favourably because of their sex than men would be treated. This in turn depends on an assessment of what amounts to 'like' treatment and 'like' circumstances; making it very difficult for legislation and the courts to move beyond 'formal' equality.[2] If men and women are treated in a like fashion there will be no breach of the law even though the manner in which society perceives the roles of men and women may mean that the treatment in question is to men's advantage and women's disadvantage. The concept of indirect discrimination, which most states employ, does increase the potential of equal treatment to secure substantive equality. Indirect discrimination occurs when men and women are subjected to identical treatment which in reality can be shown to have far more damaging consequences for women than men. The problem with indirect discrimination, however, is that it is invariably restricted to use in certain contexts and may be defined in a narrow fashion. Moreover it usually permits the offending behaviour to be defended by arguing that there is a legitimate reason for it unconnected with sex, creating uncertainty and complexity in the law.

If the concept of equal treatment fails to tackle the true reasons for inequality and to promote substantive equality then what are the alternatives? The answer is to substitute another equality outcome — most frequently equality of results — for equal treatment. Equality of results requires sensitivity to the differences between the sexes, insisting that the law accommodate them. Differences between the sexes can, however, take two forms. On the one hand there are biological differences. The most obvious of these is pregnancy and it is now well-accepted that special provision must be made for pregnant workers such as protecting them from dismissal during the course of their pregnancy. On the other hand, there are cultural differences between the sexes. These are much more difficult to classify but involve such issues as the differences in men and women's education and career choices, the extent of their participation in public life or the disproportionate share of caring for the family assumed by women. These cultural or social differences may have a biological or psychological explanation or may simply be a consequence of the way in which the role of women is perceived in society. The problem is whether, and if so how, a concept of equality can accommodate or indeed reverse them. One of the most obvious ways of

2. See Chapter Eight, this volume.

achieving this is to accord women what is variously termed as 'different' or 'special' treatment. This course of action brings with it a dilemma, namely how far such 'different' or 'special' treatment should extend.

Some feminists feel ambivalent over the argument that women should be in receipt of different treatment from men, even when it is used to address only biological differences such as pregnancy. To them, different treatment is a step on the way to admitting that men and women occupy different spheres and raises the prospect that this may be used to women's disadvantage.[3] Other feminists contend that whether these differences are biological or cultural does not matter. What does matter is that they are dealt with. Christine Littleton, in her article, *Reconstructing Sexual Equality*,[4] has argued for what she terms as 'equality as acceptance'.

> The focus of equality as acceptance, therefore, is not on the question of whether *women* are different, but rather on the question of how the social fact of gender asymmetry can be dealt with so as to create some symmetry in the lived-out experience of all members of the community. I do not think it matters so much whether differences are 'natural' or not; they are built into our structures and selves in either event. As social facts, differences are created by the interaction of person with person or person with institution; they inhere in the relationship, not in the person. On this view, the function of equality is to make gender differences, perceived or actual, costless relative to each other, so that anyone may follow a male, female, or androgynous lifestyle according to their natural inclination or choice without being punished for following a female lifestyle or rewarded for following a male one.[5]

The whole question of accommodating differences has been the focus of a vigorous exchange of views among feminists. To some feminists, however, the entire debate is mistaken since it focuses on the wrong issue.

> The pervasive argument in sex equality, until recent years at least, has been that of sameness and difference. The dominion that this debate enjoys, and the dangers which it poses, have been uncompromisingly articulated by Catherine MacKinnon.

3. See Fenwick, H. (1996), 'Special protections for women in European Union law', in Hervey, T. and O'Keeffe, D. (eds), *Sex Equality Law in the European Union*, Chichester: Wiley.
4. (1987) 75 *California Law Review* 1274
5. Ibid, p. 1280.

> The sameness/difference debate, as MacKinnon suggests, gives women just two choices; they can either aspire to be the same as men, and to enjoy the same rights, or they can campaign to have their difference from men recognised in law. Either way, women are compared with a male norm, and by presenting women with these two choices, and these two choices only, the debate immediately establishes parameters.[6]

Catherine MacKinnon asserts that differences should not be the focus of feminist analysis and concern. In her view the equality question 'is a question of the distribution of power'.[7] Gender in its turn is 'also a question of power, specifically of male supremacy and female subordination'.[8] She concludes, therefore, that

> [T]he question of equality, from the standpoint of what it is going to take to get it, is at root a question of hierarchy, which — as power succeeds in constructing social perception and social reality — derivatively becomes a categorical distinction, a difference.[9]

In other words, for whatever reasons, men are in a position to dominate women and this imbalance in power permeates society and colours reality. Laws and institutions in society reflect this power imbalance whether they do so openly or in a manner which masquerades as neutrality or impartiality. The state promotes male interests at the expense of those of women. Until this truth is faced and dealt with effectively (given that this is possible) then efforts to achieve equality between the sexes will prove fruitless.

This awareness of the layers of meaning surrounding the term 'equality' has provided the impetus for the emergence of a range of alternative strategies for addressing inequality between the sexes. Those who believe that equality of results is the goal for women and propose that women should receive special/different treatment have advocated a strategy that requires positive/affirmative action. Alternatively those who believe that the power of men over women is the key have argued that the emphasis should be placed on addressing women's subordination to men.

---

6. Ward, I. (1996), 'Beyond Sex Equality: The Limits of Sex Equality Law in the New Europe', in Hervey, T. and O'Keeffe, D. op cit, n. 3, p.370.
7. MacKinnon, C. (1987) 'Difference and Dominance: On Sex Discrimination', in *Feminism Unmodified*, Cambridge, Mass: Harvard University Press, p. 40.
8. Ibid.
9. Ibid.

> If a law, practice, or policy contributes to the subordination of women or their domination by men, it violates equality. If it empowers women or contributes to the breakdown of male domination, it enhances equality.[10]

Feminist theorising over the nature of equality suggests that alternative strategies have to be devised and acted upon if gender inequality is to be eradicated. The challenge to eliminate the adverse effects of biological, cultural and power differences between the sexes has been responded to by states resorting to positive action and mainstreaming initiatives. What follows is an analysis of these strategies as they are employed in the states featured in *Making Women Count*. Particular attention will be paid to how well they work in practice and the ease or difficulty with which states can shift from 'first generation' equality measures with their emphasis on *equal* treatment to these more sophisticated 'second and third generation' strategies.

Positive action

Measures which usually go under the description, 'positive action', are to be found in each of the states featured in *Making Women Count* and have also figured in the European Union's equal opportunities strategy. The term 'positive action' is, however, problematic[11] since it is often used in conjunction with the term 'positive discrimination'. Sometimes this is done in a manner which demonstrates that the terms are synonymous. On other occasions the terms are contrasted with one another to mark the opposite ends of a continuum of possible actions. Rather than argue over definitions and how particular policies are to be categorised, this chapter will make exclusive use of the term 'positive action'. The reason for this is that the term 'positive discrimination' carries with it the implication that one group is being deliberately disadvantaged for the benefit of another group. This misrepresents the true objective of the strategy namely to compensate for the adverse effects of differences between the sexes by putting in place *positive* initiatives to advance and improve the situation of women. The term 'positive action' more accurately reflects this objective and will therefore be used throughout this chapter.

---

10. Littleton, C. op cit, n. 4, p. 1281.
11. For a discussion of the ways in which the terms 'positive action', 'positive discrimination' and 'affirmative action' may be used see: McCrudden, C. (1986), 'Rethinking positive action', *Industrial Law Journal* 219; Rees, T. (1998) *Mainstreaming Equality in the European Union*, London: Routledge, pp 34-40; Bacchi, C. L. (1999), *Women, Policy and Politics*, London: Sage, pp 98-103.

Positive action is a strategy that can be used to address biological and cultural differences between the sexes by 'compensating' women for the disadvantages they experience. It can also represent a means of correcting the power imbalance between the sexes by ensuring that more women participate in political decision-making. Positive action can achieve these ends in a variety of ways, some more radical than others. It can require that in a particular profession or sector of society where women are underrepresented quotas are set and met. In other circumstances positive action can mean the setting of targets. A target is distinguishable from a quota since it carries with it the possibility that the target may not be reached. Targets do, however, encourage the institution or employer faced with them to examine their practices in order to identify and remove barriers which prevent that target being achieved. Positive action can also mean adopting a policy whereby, if women are underrepresented in a particular sector, they are offered special training or facilities in order to obtain the relevant qualifications or experience which will allow them access. Finally, in the case of biological differences between the sexes, positive action may take the form of awarding women special rights or protection, for instance in relation to pregnancy or maternity. Some commentators, however, would argue that this is not positive action, since there is no comparable male situation.[12]

The importance of this strategy and its standing vary considerably, with a great deal depending on the political and legal tradition of the state in question. The one issue on which states consistently singled women out for special treatment was in relation to pregnancy. This is hardly surprising since the European Union has legislation in place on this issue, namely Directive 92/85, commonly referred to as the Pregnant Workers Directive, which Member States are under a legal obligation to implement. The European Union based the Pregnant Workers Directive on the necessity to protect the health and safety of workers rather than representing it as an example of positive action. There were technical legal reasons for this[13] but

12. For a discussion of how pregnancy fits into the framework of equality laws and policies see Szyszczak, E. (1996), 'Community Law on Pregnancy and Maternity', in Hervey, T. and O'Keeffe, D. op cit, n. 3; Conaghan, J. (1993), 'Pregnancy and the workplace — a question of strategy?' 20 *Journal of Law and Society* 71; Fredman, S. (1994), 'A Difference with Distinction. pregnancy and parenthood reassessed', 110 *Law Quarterly Review* 106.

13. This was the fact that since the legal base for the Directive was Article 118A unanimity was not required among the Member States. If unanimity had been required it is doubtful whether it would have been secured. Some critics feel, however, that by relying on Article 118A the content of the Pregnant Workers Directive suffered as a consequence. See Beveridge, F. and Nott, S. (1998), 'A Hard Look at Soft Law', in Craig, P. and Harlow, C. (eds), *Lawmaking in the European Union*, London: Kluwer.

one of its consequences is that the Directive requires comparatively little of employers. A pregnant employee cannot be dismissed and she is entitled to paid maternity leave. The length set for maternity leave is short — 14 weeks — and the level of maternity pay is low – equivalent to the benefit paid by the state in respect of sick leave. Nothing is said in the Directive about supporting women once they return from maternity leave by, for example, providing adequate childcare facilities. A subsequent Directive on Parental Leave[14] has not improved matters greatly since, although it obliges states to put in place arrangements for taking parental leave when, for example, a child is ill, there is no obligation to make that leave paid leave.

State practice regarding this issue also appeared to be inspired by a variety of motives rather than the goal of compensating women for the adverse effects of biological differences. Some of the states featured in *Making Women Count*, for example the United Kingdom and Ireland, made the minimum of provision for pregnant workers compatible with their obligations under Community law. The explanation for this appeared to relate to the desire not to over-burden employers in either financial or administrative terms by transferring to them the costs of eliminating inequality. In other countries such as Sweden and Portugal, the rights accorded pregnant workers and working parents appear more generous. In the case of Sweden this could be explained by that country's long-standing tradition of generous state provision. As both Portugal and Sweden have discovered, however, such comparative generosity still does not eradicate the traditional stereotype of women as prime carers. In Sweden, for example, taking parental leave still involves a loss of income making it far more likely that the family's lower earner — usually the woman — will take advantage of such schemes.

Attempts to use positive action initiatives to tackle cultural differences between the sexes are far more problematic. They are problematic because of an inherent belief that, in their more extreme forms, such as the setting of employment quotas, they are morally unacceptable. Positive action programmes can be devised to reverse trends such as occupational segregation or to tackle the problems that may be experienced when attempting to combine work with caring for a family. Where such initiatives did exist they were low key and entirely voluntary. Both Ireland and Portugal have permissive programmes which depend on individual employers taking the lead. Neither reported that they had been a great success. One of the reasons may be that there is no pressure on employers to utilise them. Indeed there was some

14. Directive 96/34, OJ L145/4, 1996.

suspicion that employers used these schemes to encourage women into employment only when it suited their own ends. Even schemes which have government backing seemed to fare little better. In the United Kingdom, a programme known as Opportunity 2000 was launched in 1991. Opportunity 2000 consists of large and small organisations throughout the United Kingdom which are committed to a package of actions intended to promote equal opportunities. Members of this scheme sign up to three key actions. These are

- to set their own goals and action plans for women's development.
- to put into operation a set of measures through which they can monitor their progress and achievement.
- to make their progress visible through public dissemination of their results.

Opportunity 2000 has been the target of considerable criticism. In the first place it is said to be business-driven with the result that market principles outweigh equality principles. Secondly the scheme is said to avoid issues relating to women's pay and to concentrate over-much on the concerns of women in management and professional posts rather than in lower grades. Finally doubts have been raised over whether the scheme has had any lasting impact. The most recent figures show that

> amongst member organisations the share of management jobs taken by women — one of the traditional benchmarks for measuring women's progress in the workforce — remained static or declined in 1998.[15]

One area where positive action, in the form of target setting, was successful and acceptable was to increase the numbers of women in government. This may be because government based on democracy is perceived as requiring the involvement of all sectors of society. Hence increasing women's representation is perhaps regarded more as a measure to secure democracy than eliminating gender inequality. The manner in which women's rates of participation in government have increased in some countries represents a steady achievement. In the United Kingdom, for example, the number of public appointments held by women has increased steadily over the years from 19 per cent of national level appointments to 32 per cent in 1997.[16] By permitting women to play a

15. 'Fall in Opportunity 2000 Women Managers', *Equal Opportunities Review*, July/August 1999, p. 5. The members of Opportunity 2000 still, however, achieve better results as compared with national statistics.
16. See Beveridge, F., Nott, S. and Stephen, K. (1999), *Predicting the Impact of Policy: Gender-Auditing as a Means of Assessing the Probable Impact of Policy, Country Report: United Kingdom*, Liverpool: Feminist Legal Research Unit, School of Law, University of Liverpool, p. 58.

greater part in the policy and decision-making process, women's concerns and interests can be raised in a manner which is not possible whilst they are outside this process.

Positive action programmes designed to increase women's representation in any *elected* assembly can prove more difficult to implement. If increasing the numbers of women in government is simply a question of government nominating more women to sit on government boards or committees, this is comparatively straightforward. In an elected legislature, however, potential members are selected by the political parties. Much may depend, therefore, on whether a particular party believes that it can gain from such a step. In the United Kingdom, for example, it has been suggested that part of the explanation for the Labour Party's commitment to increasing women's representation in Parliament was its perception as a male-dominated party and its belief that such an initiative might bring electoral rewards.[17] On the other hand, if it has nothing to gain a party may be reluctant to face the 'bad feeling' this initiative may create among party members and voters.

The extent to which increasing women's representation in elected assemblies furthers the process of achieving equality is a moot point. One study in the United Kingdom concluded that increasing the numbers of women in the United Kingdom Parliament would produce the following gains.

> There is a strong argument that the legitimacy and authority of Parliament is undermined if it fails to reflect the diversity of British society. In the classic view of representative government, Parliament should be the main debating chamber for the nation, the forum where all voices are heard. On symbolic grounds alone, the case can be made for increasing the number of women MPs in Britain. Yet the substantive argument is harder to sustain with good evidence. The results of this study suggest that gender influences policy attitudes, priorities and legislative roles. Women tended to give stronger support for issues of women's rights, they express greater concern about social policy issues, and they give higher priority to constituency casework. This gender difference should not be exaggerated, since, as might be expected in British politics, party proved the strongest divider among politicians. The gender gap among politicians was often modest. Nevertheless the study suggests that the election of more women to Westminster has the potential to make more than just a symbolic difference.[18]

---

17. Squires, J. (1996), 'Quotas for Women: Fair Representation?', 49(1) *Parliamentary Affairs* p. 71.
18. Norris, P. (1996), 'Women Politicians: Transforming Westminster?', 49(1) *Parliamentary Affairs* p. 101.

These efforts to secure better access for women to government and the decision-making process demonstrate the success with which positive action initiatives can be deployed. This success has, however, not been repeated more generally particularly in the labour market. A number of factors may account for this, most particularly the rationale that underpins the notion of positive action. One commentator's analysis of the theoretical underpinning of positive action led him to conclude that it has three main features: namely it is a temporary anti-discrimination strategy, it is aimed at a group rather than at an individual and it has the intention of securing permanent change.[19] As a consequence positive action initiatives can sit very uneasily with equality strategies which emphasise the rights of the individual such as anti-discrimination legislation. This is illustrated by examining the national practice of the states featured in *Making Women Count*.

In Ireland and the United Kingdom a great deal of emphasis is placed on the individual and on the freedom of the market. In the context of equality between the sexes, the individual is guaranteed the right to equal treatment, with pregnant workers receiving a package of rights in recognition of their special situation. Individuals are expected to pursue their rights in the courts should they be the target of sex discrimination. This stress on individual rights and individual litigation is in direct conflict with the philosophy behind positive action. Positive action may require behaviour which is completely at variance with the notion of equal treatment. Both Ireland and the United Kingdom have, therefore, adopted legislation that specifically spells out the role to be played by positive action. Essentially that role is a permissive role. Neither state insists that employers must adopt positive action programmes. To do this would be to infringe the freedom of the market. Instead the choice is left to individual employers. What the state does, however, is to set the parameters within which such positive action programmes must function. Section 48 of the United Kingdom's Sex Discrimination Act 1975, for example, permits an employer to give women employees access to training facilities in order to allow them to take up particular kinds of work where women are under-represented. The same provision also applies to men. In addition section 47 of the 1975 Act allows employers to discriminate in providing access to training where individuals 'are in special need of training by reason of the period for which they have been discharging domestic or family responsibilities to the exclusion of regular full-time employment'. The general view seems to be that these provisions are little known and little used.

19. Casqueira Cardoso, J. (1999), 'A Critical Assessment of the European Union Approach to Positive Action', *Revista da Universidade Catolica de Brasilia*.

If an initiative is taken which falls outside these specific parameters then, however constructive it might be in promoting gender equality, there is a very great risk that it will be judged unlawful. A good example of this arose in the United Kingdom in the case of *Jepson and Dyas-Elliott v The Labour Party*.[20] Here the Labour Party adopted a policy of attempting to increase the number of female Labour MPs. It did this by insisting that when Labour Party candidates were selected to stand for election to Parliament there should be all women short-lists in some constituencies.[21] This policy was challenged as discriminatory by two men who because of it had failed to be included on a short list. Their challenge was successful and as a consequence this policy was subsequently abandoned by the Labour Party. The fact that the aim of this policy was well-intentioned and designed to tackle inequality was according to the court of no relevance to the issue of whether the arrangement results in direct unlawful sex discrimination.[22]

In other countries, such as Sweden, which do not have a tradition of vindicating rights by means of litigation, positive action has a much more central role to play. Here individual complaints of sex discrimination are rarely the subject of litigation. Instead complaints are handled either by an individual's trade union or the Equal Opportunities Ombudsman. Litigation before the Labour or District Court is seen very much as a last resort. The Swedish Equal Opportunities Act 1991 places much greater emphasis on positive action which is seen as a way in which to 'support and promote the under-represented sex as a group'.[23] Employers with ten or more employees must draw up an annual equality plan which lists the measures they intend to take to combat gender related differences in the workplace. They must also give an account of what progress they made in relation to their previous year's plan. These provisions in the 1991 Act are seen as placing an obligation on employers to promote equality. It is said of that obligation that it is

> . . . of quite a different character than what is usually implied by law. It means that the employer shall initiate affirmative (positive) actions, often by means of collective agreements, including equality plans.[24]

---

20. [1996] IRLR 116.
21. These were constituencies where the Labour Party stood some chance of winning the seat when a general election was held.
22. [1996] IRLR 116 at p. 117.
23. Eklund, R. (1996), 'The Swedish Case – The Promised Land of Sex Equality?', in Hervey, T. and O'Keeffe, D. op cit, n. 3, p. 342.
24. Ibid.

The legislation also sets out goals for an employer to achieve such as promoting 'an even distribution of men and women in various types of work and within different categories of employees'.[25] It is the task of the Equal Opportunities Ombudsman to check whether employers have arrangements of this nature, such as equality plans, in place.

This situation, whilst it clarifies the position of positive action, does not guarantee that the obligation to promote gender equality is always observed. Some employers do not bother to draw up a plan. This is revealed when the Equal Opportunities Commissioner instigates a random check in a particular economic sector. Normally the mere fact of announcing a spot check will act as a catalyst for those employers who do not have an equality plan to draw one up. Yet this still means that for a period, at least, no such plan will exist. In the case of those employers who do have an equality plan, there seems to be no quality control mechanism. In other words there is no body to review the content of these plans or to pronounce on whether or not their objectives have been met.

It has to be said, however, that whilst those countries which do not have a history of relying on litigation to vindicate individual rights may place greater emphasis on positive action, this is not always so. Portugal is another state where litigation in relation to sex discrimination is rare. Yet here the role of positive action is far from clear. Article 9(d) of the Portuguese Constitution makes it a duty of the state 'to promote . . . real equality among the Portuguese as well as the realisation of economic, social, and cultural rights by way of transforming and modernising the economic and social structures'. This Article, taken together with Portugal's adherence to the United Nations' Convention on the Elimination of all Forms of Discrimination against Women (CEDAW),[26] is assumed to make positive action lawful. Added weight is given to this view by Decree-Law 392/79 which guarantees women equality with men as regards employment and permits 'temporary provisions establishing a preference on the grounds of sex and imposed by the necessity to correct factual inequality'.[27] This dispensation also includes measures 'to protect maternity as a social value'.[28] What positive action has been taken is permissive in nature, such as providing

25. Ibid.

26. Article 4 of CEDAW specifically provides for the adoption by States Parties of temporary special measures aimed at accelerating *de facto* equality between men and women. Such measures, which include those aimed at protecting maternity, are not to be considered discriminatory.

27. Article 3(2).

28. Ibid.

financial incentives to those enterprises that create jobs for women in non-traditional occupations. There are no definite goals set. In addition positive action tends to be associated most strongly with measures related to maternity which is said to marginalise the strategy. This low-key deployment of positive action is perhaps connected with the fact that Portugal's strategy for eliminating inequality between the sexes is less developed than that of a country such as Sweden. It may also indicate that unless a state spells out what is or is not permitted under the description of positive action and compels individuals to act upon this, little is likely to be achieved. Employers, for example, may not willingly assume the costs of reversing occupational segregation unless there is a legal obligation on them to do so.

The whole question of positive action initiatives was thrown into further confusion when doubts were raised over the compatibility of such schemes with Community law. The European Union has adopted its own measure, Recommendation 84/635, on the promotion of positive actions in favour of women. This soft law initiative, whilst not binding, did seem to suggest that positive action featured in the Community's equality strategy. However in *Kalanke v Freie Hansestadt Bremen*[29] the European Court of Justice was asked to consider a case where a woman was automatically offered a job in preference to an equally well-qualified man. This was required to happen where women were under-represented, that is they did not make up at least half the staff in the relevant personnel group.[30] When the legality of this policy was questioned, the European Court of Justice determined that it constituted discrimination on the grounds of sex. This was in spite of an argument based on Article 2(4) of the Equal Treatment Directive. This provides that the

> Directive shall be without prejudice to measures to promote equal opportunity for men and women, in particular by removing existing inequalities which affect women's opportunities.

The Court held, however, that

> National rules which guarantee women absolute and unconditional priority for appointment or promotion go beyond promoting equal opportunities and overstep the limits of the exception in Art 2(4).[31]

---

29. Case 450/93 [1995] IRLR 660.
30. By a law of the Land of Breman relating to equal opportunities in the public sector. For details see the Communication from the Commission to the European Parliament and the Council on the Interpretation of the judgment of the Court of Justice on 17 October 1995 In case C-450/93, *Kalanke v Freie Hansestadt Bremen*, 27 March 1996. COM (96) 88 final.
31. Ibid.

The *Kalanke* decision was the subject of a great deal of adverse comment,[32] since it seemed to jeopardise the continuing use of schemes designed to increase the representation of women in certain professions. Very soon afterwards, yet another such scheme had its legality put to the test in *Marschall v Land Nordrhein-Westfalen.*[33] Here a teacher was refused promotion because, where there were fewer women than men in the particular grade, women were to be given priority 'in the event of equal suitability, competence and professional performance, unless reasons specific to an individual candidate tilt the balance in his favour'. This policy was found to be within the scope of Article 2(4). The reason for this was that the policy in question was not absolute and unconditional as it had been in *Kalanke*, but allowed the circumstances of individual candidates to be taken into account. Equal levels of dissatisfaction have been expressed with the ECJ's reasoning in *Marschall* as were with its conclusion in *Kalanke.*[34] The Court seems to draw an arbitrary line between acceptable and unacceptable schemes in what appears to be a knee-jerk reaction to the adverse comment which greeted its findings in *Kalanke*. Indeed these decisions expose the fact that once a body, such as the European Union, has committed itself to the concept of equal treatment how difficult it is to escape from the rhetoric which surrounds that concept. It remains to be seen whether Article 141 of the Amsterdam Treaty will clarify matters and permit more radical forms of positive action than were previously permissible under Community law.[35]

Overall, therefore, the capacity of positive action programmes to promote equality seems limited. It works best when either government instigates such a programme within the public sector or employers are legally obliged to initiate such programmes. The setting of targets and a monitoring programme would also appear to be very helpful since they allow progress to be measured. The degree of emphasis on positive action programmes depends on the political and legal traditions of individual states. Those states with a strong tradition of litigation or who lack a long-standing commitment to equality between the sexes seem most likely to regard positive action as a marginal strategy rather than central to the elimination of discrimination.

32. Ibid. See also Schiek, D. (1996), 'Positive Action in Community Law', 25 *Industrial Law Journal* 239; O'Hare, U. (1996), 'Positive action before the European Court', 2 *Web Journal of Current Legal Issues*.
33. Case 409/95 [1998] IRLR 39.
34. See 'Limited positive action allowed', (1998) 77 *Equal Opportunities Review* 38.
35. The new Article 141(4) states: With a view to ensuring full equality in practice between men and women in working life, the principle of equality shall not prevent any Member State from maintaining or adopting measures providing for specific advantages to make it easier for the under-represented sex to pursue a vocational activity or to compensate for disadvantages in professional careers.

Nor is this perception likely to be altered by the actions of the European Union, since its initiatives with respect to this strategy seem to have achieved very little except to confuse.

Mainstreaming

The failure of positive action initiatives to address and remove the deep-seated causes of gender equality has meant that the search for alternatives has continued. The most promising of these is a comparatively new strategy known as mainstreaming. It was first used with any regularity by international development agencies[36] and then achieved prominence at the United Nations World Conference on Women held at Beijing in 1995. The Platform for Action agreed at Beijing made mainstreaming, that is the need to integrate gender perspectives into legislation, public policies, programmes and projects, one of its strategic objectives.[37] The European Union (EU) has also been an enthusiastic supporter of mainstreaming. As well as endorsing the strategy in its Fourth Community Action Programme on Equal Opportunities for Women and Men (1996-2000),[38] the EU has adopted a communication on mainstreaming which defines the process in the following fashion:

> . . . not restricting efforts to promote equality to the implementation of specific measures to help women, but mobilising all general policies and measures specifically for the purpose of achieving equality by actively and openly taking into account at the planning stage their possible effects on the respective situations of men and women (gender perspective). This means systematically examining measures and policies and taking into account such possible effects when defining and implementing them: thus, development policies, the organisation of work, choices relating to transport or the fixing of school hours, etc. may have significant differential impacts on the situation of women and men which must therefore be duly taken into consideration in order to further promote equality between women and men.[39]

---

36. See, for example, Policy on Refugee Women, United Nations High Commission on Refugees, 1990 in Alfredsson, G. and Tomasevski, K. (1995), *A Thematic Guide to Documents on the Human Rights of Women*, The Hague: Martinus Nijhoff, p. 360.
37. Strategic Objective, H2.
38. It was also mentioned in the Third Medium-Term Community Action Programme on Equal Opportunities for women and men.
39. Incorporating equal opportunities for women and men into all Community policies and activities, February 1996, Com (96) 67 p. 2.

From this definition it is apparent that mainstreaming is concerned with integrating gender equality into the process of formulating and implementing policies. Unlike positive action initiatives which are regarded as 'add-ons' directed specifically at women, this is a strategy which brings gender equality into the heart of decision-making and makes it everyone's concern. Mainstreaming has a number of attributes which apparently make it ideally suited to eradicating those social and cultural perceptions regarding women that are such a barrier to substantive equality. The first of those attributes is that mainstreaming is an equality strategy which applies to all policies, not simply selected areas of activity as is the case with anti-discrimination legislation. It therefore has the potential to span the divide between the public and the private sphere represented by work and home. Feminists have regularly criticised equality strategies for ignoring the burdens placed on women by their role in the home. The promotion of family friendly policies, in the guise of job-sharing or flexible working hours, can help. However these policies, as examples of positive action initiatives, are voluntary and compensatory. By contrast mainstreaming has the ability to force each and every policy-maker to face this fact as they are in the process of formulating policies.

Mainstreaming's second attribute is that it is anticipatory. Policies are considered for their gender impact whilst they are being formulated. If it can be demonstrated that women will be adversely affected by a particular policy the opportunity is there to modify it before it causes harm. Rather than tackling the consequences of gender inequality once they have occurred this strategy requires policy-makers to eliminate them at the planning stage. Thirdly mainstreaming focuses on a policy's possible gender impact. Hence it recognises the pervasive effect of gender, that is the cultural and social constructions of the behaviour of men and women, on the content of laws and policies. Finally some commentators have suggested that, depending on the way in which the strategy is implemented, it might have even greater advantages to offer.[40] These include enhanced participation in the decision-making process by groups with specialist knowledge of gender issues, more openness in decision-making and increased government accountability.

It is perhaps an indication of mainstreaming's potential to promote gender equality that, despite its recent appearance, each of the states featured in *Making Women Count* had some procedure in place which fell within the definition of mainstreaming. What was striking, however, was the degree of variety and variation in these procedures.

---

40. McCrudden, C. (1996), *Mainstreaming Fairness — A Discussion Paper on PAFT*, Belfast: Committee on the Administration of Justice.

Portuguese Global Plan for Equal Opportunities

This Plan, which was issued in 1997, gives as its general aim the integration of 'the principle of equal opportunities between men and women into all economic, social and cultural policies.' The Plan's key elements are said to include integrating gender considerations into education and statistics as well as conducting impact studies of the measures and programmes of a variety of government departments[41] in order to evaluate the effects of these measures and programmes on the living conditions of men and women.[42] The Plan also focuses on eliminating inequalities in six areas of specific concern to women.[43] Responsibility for executing the Plan rests with individual Ministries and the High Commissioner for Matters relating to the Promotion of Equality and the Family has overall competence for encouraging its execution and evaluating progress.

Sweden's Directive 1994:124

This Directive, which was issued in 1994, requires steps to be taken to integrate equality into political decision-making. The preparatory stages which proceed the taking of Cabinet decisions should, therefore, take gender considerations into account, whilst individual Ministries should assess the gender impact of their actions. All committees of inquiry[44] should analyse and report on the consequences of suggested policies for equal opportunities and gender, budgetary matters should be analysed from a gender perspective and statistics should be disaggregated by sex. An Equality Affairs Division has been established which scrutinises proposed legislation and other decisions for their gender impact before they are referred to Cabinet, which supervises appointments to government bodies and which develops training programmes for politicians and officials as well as mainstreaming instruments. This Division also scrutinises budgetary proposals for gender impact. Mainstreaming also takes place at regional level via the use of equality experts whose task it is to follow up national initiatives and develop regional policies for integrating gender. Finally at local government level a procedure

41. See Chapter Four, this volume, pp. 104-6.
42 Ibid, Objective 1.5.
43. Ibid, Objective 1.5
44. A committee of inquiry is established in Sweden to look into law or policy initiatives before they are finally approved by Parliament. The committees, which are made up of Parliamentarian. and representatives of interest groups, are designed to ensure that when measures are finally approved they will attract popular support.

known as the '3R Method' has evolved. This considers how women and men are represented[45] on local government boards and committees, how resources[46] are distributed and the qualitative effects[47] of these quantitative variables.

Spain's Third Equal Opportunities Plan 1997

Spain's Third Equal Opportunities Plan makes a commitment to 'integrate the dimension of equal opportunities into the policies of the public administration and institutions and to foster co-operation with both non-governmental organisations and international organisations by mobilising all policies to attain equality'.[48] There is, however, no mention in this Plan of the political measures which will be required to put this objective into practice.

Ireland's Gender and Poverty Proofing Procedures

Since 1993, following a memorandum sent to all Government Departments by the Prime Minister's Office, all policy proposals in Ireland are required to include an assessment of their probable impact on women.[49] As well as this initiative on gender equality Ireland possesses a related equality initiative. This is Ireland's National Anti-Poverty Strategy (NAPS) which is a cross-departmental policy strategy designed to prioritise the needs of the poor and the socially excluded in the development of government policy. This also has a gender dimension which includes addressing the material deprivation of women and the obstacles to social participation, such as lone parenting or lack of childcare, which they face. As part of NAPS, there is a mechanism for poverty proofing. This is defined as 'the process by which government departments, local authorities and state agencies assess policies and programmes at design and review stages in relation to the likely impact that they will have or have had on poverty and on inequalities which are likely to lead to poverty, with a view to poverty reduction'.[50]

---

45. In the sense of membership and contact with these bodies.
46. In terms of time, money and space.
47. By looking at the manner in which resources and representation is distributed, an assessment can then be made of the goods, services and situations which result and the needs which are being served.
48. Instituto de la Mujer (1997), *III Plan para la Igualdad de Oportunidades entre Mujeres y Hombres 1997-2000*, Madrid: Ministerio de Trabajo y Asuntos Sociales, Instituto de la Mujer, p. 11.
49. In addition a set of guidelines has recently been produced for gender proofing within the context of the European Structural Funds. Mullally, S. (1999), Guidelines for *Gender Proofing within the Context of the European Structural Funds*, Dublin: Government Stationery Office.
50. NESF (1996), *Equality Proofing Issues*, Dublin: Government Stationery Office.

Netherlands Gender Impact Assessment (EER) Procedure

This procedure was developed in 1994 and aims to assess the potential impact on gender relations of any government policy proposal whilst it is at the planning stage. The procedure is voluntary and its content is dictated to a degree by what is politically acceptable. EER consists of a series of steps which aim to describe the gender relevance of a policy proposal,[51] to highlight current and future gender relations[52] in the given policy field and then analyse the policy proposal for its positive and negative impact on these gender relations. Those impacts are defined in terms of their effect on equal treatment, autonomy (the ability of women to decide for themselves what constitutes a 'good life') and pluriformity (a society with many differences which are not hierarchical).

The United Kingdom's Policy Appraisal Procedures

In the 1980s an initiative was launched by the Ministerial Group on Women's Issues which encouraged government Departments to develop guidelines on 'equality proofing'. The United Kingdom had two procedures – Policy Appraisal for Equal Treatment (PAET) which operated in Great Britain and Policy Appraisal and Fair Treatment (PAFT) which operated in Northern Ireland. The aim of each procedure was to ensure that issues of equality inform policy-making in all spheres and at all levels of government activity. Both PAFT and PAET required that an appraisal was undertaken when new policy proposals were made or when existing policies were reviewed. That appraisal consisted of an assessment of the impact of that policy on any of a number of target groups. Those targets included minority ethnic groups, people with or without dependants, marital status, religious belief, political affiliation, gender, sexual orientation, age, people with disabilities. An annual report was published setting out the details of any PAFT appraisals undertaken. There were no similar arrangements in relation to PAET.

PAFT has now been replaced with a statutory system of appraisal.[53] The new system[54] requires public authorities in Northern Ireland to draw up

51. That is whether it is directed at target groups and what differences exist between men and women in that particular policy area.
52. In terms of the division of labour, the organisation of intimacy/sexuality, access to resources and the existence of norms concerning gender.
53. See section 75 of the Northern Ireland Act 1998.
54. The statutory scheme was put in place as part of the Belfast (Good Friday) peace agreement in the Province. Although the operation of certain aspects of this agreement have been suspended (for example the Northern Ireland Assembly) the equality schemes have not been affected.

equality schemes indicating how they will promote equality of opportunity among a variety of groups including 'men and women generally'.[55] As part of their duty to promote equality, public authorities are obliged to undertake impact assessments of their existing and proposed policies on the target groups. As for the PAET guidelines they have been reviewed[56] and new guidelines issued. One of the major changes is that the guidelines now appear much vaguer. They no longer specifically list target groups[57] and the guidance they offer on conducting an appraisal is not as detailed as it once was. Moreover the establishment of regional assemblies in Scotland and Wales has been accompanied by the imposition on them of an obligation to promote equal opportunities.[58] This has been interpreted in a very positive fashion as requiring such actions as the mainstreaming of the policies and legislation proposed by the new assemblies.[59]

This review of national practice reveals wide variations in how exactly mainstreaming has been implemented. This is perhaps not surprising given the very different legal and political landscapes that the states featured in *Making Women Count* possess. More relevant is the extent to which these schemes have succeeded in integrating gender into the law and policy-making process. On that count there is cause for concern since, judging by the assessments made in the chapters devoted to national practice, mainstreaming seems in the main to have enjoyed only limited success. One obvious explanation relates to the sophisticated character of mainstreaming as a device for eradicating inequalities between the sexes. This means that, in order to succeed, the strategy requires a sophisticated method of implementation. Its limited achievements to date point to practical problems embedding it within the law and policy-making process.

Political commitment

Mainstreaming is a strategy for addressing gender inequality. Politicians and policy-makers may have no difficulty in making a commitment to

55. Section 75, Northern Ireland Act 1998.
56. The review was undertaken by the Women's Unit.
57. The implication is that the groups covered by PAET are those sections of the population who are specifically protected either by anti-discrimination legislation i.e. women, racial groups/nationality, the disabled, pregnant workers or by international agreement ie sexual orientation, religion. Reference is, however, also made to other groups such as the old and the young unemployed.
58. For a discussion of these obligations see Beveridge, F., Nott, S. and Stephen, K. (2000), 'Mainstreaming and the Engendering of Policy-making: A Means to an End?, 7 (4) *Journal of European Public Policy* (forthcoming).
59. Ibid.

'mainstreaming gender equality' but in practice this commitment is meaningless without the introduction into the policy-making process of the mechanisms to make mainstreaming work in practice. In some of the states featured in *Making Women Count* little progress had been made beyond the stage of rhetoric. In other states there had been an attempt to put mechanisms in place but often this had been done in an *ad hoc* fashion without recognising the need for a wholesale transformation of policy-making if mainstreaming is to be a success. Whilst acknowledging that it is not possible to state categorically — 'this is how to mainstreaming policies for their gender impact' — research has demonstrated that a state which is determined to mainstream policy-making has to pay close attention to various key aspects of the strategy.

In particular it would seem that in order to prosper mainstreaming requires a supportive political and organisational context. It should not be imagined, for example, that the introduction of mainstreaming signals the phasing out of other equality strategies such as the use of anti-discrimination legislation. Instead mainstreaming represents a way of strengthening traditional equality strategies by ensuring that they make the maximum impact.[60] What is essential if mainstreaming is to flourish is political commitment that represents more than mere political rhetoric. There needs to be the determination to put in place the resources and the processes to ensure that mainstreaming will succeed. Finance will have to be provided for such items as collecting relevant gender specific data and training personnel to be aware of the gender implications of their actions. At the same time there must be the political will to involve non-traditional actors, such as non-governmental organisations, within the decision-making process so that they can feed in data and their experiences on how the roles of the sexes are socially constructed within society. Finally political commitment is a necessary precondition for the initiation of changes to the infrastructure to ensure that the strategy works effectively. These will include procedures for assessing gender impact, for setting up channels of communication with non-traditional participants in the political process and to allow sufficient openness in government to demonstrate commitment to the procedure. Without political commitment on this scale mainstreaming will be little more than a declaration of intent or a paper exercise rather than an engine for substantive change.

60. For example, an effective mainstreaming strategy might ensure that much greater weight is given to the views of equality agencies than is currently the case. The expertise of such agencies on the impact that proposed policies would have on the respective situations of women and men would be a very valuable commodity.

The degree of political commitment to mainstreaming that could be discerned in the states featured in *Making Women Count* varied. In the case of Portugal and Spain, it appeared not to have moved beyond the stage of political rhetoric. The mainstreaming 'process' consisted of a 'plan' with no appraisal machinery or additional resources to give effect to it. It seems obvious that in such circumstances mainstreaming can be by-passed or ignored. Hence the doubts raised by the national commentators over the effectiveness of these initiatives.[61] Spain's Third Equal Opportunities Plan, for example, was condemned as lacking the operational infrastructure to put its recommendations into practice.

> Even though there is a statement of intention in the Third Plan to put into place a mainstreaming policy, there is no evidence elsewhere in the development of either the philosophy implicit in this concept or the political measures needed to enforce it.[62]

Similar criticisms were made of gender mainstreaming in Ireland. Here, although progress appeared to have been made in the shape of a specific commitment on the part of the government to assess proposed policies for their impact on women and a recognition of the desirability of gender proofing, the machinery to make this a reality had not been put in place.

> Despite this apparent commitment to gender proofing, however, systematic changes in policy-making have not yet occurred. Many of the essential features of an effective proofing procedure are lacking. Additional resources have not been made available to assist policy makers in carrying out gender impact assessments. Neither has any provision been made for training in gender analysis or gender planning. Consultation with outside bodies is not a requirement or even a general practice. Cabinet confidentiality requirements prevent impact assessment statements coming under public scrutiny, making it difficult to assess their adequacy and objectivity.[63]

---

61. See Casqueira Cardoso, J. (1999), *Predicting the Impact of Policy: Gender-Auditing as a Means of Assessing the Probable Impact of Policy, Country Report*: Portugal, Liverpool. Feminist Legal Research Unit, School of Law, University of Liverpool, section 5; Arranz, F., Quintanilla, B. and Velázquez, C. (1999) *Predicting the Impact of Policy: Gender-Auditing as a means of Assessing the Probable Impact of Policy, Country Report: Spain* Liverpool Feminist Legal Research Unit, School of Law, University of Liverpool, section 3 4
62. See Chapter Five, this volume, p 127.
63. See Chapter Two, this volume, p 45-6.

Models of mainstreaming

Other states featured in *Making Women Count* had devised procedures with the apparent intention of integrating gender into the policy-making process. Appraisal processes operated in Sweden, the Netherlands and the United Kingdom. On closer examination it appeared that these processes took one of two distinct forms. The first, typified by the Dutch Gender Impact Assessment instrument (EER), represents an *expert-bureaucratic* approach. This focuses on the use in policy-making of a gender impact assessment tool whereby a policy is subject at a particular stage or stages in its development to an analysis of its likely gender impact. This analysis is regarded as an expert task involving know-how, experience, training and a sophisticated understanding of gender relations and social theory. In Sweden, for example, the central government employs gender experts to work with regional equality officers in order to follow up national initiatives and develop regional policies for integrating gender. In the Netherlands policies are subject to scrutiny by gender experts — either from inside or outside the relevant Ministry — who raise sophisticated theoretical questions about the policy and policy area concerned. An important issue in relation to this model is how the tasks of mainstreaming are divided between experts and bureaucrats and, as discussed in Chapter Nine, how the bodies charged with contributing to or monitoring mainstreaming are constituted and where they are located. As was noted in relation to the Dutch EER, there is value both in a position of independence and distance, and in one where those involved in mainstreaming are integrated within the existing decision-making structures and able to exert influence.

A second approach — epitomised by the statutory obligation in Northern Ireland to assess policies for their impact on equality of opportunity — is a *participatory-democratic* approach, focussing on the policy-makers rather than the policy itself. In Northern Ireland though the promotion of equality is the goal, the understandings of that goal are heavily influenced by the history of exclusion from the political process experienced by many groups within the population. As a consequence inclusion in the process of policy-development has become an intrinsic component of the meaning of equality. Though the circumstances giving rise to this development are unique to Northern Ireland, the model of mainstreaming which emerges is reflected elsewhere in the United Kingdom and in Ireland. That model emphasises social partnership, conceived in a very broad fashion to include community groups, service recipients and service providers, as well as more organised interest groups such as employers, trade unions and political groupings.

Under it consultation, access to policy-making and, possibly, the devolution of decision-making are valued. In Ireland, for example, there has been a focus on increasing consultation with and securing the participation of groups such as travellers, previously excluded from the policy-making process.

The importance of consultation and participation raises the question of the relationship between gender equality policies and policies on 'other inequalities' such as race, ethnicity, religion, sexual orientation, disability and age. The *expert-bureaucratic* approach indicates that these need to be tackled separately and through distinct processes, since it is necessary to start with a firm expert understanding of the pathology of the inequality in question. Since it cannot be supposed that race discrimination is replicated and reinforced in the same ways as gender discrimination, it cannot be assumed that a model of gender impact assessment could be adapted to tackle race discrimination. Instead it will be necessary to explore and describe the pathology of race discrimination and from there to construct an approach to the promotion of racial equality. The *participatory-democratic* approach, however, indicates the opposite. Its starting point is that it is necessary to validate and value the experience of individuals affected in different ways by specific policies. The empowerment of all members of society is an inherent goal of this model. If this is carried over into the policies which emerge from that process, it could produce policies which enhance personal autonomy in a real rather than a formal sense, taking account of the real attachments, ties and situations of a range of individuals, rather than in a liberal rational detached individualist mode. Enfranchisement and the devolution of real power to the individuals affected by policies (and away from the experts) becomes an issue under this model. The *participatory-democratic* approach also validates the joining of different inequalities in the policy-making process, through the introduction of cross-cutting target definitions such as 'poverty', 'social exclusion' and 'social need'.

These two models are not necessarily mutually exclusive within any given policy-making arena but experience to date shows that governments so far have opted to focus on one or the other, rather than to seek to benefit from both approaches. A possible explanation is that states have selected the approach which is best suited to their internal political arrangements. Whilst undoubtedly policy solutions work best if they 'fit' well within the existing political and legal framework, it must be recognised that the existing political and legal framework may act as a dampener on effective action in relation to equality. As a result those fundamental changes to institutions and practices which are required if mainstreaming is to prove effective may be ignored.

The role of gender impact assessment

Despite the welcome evidence that some of the states featured in *Making Women Count* have put in place mechanisms to assess gender impact, it is not axiomatic that the process in question can then automatically be equated with mainstreaming or that this represents the supportive political climate that mainstreaming requires. Some commentators have argued that on its own an impact assessment procedure is not the equivalent of mainstreaming.[64] Whilst it is clear that 'impact assessment' is a necessary feature in operationalising mainstreaming, i.e. 'making it real in practice',[65] mainstreaming is a wider strategy since it requires gender to figure at all stages of policy development and delivery. The United Kingdom offers a good example of how the mere presence of appraisal machinery is not sufficient. PAET has been in existence for over a decade yet, since there was (until recently) no serious political commitment to mainstreaming, it merely represented a procedure that, whilst it may or may not have been taken seriously, did nothing to put gender at the heart of the policy-making process. Hence it is plain that if mainstreaming is to work there must be an effective means of assessing gender impact in place which is part of a wider obligation to integrate gender into the policy-making process.

A gender impact assessment procedure, if it is to succeed, has to possess certain characteristics. In the first place it must be integrated into a state's law and policy-making framework and become an essential part of it. Resources have to be devoted to this and most importantly it has to be clear who is responsible for defining that procedure's goals and is accountable for its successful implementation. Secondly the procedure adopted for mainstreaming gender must specify to what laws and policies it applies. If substantial areas of policy-making are excluded, particularly financial policies or budgetary matters, or all levels of policy-making – national, regional, local — are not included then the process risks being marginalised and undermined. Thirdly the objectives of a gender impact assessment, who is to carry them out and how the training needs of those responsible are to be met require clarification. If responsibilities are not spelt out and proper training given then mainstreaming may become a charade infected by the very stereotypes which it is designed to eliminate. Fourthly arrangements must be made to secure as wide a degree of participation — whether by gender experts or by interested organisations or both — in the process as is thought

64 Spencer, F. *Briefing on Mainstreaming*, Manchester: Equal Opportunities Commission.
65. Equality Proofing Administrative Procedures, 1998, p. 20.

to be appropriate. Fifthly any gender impact assessment should be open to public scrutiny in order to demonstrate if and how the procedure has been conducted. Without this doubts may be raised over the objectivity and quality of the exercise. Finally some person or agency needs to be accountable for such procedures and their actions need to be monitored either by an external body or by setting targets or goals. Without external scrutiny and the ability to hold someone to account mainstreaming may simply become an exercise in 'tokenism': a procedure which officials can point to when their equal opportunities record is challenged but which is not audited for its efficiency in eliminating inequalities between the sexes.

In those countries which do possess a gender impact assessment procedure of some kind, the qualities which are essential for success are often lacking. In Sweden, for example, it appears that, despite being required, a comprehensive analysis of the gender implications of policies is not always undertaken. In 1997 an evaluation carried out by the Equality Affairs Division concluded that only 33 per cent of the pre-legislative investigations carried out had included a thorough gender perspective in the written report. The reasons for this were identified as a lack of knowledge concerning equality issues and a lack of sanctions if a gender assessment was not properly executed.

The same doubts arose in the United Kingdom over the operation of the PAET and PAFT guidelines. The current PAET guidelines contain a rather vague description of what any appraisal will involve. In addition no information is available on what PAET appraisals have been undertaken and their findings. There is no transparency whatsoever regarding the process. The annual reports published in conjunction with PAFT did contain some information on what appraisals had been undertaken. This information, however, raised the suspicion that appraisals had often not been properly undertaken since policies were sometimes said to have had no gender impact when this was patently not the case.

In some of the countries undertaking a gender appraisal little evidence existed that expert bodies were consulted to give their views and lend their expertise in relation to the matter in hand. In Ireland the National Women's Council of Ireland indicates that it has never been consulted as part of a gender audit. In the United Kingdom the PAET guidelines list organisations which might be consulted when conducting an appraisal. These include the Equal Opportunities Commission and the Women's National Commission.[66] There is no information available on whether they have ever been involved in a PAET appraisal.

66. Policy Appraisal for Equal Treatment, 1998, Appendix B.

The gender impact procedures discussed in this chapter operated primarily at national level. In Sweden, the Netherlands and the United Kingdom there were procedures in place at other levels of government but this was very much on an *ad hoc* basis. In the United Kingdom, for example, there are mainstreaming initiatives at local government level[67] but no co-ordinated policy on their general desirability. In contrast an effort had been made when setting up devolved assemblies in Scotland and Wales to integrate the promotion of equal opportunities into their working practices.[68] This happened, however, largely as a result of external pressure from women's organisations rather than as part of some systematic approach to mainstreaming on the part of central government. Other countries such as Sweden have encouraged local government to experiment with such schemes and have provided financial support. No country, however, has made a systematic effort to ensure that a policy of mainstreaming was adopted at all levels of government.

The objectives of gender impact assessment

The appraisal procedures in Ireland, Sweden and the United Kingdom also appear vague on what they perceive to be their objective. References are made to examining policies for adverse impact or gender impact but little additional information is given on what exactly this means. The PAET guidelines, for example, refer to 'differential impact'. This apparently includes direct and indirect discrimination as it is defined in the anti-discrimination legislation since those undertaking a policy appraisal are instructed that if the differential impact is not 'legally permissible' it must be eliminated. If the differential impact is 'legally permissible', the following advice is offered.

> . . . decide whether the difference is justifiable in policy terms. If it is a programme intended specifically to address the needs of a particular group, it may be justifiable. Judge whether the differential impact is acceptable within the context of the programme. Where necessary, amend the policy or programme.[69]

If a state's definition of 'adverse impact' does not go beyond the 'equal treatment' definition of equality then it would appear that mainstreaming

67. The Equal Opportunities Commission has conducted research into such initiatives. See Equal Opportunities Commission (1997), *Mainstreaming Gender Equality in Local Government: A Framework*, Manchester, EOC.
68. See Beveridge, F., Nott, S. and Stephen, K. op cit, n. 58.
69. Policy Appraisal for Equal Treatment, The Women's Unit, London, 1998, p. 5.

will tackle neither cultural differences nor power imbalances between the sexes. In the case of the United Kingdom, the decision whether to amend a policy to eliminate a 'legally permissible' differential impact seems to be purely discretionary. In one respect this seems sensible since the differential impact may be the direct result of a deliberate effort to help a disadvantaged group. Alternatively, this discretionary power could be used in a way that defeats the objects of gender impact assessment.

In contrast, the Netherlands' EER and Sweden's 3R initiatives adopt a very sophisticated analysis of what constitutes 'adverse impact', which takes much greater account of the theoretical and practical reasons underlying inequality between the sexes. Clearly an attempt at the wholesale transfer of such detailed analyses into another legal and political context is unlikely to work. It is said of the Netherlands' EER that it is not easily exportable, not because of its academic qualities but because it is adapted to a specific political and policy context.[70] This serves as a reminder that, whilst officials may seek a 'painless' gender impact assessment procedure that is quick and requires no effort or expertise, the reality is that 'gender relations are very complex and any gender impact assessment would necessarily need a certain degree of sophistication'.[71]

Another variation in the use of gender impact assessment procedures was whether or not they were compulsory. In Sweden, Ireland and the United Kingdom the expectation was that all government policies would be assessed. In reality, however, there was evidence that this was not so.[72] In the case of Ireland there was said to be suspicion that gender proofing is carried out only on policy proposals that are clearly seen to have a differential impact on women. If this is so then it seems to defeat the whole object of gender proofing which is to appraise all policies even those which on the face of them have no apparent gender impact. In only one country, that is the United Kingdom or more specifically Northern Ireland, were steps being taken to make policy appraisal obligatory. The reason for this lies not in the desire to promote equality between the sexes but the religious/political differences that bedevil that country. In the Netherlands, however, EER is optional. This would seem to represent a major weakness since mainstreaming works best either when coverage is complete or when there is some screening mechanism in place to select the policies to be appraised.

---

70. See Chapter Three, this volume p 62.
71. Ibid, p 61.
72. See Gillberg, M. (1999) *Predicting the Impact of Policy: Gender-Auditing as a means of Assessing the Probable Impact of Policy, Country Report: Sweden* Liverpool: Feminist Legal Research Unit, School of Law, University of Liverpool, p. 41

This situation, however, represents a pragmatic response to a lack of political support for compulsion and stresses the importance of heeding the political and legal contexts within which gender impact assessment operates.

Of the states featured in *Making Women Count* only one, the United Kingdom, had a gender impact assessment which was part of a larger process of appraising policies for their impact on a variety of inequalities such as race or disability.[73] The point has already been made that a very broad procedure apparently has the advantage of addressing those very specific problems suffered by women from ethnic minority communities or who are disabled. There is, however, some evidence that where a procedure attempts to deal with many forms of inequality a hierarchy develops with the result that some forms of inequality are rarely addressed.[74] Elsewhere in this book it is argued that the analytical elements that are important for other structural inequalities,[75] such as race, are very different from those of gender. Hence difficulties may be experienced in combining impact assessment procedures. Indeed in Ireland where there are two discrete appraisal procedures for gender and poverty, reservations have been expressed regarding the relationship between the two processes.[76]

Conclusions

This chapter has been concerned to explore those equality strategies, namely positive action and mainstreaming — which attempt to address the deep-seated causes of gender inequality. What has become apparent is that positive action is often constrained in what it can achieve by the concept of equality which a state may employ. In contrast mainstreaming has far greater potential to eliminate inequalities. The key to its success, however, is the degree of thought which is given to putting this strategy into place. It should not be imagined that, once a suitable procedure is in existence, then equality between the sexes will emerge as a matter of course. Since mainstreaming is dependent on high level political commitment it is vulnerable to changes in political power or to a state's political structures. In addition mainstreaming is

73. In Ireland there are separate procedures for gender and poverty proofing.

74 See Nott, S. (1999), 'Mainstreaming Equal Opportunities: Succeeding When All Else Has Failed?', in Morris, A. and O'Donnell, T. (eds), *Feminist Perspectives on Employment Law*, London: Cavendish, p. 220.

75. See Chapter Three, this volume p. 64.

76. Donnelly, M., Mullally, S. and Smith, O. (1999) *Predicting the Impact of Policy:Gender-Auditing as a means of Assessing the Probable Impact of Policy, Country Report: Ireland* Liverpool· Feminist Legal Research Unit, School of Law, University of Liverpool.

a reactive process. It can be used to appraise only those policies which a government decides to implement. It cannot force a government which is hostile to equal opportunities to put forward helpful policy initiatives. All it can do is to draw attention to the adverse effects of those policies a government chooses to promote. Most specifically if feminist theory is correct in drawing attention to the 'maleness' of the state then mainstreaming may find this difficult to counteract. Its target is policies rather than the institutions which produce them. Finally mainstreaming is a strategy which assesses policy initiatives taken by public sector bodies. The policies of the private sector may remain untouched[77] and it may well be that they have far more effect on women than government policies.

77. Initiatives are being taken to explore the introduction of mainstreaming into the workplace. A researcł ɔroject on gender mainstreaming in human resource management is currently being undertaken for The Ministry of the Flemish Community in Belgium.

11 Moving Forward with Mainstreaming

FIONA BEVERIDGE, SUE NOTT AND KYLIE STEPHEN

Each of the contributions to *Making Women Count* has offered a view of gender equality in the late 1990s. Whether addressing practice in a particular state or dealing with cross-cutting themes, the contributors have identified trends in the evolution of equality strategies and have advanced their views about the effectiveness of the measures in question in tackling gender inequality. It is clear that despite the great diversity between the situations in different states,[1] many are facing similar challenges and similar difficulties in establishing effective mechanisms. The analyses presented above seek to explore these challenges and identify how various equality strategies can contribute to the promotion of gender equality in the future. There is acceptance that any strategies which utilise the notion of equality as equal treatment can achieve only so much. Whilst not suggesting that they should be abandoned, there is a feeling amongst the contributors to *Making Women Count* that if the struggle for gender equality is to move forward some original and innovative initiative is required — a possible candidate according to those contributors is the concept known as mainstreaming.

Mainstreaming is the most recent of the strategies developed to address these challenges. In the abstract the concept of mainstreaming can be seen both as a new development in gender politics and as an evolution of previous approaches. Mainstreaming is new insofar as it seeks to give recognition in practice to theoretical understandings about the pervasiveness of inequality and about the ways in which inequality is maintained and reproduced in the institutions and practices of societies. In so doing it turns the spotlight, not before time, away from formal rights strategies and compensatory mechanisms such as positive action, towards institutions and processes. Mainstreaming shifts attention away from the results of discrimination towards

1. The implications of this diversity for the development of EU social policy are discussed elsewhere c.f. Beveridge, F., Nott, S. and Stephen, K. (2000), 'Addressing Gender in National and Community Law and Policy-Making', in Shaw, J. (ed.), *Social Law and Policy in an Evolving European Union*, Oxford: Hart Publishing (forthcoming).

its causes. And since it is understood that the processes which reproduce inequality are continuously at work, so too it is understood that strategies to combat gender inequality must infect all areas of human activity at all levels. Tackling inequality is no longer about finding the right policy but about ensuring that all policies are right: equality is no longer an end in itself, but a value which must be respected at all times and in all activities. Mainstreaming therefore represents a new consensus about the importance of process in maintaining inequality and hence about the centrality of process-oriented strategies in tackling inequality.

Mainstreaming can also be understood as evolutionary in that it both includes and builds on the understandings of equality and inequality developed in previous generations of equality strategies. Mainstreaming can be said to take a wider view of the causes of inequality, both in a horizontal and in a vertical sense. In a horizontal sense it views the factors which characterise women's lives outside the workplace as determinants of the situation of women within the workplace, placing responsibility for the promotion of equality onto policy-makers across government, in all policy areas. In a vertical sense it views women workers as a product of their education and training, their upbringing and their employment history, and places an obligation on policy-makers to take account of such factors in the development of policies. Thus mainstreaming seeks to internalise within the policy-making system certain of the sociological truths which had previously gained acceptance as external critiques of policy.[2]

Mainstreaming is also capable of addressing, on a conceptual level, feminist critiques of law as essentialising. By focusing attention on the process of policy-making rather than its content, and by seeking to recognise the reality of women's lives rather than reducing women to the subjects of legal rights and duties, mainstreaming is at least capable of promoting and protecting both cultural and normative pluralism. Whether it does so will depend on the wider political context in which it is pursued, the specific meanings ascribed to mainstreaming and the tools developed in its name. But at its best, the case for mainstreaming is a case for good governance and evidence-led policy-making.[3] This observation does of course require caution. As noted in Chapter Ten, care must be taken not to assume that the same approaches

2. For an analysis of the 'gender mainstreaming' concept as a product of *frame alignment* see further Verloo, M. (1999), 'On the conceptual and theoretical roots of gender main streaming' in *ESRC Seminar Series: The Interface Between Public Policy and Gender Equality, Seminar One* Sheffield: Centre for Regional Economic and Social Research, Sheffield Hallam University.
3. See further Mackay, F. and Bilton, K. (2000), *Learning From Experience: Lessons in Mainstreaming Equal Opportunities*, Edinburgh: Governance of Scotland Forum, University of Edinburgh.

and tools can address, say, the gender and race dimensions of inequality.[4] But in theory, at least, mainstreaming is capable of furthering the politics of difference.

A case can also be made that mainstreaming has the potential to tackle the 'maleness' of the state and of the law. Gender mainstreaming has been held to have the ability to recognise the 'hidden, unrecognised and unremarked ways in which systems and structures are biased in favour of men'[5] and to require steady transformation of these institutions, and their working practices.[6] Thus a distinction can be drawn between mainstreaming approaches which are 'integrationist' and those which are 'agenda-setting';[7] in the latter case, '[w]omen not only become part of the mainstream, they also reorient the nature of the mainstream'.[8]

However there will undoubtedly be feminist commentators who greet mainstreaming with scepticism. And indeed, the sight of the United Nations, the Council of Europe, the Nordic Council and the European Union *inter alia* all turning to embrace the concept of mainstreaming has the unmistakable ring of modernity about it: mainstreaming has been embraced as the grand plan to encapsulate all dimensions of gender equality policies and to provide a platform for future action. Practice on the ground, on the other hand, is far from homogenous. As is clear from the foregoing chapters, the concept of mainstreaming has been seized upon enthusiastically and acted on in many different ways and by many different actors, each with their own agenda and each giving mainstreaming their own interpretation. The contributions in *Making Women Count* show that at one end of the spectrum mainstreaming initiatives can amount to little more than well-meaning policy-statements, while at the other end of the spectrum, they can provide a basis for dialogue and the introduction of genuinely transformative strategies. Opportunism plays its part in determining how particular mainstreaming initiatives will shape up.[9]

4. See also Verloo, op cit, n. 2; Rees, T. (1999), 'Managing Diversity and Mainstreaming Equality', *ESRC Seminar Series: The Interface Between Public Policy and Gender Equality, Seminar Two*, Sheffield: Centre for Regional Economic and Social Research, Sheffield Hallam University.
5. Rees, T. (1998), *Mainstreaming Equality in the European Union*, London: Routledge.
6. Mackay and Bilton, op cit n. 3.
7. Rahan, R. (1995), *The Elusive Agenda: Mainstreaming Women in Development*, London: Zed Books at p. 13.
8. Ibid.
9. See also Beveridge, F., Nott, S. and Stephen, K. (2000), 'Mainstreaming and the Engendering of Policy-Making: A Means to an End?', 7(4) *Journal of European Public Policy* (forthcoming).

Thus in some situations, at least, it would seem that mainstreaming can serve as a vehicle for change and should not be dismissed out of hand. However, there is clearly a need for scepticism and caution when advancing claims about the transformative potential of mainstreaming. In addition it is vital to be aware of the inherent limitations of mainstreaming as a strategy for addressing inequality.

Mainstreaming and the market

One of the most complex and intractable political problems is the relationship between governments and markets. The tendency of markets, regulated or otherwise, to create and replicate gender divisions through horizontal and vertical segregation, through the promotion of stereotypes and through the disenfranchisement of the economically weak in society is central to gender inequality, yet extremely difficult to tackle. Moreover the public/private division, which separates the sphere in which governments can legitimately act from that which is accepted to be beyond the reach of government, serves to ensure that only certain aspects of the market are truly recognised as public.

First generation equality laws, promoting formal equality between men and women in the political and later the economic spheres, presented little challenge to the structure and organisation of the market. Though direct discrimination was clearly unlawful this was irrelevant where there was strong horizontal and vertical segregation since it was not necessary to discriminate directly between employees to restrict women to 'women's work' — typically low-paid and concentrated in areas where the career structure was weak. Indirect discrimination in theory offers the opportunity to tackle segregation as epitomised perhaps in the *Enderby* Case[10] where the pay and conditions enjoyed by clinical psychologists and pharmacists were claimed by speech therapists, historically less-well paid and treated and predominantly female. But such cases are the exception rather than the rule and occupational segregation remains a major factor in gender discrimination in the workplace.

Second generation strategies — family-friendly policies and positive discrimination — appear to acknowledge the role of the market in disadvantaging certain groups and offer the opportunity to address this disadvantage by taking

10. Case 127/92 *Enderby v Frenchay Health Authority and the Secretary of State for Health* [1993] ECR 5535.

it into account in the recruitment and treatment of employees. However as was noted in Chapter Ten, many of the states examined in this book demonstrated a marked reluctance to transfer to employers the costs of addressing disadvantage. Even the monitoring of equal opportunities in the workplace is regarded in many states as something which should be left to the employer, or to the social partners, rather than made the subject of legal requirements.[11] Positive discrimination where it was permitted by law was usually permissive rather than required — only in Sweden were employers under a positive obligation to attempt to achieve balanced representation of the sexes in the workforce and to tackle gender divisions within it — and the general unease with 'strong' positive discrimination policies which breach the liberal conception of equality of opportunity displayed in the *Kalanke* Case[12] was replicated in a number of Member States.

Family-friendly or women-friendly policies which acknowledge the role which caring responsibilities play in perpetuating gender inequality have been the subject of more recent policy initiatives in relation, for instance, to parental leave and pregnant workers. However legislators have been unwilling to demand substantial changes in working practices, perceiving it to be inappropriate to impose the 'costs' of addressing inequality on market actors (employers). This tendency is evident both at the EU level, where legislation has on the whole left to governments the question of how leave is to be paid for, and in the Member States where when the relevant measures have been acted on, many have opted for the minimum legal requirements.[13] It should also be noted that equality policies remain heavily market-focused, that is to say that equality is granted where women participate in the market as employees or sometimes as consumers, but that equality policies are much more difficult to pursue into the domestic or 'private' sphere. Thus while it is now accepted, for instance, that the disadvantages faced by employees who are parents vis-à-vis other employees are a legitimate focus of concern, the fate of those excluded from the workforce by reason of caring responsibilities falls outside the liberal equality project. These limitations to first and second generation equality laws form the background against which the utility of mainstreaming should be analysed.

Changes to the equality provisions of EU law introduced by the Treaty of Amsterdam seem unlikely to produce much change in this respect.

---

11. Though there are good examples in both Sweden and Northern Ireland where workforce monitoring is required by law and generally accepted as non-controversial by the business community.
12. Case C-450/93 *Kalanke v Freie Hansestadt Bremen* [1995] ECR I-3051.
13. As is the case, for instance, with the measures adopted by the governments o. Ireland and the UK to give effect to the Parental Leave Directive.

As noted in Chapter Eight, the new approach of the Community institutions, seeking to balance social cohesion, competitiveness and sound public finances, may well act as a powerful constraint on the setting of higher standards of protection for workers. One writer has commented that social policy is being 'subsumed by the competitiveness agenda'.[14]

Mainstreaming is a tool which operates essentially in the political sphere, requiring policy-makers to take gender considerations into account when making public policy. Its major contribution to equality policies is the recognition that the pursuit of equality policies in the employment field may be less important than the gender impact of policies in other fields such as education, health, transport, housing and criminal law. Policies which emerge from a mainstreaming process may of course have serious implications for private parties — for instance if the policies developed impose equality obligations on employers or on the suppliers of services or goods or the recipients of government funds. But there is nothing intrinsic to mainstreaming which will ensure that that it will give rise to policies which will bridge the divide between the public and the private, or which will make governments intrinsically more likely to regard it as appropriate to impose equality policies and duties on the private sector. Mainstreaming is a tool which may be of use in the political sphere but it is not a political philosophy: while the application of mainstreaming instruments may help to expose the flaws of a dominant political philosophy it will not in itself serve as a substitute.

It is important to recognise this limitation of mainstreaming, since it should not be expected that mainstreaming will resolve questions regarding the relationship between governments and markets; hence such questions must still be addressed in the appropriate political spheres. Mainstreaming tools can be developed which will identify the likely gender implications of pursuing particular economic policies and strategies but they cannot by themselves determine the appropriate political choices.

The concept of mainstreaming can therefore be seen to offer real possibilities of change, but also to be subject to some serious limitations. As the previous chapters have shown it has proved itself popular with governments who at the level of rhetoric have been quick to commit themselves to mainstreaming and to promise to act on it. What then does mainstreaming demand in practice and what difficulties lie in transforming the general concept of mainstreaming into concrete practices?

---

14. Kenner, J. (2000), 'The paradox of the social dimension', in Lynch, P., Neuwahl, N. and Rees, W (eds), *Reforming the European Union — from Maastricht to Amsterdam*, London: Longman, p. 108 at p. 125.

Mainstreaming in Practice

An initial observation about mainstreaming is that without further development it is rather bland and vague. Though it is clear that its target is policy-makers and that its objective is the promotion of gender equality, this raises more questions than are answered about what it actually requires if it is to be successful. It will remain meaningless in real terms unless and until it is developed through the introduction into the policy-making process of rules, protocols, procedures and/or instruments to give effect to mainstreaming. Moreover until this is done and done effectively, mainstreaming can and should be viewed with suspicion as well as expectation, since it will serve well as the text for those who wish to pay lip-service to the goal of promoting equality as well as empowering and guiding those who take such a goal seriously. Already for instance, feminists in Australia have complained that 'mainstreaming' has served as a justification for removing support from institutions whose sole task was the promotion of equality with the excuse that equality was now everyone's business and that resources should be distributed accordingly. Examples also exist of states where there has been a superficial expression of commitment to 'mainstreaming' as a strategy for the promotion of equality but without the development of any concrete mechanisms to advance such a strategy.[15]

In the states where mechanisms had been introduced or developed to build on the political commitment to mainstreaming, this had usually been effected only in one sector of policy-making or at one level of government. Though there is an increasing element in the practice of states of 'self-reporting' — typically the production of an Annual Report on equality — there was little evidence of any overall mainstreaming strategy. Similarly, efforts to operationalise mainstreaming are often still regarded as being at the developmental or experimental stage, but with no clear timetable for moving forward to the next stage. And in most states tools have been developed to carry out some tasks while other tasks have been ignored completely.

But for mainstreaming to bring about any real improvement in approaches to inequality, both the context and the specific requirements of mainstreaming need to be properly addressed, and the current haphazardness

15. See for instance the criticisms of the Portuguese Global Plan for Equal Opportunities 1997 and the Spanish Third Equal Opportunities Plan 1997-2000, in Chapters Three and Four respectively. The commitments of these two states to mainstreaming are fairly typical initial responses to mainstreaming and perhaps stand out for criticism particularly because of the very formal way in which the commitments are made.

addressed. As argued in Chapter Ten, mainstreaming requires political commitment and adequate resources. It also needs also to be located within a wider culture of gender awareness. At the political level, the enhancement of gender awareness is required to enable and assist political actors, such as parliamentarians and NGOs, to play a full role in ensuring that gender issues have been addressed and to ensure the allocation of appropriate resources. On a practical level, better gender awareness can lead to the development of better information about inequalities.

Judging Mainstreaming

The identification of 'good practice' is often highlighted as necessary to further the development or successful implementation of mainstreaming guidelines or policies. This, though understandable in the context, does very clearly embody an assumption that it is possible to distinguish between 'good' and 'bad' examples in practice. So far, however, little work has been done on the development of criteria by which the success or failure of mainstreaming initiatives can be analysed. To date, most literature on mainstreaming has focused on the exchange of 'good practice', or on describing and analysing the efforts of a particular state or institution to introduce mainstreaming.[16]

There has been little attempt to develop a general theory of mainstreaming which transcends the diversity of state practice and provides a frame of reference or set of criteria by which mainstreaming may be understood and particular mainstreaming initiatives judged. Hafnoer-Burton and Pollack,[17] for instance, have detailed the extent to which the adoption of a mainstreaming initiative by the European Commission has produced results, in the sense of leading to the adoption of measures which reflect that mainstreaming concern. Their paper demonstrates that in the areas chosen by the Commission as pilots for the mainstreaming project, such results have been forthcoming. The pilot project might then be judged a success by the Commission's own terms. But the wider question raised is whether the Commission's initiative has delivered any of the advantages over previous policy-approaches which mainstreaming is said to offer. This in itself raises questions about the extent to which mainstreaming initiatives must be judged according to their specific context. How, for instance, are the European

16. See Chapter Ten and references therein.
17. Hafnoer-Burton, E. and Pollack, M. (2000), 'Mainstreaming Gender in the European Union', 7(4) *Journal of European Public Policy* (forthcoming).

Commission's initiatives to be compared with the Dutch Gender Impact Assessment initiative discussed by Verloo and Roggeband.[18] In other words, by what external criteria can the success of such initiatives be judged?

Conclusion

Mainstreaming should be recognised as an important new development in practice in the equality field. However, it raises important theoretical questions about the meaning of inequality, and about the role and aim of equality policies which require further exploration. There is room for both optimism and scepticism about mainstreaming, and a clear need for vigilance to ensure that governments' current enthusiasm for this idea are translated into meaningful gains in the policy-making arena.

18 Verloo, M and Roggeband, C (1996), 'Gender Impact Assessment: The Development of a New Instrument in the Netherlands', 14(1) *Impact Assessment* 3.

Bibliography

Official Publications

Council of Europe

Council of Europe (1998), *Gender Mainstreaming: Conceptual Framework, Methodology and Presentation of Good Practices, Final Report of the Activities of the Group of Specialists on Mainstreaming* (EG-S-MS (98) 2), Strasbourg: Council of Europe.

European Union

Commission Recommendation on the Protection of the Dignity of Men and Women at Work

Commission of the European Communities (1996), *Communication on Gender Mainstreaming*, COM 67.

Commission of the European Communities (1996), *Communication on Incorporating Equal Opportunities for Men and Women into all Community Policies and Activities*, COM (96)67, 21/02/96.

Commission of the European Communities (1999), *Annual Report on Equal Opportunities for Women and Men in the European Union 1998*, 5th March 1999, COM 106 final.

Rubenstein, M. (1987), *The Dignity of Men and Women at Work: A Report on the Problem of Sexual Harassment in the Member States of the European Community*, COM V/412/87.

Ireland

Commission on the Family (1998), *Strengthening Families for Life*, Final Report to Minister for Social Community and Family Affairs, Dublin: Government Stationery Office. Constitution Review Group (1996), *Report of the Constitution Review Group*, Dublin: Government Stationery Office.

Department of Equality and Law Reform (1996), *UN Fourth World Conference on Women: First Report on Implementation of the Platform for Action*, Dublin: Government Stationery Office.

Department of Justice, Equality and Law Reform (1999), *Discussion Document on Gender Proofing*, Dublin: Government Stationery Office.

Department of Social, Community and Family Affairs (1998), *Guidelines on Poverty Proofing within the context of the National Anti-Poverty Strategy*, Dublin: Government Stationery Office.

Department of the Taoiseach (1998), *Cabinet Handbook*, Dublin: Government Stationery Office.

First Commission on the Status of Women (1972), *Report to the Minister for Finance*, Dublin: Government Stationery Office.

Government of Ireland (1994), *A Government of Renewal: A Policy Agreement between Fine Gael, the Labour Party and Democratic Left*, Dublin: Government Stationery Office.

Government of Ireland (1996), *Delivering Better Government: A Programme of Change for th Civil Service. Second Report of the Co-ordinating Group of Secretaries*, Dublin: Government Stationery Office.

Government of Ireland (1996), *UN Fourth World Conference on Women: First Report on Implementation of the Platform for Action*, Dublin: Government Stationery Office.
Government of Ireland (1997), *Ireland's Combined Second and Third Reports under the United Nations Convention on the Elimination of All Forms of Discrimination Against Women*, Dublin: Government Stationery Office.
Government of Ireland (1998), *Employment Action Plan*, Dublin: Government Stationery Office
Government of Ireland (1999), *Third Progress Report on the Implementation of the Recommendations of the Second Commission on the Status of Women*, Dublin: Government Stationery Office.
McGinley, M. (1996), *From Employment Equality Agency to Equality Authority, Sixth Report to the Fourth Joint Oireachtas Committee on Women's Rights*, Dublin: Government Stationery Office.
Mullally, S. (1999), *Guidelines for Gender Proofing within the Context of the Structural Funds*, Dublin: Department of Justice, Equality and Law Reform.
Mullally, S. and Smith, O. (1999), *Guidelines for Equality Proofing*, Dublin: Department of Justice, Equality and Law Reform.
NESF (1996), *Equality Proofing Issues*, Dublin: Government Stationery Office.
NESF (1997), *A Framework for Partnership — Enriching Strategic Consensus through Participation*, Dublin: Government Stationery Office.
National Women's Council of Ireland (1997), *Response to the Report of the Monitoring Committee of the Second Commission on the Status of Women*, Dublin: NWCI.
National Women's Council of Ireland (1997), *Who Makes the Decisions in 1997? A Review of Gender Balance on State Boards in Ireland*, Dublin: NWCI.
Office of the Tánaiste (1997), *Report of the Task Force on Violence against Women*, Dublin: Government Stationery Office.
Partnership 2000 (1996), *Partnership 2000, for Inclusion, Employment and Competitiveness*, Dublin: Government Stationery Office.
Partnership 2000 (1999), *National Childcare Strategy: Report of the Partnership 2000 Expert Working Group on Childcare*, Dublin: Government Stationery Office.
Second Commission on the Status of Women (1993), *Report to Government*, Dublin: Government Stationery Office.

The Netherlands

Ministry of Foreign Affairs (1998), *Women and Development. Policy and Implementation in Netherlands Development Cooperation 1985-1996. Evaluation Report*, The Hague: Policy and Operations Evaluation Department, Ministry of Foreign Affairs.
Ministry of Social Affairs and Employment (1999), *The Second Report of the Netherlands to the UN Committee for the Elimination of all forms of Discrimination Against Women (CEDAW)*, The Hague: Ministry of Social Affairs and Employment.

OECD

Development Assistance Committee (1983), *Guiding Principles on Women and Development*, Paris: OECD.

Portugal

Comissão para a Igualdade e para os Direitos das Mulheres (1998), *Situação das Mulheres* — Lisbon: Commission for Equality and Women's Rights.
Commission for Equality and Women's Rights (1995), *Portugal — Status of Women — 1994*, Lisbon: High Commission for Equality and Family.

Conselho Económico e Social (1996), *O Conselho Económico e Social — Legislação e composição*, Lisbon: Conselho Económico e Social.
Conselho Económico e Social (1997), *Acordo de Concertação Estratégica 1996/1999*, Lisbon: Conselho Económico e Social.
High Commissioner for Matters relating to the Promotion of Equality and the Family (1998), Procuradoria-Geral da República (1983), *Pareceres, Volume I*, Lisbon: Ministério da Justiça.
Report on the execution of the measures announced in the Global Plan for Equal Opportunities, Lisbon: Presidência do Conselho de Ministros.

Spain

Consejo Económico y Social (1994), *Memoria de Actividades 1993*, Madrid: Consejo Económico y Social.
Consejo Económico y Social (1998), *Panorama Sociolaboral de la Mujer en España*, No. 11, Madrid: Consejo Económico y Social.
Instituto de la Mujer (IM) (1990), *Primer Plan para la Igualdad de Oportunidades de las Mujeres 1988-1990 Evaluación*, Madrid: Ministerio de Asuntos Sociales, Instituto de la Mujer.
Instituto de la Mujer (IM) (1993), *Segundo Plan para la Igualdad de Oportunidades de las Mujeres, 1993-1995*, Madrid: Ministerio de Asuntos Sociales, Instituto de la Mujer.
Instituto de la Mujer (IM) (1994), *Spanish Women on the Threshold of 21st Century. Report Submitted by Spain to the Fourth World Conference On Women, Beijing, 1995*, Madrid: Ministerio de Asuntos Sociales, Instituto de la Mujer.
Instituto de la Mujer (IM) (1997), *Memoria del Instituto de la Mujer 1996*, Madrid: Ministerio de Asuntos Sociales, Instituto de la Mujer.
Instituto de la Mujer (IM) (1997), *III Plan para la Igualdad de Oportunidades entre Mujeres y Hombres 1997-2000*, Madrid: Ministerio de Trabajo y Asuntos Sociales, Instituto de la Mujer.

Sweden

JämOs Nyhetsbrev (June 1998), No 5, Stockholm: Office of the Equal Opportunities Ombudsman. Statistics Sweden (1995), Women and Men in Sweden. Facts and Figures.
Ministry of Industry, Employment and Communications (February 1999), *Fact sheet: National Machinery for Equality Between Women and Men*.
Ministry of Labour (August 1998), *Fact Sheet: Violence Against Women and Women's Integrity*.
The Equality Affairs Division (November 1997), *Evaluation of Directive 1994:124*, Ministry of Labour and Employment.
What is JämO? (1997), Stockholm: Fact Sheet from the Office of the Equal Opportunities Ombudsman.
The Swedish Institute (September 1997), *Fact Sheet on Sweden*.

United Nations

ILO (1982), *International Labour Conventions and Recommendations, 1919-1981*, Geneva: International Labour Office.
UNESCO, *Anuario estadistico de la UNESCO 1996*, París: UNESCO.

United Kingdom

Cabinet Office, Office of Public Service — Development and Equal Opportunities Division, *Equal Opportunities in the Civil Service 1995-97*.

CCRU (1995), *Policy Appraisal and Fair Treatment Annual Report 1994*, Belfast: CCRU.
CCRU (1997), *Policy Appraisal and Fair Treatment Annual Report 1996*, Belfast: CCRU.
Equal Opportunities Commission (1995), *The Gender Impact of Compulsory Competitive Tendering*, Manchester: Equal Opportunities Commission.
Equal Opportunities Commission (1997), *Mainstreaming Gender Equality in Local Government: A Framework*, Manchester: Equal Opportunities Commission.
Equal Opportunities Commission (1998), *Equality in the 21st Century: A New Approach*, Manchester: Equal Opportunities Commission.
Equal Opportunities Commission, *Facts about Women and Men in Great Britain, Manchester: Equal Opportunities Commission.*
Freedom of Information: Consultation on Draft Legislation (May 1999), Cmnd 4355, London: HMSO.
Open Government (2nd 1997), *Code of Practice on Access to Government Information, Guidance on Interpretation*, Part V.
Report of the Committee on Reform of Section 2 of the Official Secrets Act 1911, (1972), Cmnd 5104, vol. I, London: HMSO.
Women's National Commission (1994), *A Direct Line Between Women and Government: 25 Years of the Women's National Commission*, London: WNC.
Women's Unit (1998), *Policy Appraisal for Equal Treatment*, London: Central Office of Information for the Cabinet Office.
Your Right to Know, White Paper on the Government's Proposals for a Freedom of Information Act, (December 1997) Cmnd 3818, London: HMSO.

Texts and Articles

Ackers, L. (1994), 'Women Citizenship and European Community Law: The Gender Implications of the Free Movement of Persons', *Journal of Social Welfare and Family Law* 391.
Alfredsson, G. and Tomasevski, K. (1995), *A Thematic Guide to Documents on the Human Rights of Women*, The Hague: Martinus Nijhoff Publishers.
Arranz, F. (1996), 'La epistemología y metodología feminista en los estudios e investigaciones sociológicas sobre la mujer en España (1990-1994)', *Jornadas A.U.D.E.M. Oviedo*.
Arranz, F., Quintanilla, B. and Velázquez, C. (1999), *Predicting the Impact of Policy: Gender-Auditing as a Means of Assessing the Probable Impact of Policy Initiatives on Women. Country Report: Spain*, Liverpool: Feminist Legal Research Unit, School of Law, University of Liverpool.
Ashiagbor, D. (1999), 'The Intersection between Gender and "Race" in the Labour Market: Lessons for Anti-Discrimination Law', in Morris, A. and O'Donnell, T. (eds), *Feminist Perspectives on Employment Law*, London: Cavendish.
Asscher-Vonk, I. (1995), *Equality in Law Between Men and Women in the European Community: The Netherlands*, Dordrecht/Boston/London: Martinus Nijhoff.
Astelarra, J. (1996), 'Politicas de igualdad de oportunidades en Espa a y Reino Unido' in *Sociología de las Relaciones de Género*, Madrid: Instituto de la Mujer. Serie Debate.
Bacchi, C. L. (1999), *Women, Policy and Politics*, London: Sage.
Bacik, I. (1996), 'New Developments in Irish Employment Equality Law — The New Enforcement Procedures', Paper given to EIRI Conference: Dublin.
Barnard, C. (1996), 'The Economic Objectives of Article 119', in Hervey, T. and O'Keeffe, D. (eds), *Sex Equality Law in the European Union*, Chichester: Wiley.
Barnard, C. (1999), 'Article 13: Through the Looking Glass of Union Citizenship', in O'Keeffe, D. and Twomey, P., *Legal Issues of the Amsterdam Treaty*, Oxford: Hart Publishing.
Barnard, C. and Hervey, T. (1998), 'European Union Employment and Social Policy Survey 1998', 18 *Yearbook of European Law* 613.

Berner, B. (1996), *Sakernas tillstånd. Kön, klass, teknisk expertis*, Lund: Carlsson Bokförlag.
Beveridge, F. and Nott, S. (1995), 'Women, Wealth and the Single Market', in Mayes, D. (ed.), *The Evolution of Rules for a Single European Market*, Cost A7 Vol.5, Part III, Brussels: Office for Official Publications for the EC.
Beveridge, F. and Nott, S. (1998), 'A Hard Look at Soft Law' in Craig, P. and Harlow, C. (eds), *Lawmaking in the European Union*, London: Kluwer Law International.
Beveridge, F., Nott, S. and Stephen, K. (1999), *Predicting the Impact of Policy: Gender-Auditing as a Means of Assessing the Probable Impact of Policy Initiatives on Women. Country Report: United Kingdom*, Liverpool: Feminist Legal Research Unit, School of Law, University of Liverpool.
Beveridge, F., Nott, S. and Stephen, K. (2000), 'Addressing Gender in National and Community Law and Policy-Making', in Shaw, J. (ed.), *Social Law and Policy in an Evolving European Union*, Oxford: Hart Publishing (forthcoming).
Beveridge, F., Nott, S. and Stephen, K. 'Mainstreaming and the Engendering of Policy-Making: A Means to an End?', 7(4) *Journal of European Public Policy* (forthcoming.
Birkinshaw, P. (2nd 1996), *Freedom of Information: The Law, the Practice and the Ideal*, London: Butterworths.
Bourn, C. and Whitmore, J. (1993), *Race and Sex Discrimination*, London: Sweet and Maxwell.
Brooks, D. (1994), 'A commentary on the essence of anti-essentialism in feminist legal theory', 2 *Feminist Legal Studies* 115.
Bruun, N. *et al* (eds), (1992), *The Nordic Labour Relations Model*, London: Dartmouth.
Buckley, M. and Anderson, M. (eds), (1988), *Women, Equality and Europe*, London: Macmillan.
Bueno Abad, J. R. *et al* (1995), 'Estudio longitudinal de la presencia de la mujer en los medios de comunicación de prensa escrita', en Instituto de la Mujer (ed.), *Síntesis de estudios e investigaciones del Instituto de la Mujer 1990-1994*, Madrid: Ministerio de Asuntos Sociales, Instituto de la Mujer.
Caetano, M. (1984), *Manual de Direito Administrativo, Vol. I*, Coimbra: Almedina.
Cardoso Da Costa, J. M. (2nd 1992), 'A Jurisdição Constitucional em Portugal', in *Boletim da Faculdade de Direito de Coimbra — Número Especial Estudos em Homagem ao Prof. Doutor Afonso Queiró, Vol. I*, Coimbra: Faculdade de Direito da Universidade de Coimbra.
Casqueira Cardoso, J. (1997), *Conceptions et Politiques des Mesures d'Action Positive*, Florence: European University Institute.
Casqueira Cardoso, J. (1999), 'A Critical Assessment of the European Union Approach to Positive Action', *Revista da Universidade Catolica de Brasilia*.
Casqueira Cardoso, J. (1999), *Etnicidade e Desigualdade de Género em Portugal*, Porto: Universidade Fernando Pessoa, Centre for Studies on Minorities Report 2/99.
Casqueira Cardoso, J. (1999), *Predicting the Impact of Policy: Gender-Auditing as a Means of Assessing the Probable Impact of Policy Initiatives on Women. Country Report: Portugal*, Liverpool: Feminist Legal Research Unit, School of Law, University of Liverpool.
Chubb, B. (3rd 1992), *The Government and Politics of Ireland*, London: Longman.
Collins, E. (1996), 'European Union Sexual Harassment Policy', in Elman, R. A. (ed.), *Sexual Politics and the European Union*, Oxford: Berghahn Books.
Conaghan, J. (1993), 'Pregnancy and the workplace - a question of strategy?', 20 *Journal of Law and Society* 71.
Cousins, M. (1995), *The Irish Social Welfare System Law and Social Policy*, Dublin: Roundhall Press.
Cronhult, P. (1994), 'Introduction', in Tiberg, H. *et al* (eds), Swedish Law: A Survey, Stockholm: Juristförlaget.
Cullen, H. (1994), 'The Subsidiary Woman', *Journal of Social Work and Family Law* 407.
Cunningham, S. (1992), 'The Development of Equal Opportunities Theory and Practice in the European Community', 20 *Policy and Politics* 177.

Curtin, D. M. (1999), 'The Fundamental Principle of Open-Decision Making and EU (Political) Citizenship', in O'Keeffe, D. and Twomey, P., *Legal Issues of the Amsterdam Treaty*, Oxford: Hart Publishing.

Da Fonseca, G. and Domingos, I. (1997), *Breviário de Direito Processual Constitucional — Recurso de Constitucionalidade*, Lisboa: Coimbra Editora.

De Beauvoir, S. (1949), *The Second Sex*, (ed.)Parshley, H. M. (1972), London: Penguin.

De Matos Correia, J., Leite Pinto, R. and Roboredo Seara, F. (1997), *Direito Constitucional Português Vigente — Opúsculo temáticos I: A fiscalização da constitucionalidade e da legalidade*, Lisboa: SPB Editores.

De Oliveira, A. C. (1993), *Direito das autarquias locais*, Coimbra: Coimbra Editora.

Díez-Picazo, L. M. (1994), *Source of Law in Spain: An Outline*, EUI Working Paper Law 94/10, Florence: European University Institute.

Donnelly, M., Mullally, S. and Smith, O. (1999), *Predicting the Impact of Policy: Gender-Auditing as a Means of Assessing the Probable Impact of Policy Initiatives on Women Country Report: Ireland*. Liverpool, Feminist Legal Research Unit, School of Law, University of Liverpool.

Duran, M. A. and Gallego, M. T. (1986), 'The Women's Movement in Spain and the New Spanish Democracy', in Dahlerup, D. (ed.), *The New Women's Movement: Feminism and Political Power in Europe and the USA*, London: Sage.

Eduards, M. (1995), 'En allvarsam lek med ord' in Brattström, W. E. (ed.), *Viljan att veta, viljan att förstå*, Stockholm: Fritzes.

Eklund, R. (1996), 'The Swedish Case - The Promised Land of Sex Equality?', in Hervey, T. and O'Keeffe, D. (eds), *Sex Equality Law in the European Union*, Chichester: Wiley.

El País (1999), *Anuario El País 1998*, Madrid: Prisa.

Ellis, E. (2nd 1998), *EC Sex Equality Law*, Oxford: Clarendon Press.

Employment Equality Agency (Summer 1999), 'Interview with Niall Crowley', *Equality News*, 18.

Equal Opportunities Review (1998), 'Limited positive action allowed', no. 77, Jan/Feb 1998.

Equal Opportunities Review (1999), 'Creating a unified Equality Commission — the Challenge Ahead', no. 83, Jan/Feb 1999.

Equal Opportunities Review (1999), 'NI equality body proposals', no. 84, March/April 1999.

Equal Opportunities Review (1999), 'Fall in Opportunity 2000 Women Managers', no. 86, July/August 1999.

Fahlbeck, R. (1994), 'Labour Law', in Tiberg, H. *et al* (eds), *Swedish Law: A Survey*, Stockholm: Juristförlaget.

Fenwick, H. and Hervey, T. K. (1995), 'Sex Equality in the Single Market: New Directions for the European Court of Justice'. 32 *Common Market Law Review* 443.

Fenwick, H. (1996), 'Special protections for women in European Union law', in Hervey, T. and O'Keeffe, D. (eds), *Sex Equality Law in the European Union*, Chichester: Wiley.

Fernando Loureiro, B. (1999), *Ciência Política — Guia de estudo*, Lisbon: Associação Académica da Faculdade de Direito de Lisboa.

Ferreira, V. (1998), *As mulheres em Portugal: Situação e paradoxos*, Coimbra: Oficina do CES.

Ferreira, V, Tavares, T. and Portugal, S. (eds), (1998), 'Positive Action and Employment Segregation', in *Shifting Bonds, Shifting Bounds — Women, Mobility and Citizenship in Europe*, Oeiras: Celta editora.

Ferri Dura, J. (1995), 'Las Administraciones Públicas', in Román, P. (ed.), *Sistema Político Español*, Madrid: McGraw and Hill/Interamericana de España.

Flynn, L. (1996), 'The Body Politic(s) of EC Law', in Hervey, T. and O'Keeffe D. (eds), *Sex Equality Law in the European Union*, Chichester: Wiley.

Folguera, P. (1988), 'De la transición política a la democracia: la evolución del feminismo en España durante el período 1975-1988'. in P. Folguera (ed.), *El feminismo en España: dos siglos de historia*, Madrid: Fundación Pablo Iglesias.

Fredman, S. (1992), 'European Community Discrimination Law: A Critique', 21 *Industrial Law Journal* 119.

Fredman, S. (1994), 'A Difference with Distinction: pregnancy and parenthood reassessed', 110 *Law Quarterly Review* 106.

García Cotarelo, R. (1983), 'Los principios fundamentales de la Constitución de 1978', in A. de Blas (ed.) *Introducción al Sistema Político Español*, Barcelona: Editorial Teide.

Gardiner, F. (ed.), (1997), *Sex Equality Policy in Western Europe*, London: Routledge.

Gardiner, F. and Leijenaar, M. (1997), 'The Timid and the Bold. Analysis of the "Woman-Friendly State" in Ireland and the Netherlands', in Gardiner, F. (ed.), *Sex Equality in Western Europe*, London: Routledge.

Garrido, L. J. (1992), *Las dos biografías de la mujer en España*, Madrid: Ministerio de Asuntos Sociales, Instituto de la Mujer.

Giddens, A. (1984), *The Constitution of Society*, Cambridge: Polity Press.

Gil Ruiz, J. M. (1997), *Las Políticas de Igualdad en España: Avances y Retrocesos*, Granada: Universidad de Granada.

Gillberg, M. (1998), in *Jämställdhetsmärkning — konsumentmakt för ett jämställt samhälle (Equality Labelling — Consumer Power for an Equal Society) Ds 1998:49*, Stockholm: Fritzes Offentliga Publikationer.

Gillberg, M. (1999), 'From Green Image to Green Practice. Normative Action and Self-regulation', in, *Lund Studies in Sociology of Law*, No. 6, Lund: Lund University.

Gillberg, M. (1999), *Predicting the Impact of Policy: Gender-Auditing as a Means of Assessing the Probable Impact of Policy Initiatives on Women. Country Report: Sweden*, Liverpool: Feminist Legal Research Unit, School of Law, University of Liverpool.

Gillberg, M. and Hydén, H. (1998), 'Environmental Decision-Making in Sweden', in Weidner, H. (ed.), *Alternative Dispute Resolution*, Berlin: Zigma.

Goldman, A. H. (1979), *Justice and Reverse Discrimination*, Princeton: Princeton University Press.

Gomes Canotilho, J. J. and Vital, M. (1991), *Os poderes do Presidente da República*, Coimbra: Coimbra Editora.

Gomes Canotilho, J. J. and Vital, M. (eds), (4th 1997), *Constituição da República Portuguesa*, Coimbra: Coimbra Editora.

Gonçalves Pereira, A. and De Quadros, F. (1997), *Direito Internacional* Público, Coimbra: Livraria Almedina.

Gorter and Winants (1993), *Gehandicapt en vrouw*, The Hague.

Hadden, T., Rainey, B. and McGreevy, G. (1998), 'Equal but not Separate: Communal policy appraisal', Supplement to *Fortnight* 371, (ed.) Chris Moffat, Fortnight Educational Trust.

Hafnoer-Burton, E. and Pollack, M. A. (2000), 'Mainstreaming Gender in the European Union', 7(4) *Journal of European Public Policy* (forthcoming).

Haverland, M. (1998), *National Autonomy, European Integration and the Politics of Packaging Waste*, the Netherlands School for Social and Economic Policy Research: Utrecht.

Hervey, T (1988), *European Social Law and Policy*, London: Longman.

Hervey, T. and O'Keeffe, D. (1996), *Sex Equality Law in the European Union*, Chichester: Wiley.

Hirdman, Y. (1998), 'Med kluven tunga. Lo och genusordningen', *Arbetarhistoria. Meddelande Vern Arbetarrörelsens Arkiv och Bibliotek*, No 85-86, 1- 2.

Hogan, G. and Whyte, G. (3rd 1994), *The Irish Constitution,* London: Sweet and Maxwell.

Hood Phillips, O. and Jackson, P. (7th 1987), in Hood Phillips, O. (ed.), *Constitutional and Administrative Law*, London: Sweet and Maxwell.

Hoskyns, C. (1996), *Integrating Gender*, London: Verso.

Hoskyns, C. (1992), 'The European Community's Policy on Women in the context of 1992', 15(1) *Women's Studies International Forum* 21.

Hydén, H. (ed.) (1987), *Rättsregler*, Lund: Studentlitteratur.

Janeiro, M. J. (1998), *O trabalho a tempo parcial em Portugal e a regulamentação colectiva,* Lisbon. Ministério do Trabalho e da Solidariedade.

Jansson, K. (1996), 'Kvinnofrid ur olika perspektiv. Våldtäkt, kvinnorov och andra sexuella övergrepp cirka 1600-1900', in Granström, G., Andersson, G., Jansson, K. and Oja, L. (eds), *Kvinnorna och rätten*, Uppsala: Hallgren & Fallgren Studieförlag.
Kaplan, G. (1992), *Contemporary Western Feminism*, London: UCL Press Allen and Unwin.
Kenner, J. (2000), 'The paradox of the social dimension', in Lynch, P., Neuwahl, N. and Rees, W. (eds), *Reforming the European Union — from Maastricht to Amsterdam*, London: Longman.
Keuzekamp, S. and Theunissen, A. (1990), *Emancipatie ten halve geregeld. Continuiteit en inenging in het emancipatiebeleid*, Den Haag: Vuga.
Kickert, W. and R. (1995), 't Veld. National Government, Governance and Administration', in Kickert, W. and van Vugt, F. (eds), *Public Policy and Administrative Sciences in the Netherlands*, London: Prentice Hall Harvester Wheatsheaf.
Kilpatrick, C. (1997), 'How Long is a Piece of String? European Regulation of the Post-Birth Period', in Hervey, T. and O'Keeffe, D. (eds), *Sex Equality Law in the European Union*, Chichester: Wiley.
Kingston, J., Whelan, A., and Bacik, I. (1997), *Abortion and the Law*, Dublin: Roundhall Sweet and Maxwell.
Korthal Altes, W. F. *et al* (eds), (1992), *Information Law Towards the 21st Century*, Deventer: Kluwer.
Lange, P. (1992), 'The Politics of the Social Dimension', in Sbragia, A. (ed.), *Euro-Politics: Institutions and Policy-Making in the 'New' European Community*, Washington: Brookings Institute.
Larsson, T. (ed.) (1993), *Det svenska atatsskicket*, Lund: Studentlitteratur.
Leijenaar, M. H. and Niemöller, C. (1994), 'Political participation of women: The Netherlands', in Nelson, B. and Chowdury, N. (eds), *Women and Politics Worldwide*, New Haven/London: Yale University Press.
Leijenaar, M., Niemöller, C. and Koster, A. D. S. (1994), *Het maatschappelijk tekort: vrouwen in besturen van maatschappelijke organisaties*, Den Haag: Vuga.
Leroy, P. (1995), *Milieukunde als beroep en als roeping*, Nijmegen: Katholieke Universiteit Nijmegen.
Lijphart, A., *Verzuiling, pacificatie en kentering in de Nederlandse politiek*, Amsterdam: J. H. De Bussy.
Lingnau da Silveira, L. (1989), 'O Provedor de Justiça', in Baptista Coelho, M. (ed.), *Portugal, o sistema politico e constitucional 1974-1987*, Lisboa: Instituto de Ciências Sociais da Universidade de Lisboa.
Lister, R. (1990), 'Women, Economic Dependency and Citizenship', 19(4) *Journal of Social Policy*.
Littleton, C. (1987), 'Reconstructing Sexual Equality', 75 *California Law Review* 1274.
Lovenduski, J. (1990), 'Feminism and Western European Politics: an overview', in Unwin, D. W. and Paterson, W. E. (eds), *Politics in Western Europe Today*, London: Longman.
Lovenduski, J. (1995), 'An Emerging Advocate: The Equal Opportunities Commission in Great Britain', in Stetson, D. M. and Mazur, A. (eds), *Comparative State Feminism*, London: Sage Publications.
Lucas Murillo de la Cueva, P. (1983), 'Los órganos constitucionales', in de Blas, A. (ed.), *Introducción al Sistema Politico Español*, Barcelona: Editorial Teide.
Lundkvist, H. and Thoursie, A. (1997), *Report on the Swedish Part of the Project Mainstreaming Gender Equality in Local Government*, The Swedish Association of Local Authorities.
Lundström, K. (1997), 'Women Caught in a Logical Trap in EC Law: An analysis of the use of quotas in the *Kalanke* Case', *Statsvetenskaplig Tidskrift*, No 1.
Lynch Fannon, I. (March 1999), *Annual Equality Lecture*, University College Cork.
McColgan, A. (2000), *Women Under the Law: the False Promise of Human Rights*, Harlow: Longman.
McCrudden, C. (1986), 'Rethinking Positive Action , *Industrial Law Journal* 219.

McCrudden, C. (1996), *Mainstreaming Fairness — A Discussion Paper on PAFT*, Belfast: Committee on the Administration of Justice.

McCrudden, C. (1998), 'A British Notion of responsibility on equality', *The Sunday Business Post Online*, March 16 1998.

McCrudden, C. (1999), 'Mainstreaming equality in the governance of Northern Ireland', *Fordham International Law Journal* 22.

McDonagh, M. (1998), *Freedom of Information Law in Ireland*, Dublin: Roundhall Sweet and Maxwell.

Machado Dray, G. (1999), *O Princípio da Igualdade no Direito do Trabalho — Sua Aplicabilidade no Domínio Específico da Formação de Contratos Individuais de Trabalho*, Lisbon: Almedina.

Machado Horta, R. (1996), 'A Constituição da República Portuguesa de 1976 e o Regime Semi-presidencial', in Miranda, J. (ed.), *Perspectivas Constitucionais Nos 20 Anos da Constituição de 1976 Vol I*, Coimbra: Coimbra Editora.

Mackay, F. and Bilton, K. (2000), *Learning From Experience: Lessons in Mainstreaming Equal Opportunities*, Edinburgh: Governance of Scotland Forum, University of Edinburgh.

MacKinnon, C. (1987), 'Difference and Dominance: On Sex Discrimination', in *Feminism Unmodified*, Cambridge, Mass.: Harvard University Press.

MacKinnon, C. (1989), *Towards a Feminist Theory of the State*, Cambridge, Mass.: Harvard University Press.

Magalhães, M. J. (1998), *Movimento Feminista e Educação - Portugal, décadas de 70 e 80*, Oeiras: Celta.

Majury, D. (1991), 'Strategizing in Equality', in Fineman, M. A. and Thomadsen, N. S. (eds), *At the Boundaries of Law*, London: Routledge.

Mazey, S. (1988), 'European Community Action on Behalf of Women: The Limits of Legislation', 27 *JCMS* 63.

Mill, J. S. (1869), 'The subjection of women', in Mill, J. S. and Mill, H. T. (eds), (reprinted 1970), *Essays on Sex Equality*, Chicago: University of Chicago Press.

Monteiro Fernandes, A. (1995), 'La réglementation du temps de travail au Portugal — Une approche de synthèse', European Forum, *The Regulation of Working Time in the European Union — Gender Approach*, Florence, European University Institute.

More, G. (1993), '"Equal Treatment" of the Sexes in European Community Law: What does "Equal" mean?', 1 *Feminist Legal Studies* 45.

Moreira, A. J. (1998), *Compêndio de leis do trabalho*, Coimbra: Almedina.

Morris, A. and Nott, S. (1992), 'The Legal Response to Pregnancy', 12 *Legal Studies*.

Morris, A. and Nott, S. (1995), *All My Worldly Goods*, Aldershot: Dartmouth.

Morris. A. and Nott, S. (1995), 'The Law's Engagement with Pregnancy', in Bridgeman, J. and Millns, S. (eds), *Law and Body Politics*, Aldershot: Dartmouth.

Mouraz Lopes, J. (1998), *Os Crimes Contra a Liberdade e Autodeterminação Sexual no Código Penal*, Coimbra: Coimbra Editora.

Muffat-Jeandet, D. (1991), 'The Proposed Pregnancy and Maternity Directive', 20 *Industrial Law Journal* 76.

Nederland, T. and Portegijs, W. (1996), *Bestuurders gevraagd: vrouwen en mannen over maatschappelijke participatie*, Den Haag: Vuga.

Nielsen, R. and Halvorsen, M. (1992), 'Equality Laws', in Bruun, N. *et al* (eds), *The Nordic Labour Relations Model*, Aldershot: Dartmouth.

Nielsen, R. and Szyszczak, E. (2nd 1993), *The Social Dimension of the European Community*, Handelshojskolens: Copenhagen.

Nolan, B. and Watson, D. (1999), *Women and Poverty in Ireland*, Dublin: Combat Poverty Agency.

Norris, P. (1996), 'Women Politicians: Transforming Westminster?', 49(1) *Parliamentary Affairs*.

Nott, S. (1999), 'Mainstreaming Equal Opportunities: Succeeding When All Else Has Failed?', in Morris, A. and O'Donnell, T. (eds), *Feminist Perspectives on Employment Law*, London: Cavendish.

Nunes, M. C. (1996), *Equal Opportunities and Collective Bargaining in the EU — Exploring the National Situation in Portugal*, Dublin: European Foundation for the Improvement of Living and Working Conditions, Working Paper No.: WP/96/57/EN.
O'Donnell, R. and Thomas, D. (1998), 'Partnership and Policy-Making', in Healy, S. and Reynolds, B. (eds), *Social Policy in Ireland*, Dublin: Oak Tree Press.
O'Donovan, K. (1998), *Engendering Human Rights* (paper delivered at the conference of the Society of Public Teachers of Law, 1998).
O'Hare, U. (1996), 'Positive action before the European Court', 2 *Web Journal of Current Legal Issues*.
Olías de Lima, B. (1995), 'El Gobierno', in Román, P. (ed.), *Sistema Político Español*, Madrid: McGraw and Hill/Interamericana de España.
Ostner, I. and Lewis, J. (1995), 'Gender and the Evolution of European Social Policies', in Liebfried, S. and Pierson, P. (eds), *European Social Policy: Between Fragmentation and Integration*, Washington: Brookings Institute.
Outshoorn, J. (1995), 'Administrative Accomodation in the Netherlands. The Department for Coordination of Equality Policy', in Stetson, D. M. and Mazur, A. (eds), *Comparative State Feminism*, London: Sage Publications.
Outshoorn, J. (1998), 'Paars en de ommekeer in het emancipatiebeleid', *Socialisme en democratie* 3.
Pateman, C. (1988), *The Sexual Contract*, California: Stanford University Press.
Petersson, O. (1997), *En sammanfattning av maktutredningen*, Stockholm: Allmänna Förlaget.
Pires, J. *Da Emancipação Juslaboral da Mulher*, Lisbon, Comissão para a Igualdade no Trabalho e no Emprego.
Pollak, A. (1999), 'Number of Families Where Both Parents Work Doubles', *Irish Times*, 2 June 1999.
Prins, M. (1974-1989), *Emancipatie van vrouwen in beweging. Emancipatie als besturingsvraagstuk*, Groningen: PP & STYX.
Queiroz, C. (1992), *O Sistema Político e Constitucional Português*, Lisbon, Associação Académica da Faculdade de Direito de Lisboa.
Radhl Philipp, R. M. *et al* (1995), 'Análisis sociológico de la imagen de la mujer en la televisión', in Instituto de la Mujer (ed.), *Síntesis de estudios e investigaciones del Instituto de la Mujer 1990-1994*, Madrid: Ministerio de Asuntos Sociales, Instituto de la Mujer.
Rahan, R. (1995), *The Elusive Agenda: Mainstreaming Women in Development*, London: Zed Books.
Rees, T. (1998), *Mainstreaming Equality in the European Union*, London: Routledge.
Rees, T. (1999), 'Managing Diversity and Mainstreaming Equality' *ESRC Seminar Series: The Interface Between Public Policy and Gender Equality, Seminar Two,* Sheffield: Centre for Regional Economic and Social Research, Sheffield Hallam University.
Ridley, F. F. (1988), 'There is no British Constitution: A Dangerous Case of the Emperor's Clothes', *Parliamentary Affairs* 41.
Robinson, R. A. H. (1993), 'O Indivíduo e o Estado no Portugal Contemporâneo', in Brettell, C. B. (ed.), *Portugal — O Indivíduo e o Estado*, Lisbon: Editorial Fragmentos.
Roboredo Seara, F., de Matos Correia, J. and Leite Pinto, R. (1995), *Ciência Política e Direito Constitucional*, Lisbon: Universidade Lusíada.
Rodriguez Pineiro, M. (1986), 'Principo de Iqualdad y Derecho del Tradajo', in Rodriguez Pineiro, M. and Fernandez Lopez, M. F. (eds), *Iqualdad y descriminacion*, Madrid: Tecnos.
Roelofs, E. (1995), 'The European Equal Opportunities Policy', in van Doorne-Huiskes, A., van Hoof, J. and Roelofs, E., *Women and the European Labour Markets*, London: Chapman.
Román Marugán, P. (1995), 'La Jefatura del Estado', in Román, P. (ed.), *Sistema Político Español,* Madrid: McGraw and Hill/Interamericana de España.
Ross, G. (1995), 'Assessing the Delors Era and Social Policy', in Liebfried, S. and Pierson, P. (eds), *European Social Policy: Between Fragmentation and Integration*, Washington: Brookings Institute.

Rovira Viñas, A. (1983), 'Los derechos y libertades fundamentales en la Constitución española de 1978', in de Blas, A. (ed.), *Introducción al Sistema Político Español*, Barcelona: Editorial Teide.
Ruane, F. and Sutherland, J. (1999), *Women in the Labour Force*, Dublin: Employment Equality Agency.
Sahlström, O. (1998), *Den röde patriarken. En essä om arbetarrörelsens auktoritära tradition*, Uddevalla: Atlas Förlag.
Sánchez de Dios, M. (1995), 'Las Cortes Generales', in Román, P. (ed.), *Sistema Político Español*, Madrid: McGraw and Hill/Interamericana de España.
Sánchez de Dios, M. (1995), 'El Poder Judicial y la Jurisdicción Constitucional', in Román, P. (ed.), *Sistema Político Español*, Madrid: McGraw and Hill/Interamericana de España.
Sannerstedt, A. and Sjölin, M. (1994), *Den moderna demokratins problem*, Lund: Studentlitteratur.
Scanlon, G. M. (1990), 'El movimiento feminista en España 1900-1985: logros y dificultades', in J. Astelarra (ed.), *Participación Política de las Mujeres*, Madrid: Centro de Investigaciones Sociológicas y Siglo XXI.
Scheiwe, K. (1994), 'EC Law's Unequal Treatment of the Family: The Case Law of the European Court of Justice on Rules Prohibiting Discrimination on Grounds of Sex and Nationality', 4 *Social and Legal Studies* 243.
Schiek, (1996), 'Positive Action in Community Law', 25 *Industrial Law Journal* 239.
Sensat, N. and Varella, R. (1998), 'Las políticas dirigidas a las mujeres: la acción pública para la igualdad entre los sexos', in Gomá, R. and Subirats, J. (eds), *Políticas públicas en España*, Barcelona: Ariel.
Shaw, J. (1994), 'Twintrack Social Europe — The Inside Track', in O'Keeffe, D. and Twomey P. (eds), *Legal Issues of the Maastricht Treaty*, London: Chancery.
Silva, M. and Perista, H. (1995), *As Portuguesas e a União Europeia — Prospectivas para a Acção*, Lisbon: Comissão para a Igualdade e para os Direitos das Mulheres.
Sjölin, M. (1988), *Coalition Politics and Parliamentary Power*, Lund: Studentlitteratur *Sociaal en Cultureel rapport*, SCP: Den Haag.
Smart, C. (1989), *Feminism and the Power of Law*, London: Routledge.
Smart, C. (1992), 'The woman of legal discourse', 1 *Social and Legal Studies* 29.
Smith, O., Mullally, S. and Donnelly, M. (2000, forthcoming), 'Case Study: Ireland's Legal and Extra-Legal Responses to the European Commission's Recommendation and Code of Practice on Protecting the Dignity of Men and Women at Work'.
Spencer, F., *Briefing on Mainstreaming*, Manchester: Equal Opportunities Commission.
Squires, J. (1996), 'Quotas for Women: Fair Representation?', 49(1) *Parliamentary Affairs* 71.
Sterzel, F. (1994), 'Public Administration', in Tiberg, H. *et al* (eds), *Swedish Law: A Survey*, Stockholm: Juristförlaget.
Sterzel, F. (1994), 'The Constitution', in Tiberg, H. *et al* (eds), *Swedish Law: A Survey*, Stockholm: Juristförlaget.
Stetson, D. M., and Mazur, A. (1995), 'Introduction', in Stetson, D. M. and Mazur, A. (eds), *Comparative State Feminism*, London: Sage Publications.
Szyszczak, E. (1994), 'Social Policy; A Happy Ending or a Reworking of the Fairy Tale?', in O'Keeffe, D. and Twomey, P. (eds), *Legal Issues of the Maastricht Treaty*, Chichester: Wiley.
Szyszczak, E. (1997), 'Community Law on Pregnancy and Maternity', in Hervey, T. and O'Keeffe, D. (eds), *Sex Equality Law in the European Union*, Chichester: Wiley.
Threfall, M. (1998), 'State Feminism or Party Feminism?', *The European Journal of Women's Studies Vol. 5*.
Toonen, T. A. J. (1988), 'The Netherlands: A Decentralised Unitary State in a Welfare Society', *Western European Politics* 8(10).
Ulmanen, P. (1998), *(S)veket mot kvinnorna och hur högern stal feminismen*, Uddevalla: Atlas Förlag

Unit for the Study of Government in Scotland (1988), *Mainstreaming Equal Opportunities, Report to the Consultative Steering Group to the Scottish Parliament*, Edinburgh: University of Edinburgh.
Valiente, C. (1995), 'The Power of Persuasion: The Instituto de la Mujer in Spain', in Stetson, D. M. and Mazur, A. (eds), *Comparative State Feminism*, London: Sage Publications.
Valiente, C. (1996), 'El feminismo institucional en España: El Instituto de la Mujer, 1983-1994', *Revista Internacional de Sociología* 13.
Valiente, C. (1997), 'State Feminism and Gender Equality Policies: the Case of Spain (1983-1985)', in Gardiner, F. (ed.), *Sex Equality Policy in Western Europe*, London: Routledge.
van de Graaf, H., Mossink, M. and Gröflin, J. (1998), *Van de EER geleerd*, Den Haag: Vuga.
van Waarden, F. (1995), 'Persistence of National Policy Styles: A Study in their Institutional Foundations', in Unger, B. and van Waarden, F. (eds), *Convergence or Diversity*, Avebury: Aldershot.
Verloo, M. (1986), 'Emancipatie, de bouwbaarheid van een feministische visie', in Nelissen, N., Geurts, J. and de Wit, H. (eds), *Het verkennen van beleidsproblemen*, Zeist: Kerckebosch.
Verloo, M. (1998), 'Alle goede dingen in drieen', *Tijdschrift voor genderstudies*.
Verloo, M. (1999), 'On the conceptual and theoretical roots of gender mainstreaming', in *ESRC Seminar Series: The Interface Between Public Policy and Gender Equality, Seminar One* , Sheffield: Centre for Regional Economic and Social Research, Sheffield Hallam University.
Verloo, M. and Hijmans, E. (1995), *Kwaliteit van onderzoe*, Den Haag: Vuga.
Verloo, M. and Roggeband, C. (1996), 'Gender Impact Assessement: The Development of a New Instrument in the Netherlands', 14(1) *Impact Assessement* 3.
Verloo, M., Fontein, E. and Krops, C. (1997), *State of the Art of Women in Political, Economic and Social Decision Making in the Netherlands*, Nijmegen: KUN.
Walby, S. (1994), 'Is Citizenship Gendered?', *Sociology* 28(2).
Walker, D. (1992), *The Scottish Legal System: An Introduction to the Study of Scots Law*, Edinburgh: Green.
Wängnerud, L. (1998), *Politikens andra sida. Om kvinnorepresentation i Sveriges riksdag*, Kungälv: Göteborg Studies in Politics 53.
Ward, I. (1996), 'Beyond Sex Equality: The Limits of Sex Equality Law in the New Europe', in Hervey, T. and O'Keeffe, D. (eds), *Sex Equality Law in the European Union*, Chichester: Wiley.
Weiler, J. H. H. (1991), 'The Transformation of Europe', 100 *Yale Law Journal* 2403.
Widerberg, K. (1980), *Kvinnor, klasser, lagar*. 1750-1980, Helingborg: Publica.
Woodward, A. and Meier, P. (1997), *Gender Impact Assessment: Tool in Mainstreaming or Tool to Begin Mainstreaming? A Comparison of Dutch and Flemish Approaches*, Paper for the ECPR Joint Sessions: Bern.
Young, I M. (1991), *Justice and the Politics of Difference*, Princeton: Princeton University Press.

Index